Distributed Computing and Cryptography

DIMACS
Series in Discrete Mathematics
and Theoretical Computer Science

Volume 2

Distributed Computing and Cryptography

Proceedings of a DIMACS Workshop
October 4–6, 1989

Joan Feigenbaum
Michael Merritt
Editors

NSF Science and Technology Center
in Discrete Mathematics and Theoretical Computer Science
A consortium of Rutgers University, Princeton University,
AT&T Bell Labs, Bellcore

American Mathematical Society
Association for Computing Machinery

The DIMACS Workshop in Distributed Computing and Cryptography was held at the Nassau Inn in Princeton, New Jersey on October 4–6, 1989.

1980 *Mathematics Subject Classification* (1985 *Revision*). Primary 68M10, 68P25, 94A60; Secondary 03B45, 03B70, 68M20, 68N99, 68Q15, 68Q60, 68S15.

Library of Congress Cataloging-in-Publication Data

DIMACS Workshop in Distributed Computing and Cryptography (1989: Princeton, N.J.)
Distributed computing and cryptography: proceedings of a DIMACS workshop held at the Nassau Inn in Princeton, New Jersey, October 4–6, 1989/Joan Feigenbaum, Michael Merritt, editors.
p. cm.—(DIMACS series in discrete mathematics and theoretical computer science, ISSN 1052-1798; v. 2)
"The DIMACS Workshop in Distributed Computing and Cryptography"—T.p. verso.
Includes bibliographical references.
AMS: ISBN 0-8218-6590-0 (alk. paper)
ACM: ISBN 0-89791-384-1
1. Electronic data processing—Distributed processing—Congresses.
2. Cryptography—Congresses. I. Feigenbaum, Joan, 1958- . II. Merritt, Michael, 1957- .
III. Title. IV. Series.
QA76.9.D5D43 1991 90–49828
005.8′2—dc20 CIP

To order through AMS contact the AMS Customer Services Department, P.O. Box 6248, Providence, Rhode Island 02940-6248 USA. For VISA or MASTERCARD orders call 1-800-321-4AMS. Order code DIMACS/2.

To order through ACM contact ACM Order Department, P.O. Box 64145, Baltimore, Maryland 21264. Phone 301-528-4261. Order number 222910.

Printed in the United States of America.
The paper used in this book is acid-free and falls within the guidelines established to ensure permanence and durability. ♾

This publication was typeset using $\mathcal{A}_{\mathcal{M}}\mathcal{S}$-TEX, the American Mathematical Society's TEX macro system.

10 9 8 7 6 5 4 3 2 1 95 94 93 92 91

Contents

Preface

On October 4, 5, and 6, 1989, seventy-four people from twenty-three institutions in five countries met at the Nassau Inn in Princeton, New Jersey, to take a critical look at current research and development efforts in the fields of distributed computing and cryptography. Much of the material covered at this highly successful workshop is contained in this volume.

The first item in these proceedings is a technical report containing a summary of the open questions raised during informal discussions, short abstracts of the formal presentations, names and addresses of the participants, and a bibliography. The rest of the proceedings consists of fifteen papers based on talks presented at the workshop and two additional contributed papers on related topics. [1] These are unrefereed papers, many of which describe ongoing research; we expect authors to write longer, more formal papers on some of these projects for refereed journals.

We would like to thank the DIMACS executive committee for sponsoring the Workshop and all of the participants for making it so successful and enjoyable.

Joan Feigenbaum
Michael Merritt
Murray Hill, New Jersey
June, 1990

---

[1] The two papers that were not presented at the workshop are "Formal Definitions for Secure Distributed Protocols," by Donald Beaver, and "On expected polynomial time simulation of zero knowledge protocols," by Uriel Feige and Adi Shamir.

Foreword

This DIMACS volume on Distributed Computing and Cryptography contains the proceedings of a workshop held at DIMACS October 4–6, 1989. We especially thank the Workshop organizers, Joan Feigenbaum and Michael Merritt, for organizing a workshop that brought together many of the major figures in a variety of research fields, both theoretical and applied, related to distributed computing and cryptography.

Daniel Gorenstein, Director
Robert Tarjan, Co-Director
Fred S. Roberts, Associate Director

DIMACS Series in Discrete Mathematics
and Theoretical Computer Science
Volume 2, 1991

Open Questions, Talk Abstracts, and Summary of Discussions

JOAN FEIGENBAUM AND MICHAEL MERRITT

The DIMACS Workshop on Distributed Computing and Cryptography was held at the Nassau Inn in Princeton, New Jersey, on October 4, 5, and 6, 1989. Participants took a critical look at the results, choice of problems, guiding philosophies, research methodology, and engineering projects that currently absorb much of the effort of people working in "cryptography" and "computer system security." This report summarizes both the formal presentations and the informal discussions that took place.

Section 1 contains our account of the group discussions and statements of open questions, both general and specific, that we think are important. This report on the workshop is based on our recollections, our notes, and notes taken by the graduate-student participants; we assume responsibility for any inaccuracies in our account. Section 2 contains abstracts of the talks presented at the workshop; whenever possible, these abstracts are accompanied by references to complete papers or extended abstracts that the speaker has published. Names and addresses of participants are given in Section 3.

1. Open questions and summary of discussion

1.1. Questions raised during talks and discussions

1.1.1. *Wednesday, October 4, 1989.* The part of the theoretical computer science community that studies cryptography has created a large amount of terminology. Many of these terms were used in Wednesday morning's talks. The lexicon includes *authentication*, *bit commitment*, *blobs*, *claw-free one-way permutations*, *coherence*, *cryptographically secure pseudorandom number generation*, *digital signature scheme*, *distributed function evaluation*, *envelopes*, *instance-hiding scheme*, *locally random reducibility*, *noninteractive*

1980 *Mathematics Subject Classification* (1985 *Revision*). Primary 68M10, 68P25, 68Q05, 68Q15.

zero-knowledge proof system, oblivious transfer, obliviously cryptographic multiparty unconditionally secure protocols, one-way authentication, one-way function, one-way hash function, one-way permutation, probabilistic encryption, public-key cryptosystem, random-self-reducibility, secret sharing, secret-key exchange, secure circuit evaluation, trapdoor function, zero-knowledge proof system, etc. Many specific questions were raised at the workshop about various terms on this list, and some of them appear both in this section and in the next one. Here, we would also like to raise a general issue – for a lengthier discussion, see the article by Merritt in these proceedings.

We have seen an outpouring of papers proving the equivalence (via polynomial-time reduction), the inequivalence (via standard techniques such as diagonalization or counting arguments) or the probable inequivalence (in various technical senses) of some pairs of these terms. One example of such a result is Naor's theorem that one-way functions suffice for bit commitment **[89]**. Within computer science, it is the structural complexity theory community that is traditionally concerned with abstract classes of objects, polynomial-time reductions among members of a single class, and equality or inequality of classes. Theirs are usually language classes and function classes defined by time- and space-bounds, whereas the classes studied by cryptographers are defined by the terms listed above.

QUESTION 1. *Is cryptography theory a branch of structural complexity theory? If not, then what is the end goal of this sizable effort to prove the equivalence or inequivalence of all of the terms we have defined?*

One aspect of Question 1 is "what is the goal of crypto-theory and is it satisfying as a pure theory?" There are traditional criteria by which to judge a pure theory; examples include depth, elegance, and technical difficulty.

Another aspect of this issue is summarized in the next question, which was raised explicitly during the discussion on Wednesday and sparked a long, animated discussion.

QUESTION 2. *Which of the ideas studied by the cryptography-theory community are (or should be) valued by practitioners?*

Practitioners offered three specific answers almost immediately: **public-key systems**, **hard-to-invert hash functions**, and **digital signatures**. This was very heartening for some of us. Are there other examples of practically useful contributions of the theory?

Many of the talks abstracted in Section 2.1 concern what we will call *secure distributed function evaluation*. The question addressed in this work is whether players $P_1, \ldots, P_n$, each with a private input $x_1, \ldots, x_n$, can together compute a function $y = f(x_1, \ldots, x_n)$ in such a way that each player learns y and no player P_i learns anything about x_j except what is implied by y. There have been a number of papers on this subject in recent years. In many of these papers, the model of computation and communication is a complete, synchronous network of arbitrarily powerful processors in which each pair of processors has a private channel over which to communicate. (This is often referred to as "the noncryptographic model.") The questions addressed include the number of malicious participants that can be thwarted, the number of rounds of communication needed, the lengths of the messages sent, and the local processing cost.

Feigenbaum posed the following question explicitly.

QUESTION 3. *Is secure distributed function evaluation ever done in practice? If not, is it because the model of computation and communication is unrealistic, or is it because there is no real motivation for doing it?*

There was a lengthy discussion following this question. Its length was probably due in large part to Lampson's initial answer: "I am glad that you asked that question, because it has always been a complete mystery to me why anyone would ever want to do such a thing."

The prototype pedagogical example of a situation in which one would use secure distributed function evaluation is voting: Everyone finds out who won but no one finds out who voted for whom. No one at the workshop mentioned an actual implementation of such a voting protocol. We would like to know whether anyone actually uses secure distributed function evaluation to do voting.

Yung suggested the following answer to Question 3. The Feige-Fiat-Shamir identification scheme [**51**] requires the generation of a modulus of the form $n = pq$, where both p and q are primes, that will be used by all of the participants. The participants can use a secure distributed function evaluation protocol to generate n; each participant will know n, none will know p and q, and there will be no need for a trusted server that does key-generation, as there is in most identification schemes. Is this a realistic suggestion?

The discussion about whether or not massive amounts of theoretical work on secure, distributed function evaluation is justified by the practical importance of the problem ended without any general conclusions. However, the practitioners' response to Question 2 convinced us that the theory of cryptography has had something to contribute to computing practice.

We have mentioned the noncryptographic model of secure distributed function evaluation. Not surprisingly, there is also a "cryptographic model" of secure distributed function evaluation (see, for example, the talk of Rogaway, abstracted in Section 2.1). More surprisingly, there are also other models (e.g., [**72**]). This proliferation of models and formalism is making it impossible (even for the people speaking and listening in the Wednesday morning session, many of whom have worked on these problems) to read papers in the field. More than one participant made the following suggestion.

QUESTION 4. *Consolidate the existing work on secure distributed function evaluation. Narrow down to as few models as are needed to prove the essential results. Make clear the relationships (if any) among results in different models. Make clear the relationship between theoretical work on this problem and actual distributed computations.*

In some sense, secure distributed function evaluation is a generalization of *oblivious transfer* (OT), which was introduced by M. Rabin **[97]** in 1981 and which has also been the subject of a number of theoretical papers (and of some talks at this workshop).

QUESTION 5. *Is OT ever used in practice?*

On Wednesday afternoon, Lampson, Reeds, and Tsudik all talked about designs of networks, both local-area and wide-area, that provide mechanisms for secure computation and communication. Bishop spoke about plans to add a mechanism for secure communication to the internet. All of the networks or designs discussed include some concept of "physically secure" or "trusted" components. Tygar asked whether the role of such components can be formalized in a general way:

QUESTION 6. *What exactly is "secure hardware" and how much of it is needed? What trade-offs are involved?*

Results on some aspects of this question have been proven. See, for example, Ostrovsky and Yung's paper in these proceedings for results on the question of whether "secure communication channels" are necessary in certain situations.

1.1.2. *Thursday, October 5, 1989.* The talks of Burrows and Abadi provoked a lot of discussion. Merritt observed that this logical approach reveals weaknesses in protocols via an inability to derive a proof of authentication. He noted that such independence arguments are often technically difficult; moreover, they do not in themselves provide a construction of a successful attack on the insecure protocol.

Merritt also noted that if a protocol were modified so that all participants initially broadcast their secret keys, a proof of correctness would still go through. The apparent paradox is resolved by noting that the axioms of the logic no longer apply to the modified protocol. The speakers noted that the logic does not check for unauthorized release of secrets.

Most of the ensuing discussion concerned the general question of whether formal systems, and in particular those based on logic, that claim to "analyze protocols" and "prove them correct (resp. secure)" are really convincing. The following sociological observation was made repeatedly: When a formal system finds a bug in a protocol, everyone believes that it is a bug; when a formal system finds a "proof of correctness (resp. security)," people seem to have trouble believing that it is a proof.

Every logical system consists of a set of rules of inference and a set of axioms. To apply the conclusions of the logic to an actual computer system, the axioms have to be interpreted within that domain. Inevitably, simplifying assumptions are made that may invalidate the conclusions.

QUESTION 7. *Why should cryptographers have confidence in any particular set of axioms or inference rules?*

More specifically,

QUESTION 8. *Logical systems allow us to prove that one set of symbols implies some other set of symbols, according to some well-defined notion of "implies." How do we convince ourselves that these symbols or this "proof" bears any meaningful relationship to the bits floating around in our network? If it still requires "magic" on the part of a human being to describe these bits in terms of "axioms," then what is the advantage of automating the inference stage of the proof?*

From a purely logical perspective, this is a question of the semantics of the logic. Logics express properties of families of formal systems, the *models* or *interpretations* of the logic. Burrows, Abadi, and Needham have devised a simple semantics for their logic of authentication [**31**] that suffices to establish the consistency of the logic, but it has a simple syntactic character with no apparent relation to authentication protocols.

QUESTION 9. *Does the Burrows-Abadi-Needham logic of authentication have a semantics more apparently related to authentication protocols?*

Two specific avenues of investigation were suggested: Tuttle suggested that an explicit complexity-theoretic semantics similar to those in [**67**] might be possible. Rackoff also made the point that complexity theory is the appropriate mechanism for bridging logic and practice. Merritt suggested a simpler "ping-pong" semantics along the lines of [**47**, **48**, **49**, **41**, **86**]. Such a semantics models the cryptosystem as a black-box, with perfect information-hiding properties.

Lamport noted that a hierarchical theory can, in principle, bridge the gap between physical systems and high-level formalisms. Presumably, one starts from such a low-level formal model that the relationship to the physical world is clear. Next, one constructs a hierarchy of formal systems at increasing levels of complexity and heights of abstraction, and constructs proofs by relating properties of systems at adjacent levels. (See, for example, [**77**, **33**, **83**].) Observing that cryptosystems are designed to baffle a very similar analysis, we pose the following:

QUESTION 10. *Can these hierarchical proof techniques be applied to cryptographic systems?*

Lipton later presented a list of axioms for intuitionist logic and noted the difficulty of appreciating the theory from its axioms alone. He argued that the semantics are crucial in considering the "correctness" of a theory. (This was echoed later in Weinberger's presentation, in which Weinberger noted that people may naïvely accept an axiom that "trust" is transitive but object to conclusions drawn from that axiom.)

Some of the issues raised during this discussion at the workshop are considered in Burrows's, Abadi's, and Needham's article in these proceedings.

One of the protocols discussed in Abadi's talk assumed an encryption function with the following property: Given the ciphertext $E(x)$, it is infeasible to generate the ciphertext $E(x+1)$. Of course, $x+1$ could be replaced with any simple function of x. The existence of such an encryption function is an open question. The RSA encryption function $E : x \mapsto x^e \bmod n$ is a multiplicative homomorphism, and so it is easy to compute $E(xy)$ given $E(x)$ and $E(y)$. The Diffie-Hellman encryption function $E : x \mapsto g^x \bmod p$ is an additive homomorphism, and so it is easy to generate $E(x+y)$ given $E(x)$ and $E(y)$. For both functions, it is assumed to be difficult to generate the other combination of ciphertexts.

An encryption function with the property that it is easy to compute both $E(x+y)$ and $E(xy)$ from $E(x)$ and $E(y)$ could not be used in the protocol discussed by Abadi. However, it could be used to accomplish *noninteractive, two-player secure circuit evaluation* in the cryptographic model (cf. [**1**, **26**]).

In summary, we have the following related questions.

QUESTION 11.

(a) *Is there an encryption function* $E()$ *such that both* $E(x+y)$ *and* $E(xy)$ *are easy to compute from* $E(x)$ *and* $E(y)$*?*

(b) *Is there any other way to accomplish noninteractive, two-player secure circuit evaluation in the cryptographic model?*

(c) *Alternatively, prove a nontrivial lower bound on the round complexity of two-player secure circuit evaluation in this model.*

Tygar's talk focussed on issues of notation and formal manipulation of security policies. Echoing previous discussion, questions were raised as to the semantics of such notation. Tygar commented that typically each permission allows the holder to execute a specific system call, which provides its *de facto* semantics. Discussion centered on the difficulty of deciding security properties such as secrecy using this approach, particularly as specifics of system calls vary between operating systems. Again, the theme was the distance between formalism and reality.

QUESTION 12.

(a) *Can access matrices be augmented usefully by precise interpretation for specific permissions?*

(b) *Could a small, orthogonal set of such permissions support a rich operating environment and still allow the simple derivation of meaningful security-related conclusions?*

(c) *Consider* (a) *and* (b) *specifically in the context of a networked computing environment.*

A later talk by Weinberger explored the problems of engineering security in real network environments, reinforcing both the importance and difficulty of resolving these questions. Noting the inadequacies of simple client-server models, he posed the following question.

QUESTION 13. *Can the abstraction and theory of transactions be applied to security problems, particularly in networks?*

The talks of Odlyzko and A. Lenstra about recent practical experience with discrete-log and factoring algorithms provoked two sorts of questions. One sort were straightforward questions to the speakers about what length keys they recommend for current use of Diffie-Hellman key-exchange and RSA, respectively. Odlyzko recommended moduli of length at least 300 decimal digits for use in the Diffie-Hellman scheme; this estimate takes into account the current work on the number-field sieve method [**78**]. A. Lenstra would not be pinned down on a key-length for RSA.

Odlyzko's talk also spurred a sociological discussion. The discrete-log algorithm that he and LaMacchia used to break the commercial system had been published in a mainstream journal more than three years before they conducted their experiment [**37**]. The published paper contained enough detail to suggest that primes of the size used in this commercial system were too small.

QUESTION 14. *Are the vendors of commercial systems that rely on the difficulty of the discrete-log problem aware of the literature on discrete-log algorithms? If not, is there something that the research community can do about this?*

1.1.3. *Friday, October 6, 1989.* The talks by Blum, Kannan, Rubinfeld, and Lipton led to a lot of discussion about their definitions of program-checking and program-testing. Much of the discussion focussed on the "little-oh" condition imposed on some checkers in [**21**].[1] The little-oh condition is designed to ensure that the checker will be different from the program being checked (i.e., that it will not just run the same code twice and compare the answers) and, more controversially, that it will be "simpler to debug" than the program being checked. If the checker is not simpler to debug, then one has not gained anything, since the checker is itself a program.

[1] In Section 1.2, our open questions address the complexity-theoretic definition of checking: The checker is just a probabilistic polynomial-time machine, and it interacts with the program in the same way that a verifier interacts with the prover in an interactive proof system. The little-oh condition is imposed by Blum et al. in some circumstances when they are attempting to design checkers that would be used in practice.

QUESTION 15.

(a) *Why should one believe that programs with lower asymptotic running-times are simpler to debug than programs with higher asymptotic running-times? In fact, it seems that there is evidence that the opposite is the case: Algorithms that use sophisticated techniques to compute things fast are often the hardest to code up correctly.*

(b) *Is there a better formal definition of "simpler to debug" that can be used to enhance the theory of checking?*

Goldwasser presented a signature scheme implemented from one-way permutations [**60**]. She posed the following problem.

QUESTION 16. *Can the assumption of one-way permutation be weakened to one-way function in* [**15**]*?*

These signatures have the property that each is independent of previous signatures. In previous solutions, the signature of each message essentially contains all previous signatures [**62**, **16**, **90**]. Goldwasser criticized these schemes as resulting in huge signatures and used the independence property to motivate her solution as more efficient. Merritt objected that only polynomially many messages can be signed in any such cryptographic scheme, so that the size of the "huge" messages is still polynomial in the security parameter. Indeed, if early signatures are padded to the length of the last signature, then the length of all signatures is the same, and still polynomial in the security parameter. Goldwasser accepted the point, and described the independence property as an issue of aesthetics, not efficiency.

QUESTION 17. *Which "provably secure" signature scheme is most efficient?*

QUESTION 18. *If two implementations of the same cryptographic primitive are constructed from different asymptotic complexity assumptions, can their efficiency be compared meaningfully?*

1.2. Complexity theory. Throughout this section, we use $\mathrm{AM}(r)$ to denote the class of languages recognizable by r-round Arthur-Merlin games (cf. [**6**]) and $\mathrm{IP}(r)$ to denote the class of languages recognizable by r-round interactive proof systems with polynomial-time Turing Machine verifiers (cf. [**61**]). $\mathrm{AM}(poly)$ (resp. $\mathrm{IP}(poly)$, also known simply as IP) denotes the union, over all polynomials r, of $\mathrm{AM}(r)$ (resp. $\mathrm{IP}(r)$). We use Σ_i^p and Π_i^p to denote the levels of the polynomial hierarchy and PH to denote the entire hierarchy. If C is a complexity class of languages, we use fC to denote the corresponding class of total functions. For example, fNP is the class of total functions computable in nondeterministic polynomial time.

The following relationships are known (cf. [**6**, **23**, **64**, **81**, **102**]): For any constant k, $\mathrm{AM}(k) = \mathrm{AM}(2)$; for any polynomial r, $\mathrm{AM}(r) \subseteq \mathrm{IP}(r)$ and $\mathrm{IP}(r) \subseteq \mathrm{AM}(r+2)$; $\mathrm{AM}(2) \subseteq \Pi_2^p$; if $\mathrm{coNP} \subseteq \mathrm{AM}(2)$, then $\Sigma_2^p = \Pi_2^p = \mathrm{AM}(2)$; finally, $\mathrm{AM}(poly) = \mathrm{IP}(poly) = \mathrm{PSPACE}$.

QUESTION 19. *What does the AM hierarchy really look like? For example,*
(a) *Is* $\mathrm{AM}(2) \subsetneq \mathrm{AM}(\log n)$?
(b) *Is* $\mathrm{AM}(2) \subsetneq \mathrm{AM}(\sqrt{n})$?
(c) *Is* $\mathrm{AM}(\log n) \subsetneq \mathrm{AM}(\sqrt{n})$?
(d) *Is* $\mathrm{AM}(\log n) \subsetneq \mathrm{PH}$?
(d) *Is* $\mathrm{AM}(\sqrt{n}) \subsetneq \mathrm{PH}$?

Blum and Kannan [**21**] have defined the language class $\mathrm{frIP} \cap \text{fr-coIP}$; it contains exactly the languages that have *program checkers* as defined in [**21**] and discussed in three of the talks abstracted in Section 2.3 below. Essentially, the difference between IP and frIP is that, in the latter, the behavior of both legitimate provers and cheating provers is restricted. The restriction is that they must be functions—the answer to the verifier's ith query q_i must depend only on q_i, rather than on $\langle q_1, \dots, q_i \rangle$, as it can in ordinary IP. This restriction is intended to capture the idea that the prover is a non-self-modifying, functional program; either the program computes the right function (i.e., is a legitimate prover), or it has a bug (i.e., computes the wrong function or is a cheating prover). It is asked in [**21**] whether frIP is the same as IP. This question has been answered conditionally: $\mathrm{frIP} \not\subseteq \mathrm{IP}$ if $\mathrm{PSPACE} \neq \mathrm{EXPTIME}$ (cf. [**4**, **81**, **102**]), and $\mathrm{frIP} \cap \text{fr-coIP} \not\subseteq \mathrm{NP}$ (and, *a fortiori*, is not contained in IP), if $\mathrm{NEEEXPTIME} \not\subseteq \mathrm{BPEEEXPTIME}$ (cf. [**14**]. BPEEEXPTIME is the triply exponential-time analogue of BPP; hence this condition is the triply exponential-time analogue of $\mathrm{NP} \not\subseteq \mathrm{BPP}$.)

QUESTION 20. *Is there a program-checker for SAT? Because SAT is clearly in frIP, this question boils down to "is SAT in fr-coIP?"*

The answer to Question 20 would be "yes" if there were an interactive proof system for coSAT in which the prover's computational power was limited to P^{NP}. The best-known upper bound on the power needed by the prover in an interactive proof system for coSAT is $\oplus\mathrm{P}$ (cf. [**112**]). By Toda's theorem [**108**], such a prover is powerful enough to recognize all of PH, which is (presumably) quite a bit more than P^{NP}. This suggests the following question, which is less ambitious than the previous one.

QUESTION 21. *Is there an interactive proof system for coSAT in which the prover is less powerful than* $\oplus\mathrm{P}$?

The notion of *random-self-reducibility* plays a role in many of the results presented at this workshop. The random-self-reducible sets are far from fully characterized. For convenience, we repeat the following definition from [**52**]. It is a generalization of the original definition given in [**2**].[2]

[2] Abadi, Feigenbaum, and Kilian (STOC, 1987) gave the first formal definition of random-self-reducible sets; their definition corresponds to what are now called 1-rsr sets, in the language of [**52**, **113**]. Subsequently, Tompa and Woll [**109**] considered random-self-reducible relations; they showed that relations $\{(x, y)\}$ for which there are random-self-reductions, efficient probabilistic algorithms that produce uniformly distributed pairs (x, y), and efficient

DEFINITION 1.1. Let $|x| = n$ and r be an element of $\{0, 1\}^m$, where m is bounded by a polynomial in n. A set S is *k-random-self-reducible* (abbreviated k-rsr) if there are polynomial-time computable functions ϕ, $\sigma_1, \ldots, \sigma_k$ such that

(1) for all n, all $x \in \{0, 1\}^n$, and all $r \in \{0, 1\}^m$,

$$\chi_S(x) = \phi(x, r, \chi_S(\sigma_1(x, r)), \ldots, \chi_S(\sigma_k(x, r))),$$

and

(2) if r is chosen uniformly at random from $\{0, 1\}^m$, then each $\sigma_i(x, r)$ is uniformly distributed over $\{0, 1\}^n$.

Note that, in general, k is a function of n, and the σ_i's are *dependent*, although individually each is uniform. χ_S denotes the characteristic function of S.

We denote by poly-RSR[3] the class of sets that are k-rsr for some polynomial k. Several negative results about poly-RSR are given in **[52]**. In particular, it is shown that any set that is 2-rsr is in $\mathrm{NP}/poly \cap \mathrm{coNP}/poly$. Thus, if SAT is 2-rsr, the PH collapses at the third level (see **[52]** for details).

QUESTION 22. *Is SAT k-rsr for any constant k? More generally, is SAT in poly-RSR?*

Added in proof: The answer to both parts of Question 22 is "Not unless the PH collapses." Refer to **[113]** for these and other recent developments on random-self-reducibility.

QUESTION 23. *Clearly every set that is $k(n)$-rsr is $(k(n)+1)$-rsr. Is this hierarchy strict?*

Note, in Question 23, that 1-rsr functions are probably a proper subset of poly-RSR: By the results in **[10, 80]**, the *permanent* function is in poly-RSR; however, by the main result in **[2]**, the permanent function is not 1-rsr, unless the PH collapses.

The definition of *coherent* sets (cf. Yao **[111]**) was motivated by, among other things, the definitions in **[2, 21, 52]**. The following relationships among coherence, checkability, and random-self-reducibility are known (cf. **[14, 111]**): All checkable sets are coherent; there is a coherent set that is not checkable; all

---

probabilistic algorithms that test whether a pair (x, y) is in the relation give rise to "perfect zero-knowledge proofs of possession of information." Note that any relation R that satisfies all of these properties corresponds to a set $S = \{x : \exists y \text{ such that } (x, y) \in R\}$ that is in NP. Thus these sets are a proper subclass of the 1-rsr sets, some of which are not even r.e.; see **[2]** for more details. The key point is that random-self-reducibility is a way of upper-bounding the worst-case complexity of a set in terms of its average-case complexity; since the average-case complexity may be arbitrarily high, random-self-reducibility certainly does not give an absolute upper bound on the complexity of the set.

[3] In **[52]**, poly-RSR actually denotes a class of *functions*, not just sets. We consider only the special case of boolean functions in this report; more details can be found in **[52]**.

sets in poly-RSR are coherent; there is a coherent set that is not in poly-RSR; there is a set in poly-RSR that is not checkable.

QUESTION 24. *Is there a checkable set that is not in poly-RSR? Good candidates may be the number-theoretic sets (see, e.g.,* **[3]**) *in which the checkers randomize only part of the input instance and leave the rest fixed.*

Part of Yao's motivation in defining coherence was to provide a way of proving that sets are not checkable. The best negative results that this approach has yielded so far are those in **[14]**: There is an incoherent (and hence uncheckable) set in DSPACE($n^{\log^* n}$); furthermore, if NEEEXPTIME $\not\subseteq$ BPEEEXPTIME, then there is an incoherent (and hence uncheckable) set in NP. Because all sets in BPP are coherent, the result that there is an incoherent set "just about PSPACE" cannot be improved without separating BPP from PSPACE.

On the other hand, all NP-complete sets (and indeed all sets that are complete for any level of the PH) are coherent (cf. **[14]**). Thus, if the answer to Question 20 is "no," the concepts of coherence and checkability are different even for sets in NP; the uncheckable, coherent sets in **[14]** are uncheckable because they are outside of NEXPTIME. (Fortnow, Rompel, and Sipser **[53]** show that all checkable sets are in NEXPTIME.)

Say that a set is *weakly coherent* if it satisfies exactly the conditions of Yao's definition, except that the examiner is a circuit family instead of a Turing machine. A set is called *strongly incoherent* if it is not weakly coherent. The incoherent sets in NP that are constructed in **[14]** are extremely sparse, and hence they are weakly coherent. Diagonalization can be used to construct a strongly incoherent set in DSPACE($n^{\log^* n}$), but the proof yields nothing about NP.

QUESTION 25. *Is there a strongly incoherent set in NP?*

QUESTION 26. *Yao's definition of coherence has proved very useful in deriving negative results on checkability and random-self-reducibility. Can it be used to derive results about other complexity-theoretic concepts?*

Examples of random-self-reducible functions were part of the motivation for the definition of *one-oracle instance-hiding schemes* (defined in **[2]**, where they are called "encryption schemes for functions"). There, it is shown that no NP-hard function has such a scheme, unless the PH collapses to the third level. More recently, *multioracle instance-hiding schemes* were introduced in **[10]**. We give an intuitive explanation of what they are here; a precise definition appears in **[10]**.

An m-oracle instance-hiding scheme for the function f is a synchronous protocol executed by a probabilistic, polynomial-time querier A and m all-powerful oracles $B_1, \ldots, B_m$. The goal is for A to use the power of the B_i's to compute $f(x)$, for some hard-to-compute function f, without revealing

x to the oracles. In each round of the protocol, A can send a message to each B_i and receive a response from each B_i; there is no bound on the amount of computation used by the oracles in each round, and in fact the responses may not even be computable (hence the term "oracle"); the querier, of course, can only do a polynomial-time computation in each round. B_i cannot communicate with B_j during the protocol, for all pairs $i \neq j$, nor does B_i see the messages sent between A and B_j. At the end of the protocol, A computes $f(x)$, using x, its private coin tosses, and the oracles' responses. The requirement that the protocol be instance-hiding means that, for any x and x' such that $|x| = |x'|$, for all oracles B_i, the distribution of messages exchanged by A and B_i is identical.[4] Thus no B_i learns anything about A's private input x except its length. An instance-hiding scheme is allowed to be adaptive, in that both queries and answers in any round may depend on the messages exchanged in previous rounds.

It is shown in **[10]** that *every* boolean function, even those that are non-r.e., has an $(n - c\log n)$-oracle instance-hiding scheme, for any constant c, where n is the length of A's input x. This general upper bound was improved to $n/(c\log n)$ in **[11]**.

The multioracle instance-hiding schemes in **[10, 11]** do not use the full, adaptive power available to them. They have the following special form.

DEFINITION 1.2. A function $f : \{0, 1\}^* \to \{0, 1\}^*$ is $(1, k)$-*locally-random-reducible* (abbreviated $(1, k)$-lrr) to a function $g : \{0, 1\}^* \to \{0, 1\}^*$ if there are polynomial-time computable functions ϕ, $\sigma_1, \dots, \sigma_k$ and polynomially-bounded functions $m(n)$ and $w(n)$ such that

(1) for all n, all $x \in \{0, 1\}^n$, and all $r \in \{0, 1\}^{m(n)}$,

$$f(x) = \phi(x, r, g(\sigma_1(x, r)), \dots, g(\sigma_k(x, r))),$$

and

(2) if r is chosen uniformly from $\{0, 1\}^{m(n)}$, then each $\sigma_i(x, r)$ is distributed uniformly over $\{0, 1\}^{w(n)}$.

Once again, k is a function of n, and the σ_i's are dependent.

Clearly, a locally random reduction can be thought of as a one-round instance-hiding scheme: Querier A chooses r, computes the random instances $\sigma_i(x, r)$, sends $\sigma_i(x, r)$ to oracle B_i (for all i), receives the responses $\{g(\sigma_i(x, r))\}$, and uses them to deduce $f(x)$.

QUESTION 27. *Is every boolean function* $(1, k)$-*lrr to some other function, where* $k(n) = o(n/\log n)$?

[4]Not polynomial-time indistinguishable, but truly identical; these are all-powerful *oracles*, and hence polynomial-time indistinguishability is useless. See **[2, 10]** for further discussion of this issue.

QUESTION 28. *The upper bound of* $n/(c \log n)$ *holds for all boolean functions, even those that are non-r.e. Is there a better upper bound for recursive functions? Is there a better upper bound for functions in fNP?*

QUESTION 29.
(a) *Characterize precisely the functions that have two-oracle instance-hiding schemes.*
(b) *Characterize precisely the functions* f *for which there is a* g *such that* f *is* $(1, 2)$*-lrr to* g.[5]

QUESTION 30. *So far, there is no known way to take advantage of the adaptive nature of instance-hiding schemes. In* [**2**], *it is shown that NP-hard functions have no one-oracle instance-hiding schemes, with or without adaptiveness, unless the PH collapses. On the other hand, the multioracle instance-hiding schemes given in* [**10**, **11**] *are nonadaptive. Is there any way to use adaptiveness? In particular, can it be used to reduce the number of oracles?*

Zero-knowledge proof systems are two-player games in which the powerful player hides the answer from the weak player. Instance-hiding schemes are two-player games in which the weak player hides the question from the powerful player. It is natural to ask whether both of these objectives can be obtained in the same game.

Towards this end, Blum, Luby, and Rubinfeld (see Section 2.3 below) have defined *private/adaptive checkers*, and Beaver, Feigenbaum, and Shoup [**12**] have defined *zero-knowledge, instance-hiding proof systems.* It is shown in [**12**] that any function that has a multiprover interactive proof system also has one that is both zero-knowledge and instance-hiding. Several questions remain open.

QUESTION 31. *Reduce the number of provers needed for the zero-knowledge, instance-hiding proof systems constructed in* [**12**].

QUESTION 32. *Characterize precisely the functions that have private/adaptive checkers, as defined by Blum, Luby, and Rubinfeld in these proceedings.*

[5] A partial result along these lines was recently obtained by Yao: There is a boolean function $f \in \mathrm{fDSPACE}(2^{n^{\log\log n}})$ that is not $(1, 2)$-lrr to any boolean function g. Note that the target functions g in [**10**, **11**] are not boolean.

2. Talk abstracts

2.1. Wednesday, October 4, 1989

Joan Feigenbaum: Welcoming remarks and open problems. Abadi, Feigenbaum, and Kilian [2] considered the following general question. Suppose that processor A is insufficiently powerful to compute a function f, and processor B is sufficiently powerful to compute f. B is willing to compute f for A, but B is a public resource and cannot guarantee the privacy of a query that A sends him. Can A transform an element x in the domain of f to another element y, send y to B, get back B's answer, and infer from it $f(x)$ in such a way that B cannot infer x from y? If so, then f is said to have a *one-oracle instance-hiding scheme.*

It is shown in [2] that if f is NP-hard, then it does not have a one-oracle instance-hiding scheme, unless the polynomial hierarchy collapses. Abadi, Feigenbaum, and Kilian left open the following question, due to Rivest: Suppose A can query several oracles $B_1, \dots, B_k$ that are not allowed to talk to each other. In other words, do NP-hard functions have *multioracle instance-hiding schemes*?

Beaver and Feigenbaum [**10**] recently obtained positive answers to Rivest's question, in two models. In Model 1, in which distinct B's may communicate before, but not during, the protocol with A, they showed that n oracles suffice for *any* function f, where $n = |x|$. In Model 2, in which distinct B's may not communicate at all, either before or during the protocol, they showed that two oracles suffice for any f.

I will review briefly the results of [**2**, **10**] and then state open problems in this area.

(These open problems are stated in Section 1. Further discussion of these questions can be found in, e.g., [**11**, **12**, **52**, **113**].)

Moti Yung: On the impossibility of basing cryptography on oblivious transfer. Oblivious Transfer (OT) is a basic two-party protocol introduced by M. Rabin. It enables one user to transmit a secret with success probability 1/2, without knowing the result of the transmission. It is analogous to sending a letter that arrives with probability 1/2. Kilian [**72**] showed that OT is complete for the set of protocols for secure distributed circuit evaluation. In the absence of any kind of physical channel security, the only known mechanisms for achieving OT are based on mathematical (cryptographic) assumptions. This is the classical cryptographic context, and it is the context of this work. It is known that OT is possible if a trapdoor function exists.

Recently, OT was proposed as a way to achieve noninteractive (or limited-interaction) procedures. This led us to ask what the round complexity of a (mathematically-based) OT protocol is. We show in this paper that OT is inherently interactive.

We also show the impossibility of implementing "perfect" OT (that is, perfect in an information-theoretic sense). We give a strong indication (in the sense of Impagliazzo-Rudich [**68**]) that OT will be hard to implement under the assumption that a one-way function exists. Finally, we investigate consequences of these results.

(Joint work with R. Ostrovsky. A paper based on this talk appears in these proceedings.)

Stuart Haber: Security against chosen-ciphertext attack. Since zero-knowledge proofs were proposed [**61**], they have seen several different uses in cryptography. In a number of extended abstracts published in conference proceedings, zero-knowledge proofs have been used in one or another way in order to specify a public-key cryptosystem that achieves one or another sort of security against chosen-ciphertext attack (for example, the speaker did this, along with his coauthors, at Crypto '85 [**54**]). None of these published claims included a precise definition of the security achieved, let alone a proof (for example, ditto).

In this talk I would like to suggest a formal definition for chosen-ciphertext security, hoping to elicit comment and criticism. Then I will show how I can use the properties of zero-knowledge proofs of knowledge (as formalized by Tompa-Woll [**109**] and Feige-Fiat-Shamir [**51**]) in order to prove, while waving only one of my hands, that the interactive cryptosystem we proposed at Crypto '85 actually satisfies the proposed definition.

(Joint work with Z. Galil and M. Yung. A paper based on this talk appears in these proceedings.)

Lenore Cowen: On the structure of secret key exchange protocols. A secret-key-exchange protocol, which enables two parties to establish a common and secret key over public channels, is a fundamental primitive for private communication. We show here that any secret-key-exchange protocol has strong structural properties. Our results imply that one-way functions are necessary for secret key exchange. As a corollary we obtain that one-way functions are also necessary for oblivious transfer.

Our results also imply that the existence of a secret-key-exchange protocol implies the existence of strong bit commitment schemes, and that perfect secret key exchange (i.e., in the "information-theoretic sense") is impossible.

(Joint work with M. Bellare and S. Goldwasser. A paper based on this talk appears in these proceedings.)

Judit Bar-Ilan: Noncryptographic fault-tolerant computing in a constant number of rounds of interaction. Given a circuit C with bounded fan-in, there are noncryptographic protocols by which a collection of n processors can evaluate C at secret values $x_1, \dots, x_n$, without revealing anything about the arguments except what the final result provides (cf. Ben-Or–Goldwasser–Wigderson [**20**] and Chaum-Crépeau-Damgård [**35**]). Unfortunately, evaluating a circuit of depth d and size s requires $O(d)$ rounds of communication and messages of size polynomial in s and n.

We show that a completely connected network with private communication lines can secretly evaluate a circuit of arbitrary depth in a constant expected number of rounds. Our results are based on three new techniques for multiparty computations, including secretly computing multiplicative inverses over a field, simulating polynomially-bounded fan-in multiplicative (or AND) gates, and secretly computing compositions of polynomially many secret permutations. No method to evaluate unbounded fan-in multiplicative (or AND) gates was previously known, though unbounded addition is trivial.

There is a concomitant increase in message size, but for any function in NC^1 the number of bits required is polynomial in n. For arbitrary circuits we exhibit a tradeoff in time complexity and message complexity.

For $3t < n$, our methods tolerate up to t faulty processors, with Byzantine faults and a dynamic adversary who coordinates the processors.

(Joint work with D. Beaver. An extended abstract of these results appears in the proceedings of the 8th PODC [**8**].)

Phillip Rogaway: Secure distributed computation in a constant number of rounds. Goldreich, Micali, and Wigderson [**59**] give a cryptographic protocol that securely carries out any multiparty computation, assuming that the majority of the players in the computation follow the protocol faithfully. Subsequent work by Ben-Or, Goldwasser, and Wigderson [**20**] and by Chaum, Crépeau, and Damgård [**35**] remove the need for cryptography (assuming we have private channels) when more than two thirds of the participants in the protocol are honest. Work by T. Rabin [**99**] on verifiable secret sharing has allowed the extension of these noncryptographic results to the case of honest majority; see Beaver [**9**] and Rabin–Ben-Or [**100**].

In a high bandwidth network of powerful processors, the round complexity of a distributed protocol is a measure of the time necessary to carry out the computation. Reducing round complexity while retaining feasibility of local computation is therefore an important goal.

The cryptographic protocol of [**59**] requires $\Theta(dn^2)$ communication rounds, where d is the depth of the circuit evaluating the function, and n is the number of players. A variant by Haber [**66**] makes due with $\Theta(d)$ rounds. The dependency in these protocols on the depth of the circuit being evaluated is due to the fact that the protocols distributively evaluate the circuit gate-by-gate, working their way from the leaves to the root. As time progresses, the community shares the values on wires closer and closer to the root.

The noncryptographic protocols of [**20**, **35**] share this gate-by-gate approach and require $\Theta(d)$ rounds. In fact, it might seem reasonable to believe that the depth of the underlying circuit family lower bounds (up to a constant) the required number of communication rounds, both for the cryptographic and noncryptographic case. However, Bar-Ilan and Beaver [**8**] show how a log-depth circuit family can be evaluated noncryptographically in a *constant* expected number of rounds, retaining polynomial computation for each player. This allows arbitrary circuit families to be distributively evaluated in $\Theta(d/\log m)$ expected rounds, where m is the number of leaves.

The work contained here was motivated by **[8]**, but reverts to the cryptographic setting. We show how an *arbitrary* circuit can be securely collaboratively evaluated using only a constant number of rounds of interaction. That is, the number of rounds is independent of both the complexity of the circuit being evaluated and the security parameter. The local computation to be performed by each player is polynomial in the size of the circuit and in the security parameter. To achieve this, we assume that a one-way function exists and that the majority of participants are honest. The scheme necessarily departs from the gate-by-gate approach to collaborative circuit evaluation.

(Joint work with D. Beaver and S. Micali. An extended abstract of these results appears in the Proceedings of the 22nd STOC **[13]**. For further discussion of the power of constant-round secure protocols, see **[11]**.)

Donald Beaver: Privacy for general two-party protocols. We examine the problem of computing functions in a distributed manner based on private inputs, revealing the value of a function without revealing any additional information about the inputs. A function $f(x_1, \dots, x_n)$ is *t-private* if there is a protocol whereby n parties, each holding an input value, can compute f, and no subset of t or fewer parties gains any information other than what is computable from $f(x_1, \dots, x_n)$.

The class of t-private boolean functions, for $t \geq \lceil n/2 \rceil$, was characterized by Chor and Kushilevitz **[36]**.

In this talk, we give a characterization of 1-private functions for two parties, *without* the restriction to the boolean case. We also examine a restricted form of private computation in the n-party case, and show that addition is the only privately computable function in that model.

We also present an open problem concerning the existence of private n-party protocols for computing nonboolean functions of $n > 2$ variables.

(A paper based on this talk appears in these proceedings. The same result was obtained independently by Kushilevitz **[74]**.)

Butler Lampson: User authentication and delegation in distributed systems. A basic primitive for secure distributed computing is the ability of a system A to delegate to another system B the authority to act on A's behalf. User authentication is a special case in which the user delegates to a machine. When B requests service from another machine C, B will present credentials that are supposed to demonstrate to C that B is making the request and that A has delegated to B. We would like to be sure that the credentials cannot be forged (i.e., the request must have come from B, and the delegation must have been made by A). Also, when B has finished acting on behalf of A it should be able to relinquish its right to do so in such a way that even if B is later compromised, it will not be able to regain the right.

Public key encryption can be used to implement delegation. B makes up a fresh "delegation key pair," keeps the private key secret, and sends the public key to A. A signs a "delegation certificate" that authorizes B to act on A's behalf (perhaps for limited purposes only), provided that B's requests are signed by the delegation key. B signs his requests with both its own key and the delegation key. To relinquish its authority, B just forgets the private delegation key. The only problem is that with RSA public key encryption, things are not as fast as we would like.

User authentication is not exactly the same, since the user cannot do public key encryption in his head. There are various ways of getting around this defect.

Matt Bishop: Enhancing security in electronic mail. The security of electronic mail sent through the Internet may be summed up in three words: there is none. The Privacy Task Force has recently released a proposal designed to remedy this situation. The mechanism provides both authentication and privacy for electronic mail using a certificate-based key management scheme.

To send such a message, it must first be encrypted using a *data encryption key* (DEK), which is itself encrypted using an *interchange key* (IK). The DEKs are chosen on a per-message basis, whereas the IKs remain fixed (unless changed by the party or parties involved) for a given sender and a given recipient. The DEKs may use either private or public key systems; the IKs use the RSA cryptosystem. Each user has a certificate consisting of that user's public key, user identification information (such as organizational affiliations), and the identity of the organization whose notary has signed the certificate; this is encrypted using the notary's private key. To transmit a message, the sender obtains the certificate of the recipient and the public key of the notary who signed the certificate; the sender then obtains the recipient's public key from the certificate, encrypts the DEK using the public key as the IK, and places that in a header in the message.

The key management system is hierarchical, involving certifying authorities who sign certificates and who may delegate authority to identify (potential) users by affiliation to organizational notaries, so (for example) an employee of Dartmouth College would not need to convince the certifying authority itself that the stated affiliation is in fact correct, but would be able to do so to an organizational notary of Dartmouth College who could in turn inform the certifying authority that the affiliation is correct. Similarly, the certifying authority may cooperate with other certifying authorities to provide secure mail between users certified by different authorities. A mechanism for revocation and for notifying users that specific certificates are no longer valid is also provided.

(A paper based on this talk appears in these proceedings.)

Gene Tsudik: Secure control of internetwork traffic. In order to preserve autonomy in an increasingly open and heterogeneous internetwork environment, controls must be added to internetwork protocols at the expense of packet processing speed. Neither traditional network access control methods nor current routing protocols are suited for secure control of transit traffic on an internetwork. This talk explores the design and performance of a new generation of internetwork protocols that support secure control of transit traffic.

(Joint work with D. Estrin. A paper based on this talk appears in these proceedings.)

Jim Reeds: Building a secure network based on power of attorney. In a large-scale, multilevel, secure, distributed computer system you need to have a convenient way of handling a wide range of special privileges, rights, and authorizations. These rights will not all originate from a central control computer. Some will be nonce rights, forgotten soon after granting. Some will originate with the owners of the computers, some with the operators, some with the users. Some will be passed from computer to computer, in possibly delegated or diluted form. Some will be derived from others. It will be possible to be confused. Given a substratum of trusted computers connected by a trusted network, how can we build up a distributed system for creating, negotiating, storing, transmitting, and exercising rights?

A small project at Bell Labs is experimenting with some of these ideas. For example, we are trying to find a minimal set of substratum (operating system and networking) services needed to extend the file access controls (and associated administration functions) found in a trusted multilevel secure computer system to a distributed network file system.

One assumption is that almost all sensitive security actions (such as changing a user's clearance level, creating a new security classification, declassifying data, etc.) will involve use of a "power of attorney" (or "delegation" or "proxy") protocol, whereby a server acts on behalf of one entity (user, say) by exercising a right received from another entity. We have identified two substratum services that seem to be crucial ingredients for a power-of-attorney-based distributed secure system: a method of establishing secure inter-process, cross-machine communications "pipes," and a notation for recording rights. Since standard versions of (say) the UNIX[6] operating system provide neither service, we have been forced to design our own.

(A paper based on this talk appears in these proceedings.)

2.2. Thursday, October 4, 1989

Michael Merritt: Open problems. This talk is primarily concerned with research methodology in the overlap of distributed computing and cryptography. A paper based on it appears in these proceedings.

[6]UNIX is a trademark of AT&T Bell Laboratories.

Mike Burrows: User authentication with smart-cards. The authentication of users in distributed systems poses special problems because users lack the ability to encrypt and decrypt. In a popular approach, the user is forced to trust the node he wants to use; in a more satisfactory solution, a smart-card assists the user.

Authentication is relatively straightforward with a sufficiently powerful smart-card. However, for economic reasons, authentication protocols that place weaker demands on the smart-cards should be considered. These protocols are subtler, as they rely on intricate trust relationships among the principals in the system. We discuss a range of smart-card authentication protocols, and make precise their assumptions and the guarantees they offer, using the Burrows-Abadi-Needham logic of authentication [**31**] where appropriate.

(Joint work with M. Abadi, C. Kaufman, and B. Lampson.)

Martín Abadi: A logic of authentication. Questions of belief are essential in analyzing protocols for authentication in distributed computing systems. We describe a simple epistemic logic specifically designed for this analysis. The formalism enables us to isolate and express differences between protocols, and it draws attention to subtle features. For instance, it highlights some redundancies in both information and encryption, as well as undesirable assumptions sometimes required to achieve authentication.

In this talk we review the basics of the logic. We emphasize public-key reasoning, and, as an example, describe the CCITT X.509 authentication protocols and some flaws the logic has helped uncover.

(Joint work with M. Burrows and R. Needham. Papers based on this work appear in these proceedings, in the Proceedings of the 2nd TARK Conference [**30**], and in the Proceedings of the Royal Society of London [**31**].)

Marie-Jeanne Toussaint: Reasoning about participants' knowledge in cryptographic protocols. So far, a lot of effort has been devoted to the study of cryptographic systems. Unfortunately, if the cryptosystem is used in an incorrect protocol, security can be compromised even if the cryptosystem is perfect.

Assuming the underlying cryptographic system to be perfect, we present a modelization of the probabilistic knowledge of the participants in cryptographic protocols. This modelization is an extension of the "Hidden Automorphism Model" introduced by Merritt [**86**]. We use it to analyze and find the possible weaknesses of a number of examples. Finally, we present an attempt to systematically derive the representation of the participants' knowledge from the protocol.

(Joint work with P. Wolper. A paper based on this talk appears in these proceedings.)

Doug Tygar: Protection models in the security toolkit. I will discuss issues of notation, implementation, and semantics of security policies. I will present examples from two real systems, the ITOSS system implemented at Harvard and the MIRO system implemented at CMU.

(For further discussion of ITOSS, refer to M. Rabin and Tygar [**98**].)

Jurjen Bos: Detecting disrupters in the DC untraceable sending network. *Untraceable sending* is a transmission system in which it is impossible to trace the sender of a message. David Chaum proposed an implementation of this mechanism in [**34**]. There he addresses the problem of *disruption*, where a malicious sender uses anonymity to disrupt the system without being caught.

Here we present a new implementation that uses a method from coding theory in a completely new way. The resulting solution is much more efficient than Chaum's original one.

(Joint work with B. den Boer. A paper based on this talk appears in the Proceedings of Eurocrypt89 [**24**].)

Andrew Odlyzko: Linear equations over finite fields and the discrete logarithm problem. Experience with implementing the best-known practical algorithms for computing discrete logarithms in prime fields shows that they are only slightly less efficient than the quadratic sieve for factoring integers of the same size. Neither the sieving procedure nor the problem of solving a sparse system of linear equations over finite fields presents a serious difficulty. What this implies is that to obtain reasonable security, implementations of the Diffie-Hellman algorithm and its variants require the use of very large primes.

(Joint work with B. A. LaMacchia. More information about the work described in this talk can be found in [**75**, **76**].)

Arjen Lenstra: Experimental work on factoring. Last spring we factored a 106-digit number using otherwise idle cycles of approximately 600 machines all over the U.S., Australia, Canada, Europe, and Japan. The machines on our "factoring-network" used electronic mail to exchange messages. There are more than 600 machines on the electronic mail networks. How safe is the RSA-challenge if we could use all idle cycles on all those machines worldwide?

(Joint work with H. W. Lenstra, M. Manasse, and J. Pollard. More information about the factoring network and the recent number-field sieve factoring method can be found in [**78**, **79**].)

Matt Bishop: Preliminary statistical analysis of the UNIX password algorithm. Lately, concern about the strength of the UNIX operating system's password encryption algorithm has led to some proposals for altering it. The proposals are aimed at increasing the time required to test guesses of passwords to see if they are accurate.

However, a more fundamental question has not been explored: Is it possible to deduce information about a password from its encrypted form? Although based on the DES, for which statistical studies have been conducted, the UNIX password scheme alters that algorithm by perturbing a table. How does this affect the cryptographic strength of the one-way function?

Some very preliminary results of a statistical analysis are presented. The methodology will be discussed, as will the results, and suggestions for future work will also be presented.

Peter Weinberger: Security in distributed file systems. I will present a view of distributed systems that questions some of the views described above. Two of the underlying assumptions questioned will be the feasibility of managing a global naming scheme and the transitivity of a binary relation formalizing "A trusts B," where A and B are computer systems with both human users and privileged programs.

Alon Orlitsky: Feedback in discrete communication. X and Y are random variables distributed according to some joint probability distribution $p(x, y)$. Person P_X knows X and Person P_Y knows Y. They communicate in order for P_Y to learn X. P_X may or may not learn Y. How many bits must be transmitted (by both persons) in the worst case?

$C_1(p)$ is the number of bits required when at most one message is allowed, necessarily from P_X to P_Y. $C_2(p)$ is the number of bits required when at most two messages are permitted: P_Y transmits a message to P_X, then P_X responds with a message to P_Y. $C_\infty(p)$ is the number of bits required when P_X and P_Y can communicate back and forth. Messages from P_Y to P_X are called feedback.

The maximal reduction in communication achievable via feedback is logarithmic: all probability distributions p have $C_\infty(p) \geq \log C_1(p)$ while there are distributions for which equality holds. Therefore, $C_1(p)$ can be exponentially larger than $C_\infty(p)$. Yet $C_2(p)$ cannot. With just one feedback message the number of bits required is at most four times larger than the minimal: $C_2(p) \leq 4C_\infty(p)$. For some distributions, $C_2(p) \geq 2C_\infty(p)$.

Surprisingly, for almost all sparse distributions, P_Y (who has nothing to say at the beginning of the protocol) must transmit almost all the bits in order to achieve the minimal number: $C_\infty(p)$. The number of bits transmitted by P_Y can be appreciably reduced only if P_X transmits exponentially more than $C_\infty(p)$ bits.

(A paper based on this talk appears in these proceedings.)

Cynthia Dwork: The Secret Message Transmission problem. In the Secret Message Transmission problem there are two synchronized nonfaulty processors, A and B, connected by some number n of wires. A has a secret message m drawn from a finite set Q of values. There are two parameters, σ (for secrecy) and ρ (for resiliency). The problem is for A to convey m to B while satisfying:

Perfect secrecy: For all sets S of at most σ of the n wires, no listening adversary $\mathscr{A}_L$, listening to all the wires of S, learns anything about m (secrecy must be information-theoretic).

Perfect resiliency: For all sets R of at most ρ wires (possibly, but not necessarily, disjoint from S), B correctly learns m, regardless of the disrupting adversary $\mathscr{A}_D$ controlling and coordinating the behavior of the wires in R.

We obtain tight bounds on n, the required connectivity between A and B, for this problem, for both the *one-way* case (information flows only from A to B) and the *two-way* case (A and B "converse"), under the assumption that the coordination between the listening and disrupting adversaries is restricted. Specifically, we show that the bounds on n decrease by ρ even with just one extra round of communication; moreover, both algorithms have cost polynomial in σ and ρ.

We also study how the lower bounds on n are affected by the degree of coordination between $\mathscr{A}_L$ and $\mathscr{A}_D$. Unlimited coordination yields an increase of ρ for both the one-way and two-way cases, and these bounds are tight. Prior agreement between the two adversaries, on a disrupting strategy, yields increases of $\rho - 1$ or ρ wires, tight in the one-way case and for two-round two-way algorithms (our two-way algorithm for this model also requires only two rounds). Our lower and upper bounds differ by exactly one wire for two-way algorithms of three or more rounds.

Finally, we discovered an interesting relationship between secret message transmission and *Verifiable Secret Sharing*. The results for one-way transmission imply that the lower bound of $3t + 1$ processors needed for verifiable secret sharing (obtained by Ben-Or, Goldwasser, and Wigderson [**20**]) holds even in the presence of a broadcast channel. The previous proof is by reduction to Byzantine agreement and therefore does not apply in the model with a broadcast channel.

(Joint work with D. Dolev, O. Waarts, and M. Yung. An extended abstract based on these results appears in the Proceedings of the 31st FOCS [**46**].)

2.3. Friday, October 6, 1989

Manuel Blum: Designing programs that check their work. This talk describes an approach that I have recently initiated to ensure correctness of computation. The idea, which is distinct from verification or testing, is to design programs to check their work. The lack of such checks by programs is, in my view, an oversight. Scientists, engineers, and programmers are all taught to check their work. Programs can benefit equally well from the same sort of activity; they can detect their errors by checking their results.

This talk first defines *program result checkers* and suggests how to construct checkers for a variety of interesting problems. It points out the importance of randomization in the design of checkers and the close tie between checkers and *probabilistic interactive proofs.* The idea of checking leads one naturally to try to design programs that correct their errors. As an example of what is possible, I show how to convert a package of fast but faulty programs for matrix multiplication, inversion, and determinant into a package that works correctly and fast on all inputs without exception.

(Joint work with S. Kannan and R. Rubinfeld. For further discussion of the notions of checking, testing, and self-correcting that form the basis of this and the next two talks, see, e.g., [**3**, **14**, **21**, **22**, **70**, **111**].)

Ronitt Rubinfeld: Stronger checkers and general techniques for numerical problems. The theory of checking is a technique for designing a simple program, called the checker, which verifies that a possibly faulty program for a problem outputs the correct answer on given inputs. In the first part of the talk, we present a general technique for designing efficient checkers for arithmetic problems. This technique gives very simple checkers that conceptually only rely on the ability to add, shift, and compare. We show how to apply this technique to get efficient checkers for integer multiplication, integer division, integer mod, modular multiplication, modular exponentiation, polynomial multiplication, squaring, and matrix multiplication.

In the second part of the talk, we discuss stronger notions of checking: We first define what it means to check a self-modifying program, and then show how to construct such checkers for the aforementioned problems. We then alter the definition of checking to allow the checking of private computations, i.e., ones in which the program calls made by the checker do not reveal the computation that is being checked. We show how to construct such private checkers for the aforementioned problems.

(Joint work with M. Blum and M. Luby. A paper based on the material in the second part of this talk appears in these proceedings.)

Sampath Kannan: Checkers in group theory. Group theory is an interesting area for developing program checkers for several reasons:

- Computational group theorists often worry about the reliability of computer-produced results.
- The structure of group theoretic problems can be exploited in the design of efficient program checkers.
- The rich polynomial equivalence structure among group-theoretic problems allows for the design of checkers for several problems at once.

In the first half of the talk, these and other general issues in checking group-theoretic computation are discussed. In the second half, we focus on the problem of group isomorphism. We provide an interactive proof for the nonisomorphism of groups given as permutation groups. This goes part way towards a checker for the problem.

(An extensive discussion of checkers for group-theoretic problems appears in **[70]**. The interactive proof system for group nonisomorphism appears in **[5]**.)

Richard J. Lipton: New directions in testing. We present a new theory of randomly testable functions. This theory is distribution-free; i.e., it makes no assumptions about the distribution of values used at run time. It demonstrates that testing can *prove* that programs are correct.

(A paper based on this talk appears in these proceedings.)

Michael Fischer: Secret bit transmission using a random deal of cards. In the game of bridge, players use open bids to communicate information about their hands to their partners. It is to their advantage to use a bidding strategy that releases as little useful information as possible to the opponents.

We abstract from bridge to consider the following problem: Player A has a secret bit s (independent of her hand) which she wants to communicate to her partner, player B, but she doesn't want her opponents to gain any information at all about s. Players are dealt hands at random from a deck of size n, with player A receiving p cards, player B receiving q cards, and the remaining $r = n - p - q$ cards going to the opponents. Players A and B then carry on a conversation in which they can make arbitrary statements, but everything they say is public and is heard by the opponents.

We present several protocols for A and B that solve this problem under various assumptions. The easiest assumes that A and B have access to random number generators. (Note that public key cryptography is not applicable here because we place no limit on the computational power of the opponents.) This protocol works whenever $p, q \geq 1$ and $p + q \geq r + 2$, so the partners together have more than half the cards in the deck. Rather surprisingly, it is sufficient for the partners to receive any fixed fraction of the cards (say $1/10$) if the deck is sufficiently large. We also establish a general condition on p, q, and r that implies that no protocol exists, and we discuss the effects of requiring that the protocols for A and B be deterministic.

(Joint work with M. Paterson and C. Rackoff. A paper based on this talk appears in these proceedings.)

Rafail Ostrovsky: Efficient computation on oblivious RAMs. A machine is *oblivious* if the sequence in which it accesses memory locations is equivalent for any two programs with the same running time. For example, an oblivious Turing machine is one for which the movement of the heads on the tapes is identical for each computation. (Thus, it is independent of the actual input.) What is the slowdown in the running time of any machine, if it is required to be oblivious?

In 1979, Pippenger and Fischer **[96]** showed how a two-tape Turing machine can simulate, on-line, a one-tape Turing machine, with a logarithmic slowdown in the running time. We show a similar result for the random-access memory (RAM) model of computation. In particular, we show how to do an on-line simulation of an arbitrary RAM program by a probabilistic RAM whose memory access pattern is independent of the program that is being executed, and only with a poly-logarithmic slowdown in the running time.

Our proof yields a technique of efficiently hiding (through randomization) the access pattern into any composite data-structure. We exhibit applications of our technique to secure distributed databases and to software protection, solving an open problem posed by Goldreich **[56]**.

Our result can be strengthened in the practical world by using *any* one-way function to simulate a random oracle **[57]**. We stress, though, that cryptography is *not* needed in the proof of our main result. We now list some of the applications of our technique.

One of the applications of our result deals with a distributed database in which no user can hold at one time more than a small part of the database, and in which a polynomial-time adversary can monitor all communication lines. Encryption hides the contents of the messages, but does not hide which communication lines are used. Thus, indirectly, some information about the database is revealed to an adversary. For example, an adversary can learn which part of the database is most useful (i.e., most frequently read and updated), and which part of the database is most useful to a particular user. How can users hide the access sequence without sending too many additional messages? Our technique yields a simple and efficient solution to this problem.

Another application concerns *software protection*, one of the most important issues in computer practice. A theoretical formulation of the problem for a generic one-processor, random-access machine (RAM) model of computation was given by Goldreich **[56]**. In this paper, we present a simple and efficient software protection scheme for this model. In particular, we show how to protect any program at the cost of a poly-logarithmic slowdown in the running time of the protected program.

Software is very expensive to create and very easy to steal. "Software piracy" is a major concern (and a major loss of revenue) to all software-related companies. Software pirates borrow/rent software they need, copy it to their computer and use it without paying anything for it. The question of how one prevents a pirate from illegal copying of software is a question of "software protection." Let us examine various options that any software company has when considering how to protect its software. On one hand, it can sell a *physically shielded* computer with all the software installed, which self-destructs if ever opened. Clearly, such a "solution" eliminates the problem of software piracy at the price of forcing customers to purchase a new computer for each new task. We consider such a "solution" infeasible and contradictory to a general-purpose machine paradigm. One would want to sell just the software, that runs on any general-purpose computer, but which is impossible to copy. This, however, is unachievable: if one sells software that runs on any general-purpose computer, the software can always be duplicated. Thus, we always need some physically-shielded hardware to prevent the duplication. What is the minimal amount of protected hardware one needs? We require only a constant number of registers to be physically protected. That is, only a single *chip* with a fixed number of registers is protected while the entire memory is open to the pirate, who can inspect it and alter it, in order to learn something about the protected program. Thus, we assume that a physically shielded chip is connected to a random access memory (RAM) to which the pirate has a complete read/write access.

The next question we turn to is the interpretation of "software protection." Let us consider the following hypothetical situation: suppose you are a software producer selling a protected program that took you an enormous effort to write. Your competitor purchases your program, experiments with it widely and learns some partial information about your implementation. Intuitively, if the information he gained through experimentation with your protected program simplifies his task of writing a software package, then we consider the protection scheme to be insecure. Thus, the software protection must hide *all* the information about the implementation. Software protection is secure if, intuitively, whatever any poly-time adversary can do when having access to an (encrypted) program running on a protected chip, he can also do when having access to a "specification oracle" (such an oracle on any input "magically" gives the output and the running time). Essentially, the protected program must behave like a black box, which, on any input, hums for a while and gives an output and such that no information except its I/O behavior and running time can be extracted. Thus, not only the values stored in the general-purpose memory must be hidden (using encryption) but also the *sequence* in which memory locations are accessed during program execution must be hidden. Notice that if this is not the case, the program "loop structure" is revealed to the adversary, even if all the memory locations are securely encrypted. Surely, the information about the "loop structure" does provide some information about the structure of the code. To prevent this, the memory *access pattern* should be *independent* of the program that is being executed.

Nothing comes without a price. What is the price one has to pay for protecting the software? The answer is "speed." The protected program will run more slowly than the unprotected one. What is the minimal slowdown we can achieve without sacrificing the security of the protection? *Software protection overhead* is defined as the number of steps the protected program must make for each step of the source-code program. The key problem of efficient software protection is to be able to hide the access pattern efficiently.

Goldreich shows how to achieve $O((\log m)^c \cdot 2^{\sqrt{2\log m \cdot \log\log m}})$ overhead for hiding the access pattern, where m is the total (RAM) memory size and c is some small constant. He conjectures that a poly-logarithmic (in m) overhead is impossible to achieve.

We show how to achieve a poly-logarithmic overhead of hiding the access pattern. Actually, our result is even stronger: we show how to achieve a poly-logarithmic overhead as a function of the program running time for hiding the access pattern, instead of poly-logarithmic overhead of total RAM memory size, which could be much bigger than the program running time.

(An extended abstract of these results appears in the Proceedings of the 22nd STOC **[93]**.)

Rebecca N. Wright: Experimental work on database encryption. We consider the question of controlled access to large, valuable databases. Suppose that D is a database and that P is a program used to query D. We wish to construct an encrypted database D' and a corresponding program P' with the following properties:

- For any valid query q, $P(q, D) = P'(q, D')$.
- Given P' and D', it is computationally infeasible to reconstruct D.

This talk describes

- a simple cryptographic solution for protecting table-structured databases;
- experimental work that applies this table-encryption technique to natural language databases and the automata-based programs that access them;
- open problems concerning this specific example of database encryption and its relationship to the more general software-protection question.

(Joint work with J. Feigenbaum and M. Liberman. A paper based on this talk appears in these proceedings.)

Shafi Goldwasser: Noninteractive zero-knowledge proofs and digital signatures. Using noninteractive zero-knowledge proofs, we provide a simple new paradigm for digital signing and message authentication secure against adaptive chosen-message attack. In contrast to previous work, our signatures are independent of previous signatures.

For digital signatures, we require that the noninteractive zero-knowledge proofs be publicly verifiable: they should be checkable by anyone rather than directed at a particular verifier. We accordingly show how to implement noninteractive zero-knowledge proofs in a network so that anyone in the network can check correctness unilaterally, while the proof is zero-knowledge with respect to any sufficiently small coalition.

(Joint work with M. Bellare. An extended abstract of these results appears in the Proceedings of the 9th CRYPTO **[15]**.)

Andrew C. Yao: On the complexity of inverting one-way functions. I will address the relationship between secret-sharing schemes and monotone circuit size. I conjecture that a family of subsets has a computationally feasible secret sharing scheme (cfsss) iff it has a polynomial-size monotone circuit for the membership problem. What can be proved is that

- the existence of a cfsss implies a polynomial-size nonmonotone circuit for the membership problem, and
- if a one-way function exists, then a monotone circuit for the membership problem implies a cfsss.

Rafail Ostrovsky: Comparison of bit-commitment and oblivious transfer protocols when players have different computing power. We study the hardness of complexity-based implementations of bit-commitment and oblivious transfer protocols when players are of different computing power. We show that the hardness in the following three cases is equivalent:

- Bit-commitment from a polynomially-bounded player to an infinitely-powerful player.
- Oblivious Transfer from a polynomially-bounded to an infinitely-powerful player.
- Oblivious Transfer from an infinitely-powerful player to a polynomially-bounded one.

That is, given an implementation of any one of these three protocols, we show how to construct an implementation of the other two, *without any additional assumptions.*

We start with an informal description of Bit-Commitment (BC) and Oblivious Transfer (OT) primitives:

BC may be thought of as a way for player S (the Sender) to commit a bit b to player R (the Receiver) in such a way that the bit may be revealed to R at a later point in time. Before b is revealed (but even after b has been committed), no information about b is revealed to R. When b is revealed, it is guaranteed to be the same as the value to which it was originally committed.

In OT, as defined by M. Rabin **[97]**, Player S (the Sender) has an input bit b. After the protocol, player R (the Receiver) gets b with a probability of $1/2$. R must know whether or not he got the bit, while S must not know.

In 1-2-OT, as defined by Even, Goldreich, and Lempel **[50]**, Player S has two bits b_0 and b_1, and R has a selection bit i. After the transfer, R gets only b_i, while S does not know the value of i.

Crépeau and Kilian **[39]** defined α-1-2-OT. This is similar to 1-2-OT, but a malicious S can guess R's selection bit i with probability α at the end of the protocol, $1/2 \leq \alpha < 1$.

1-2-string-OT is similar to 1-2-OT, but here S has two strings, instead of two bits.

Yao [**110**] defined Combined-OT. As a common input, S and R are given a poly-size circuit $C(\cdot, \cdot)$. S has a private input x, and R has a private input y. After the protocol, R gets $C(x, y)$, while S gets nothing.

The notions of OT, 1-2-OT, α-1-2-OT, 1-2-string-OT, and Combined-OT were all shown to be equivalent to each other [**38, 28, 72, 39**]. That is, given any one of these protocols, one can implement the other ones. Thus, by "OT" we can refer to any one of them. It was shown that, independent of the power of the players, OT $\Longrightarrow$ BC [**38**]; the existence of any one-way function $\Longrightarrow$ BC from an infinitely-powerful (STRONG) player to a polynomially-bounded (WEAK) player [**89**].

In many cases, BC and OT protocols are needed in the asymmetric scenario. For example, in zero-knowledge proofs [**61**], the prover, who is infinitely-powerful, may wish to execute OT with a poly-bounded verifier [**73**]. In some cases, the verifier needs to commit bits to the prover [**29, 17**]. What are the most general complexity assumptions necessary to implement BC and OT when players have different computing power? There are four cases: (1) (STRONG $\xrightarrow{\text{BC}}$ WEAK); (2) (WEAK $\xrightarrow{\text{BC}}$ STRONG); (3) (STRONG $\xrightarrow{\text{OT}}$ WEAK); and (4) (WEAK $\xrightarrow{\text{OT}}$ STRONG). The existence of a hard on the average problem for PSPACE is known to be sufficient for (1) [**94**]. For (2), an implementation is known using claw-free permutations and trapdoor permutations [**27, 63**] and for (3) using trapdoor permutations [**59**]. In this work, we show that the difficulty of implementing any one of (2), (3), or (4) is equivalent to implementing all of them:

THEOREM.

$$(\text{WEAK} \xrightarrow{BC} \text{STRONG}) \Longleftrightarrow (\text{WEAK} \xrightarrow{OT} \text{STRONG}) \Longleftrightarrow (\text{STRONG} \xrightarrow{OT} \text{WEAK})$$

PROOF OUTLINE. (WEAK $\xrightarrow{\text{BC}}$ STRONG) $\Longleftrightarrow$ (STRONG $\xrightarrow{\text{OT}}$ WEAK): Observe that BC to a STRONG player implies a function of a special form: given a transcript of the "bit-committal-conversation" (which may not even be sampleable), it can be "decommitted" as both a zero and a one. (Otherwise the STRONG player can guess which value is being committed.) On the other hand, the WEAK player, who knows one of the decommittals, should not be able to compute the other decommittal (otherwise he can change his decommittal). Let the number of random bits used by the WEAK player during both the committal and decommittal stage be bounded by l. WLOG, decommittal of zero/(one) is the set of all strings of length l that could be used consistently for committal/decommittal of zero/(one) by the WEAK player. The players agree on single hard-core bit of a single "decommittal" string for both zero and one (utilizing [**102, 58**]). Subsequently, the STRONG player sends his two input bits XOR the agreed-upon hard bits to the WEAK player. This can be shown to yield α-1-2-OT.

(The implication in the opposite direction is straightforward: the STRONG player selects two random strings and plays 1-2-string-OT with the weak player. The "selection-bit" of a weak player serves as his committal. This was first observed by Brassard.) □

(WEAK $\xrightarrow{\text{BC}}$ STRONG) $\Longleftrightarrow$ (WEAK $\xrightarrow{\text{OT}}$ STRONG) : Since BC follows from OT, one direction is done. In the other direction, the WEAK player has two bits b_0 and b_1 and he wishes to execute 1-2-OT to the STRONG player. Since we assume (WEAK $\xrightarrow{\text{BC}}$ STRONG), it follows that the STRONG player can do both OT and BC to the WEAK player. The main idea of the protocol is as follows: the STRONG player commits 2 pairs of bits. For each pair, one committed bit is denoted as "encoding of zero" and the other as "encoding of one." One pair contains identical bits, and the other pair contains different bits. Using *Combined-OT* the STRONG player convinces the WEAK player that this is indeed so, without revealing which is an identical pair of bits. Then, using 1-2-OT from STRONG to WEAK, the WEAK player selects "encoding of b_0" from the first pair, and "encoding of b_1" from the second pair and sends back to the STRONG player the two (ordered) bits that he got from each pair. Note that for the pair in which bits are equivalent, the STRONG player learns nothing, while for the pair in which bits are different, the STRONG player gets the bit while the WEAK player does not know which bit b_i the STRONG player got. □

Building on the above result, we have recently shown that all three protocols (that are stated in the above theorem) can be implemented, based on *any* one-way function [**94**].

Judit Bar-Ilan: A note on the Random-Function model. In this note, we consider the *Information Theoretic Random Function* (ITRF) model, which was studied in [7, **68**]. The participants, A, B, and C, are infinitely powerful and are only charged for asking questions of a "black-box." The box evaluates the values of a function. This function is chosen uniformly from the set of all functions from the given domain to the given range. Communication to and from the box is private. All other communication is through an open communication channel. In this model, two participants A and B execute a key-agreement protocol, in the presence of an eavesdropper, C. In such a protocol, each participant does local computation, tosses coins, asks questions of the box, and sends messages to the other participant. By the end of the protocol, each party prints a key. The protocol is successful if A and B print the same key. The eavesdropper sees only the messages (i.e., not the messages between participants and the box), but he too can ask questions of the box.

Merkle presented a protocol [**84, 85**] in a variant of the ITRF model in which a quadratic gap is achievable between the number of questions A and B ask of the box and the number of questions C asks of the box. This protocol is based on the observation that two random subsets of size n of a set of size n^2 intersect with high probability. The intersection point is the common key. The subsets are encrypted with the black-box function; therefore A and

B have to ask n questions each. C has to find the intersection point, and since the black-box function is random, he has to ask $n^2/2$ questions on the average.

In [**84**], Merkle asked whether an exponential gap is achievable. This question was answered in [7, **68**]: For any key-agreement protocol, one can construct an eavesdropper C, who can (with high probability) compute the agreed-upon key by investing computational effort that is polynomially related to the effort spent by A and B. By polynomially related, we mean that if A and B ask n questions, then C asks $poly(n)$ questions.

The impossibility of an exponential gap is often interpreted as an indication that key-agreement is impossible in this model. However, in some cases it may be possible to choose a particular n for which the computational effort spent by A and B is reasonable, while C's computational effort is forbiddingly high (even though the gap is only quadratic).

Next, let us consider the case in which all participants are probabilistic polynomial machines and each question of the box costs one unit. In this case, Merkle's protocol still guarantees a quadratic gap. It is not known whether there exists a protocol achieving a larger, possible exponential gap. It was emphasized in [**68**] that even if an exponential gap is achievable, proving the existence of such a gap will be difficult in our current state of knowledge. The random function may be viewed as an "ideal" one-way function: for every image, each preimage is equally likely, and the only way to invert it is by exhaustive search. A natural question that arises is what gap can be achieved when we exchange the random function with the weaker notion of a one-way function. The stronger assumption that trapdoor functions exist is sufficient for achieving a superpolynomial gap (see [**45**]). On the other hand, we do not know whether even a polynomial gap is possible under the sole assumption that one-way functions exist, because Merkle's proof does not work in this case. So, is the one-way function model sufficient for an exponential, or at least, a polynomial gap?

3. Participants

Martín Abadi
Member of Research Staff
DEC Systems Research Center
130 Lytton Avenue
Palo Alto, CA 94301 USA
415-853-2196
ma@src.dec.com

Bill Aiello
Member of Technical Staff
Bellcore
445 South Street
Morristown, NJ 07960 USA
201-829-4872
aiello@bellcore.com

Eric Allender
Professor
Department of Computer Science
Rutgers University Busch Campus
Hill Center for the Mathematical Sciences
Piscataway, NJ 08855 USA
201-932-3629
allender@aramis.rutgers.edu

Sigal Ar
Graduate Student
Computer Science Department
Princeton University
Princeton, NJ 08544 USA
shr@princeton.edu

Judit Bar-Ilan
Postdoctorate Student
Weizmann Institute
Applied Math Department
Rehovot, ISRAEL
judit@wisdom.bitnet

Eric Baum
Senior Research Scientist
NEC Research Institute
4 Independence Way
Princeton, NJ 08540 USA
609-520-1559

Donald Beaver
Graduate Student
Aiken Computation Laboratory
Harvard University
Cambridge, MA 02138 USA
617-495-2662
beaver@harvard.harvard.edu
(As of August, 1990:
AT&T Bell Laboratories,
Murray Hill, NJ 07974 USA.)

Mihir Bellare
Graduate Student
MIT Laboratory for Computer Science
545 Technology Square
Cambridge, MA 02139 USA
bellare@theory.lcs.mit.edu

Andrew Berman
Graduate Student
Computer Science Department
Yale University
New Haven, CT 06520 USA
berman-andrew@cs.yale.edu

Matt Bishop
Professor
Dept. of Mathematics and Computer Science
Dartmouth College
Hanover, NH 03755 USA
Matt.Bishop@dartmouth.edu

Manuel Blum
Professor
Computer Science Division
University of California
Berkeley, CA 94720 USA
415-642-1662
blum@ernie.berkeley.edu

Geza Bohus
Graduate Student
Department of Mathematics
Rutgers University Busch Campus
Hill Center for the Mathematical Sciences
Piscataway, NJ 08855 USA
bohus@math.rutgers.edu

Jurjen Bos
Graduate Student
Center for Mathematics
and Computer Science
Kruislaan 413
Amsterdam, THE NETHERLANDS
jurjen@cwi.nl

Mike Burrows
Member of Research Staff
DEC Systems Research Center
130 Lytton Avenue
Palo Alto, CA 94301 USA
burrows@src.dec.com

Brian Coan
Member of Technical Staff
Bellcore, MRE-2Q-244
445 South Street
Morristown, NJ 07960-1910 USA
201-829-4489
coan@faline.bellcore.com

Lenore Cowen
Graduate Student
MIT Laboratory for Computer Science
545 Technology Square
Cambridge, MA 02139 USA
lenore@theory.lcs.mit.edu

Richard Draper
Supercomputer Research Center
17100 Science Drive
Bowie, MD 20715-4300 USA
draper@super.org

Cynthia Dwork
Research Staff Member
IBM Almaden Research Center
650 Harry Road
San Jose, CA 95120 USA
408-927-1752
dwork@ibm.com
(1989/90 academic year:
dwork@holmes.lcs.mit.edu)

Joan Feigenbaum
Member of Technical Staff
AT&T Bell Labs, Room 2C473
600 Mountain Avenue
Murray Hill, NJ 07974 USA
201-582-6910
jf@research.att.com

Charles Fiduccia
Supercomputing Research Center
17100 Science Drive
Bowie, MD 20715-4300
301-805-7374
fiduccia@super.org

Michael Fischer
Professor
Computer Science Department
Yale University
New Haven, CT 06520 USA
203-432-1268
fischer-michael@cs.yale.edu

Shafi Goldwasser
Professor
MIT Laboratory for Computer Science
545 Technology Square
Cambridge, MA 02139 USA
617-253-5914
shafi@theory.lcs.mit.edu

Mordecai Golin
Graduate Student
Computer Science Department
Princeton University
Princeton, NJ 08544 USA
mjg@princeton.edu

Jim Gosler
NSA
Mail Stop X2
9800 Savage Road
Fort Meade, MD 20755 USA

Richard Graveman
Member of Technical Staff
Bellcore, Room 2A-233
445 South Street
Morristown NJ 07960-1910 USA
201-829-5160
rfg@bellcore.com

Bill Griffeth
Member of Technical Staff
AT&T Bell Laboratories, Room 4213
190 River Road
Summit, NJ 07901-1444 USA
201-522-6531
billg@attunix.att.com

Stuart Haber
Member of Technical Staff
Bellcore, Room 2P374
445 South Street
Morristown, NJ 07960 USA
201-829-4652
stuart@bellcore.com

Doug J. Ierardi
Postdoctoral Student
Department of Computer Science
Princeton University
Princeton, New Jersey 08544 USA
dji@princeton.edu

Sampath Kannan
Graduate Student
Computer Science Division
University of California
Berkeley, CA 94720 USA
kannan@ernie.berkeley.edu
(As of September, 1990:
Princeton Comp. Sci. Dept.
Princeton, NJ 08544 USA)

Sarantos Kapidakis
Graduate Student
Computer Science Department
Princeton University
Princeton, New Jersey 08544 USA
609-258-6126
sarantos@princeton.edu

Claire Kenyon-Mattieu
Postdoctorate Student
Rutgers University Busch Campus
Computer Science Department
Hill Center for the Mathematical Sciences
Piscataway, NJ 08855 USA
cmm@princeton.edu

Myong-Hi Kim
Member of Technical Staff
Bellcore, Room 2P370
445 South Street
Morristown , NJ 07960 USA
201-829-4322
myonghi@bellcore.com

Doyle Knight
Director
John von Neumann Supercomputer Center
Consortium for Scientific Computing, Inc.
P. O. Box 3717
Princeton, NJ 08543 USA
609-520-2000

David Kravitz
IDA-CRD
Thanet Road
Princeton, NJ 08540 USA
609-924-4600 x310

Shay Kutten
Research Staff Member
IBM Research, Room HA-E51
P.O. Box 704
Yorktown Heights, NY 10598 USA
914-784-7346
kutten@ibm.com

Leslie Lamport
Member of Research Staff
DEC Systems Research Center
130 Lytton Avenue
Palo Alto, CA 94301 USA
lamport@src.dec.com

Butler Lampson
Member of Research Staff
DEC Cambridge Research Lab
1 Kendall Square
Cambridge, MA 02139 USA
617-621-6619
lampson@crl.dec.com

Pil Joong Lee
Member of Technical Staff
Bellcore
445 South Street
Morristown, NJ 07960-1910 USA
201-829-4512
pjl@thumper.bellcore.com

Arjen K. Lenstra
Member of Technical Staff
Bellcore, Room 2Q-334
435 South Street
Morristown, NJ 07960-1910 USA
201-829-4878
lenstra@bellcore.com

John Leo
Graduate Student
MIT Laboratory for Computer Science
545 Technology Square
Cambridge, MA 02139 USA
leo@tds.lcs.mit.edu

Richard Lipton
Professor
Computer Science Department
Princeton University
Princeton, NJ 08544 USA
609-258-4646
rjl@princeton.edu

Nancy Lynch
Professor
MIT Laboratory for Computer Science
545 Technology Square
Cambridge, MA 02138 USA
617-253-7225
lynch@holmes.lcs.mit.edu

Yishay Mansour
Graduate Student
MIT Laboratory for Computer Science
545 Technology Square
Cambridge, MA 02139 USA
mansour@theory.lcs.mit.edu

Nick Maxemchuk
Department Head
AT&T Bell Lab., Room 3D402
600 Mountain Avenue
Murray Hill, NJ 07974 USA
201-582-6240
nfm@research.att.com

Michael Merritt
Member of Technical Staff
AT&T Bell Lab., Room 3D458
600 Mountain Avenue
Murray Hill, NJ 07974 USA
201-582-5334
mischu@research.att.com

Francesmary Modugno
Graduate Student
Computer Science Department
Carnegie-Mellon University
Pittsburg, PA 15213 USA
412-268-5728
fmm@cs.cmu.edu

Andrew Odlyzko
Department Head
AT&T Bell Lab., Room 2C355
600 Mountain Avenue
Murray Hill, NJ 07974 USA
201-582-7286
amo@research.att.com

Alon Orlitsky
Member of Technical Staff
AT&T Bell Lab., Room 2C370
600 Mountain Avenue
Murray Hill, NJ 07974 USA
201-582-2285
alon@research.att.com

Peter Ostapenko
Graduate Student
Department of Mathematics
Rutgers University Busch Campus
Hill Center for the Mathematical Sciences
Piscataway, NJ 08855 USA
postapen@math.rutgers.edu

Rafail Ostrovsky
Graduate Student
MIT Laboratory for Computer Science
545 Technology Square
Cambridge, MA 02139 USA
raf@theory.lcs.mit.edu

Leonidas Palios
Graduate Student
Computer Science Department
Princeton University
Princeton, NJ 08544 USA
lap@princeton.edu

Charles Rackoff
Professor
Computer Science Department
University of Toronto
Toronto, Ontario MS5 1A4
CANADA
rackoff@theory.toronto.edu

James Reeds
Member of Technical Staff
AT&T Bell Lab., Room 2C357
600 Mountain Avenue
Murray Hill, NJ 07974 USA
201-582-7066
reeds@research.att.com

Phillip Rogaway
Graduate Student
MIT Laboratory for Computer Science
545 Technology Square
Cambridge, MA 02139 USA
rogaway@theory.lcs.mit.edu

Ronitt Rubinfeld
Graduate Student
Computer Science Division
University of California
Berkeley, CA 94720 USA
ronitt@ernie.berkeley.edu
(As of Sept., 1990:
Princeton Comp. Sci. Dept.
Princeton, NJ 08544 USA)

Jeanette Schmidt
Visiting Professor
Polytechnic Institute of New York
333 Jay Street
Brooklyn, NY 11201 USA
jps@pucs4.poly.edu

Ron Shamir
Postdoctorate Student
Department of Mathematics
Rutgers University Busch Campus
Hill Center for the Mathematical Sciences
Piscataway, NJ 08855 USA
shamir@math.rutgers.edu

Dan Simon
Graduate Student
Computer Science Department
University of Toronto
Toronto, Ontario MS5 1A4 CANADA
me@theory.toronto.edu

Ramesh Sitaraman
Graduate Student
Computer Science Department
Princeton University
Princeton, NJ 08544 USA
rks@princeton.edu

Larry Stockmeyer
Research Staff Member
IBM Almaden Research Center
650 Harry Road
San Jose, CA 95120 USA
stock@ibm.com
(1989/90 academic year:
stock@theory.lcs.mit.edu.)

Marie-Jeanne Toussaint
Graduate Student
Université de Liège
Institut d'Electricité Montefiore
Informatique (Systèmes et Modelisation)
SART TILMAN, B 28
B-4000 Liège, BELGIUM
u515902@bliulg11.bitnet

Greg Troxel
Graduate Student
MIT Laboratory for Computer Science
545 Technology Square
Cambridge, MA 02139 USA
617-253-5905
gdt@tds.lcs.mit.edu

Gene Tsudik
Graduate Student
Computer Science Department
University of Southern California
Los Angeles, CA 90089 USA
tsudik@jerico.usc.edu

Mark Tuttle
Member of Research Staff
DEC Cambridge Research Laboratory
1 Kendall Square
Cambridge, MA 02139 USA
617-354-7395
tuttle@crl.dec.com

Doug Tygar
Professor
Computer Science Department
Carnegie Mellon University
Pittsburg, PA 15213 USA
412-268-6340
tygar@cs.cmu.edu

Peter Weinberger
Director
AT&T Bell Lab., Room 2T502
600 Mountain Avenue
Murray Hill, NJ 07974 USA
201-582-7214
pjw@research.att.com

Steve R. White
Research Staff Member
IBM Research
P.O. Box 704
Yorktown Heights, NY 10598 USA
914-784-7368
srwhite@ibm.com

Peter Winkler
District Manager
Bellcore
445 South Street
Morristown, NJ 07960 USA
pw@bellcore.com

Heather Woll
Professor
Department of Computer Science and Engineering, C-014
University of California
La Jolla, CA 92092-0114 USA
619-534-4725
woll@cs.ucsd.edu

Rebecca Wright
Graduate Student
Computer Science Department
Yale University
New Haven, CT 06520 USA
203-432-1239
wright-rebecca@cs.yale.edu

Yacov Yacobi
Member of Technical Staff
Bellcore, Room 2A-217
445 South Street
Morristown, NJ 07960 USA
yacov@thumper.bellcore.com

Andrew Yao
Professor
Computer Science Department
Princeton University
Princeton, NJ 08544 USA
609-258-5182
yao@princeton.edu

Neal Young
Graduate Student
Computer Science Department
Princeton University
Princeton, NJ 08544 USA
ney@princeton.edu

Moti Yung
Research Staff Member
IBM Research, Room H3A09
P. O. Box 704
Yorktown Heights, NY 10598 USA
914-784-7196
moti@ibm.com

Jenny Zhao
Graduate Student
Computer Science Department
Princeton University
Princeton, NJ 08544 USA
zhz@princeton.edu

References

This bibliography contains references for the articles mentioned in Sections 1 and 2 above, as well as some other articles and books that we think would be useful to researchers and practitioners. We have not attempted a complete bibliography on cryptography theory; many such attempts have already been made – for example, we refer the reader to Goldreich's course outline **[55]** for additional references.

1. M. Abadi and J. Feigenbaum, *Secure circuit evaluation: A protocol based on hiding information from an oracle*, J. Cryptology **2** (1990), 1–12.
2. M. Abadi, J. Feigenbaum, and J. Kilian, *On hiding information from an oracle*, J. Comput. System Sci. **39** (1989), 21–50.
3. L. Adleman, M. Huang, and K. Kompella, *Efficient checkers for number theoretic problems*, manuscript, October, 1989.
4. L. Babai, L. Fortnow, and C. Lund, *Nondeterministic exponential time has two-prover interactive protocols*, Proceedings of the 31st FOCS (St. Louis, MO; October, 1990), IEEE.
5. L. Babai, S. Kannan, and E. Luks, *A zero-knowledge proof for group nonisomorphism*, manuscript, October, 1989.
6. L. Babai and S. Moran, *Arthur-Merlin games: A randomized proof system and a hierarchy of complexity classes*, J. Comput. System Sci. **36** (1988), 254–276.
7. J. Bar-Ilan, *Applications of one-way functions and randomization in security protocols*, Ph.D. thesis, Hebrew University of Jerusalem, 1989.
8. J. Bar-Ilan and D. Beaver, *Noncryptographic fault-tolerant computing in a constant number of rounds of interaction*, Proceedings of the 8th PODC (Edmonton, Alberta; August, 1989), ACM, 201–209.
9. D. Beaver, *Multiparty protocols tolerating half faulty processors*, Proceedings of the 9th CRYPTO (Santa Barbara, CA; August, 1989), Springer-Verlag, LNCS, 560–572.
10. D. Beaver and J. Feigenbaum, *Hiding instances in multioracle queries*, Proceedings of the 7th STACS (Rouen, France; February, 1990), Springer-Verlag, LNCS 415, 37–48.
11. D. Beaver, J. Feigenbaum, J. Kilian, and P. Rogaway, *Security with low communication overhead*, Proceedings of the 10th CRYPTO (Santa Barbara, CA; August, 1990), Springer-Verlag, LNCS.
12. D. Beaver, J. Feigenbaum, and V. Shoup, *Hiding instances in zero-knowledge proof systems*, Proceedings of the 10th CRYPTO (Santa Barbara, CA; August, 1990), Springer-Verlag, LNCS.
13. D. Beaver, S. Micali, and P. Rogaway, *Cryptographically secure distributed computation in a constant number of rounds*, Proceedings of the 22nd STOC (Baltimore, MD; May, 1990), ACM, 503–513.
14. R. Beigel and J. Feigenbaum, *Improved bounds on coherence and checkability*, YALEU/DCS/TR-819, Yale University, September 11,1990.
15. M. Bellare and S. Goldwasser, *New paradigms for digital signatures and message authentication based on noninteractive zero knowledge proofs*, Proceedings of the 9th CRYPTO (Santa Barbara, CA; August, 1989), Springer-Verlag, LNCS, 194–211.
16. M. Bellare and S. Micali, *How to sign given any trapdoor function*, Proceedings of the 20th STOC (Chicago, IL; May, 1988), ACM, 32–42.
17. M. Bellare, S. Micali, and R. Ostrovsky, *The (true) complexity of statistical zero knowledge*, Proceedings of the 22nd STOC (Baltimore, MD; May, 1990), ACM, 494–502.
18. S. M. Bellovin and M. Merritt, *An attack on password-authenticated exponential key exchange*, AT&T Bell Laboratories Technical Memorandum, May 1990.
19. S. M. Bellovin and M. Merritt, *Limitations of the Kerberos protocol*, AT&T Bell Laboratories Technical Memorandum, May 1990.
20. M. Ben-Or, S. Goldwasser, and A. Wigderson, *Completeness theorems for noncryptographic fault-tolerant distributed computation*, Proceedings of the 20th STOC (Chicago, IL; May, 1988), ACM, 1–10.
21. M. Blum and S. Kannan, *Designing programs that check their work*, Proceedings of the

21st STOC (Seattle, WA; May, 1989), ACM, 86–97.

22. M. Blum, M. Luby, and R. Rubinfeld, *Self-testing and self-correcting programs with applications to numerical problems*, Proceedings of the 22nd STOC (Baltimore, MD; May, 1990), ACM, 73–83.
23. R. Boppana, J. Håstad, and S. Zachos, *Does coNP have short interactive proofs?*, Inform. Proc. Lett. **25** (1987), 127–132.
24. J. Bos and B. den Boer, *Detection of disrupters in the DC protocol*, Proceedings of Eurocrypt89 (Houthalen, Belgium; April, 1989), Springer-Verlag, LNCS.
25. G. Brassard, *Modern cryptography: A tutorial*, Springer-Verlag, LNCS 325, 1988.
26. G. Brassard, D. Chaum, and C. Crépeau, *Minimum disclosure proofs of knowledge*, J. Comput. System Sci. **37** (1988), 156–189.
27. G. Brassard and C. Crépeau, *Nontransitive transfer of confidence: a perfect zero-knowledge interactive protocol for SAT and beyond*, Proceedings of the 27th FOCS (Toronto, Ontario; October, 1986), IEEE, 188–195.
28. G. Brassard, C. Crépeau, and J.-M. Robert, *Information theoretic reductions among disclosure problems*, Proceedings of the 27th FOCS (Toronto, Ontario; October, 1986), IEEE, 168–173.
29. G. Brassard , C. Crépeau, and M. Yung, *Everything in NP can be argued in perfect zero knowledge in a bounded number of rounds*, Proceedings of the 16th ICALP (Stresa, Italy; July, 1989), Springer-Verlag, LNCS 372, 123–136.
30. M. Burrows, M. Abadi, and R. Needham, *Authentication: A practical study in belief and action*, Proceedings of the 2nd Conference on Theoretical Aspects of Reasoning about Knowledge (Pacific Grove, CA; March, 1988), Morgan Kaufmann, 325–342.
31. M. Burrows, M. Abadi, and R. Needham, *A logic of authentication*, Proceedings of the Royal Society of London A **426** (1989), 233–271.
32. CCITT, *The directory-authentication framework, version 7*, Technical Report, Draft Recommendation X.509, November 1987.
33. K. M. Chandy and J. Misra, *Parallel program design: A foundation*, Addison-Wesley, Reading, MA, 1988.
34. D. Chaum, *The dining cryptographers problem: unconditional sender and receiver untraceability*, J. Cryptology **1** (1988), 65–75.
35. D. Chaum, C. Crépeau, and I. Damgård, *Multiparty unconditionally secure protocols*, Proceedings of the 20th STOC (Chicago, IL; May, 1988), ACM, 11–19.
36. B. Chor and E. Kushilevitz, *A zero-one law for boolean privacy*, Proceedings of the 21st STOC (Seattle, WA; May, 1989), ACM, 62–72.
37. D. Coppersmith, A. Odlyzko, and R. Schroeppel, *Discrete logarithms in* GF(p), Algorithmica **1** (1986), 1–15.
38. C. Crépeau, *Equivalence between two flavors of oblivious transfer*, Proceedings of the 7th CRYPTO (Santa Barbara, CA; August, 1987), Springer-Verlag, LNCS 293, 350–354.
39. C. Crépeau and J. Kilian, *Achieving oblivious transfer using weakened security assumptions*, Proceedings of the 29th FOCS (White Plains, NY; October, 1988), IEEE, 42–52.
40. D. W. Davies and W. L. Price, *Security for computer networks*, John Wiley & Sons, 1984.
41. R. DeMillo, N. Lynch, and M. Merritt, *Cryptographic protocols*, Proceedings of the 14th STOC (San Fransisco, CA; May, 1982), ACM, 383–400.
42. R. DeMillo and M. Merritt, *Protocols for data security*, Computer **16** (1983), 39–50.
43. D. Denning, *Cryptography and Data Security*, Addison-Wesley, Reading, MA, 1983.
44. D. Denning and G. Sacco, *Timestamps in key distribution protocols*, Commun. Assoc. Comput. Mach. **24** (1981), 533–536.
45. W. Diffie and M. E. Hellman, *New directions in cryptography*, IEEE Trans. Inform. Theory, **IT-22** (1976), 644–654.
46. D. Dolev, C. Dwork, O. Waarts, and M. Yung, *Perfectly secure message transmission*, Proceedings of the 31st FOCS (St. Louis, MO; October, 1990), IEEE. Expanded version available as IBM Research Report RJ7496 (70011), May 23, 1990.
47. D. Dolev, S. Even, and R. M. Karp, *On the security of ping-pong protocols*, Inform. and

Control 55 (1982), 57–68.

48. D. Dolev and A. Yao, *On the security of public key protocols*, IEEE Trans. Inform. Theory **IT-29** (1983), 198–208.
49. S. Even and O. Goldreich, *On the security of multi-party ping-pong protocols*, Proceedings of the 24th FOCS (Tuscon, AZ; November, 1983), IEEE, 34–39.
50. S. Even, O. Goldreich, and A. Lempel, *A randomized protocol for signing contracts*, Commun. Assoc. Comput. Mach. **28** (1985), 637–647.
51. U. Feige, A. Fiat, and A. Shamir, *Zero knowledge proofs of identity*, J. Cryptology **1** (1988), 77–94.
52. J. Feigenbaum, S. Kannan, and N. Nisan, *Lower bounds on random-self-reducibility*, Proceedings of the 5th Structures (Barcelona, Spain; July, 1990), IEEE, 100–109.
53. L. Fortnow, J. Rompel, and M. Sipser, *On the power of multiprover interactive protocols*, Proceedings of the 3rd Structures (Washington DC; June, 1988), IEEE, 156–161.
54. Z. Galil, S. Haber, and M. Yung, *Symmetric public-key encryption*, Proceedings of the 5th CRYPTO (Santa Barbara, CA; August, 1985), Springer-Verlag, LNCS 218, 128–137. Expanded version available as Bellcore Technical Memorandum ARH-013-160, 1989.
55. O. Goldreich, *Foundations of Cryptography*, class notes, Technion, Haifa, Spring, 1989.
56. O. Goldreich, *Towards a theory of software protection*, Proceedings of the 19th STOC (New York, NY; May, 1987), ACM, 182–194.
57. O. Goldreich, S. Goldwasser, and S. Micali, *How to construct random functions*, J. Assoc. Comput. Mach. **33** (1986), 792–807.
58. O. Goldreich and L. Levin, *A hard-core predicate for ANY one-way function*, Proceedings of the 21st STOC (Seattle, WA; May, 1989), ACM, 25–32.
59. O. Goldreich, S. Micali, and A. Wigderson, *How to play ANY mental game*, Proceedings of the 19th STOC (New York, NY; May, 1987), ACM, 218–229.
60. S. Goldwasser and S. Micali, *Probabilistic encryption*, J. Comput. System Sci. **28** (1984), 270–299.
61. S. Goldwasser, S. Micali, and C. Rackoff, *The knowledge complexity of interactive proof systems*, SIAM J. Comput. **18** (1989), 186–208.
62. S. Goldwasser, S. Micali, and R. Rivest, *A digital signature scheme secure against adaptive chosen-message attacks*, SIAM J. Comput. **17** (1988), 281–308.
63. S. Goldwasser and N. Nisan, private communication to R. Ostrovsky.
64. S. Goldwasser and M. Sipser, *Private coins vs. public coins in interactive proof systems*, Advances in Computing Research – Vol. 5: Randomness and Computation, JAI Press, Greenwich, CT, 1989, 73–90.
65. L. Gong, R. Needham, and R. Yahalom, *A methodology for analyzing cryptographic protocols*, Technical Report, University of Cambridge Computer Laboratory, Cambridge CB2 3QG, England, March, 1990.
66. S. Haber, *Multi-Party cryptographic computation: Techniques and applications*, Ph.D. Thesis, Columbia University, 1988.
67. J. Halpern, Y. Moses, and M. Tuttle, *A knowledge-based analysis of zero knowledge*, Proceedings of the 20th STOC (Chicago, IL; May, 1988), ACM, 132–147.
68. R. Impagliazzo and S. Rudich, *Limits on the provable consequences of one-way permutations*, Proceedings of the 21st STOC (Seattle, WA; May, 1989), ACM, 44–56.
69. D. Kahn, *The Codebreakers*, Macmillan and Co., New York, 1967.
70. S. Kannan, *Program checkers for algebraic problems*, Ph.D. Thesis, UC Berkeley. Available as International Computer Science Institute TR-89-064, December 22, 1989.
71. R. A. Kemmerer, *Analyzing encryption protocols using formal verification techniques*, IEEE J. Selected Areas in Commun. **7** (1989), 448–457.
72. J. Kilian, *Founding cryptography on oblivious transfer*, Proceedings of the 20th STOC (Chicago, IL; May, 1988), ACM, 20–31.
73. J. Kilian, S. Micali, and R. Ostrovsky, *Minimum resource zero-knowledge*, Proceedings of the 30th FOCS (Research Triangle Park, NC; October, 1989), IEEE, 474–479.
74. E. Kushilevitz, *Privacy and communication complexity*, Proceedings of the 30th FOCS (Research Triangle Park, NC; October, 1989), IEEE, 416–421.

75. B. A. LaMacchia and A. M. Odlyzko, *Computation of Discrete Logarithms in Prime Fields*, AT&T Bell Laboratories Technical Memorandum, June, 1990.
76. B. A. LaMacchia and A. M. Odlyzko, *Solving large sparse linear systems over finite fields*, Proceedings of the 10th CRYPTO (Santa Barbara, CA; August, 1990), Springer-Verlag, LNCS.
77. L. Lamport, *On interprocess communication*, Distributed Computing **1** (1986), 77–101.
78. A. Lenstra, H. Lenstra, M. Manasse, and J. Pollard, *The number field sieve*, Proceedings of the 22nd STOC (Baltimore, MD; May, 1990), ACM, 564–572.
79. A. Lenstra and M. Manasse, *Factoring by electronic mail*, Proceedings of Eurocrypt89 (Houthalen, Belgium; April, 1989), Springer-Verlag, LNCS.
80. R. Lipton, *New directions in testing*, these proceedings.
81. C. Lund, L. Fortnow, H. Karloff, and N. Nisan, *Algebraic methods in interactive proof systems*, Proceedings of the 31st FOCS (St. Louis, MO; October, 1990), IEEE.
82. W. P. Lu and M. K. Sundareshan, *Secure communication in internet environments*, IEEE Trans. Commun. **37** (1989), 1014–1023.
83. N. Lynch and M. Tuttle, *Hierarchical correctness proofs for distributed algorithms*, Proceedings of 6th PODC (Vancouver, BC; August, 1987), ACM, 137–151. Expanded version available as MIT Laboratory for Computer Science Technical Report MIT/LCS/TR-387, 1987.
84. R. C. Merkle, *Secure communications over insecure channels*, Commun. Assoc. Comput. Mach. **21** (1978), 294–299.
85. R. C. Merkle, *Authentication and Public Key Systems*, UMI Research Press, 1982.
86. M. Merritt, *Cryptographic Protocols*, Ph.D. Thesis, Georgia Institute of Technology, 1983, Report # GIT-ICS-83/06.
87. S. Micali, C. Rackoff, and B. Sloan, *The notion of security for probabilistic cryptosystems*, SIAM J. Comput. **17** (1988), 412–426.
88. J. H. Moore, *Protocol failures in cryptosystems*, Proceedings of the IEEE **76** (1988), 594–602.
89. M. Naor, *Bit commitment using pseudo-randomness*, J. Cryptology, to appear. Extended Abstract in Proceedings of the 9th CRYPTO.
90. M. Naor and M. Yung, *Universal one-way hash functions and their cryptographic applications*, Proceedings of the 21st STOC (Seattle, WA; May, 1989), ACM, 33–43.
91. R. Needham and M. Schroeder, *Using encryption for authentication in large networks of computers*, Commun. Assoc. Comput. Mach. **21** (1978), 993–999.
92. R. Needham and M. Schroeder, *Authentication revisited*, Operating Systems Review **21** (1987), 7.
93. R. Ostrovsky, *Efficient computation on oblivious RAMs*, Proceedings of the 22nd STOC (Baltimore, MD; May, 1990), ACM, 514–523.
94. R. Ostrovsky, R. Venkatesan, and M. Yung, *On the Complexity of Asymmetric Games*, manuscript, April, 1990.
95. D. Otway and O. Rees, *Efficient and timely mutual authentication*, Operating Systems Review **21** (1987), 8–10.
96. N. Pippenger and M. Fischer, *Relations among complexity measures*, J. Assoc. Comput. Mach. **26** (1979), 361–381.
97. M. Rabin, *How to exchange secrets by oblivious transfer*, Aiken Computation Laboratory Technical Report, Harvard University, 1981.
98. M. Rabin and D. Tygar, *An integrated toolkit for operating system security*, Aiken Computation Laboratory TR-05-87, Harvard University, 1987.
99. T. Rabin, *Robust sharing of secrets when the dealer is honest or cheating*, M.Sc. Thesis, Hebrew University, 1988.
100. T. Rabin and M. Ben-Or, *Verifiable secret sharing and multiparty protocols with honest majority*, Proceedings of the 21st STOC (Seattle, WA; May, 1989), ACM, 73–85.
101. R. L. Rivest, A. Shamir, and L. Adleman, *A method of obtaining digital signatures and public-key cryptosystems*, Commun. Assoc. Comput. Mach. **21** (1988), 120–126.
102. A. Shamir, IP = PSPACE, Proceedings of the 31st FOCS (St. Louis, MO; October, 1990), IEEE.

103. A. Shamir, *How to share a secret*, Commun. Assoc. Comput. Mach. **22** (1979), 612–613.
104. A. Shamir, R. Rivest, and L. Adleman, *Mental poker*, Mathematical Gardner, D. E. Klarner (ed.), Wadsworth, New York, 1981. Also MIT Laboratory for Computer Science Technical Memorandum MIT/LCS/TM-125, 1979.
105. C. Shannon, *Communication theory of secrecy systems*, Bell System Tech. J. **28** (1949), 656–715.
106. J. Steiner, C. Neuman, and J. I. Schiller, *Kerberos: An authentication service for open network systems*, Proceedings of the Winter USENIX Conference (Dallas, TX; February, 1988), 191–202.
107. Brad Taylor, *A framework for network security*, Sun Technology **1** (1988), 47–49.
108. S. Toda, *On the computational power of PP and $\oplus P$*, Proceedings of the 30th FOCS (Research Triangle Park, NC; October, 1989), IEEE, 514–519.
109. M. Tompa and H. Woll, *Random self-reducibility and zero knowledge interactive proofs of possession of information*, Proceedings of the 28th FOCS (Los Angeles, CA; October, 1987), IEEE, 472–482.
110. A. C. Yao, *How to generate and exchange secrets*, Proceedings of the 27th FOCS (Toronto, Ontario; October, 1986), IEEE, 162–167.
111. A. C. Yao, *Coherent functions and program checkers*, Proceedings of the 22nd STOC (Baltimore, MD; May, 1990), ACM, 84–94.

(Added in proof)

112. L. Babai and L. Fortnow, *A characterization of #P by arithmetic straight line programs*, Proceedings of the 31st FOCS (St. Louis, MO; October, 1990), IEEE.
113. J. Feigenbaum and L. Fortnow, *On the random-self-reducibility of complete sets*, University of Chicago Technical Report 90-22. Computer Science Department, August 20, 1990.

AT&T Bell Laboratories, Murray Hill, NJ 07974

DIMACS Series in Discrete Mathematics
and Theoretical Computer Science
Volume 2, 1991

Formal Definitions for Secure Distributed Protocols

Extended Abstract

DONALD BEAVER

ABSTRACT. The problem of secure multiparty computations is described abstractly as follows: n players in a network wish to compute a function $F(x_1, \ldots, x_n)$ without revealing the inputs, where each player supplies a private input x_i. Though much recent research has delved into secure and reliable multiparty computations, a formal and unified treatment is lacking. We give precise definitions of correctness and privacy, and introduce the concept of a *fault oracle* in order to measure exactly the information disclosed during the execution of a protocol. A fault oracle also provides a direct way to analyze protocols designed to be resilient against dynamic adversaries (a property that is often claimed but not formally defined or proven). We collect and formalize various approaches that have often been described only intuitively, in order to provide a unified framework for defining, proving, and comparing the variety of solutions and models for multiparty computations.

1. Introduction

A network of n players wishes to compute a function $F(x_1, \ldots, x_n)$, where each player i supplies a private input x_i, without revealing anything more than $F(x_1, \ldots, x_n)$. In other words, even though any member of the network might be unreliable, and a trusted party may not be available, the players would like to simulate a trusted party who collects their inputs, computes $F(x_1, \ldots, x_n)$, and reveals only the result.

The recent interest in secure and reliable multiparty computations has spurred a great many new ideas and methods. Protocols abound; but proofs and formal definitions do not. Often only intuitive arguments are given, and the underlying models are rarely stated clearly and formally.

1980 *Mathematics Subject Classification* (1985 *Revision*). Primary 68-06, 68M10, 68Q05, 68Q75, 68Q99, 94A05, 94A60.

This research was supported in part under NSF grant CCR-870-4513.

This abstract is excerpted from an article to appear in *J. Cryptology* **[Bea88]**.

In order to appreciate and to compare the variety of protocols under the broad and varied set of assumptions and network models, a unifying model is needed. We give a framework to define and describe the properties of multiparty computations.

The important aspects of a model and solution can be listed in a few dimensions. The participants may be resource-unbounded automata, having a finite or even an infinite number of states (the "information-theoretic" model), or Turing machines with limited resources (the "complexity-based" model). The network may connect the participants completely, and it may also support a range of communication channels, broadcast and private channels being the most important but by no means exclusive. "Cryptographic" or "complexity-theoretic" assumptions may be made; often, for example, protocols are based on the unproven existence of one-way or trapdoor functions.

Normally, one allows an adversary to observe and perhaps to change the communications to and from various participants. The adversary may be unbounded or bounded, static or dynamic in its choice of participants to corrupt, and passive or malicious in its actions.

Once a network model has been described and the assumptions have been stated, the properties that a protocol achieves can be described. Correctness is the most important property, yet it has received the least direct attention (in terms of definitions). Inputs and outputs are far more subtle than the established study of single-processor computations would suggest, and often, rather than delve into the subtleties, researchers make particular assumptions (e.g., all inputs are encrypted and broadcast, or every input is "secretly shared") in order to finesse the issue. Similar definitions for Byzantine Agreement do not suffice, since the goal of that problem is simply to agree on a common value (a process which is fairly insensitive to individual variations in a fraction of the input values) as opposed to determining a value that may be extremely sensitive to individual inputs.

After correctness, privacy is the next most desirable property, and also needs careful treatment. The definitions appearing in the literature often concentrate too closely on the privacy of the inputs and make little reference to other information that may be leaked. ([**Hab88**] is a notable exception. Also [**AFK89**] and [**BF90**] introduce a specific measure of information that is hidden or leaked for the related problem of instance-hiding schemes.) Since the protocols often happen to satisfy the stronger requirement that no information except $F(x_1, \ldots, x_n)$ is leaked, this issue is overlooked. In order to compose protocols, however, a careful measure of the information leaked by each subprotocol is necessary. Each protocol might hide its own inputs, but one might leak the entire knowledge of another protocol if the definitions are not made carefully.

Other issues, such as the independence of the choice of inputs and a measure of fairness when faulty participants may halt the protocol before reliable participants learn the output, require formal treatment as well.

We present a unified framework in which multiparty protocols can be described, compared, and their properties proven. We collect and formalize ideas and definitions that are often only intuitively stated, sometimes finessed or ignored, and at best, scattered in the literature. Some of the definitions for protocols and protocol executions herein may seem weighty; but we wish to specify exactly what occurs during a multiparty computation.

The collection of formal definitions for properties such as correctness and privacy make for more interesting and, fortunately, somewhat lighter reading. We introduce the concept of a *fault oracle,* which makes the analysis of information leaked by a protocol very straightforward. It also provides a concrete definition for privacy against dynamic adversaries. The precise definitions of protocol properties are a necessary prerequisite to proving the resilience of any of the protocols that have appeared in the literature.

2. Notation

We use a vector notation to represent a list of items: $\vec{x} = \{ x_1, \dots, x_n \}$. We use a subscript to denote a subset of those values: $\vec{x}_T = \{ x_i \mid i \in T \}$. Bars indicate complements: $\overline{T} = [n] - T$, where $[n] = \{ 1, \dots, n \}$.

Let $\Sigma = \{ 0, 1 \}$. For notational convenience, we define $H_m = (\Sigma^\star)^m$, the set of m-tuples of strings, and we let $H = \bigcup_{i=1}^{\infty} H_i$.

The set of all distributions on a set X is denoted by $\mathrm{dist}(X)$. If P and Q are distributions on a set X, define their difference by $|P - Q| = \sum_{x \in X} |P(x) - Q(x)|$, where $P(x)$ denotes $\Pr[P = x]$. We denote a sample x taken according to P by $\{ x \leftarrow P \}$. Let f be a function from some number j of arguments to a range X; we denote by

$$\{ x_1 \leftarrow P_1 ; x_2 \leftarrow P_2 ; \dots ; x_j \leftarrow P_j : f(x_1, x_2, \dots, x_j) \}$$

the distribution on X induced by running the j experiments in order and applying f to the results. Where clear from the context, we use the same notation to describe a sample drawn from that distribution.

An ensemble $\mathscr{P} = \{ P(z) \}$ parametrized by $z \in \Sigma^\star$ is a set of distributions on $\Sigma^{p(|z|)}$, where $p(k)$ is polynomially bounded. As with many of the definitions presented here, there are different versions describing the indistinguishability of ensembles, one information-theoretic, one statistical, and one computational.

Ensembles $\mathscr{P}$ and $\mathscr{Q}$ are $\delta(k)$-indistinguishable if, for all sufficiently large z,

$$|\mathscr{P}(z) - \mathscr{Q}(z)| \leq \delta(|z|).$$

The ensembles are identical if they are 0-indistinguishable. They are *statistically* indistinguishable if for any c and for k sufficiently large, $\delta(k) \leq k^{-c}$.

Computational distinguishability is based on a notion of a resource-bounded machine that tries to distinguish strings sampled from one distribution or the other. A *distinguisher* A is a probabilistic polynomial time algorithm that outputs either 0 or 1. Let $P^0_{\mathcal{P}(z)}$ denote the probability that A outputs a 0 on an input selected according to $\mathcal{P}(z)$ and let $P^0_{\mathcal{Q}(z)}$ denote the probability that A outputs a 0 on an input selected according to $\mathcal{Q}(z)$. Then ensembles $\mathcal{P}$ and $\mathcal{Q}$ are *computationally* indistinguishable if, for any c and for all sufficiently large z, $|P^0_{\mathcal{P}(z)} - P^0_{\mathcal{Q}(z)}| \leq |z|^{-c}$.

3. Players, protocols, and adversaries

We begin by giving formal definitions of players in the most general sense, describing them as automata that may have a finite or infinite number of states, and ignoring bounds on available resources. This corresponds to the "information-theoretic" model, in which one is concerned with "perfect" secrecy; any difference or dependence among distributions on messages sent from player to player is considered to give away information, regardless of the resources needed to detect it. Our use of the term "automaton" extends beyond the common, finite-state machine. The information-theoretic model does not restrict the power of the players and malicious adversaries to compute recursive functions on the messages they see; in fact, each player could more generally be defined as a function from inputs to outputs. The concept of an automaton, even one having an infinite control (thereby enabling it to compute nonrecursive functions or functions of real numbers, for example), is more convenient and more easily applied when we study a particular sort of player, the interactive Turing machine.

Turing machines can be regarded as a special case of the broader definition for players, in which the players are described by finite-state transition functions along with work tapes and random tapes. (A Turing machine is thus an automata having an infinite number of states if one includes the configuration of its tapes.) The "complexity-based" model permits only a bounded (polynomial) amount of resources to derive extra information.

In this section we describe protocols and specify the sequence of steps that occur, and then examine protocols run in the presence of an adversary who may corrupt some portion of the players. Properties related to computing a function, such as correctness and privacy, are discussed in §4.

3.1. Players. Each player has a state set Q, a standard input set $X \subseteq \Sigma^\star$, and an auxiliary input set Z. The auxiliary input set is useful in composing different protocols and in proving properties of the protocols. It may encode previous inputs given to the player, computations performed by the player in previous protocols, or other information. Rather than combine X and Z into some general input set, we maintain them as separate entities in order to facilitate defining the correct output of a protocol according to the given inputs in X. The auxiliary inputs are often external information that has nothing to do with the protocol at hand or the function it needs to compute, but which must be taken into account when considering the security and reliability of the protocol at hand.

The initial state of a player is selected according to the input and auxiliary input; that is, each player has a function $q^0 : X \times Z \to Q$.

During each round of a protocol, each player performs a randomized computation and sends messages distributed according to the results. The sets of incoming and outgoing messages depend on the types of communication channels and the number of other players in the network. In particular, each player is described by a transition function δ that produces a *distribution* on new states and new messages based on the current state and incoming messages:

$$\delta : Q \times H \to \mathrm{dist}(Q \times H).$$

In other words, given a state and the messages of the previous round, δ produces a distribution on new states and messages from which distribution the subsequent state and outgoing messages of the player are drawn.

Note that the transition function produces a *distribution* on outputs, in analogy to the computation of a probabilistic Turing machine, which need not compute a *function* of its inputs, but rather produces a distribution on outputs based on its input and induced by the uniformly random bits on its random tape. A Turing machine can also be regarded as producing a *sample* from that distribution. (In particular, a Turing machine *is* a function of its input and random input.) We consider a player in a similar, dual fashion: as producing a distribution, or as producing a sample from that distribution. This will allow us to describe protocol executions in terms of the distributions on messages as well as in terms of particular message histories generated by sampling from those distributions.

We may describe a *player* concisely by a tuple (Q, X, Z, q^0, δ).

3.2. Networks. A network is a graph describing the connections between players, where each edge is labelled according to the type of communication channel it supports. In general, networks are taken to be completely connected graphs, though restrictions to $(t+1)$-connected graphs, where t is a fault-tolerance parameter, are sometimes considered.

3.2.1. *Channels.* The most common sorts of communication lines fall into three categories: private channels, broadcast channels, and oblivious transfer channels. We describe a message sent to player j by the pair (j, m_j). Let

$$M = \{ A \mid A \subseteq N \times \Sigma^\star \}$$

be the collection of sets of messages (j, m_j).

A *channel* C is a family $\{ C_m \mid m \in \Sigma^\star \}$ of distributions on M, where m denotes the message applied to the channel.

When a player sends message m over channel C, a set of strings

$$\{(j_1, m_{j_1}), \ldots, (j_k, m_{j_k})\}$$

is selected according to distribution C_m, and each m_{j_l} is given to player l.

A *private* channel between a player i and a player j is described by a family of distributions $\{C_m\}$ where each C_m assigns probability 1 to $\{(j, m)\}$. A *broadcast* channel gives probability 1 to $\{(1, m), \ldots, (n, m)\}$. An *oblivious transfer* channel delivers messages with a 50-50 chance, represented by

$$\Pr_{C_m}[\{(j, m)\}] = \frac{1}{2};$$
$$\Pr_{C_m}[\emptyset] = \frac{1}{2}.$$

Note that a sender is identified by delivering the string $i\#m_j$ for each (j, m_j) appearing in the selected set of messages; an anonymous channel is modeled by supplying the recipient simply with m_j. The sender does not know what message is actually delivered (unless, as in the case of private and broadcast channels, the channel defines it uniquely).

3.3. Protocols. An n-player protocol is a set of players, channels, and input and output functions: $\Pi_n = \{(P_1, \mathscr{C}_1, I_1, O_1), \ldots, (P_n, \mathscr{C}_n, I_n, O_n)\}$. Player P_i is described by $P_i = (Q_i, X_i, Z_i, q_i^0, \delta_i)$. Each $\mathscr{C}_i$ denotes a set $\{C^1, \ldots, C^k\}$ of channels for player P_i. The input and output functions concern the function that the protocol is intended to compute, and are discussed in §4. For now, we shall examine the sequence of events and the various histories generated by an execution of the protocol, and leave the nature of its computation for later.

Since the purpose of this work is to specify *precisely* the nature of a protocol and its execution rather than to become immersed in formalism, let us use some shorthand to relieve the burden of the notation. As mentioned, during each round of a protocol, a player performs a computation and then sends messages over its various channels. Let $\mu^{\text{out}}(U, V, r)$ denote the set of messages sent from players in set U to players in set V during round r. Let $\mu(U, V, r)$ denote the set of messages actually received by players in set V from players in set U, that is, those messages drawn according to the various channel distributions acting on $\mu^{\text{out}}(U, V, r)$. Denote the messages received by V from U and U from V by $\mathscr{M}(U, V, r) = \mu(U, V, r) \cup \mu(V, U, r)$.

Let $\text{SEND}(\{m_1, \ldots, m_k\}, \{C_1, \ldots, C_k\})$ denote the set of messages generated by applying each message m_i to channel C_i.

3.3.1. *Reliable execution.* An execution of a synchronous R-round protocol Π_n on inputs $\vec{x}$ and auxiliary inputs $\vec{a}$ is the sequence of states and messages obtained from the following experiment. Initialize all states according to $\vec{x}$ and $\vec{a}$. At each round, select the new states and outgoing messages using the transition functions of each player, apply the messages to the channels, and generate the messages actually sent. Finally, after round R, allow one final computation.

More formally, but still using a somewhat loose notation, consider the case of a network with private lines and broadcast channels. We denote the messages sent over private lines by $\mu_{\text{priv}}(U, V, r)$ and those sent over broadcast lines by $\mu_{\text{broad}}(U, [n], r)$. Let $\mathscr{C}_{\text{priv}}$ and $\mathscr{C}_{\text{broad}}$ denote the private and broadcast channels. An execution of the protocol is generated by the following experiment:

- **For** $i = 1..n$ **do** set $q_i^0 = q_i^0(x_i, a_i)$.
- **For** $r = 1..R$ **do** **For** $i = 1..n$ **do**

$$(q_i^{r+1}, \mu_{\text{priv}}^{\text{out}}(i, [n], r+1), \mu_{\text{broad}}^{\text{out}}(i, [n], r+1)) \leftarrow \delta_i(q_i^r, \mu([n], i, r))$$

$$(\mu_{\text{priv}}(i, [n], r+1), \mu_{\text{broad}}(i, [n], r+1))$$

$$\leftarrow \text{SEND}(\mu_{\text{priv}}^{\text{out}}(i, [n], r+1) \cup \mu_{\text{broad}}^{\text{out}}(i, [n], r+1), \mathscr{C}_{\text{priv}} \cup \mathscr{C}_{\text{broad}})$$

- **For** $i = 1..n$ **do** /* final computation after protocol */

$$q_i^f \leftarrow \delta_i(q_i^R, \mu([n], i, R))$$

3.3.2. *Views.* A global state vector is a sequence of n states, one for each player. In general, we may consider state vectors for arbitrary subsets of the n players. Let $\widetilde{Q}$ be the set of all partial state vectors:

$$\widetilde{Q} = \{ \vec{q}_B \mid \vec{q} \in Q_1 \times \cdots \times Q_n, B \subseteq [n] \}.$$

We call the state vector and messages seen by a subset B of the players at a given round r a *view*:

$$\text{VIEW}_B^r = (\vec{q}_B^{\,r}, \mathscr{M}(B, [n], r)).$$

The set of all possible views is

$$\widetilde{V} = \widetilde{Q} \times H.$$

A *history* or *execution* of the protocol is a set of initial states, inputs, auxiliary inputs, a sequence of views, and a set of final states:

$$\text{EXEC} = \widetilde{X} \times \widetilde{Z} \times \widetilde{Q} \times (\widetilde{V})^R \times \widetilde{Q}.$$

A protocol induces a distribution on executions according to the experiment described above.

3.3.3. *Memoryless protocols and players.* As described thus far, a protocol is *memoryless*; the current states and messages are all that matter to the execution of the protocol. The final states of the players do not necessarily reflect the history of the protocol.

In practical situations it is often impossible to assure that no record is kept of previous operations. Backups are kept; transactions must be rolled back to consistent states when failures occur; and a wide variety of reasons make it extremely risky to assume that a history of previous behavior is erased before an adversary gains control of an installation.

In order to assure maximal security, we consider a stronger model in which each player is replaced by a modified player that records its view of the history of the protocol in its current state. In other words, the state q_i^r of player i at round r determines the sequence

$$(q_i^0, \mathcal{M}(i, [n], 1), q_i^1, \ldots, \mathcal{M}(i, [n], r), q_i^r).$$

The transition function δ_i is easily modified to accommodate this record, giving rise to a player whose behavior is identical but whose state determines the sequence of states and messages seen by that player.

We adopt this as the *standard* model, and assume that all players are transformed in this manner. In the standard model, the set of states of players in some coalition T at round r defines not only their current view, VIEW_T^r, but the history of the protocol up to that point: $\vec{x}_T, \vec{a}_t, \vec{q}^{\,0}, \text{VIEW}_T^1, \ldots, \text{VIEW}_T^r$. We distinguish the weaker model, in which players may forget previous state information, by specifically noting it as the *memoryless* model. Though the memoryless model has advantages in proving privacy against dynamic adversaries in cryptographic models [**BHY89**] because it permits easier simulations of the knowledge of corrupted players, we shall not discuss it further.

3.4. Adversaries (Fault class). A *fault class* $\mathcal{T}$ is a collection of allowable coalitions, namely a collection of subsets of $[n]$. We require that if $T \in \mathcal{T}$ and $U \subseteq T$, then $U \in \mathcal{T}$. Most protocols in the literature are designed to be resilient against a class described simply by $\mathcal{T} = \{ T \subseteq [n] \mid |T| \leq t \}$ for a given fault-tolerance parameter t.

3.4.1. *Passive adversaries.* Formally, a passive adversary is a tuple $(Q_A, Z_A, q_A^0, \delta_A, T)$, where Q_A is a set of states, q_A^0 is a function mapping auxiliary inputs in Z_A to initial states in Q_A, δ_A is a transition function to be described shortly, and T is a function mapping Q_A to $[n]$, describing the current coalition that the adversary chooses to corrupt. The passive adversary does not generate messages but it does choose a new state and new coalition based on its current state and the view of the coalition it currently corrupts:

$$\delta_A : Q_A \times \widetilde{V} \to \text{dist}(Q_A).$$

A passive $\mathcal{T}$-adversary for a fault class $\mathcal{T}$ is a passive adversary for which (1) for all $q_A \in Q_A$, $T(q_A) \in \mathcal{T}$, and (2) it always chooses a new coalition that is a superset of the current one (i.e., for all $q_A \in Q_A$, for all partial views $\text{VIEW}_{T(q_A)}^r$, for all states q_A' having nonzero probability weight in $\delta_A(q_A, \text{VIEW}_{T(q_A)}^r)$, $T(q_A) \subseteq T(q_A')$). Since we shall be concerned with fault classes containing all coalitions of size t or less, we also refer to this as a passive t-adversary.

3.4.2. *Execution with passive adversary.* An R-round protocol is executed synchronously in the presence of a passive adversary as follows:

- **For** $i = 1..n$ **do** set $q_i^0 = q_i^0(x_i, a_i)$.
- **For** $r = 1..R$ **do** **For** $i = 1..n$ **do** set

$$(q_i^{r+1}, \mu^{\text{out}}(i, [n], r+1)) \leftarrow \delta_i(q_i^r, \mu([n], i, r))$$
$$\mu(i, [n], r+1) \leftarrow \text{SEND}(\mu^{\text{out}}(i, [n], r+1), \mathscr{C}_1 \cup \cdots \cup \mathscr{C}_n)$$

- **For** $i = 1..n$ **do** set

$$(q_i^f) \leftarrow \delta_i(q_i^R, \mu([n], i, R))$$

It is straightforward to include the state and messages seen by the adversary in the definitions of views and histories.

3.4.3. *Dynamic vs. static adversaries.* A passive adversary is *static* if T is constant, and thus fixed before the protocol. A passive adversary is *dynamic* if T varies with the state of the adversary.

3.5. Byzantine adversaries. A Byzantine or malicious adversary $(Q_A, Z_A, q_A^0, \delta_A, T)$ has the added capability of overwriting the messages sent by players in the coalition it has corrupted. We thus extend its transition function to allow it to generate malicious messages:

$$\delta_A : Q_A \times \widetilde{V} \to \text{dist}(Q_A \times H).$$

As before, a Byzantine adversary is static if T is a constant function and dynamic if T depends on the state. A Byzantine t-adversary is allowed the fault class $\mathscr{T} = \{T \mid |T| \leq t\}$.

3.5.1. *Rushing.* A more severe sort of Byzantine adversary may *rush* messages, meaning it has access to the messages sent from reliable players before it chooses the messages sent from the corrupted coalition and before it chooses the new coalition for the subsequent round:

$$\delta_A : Q_A \times \widetilde{V} \times H \to \text{dist}(Q_A \times H).$$

The input strings in the domain H contain the rushed messages from reliable players.

3.5.2. *Execution with Byzantine adversary.* An execution of the protocol with a rushing, Byzantine adversary on inputs $\vec{x}$, auxiliary inputs $\vec{a}$, and adversary auxiliary input a_A occurs as follows:

- **For** $i = 1..n$ **do** set $q_i^0 = q_i^0(x_i, a_i)$.
- Set $q_A^0 = q_A^0(a_A)$.
- **For** $r = 1..R$ **do**

- **For** $i \notin T(q_A^r)$ **do** /* allow rushing of $\mu(\overline{T}(q_A^r), T(q_A^r), r+1)$ */

$$(q_i^{r+1}, \mu^{\text{out}}(i, [n], r+1)) \leftarrow \delta_i(q_i^r, \mu([n], i, r))$$
$$\mu(i, [n], r+1) \leftarrow \text{SEND}(\mathscr{C}_1 \cup \cdots \cup \mathscr{C}_n, \mu^{\text{out}}(i, [n], r+1)).$$

- Set

$$(q_A^{r+1}, \mu^{\text{out}}(T(q_A^{r+1}), [n], r+1)) \leftarrow \delta_A(q_A^r, \text{VIEW}^r_{T(q_A^r)}, \mu(\overline{T}(q_A^r), T(q_A^r), r+1))$$
$$\mu(T(q_A^{r+1}), [n], r+1) \leftarrow \text{SEND}(\bigcup_{T(q_A^{r+1})} \mathscr{C}_i, \mu^{\text{out}}(i, [n], r+1)).$$

- **For** $i \notin T(q_A^R)$ **do** /* final computation after protocol */

$$q_i^f \leftarrow \delta_i(q_i^R, \text{VIEW}_i^R)$$

- Set $(q_A^f) \leftarrow \delta_A(q_A^R, \text{VIEW}^R_{T(q_A^R)})$

4. Correctness, privacy, and other properties

With all this formalism intended to specify exactly how a protocol proceeds, we have yet to discuss what the protocol is intended to compute.

Let F be a function that produces a *distribution* on outputs:

$$F : X_1 \times X_2 \times \cdots \times X_n \to \text{dist}(Y_1 \times Y_2 \times \cdots \times Y_n),$$

where each $Y_i \subseteq \Sigma^\star$, and let $m = \sum_i \log|X_i|$ be the number of bits for the inputs. Notice that, as in the example of the probabilistic Turing machine discussed above, we may discuss the result of a computation as a *distribution* on outputs or as a *sample* taken from such a distribution.

We would like a protocol Π to compute a vector $(y_1, y_2, \ldots, y_n)$ selected according to the distribution $F(x_1, x_2, \ldots, x_n)$, and to provide player i with the correct value y_i. Denote the ith output of F by $F_i(x_1, \ldots, x_n)$. Often, F can be regarded as a *function* of $x_1, \ldots, x_n$, as in the case of a secret ballot, for instance. For the purposes of developing modular protocols, it is useful to express the output of a subprotocol as a distribution on individual outputs. For instance, if a protocol is based on a threshold scheme such as secret-sharing [**Sha79**, **BGW88**, **CCD88**], and its output is a collection of pieces of a new secret for the various players, then the output is not a function of the inputs but a result generated according to some appropriate distribution.

There are some important subtleties in the formal definition of correctness. In particular, the issues of defining inputs and outputs introduce several problems that are not evident at first glance. It might seem easy simply to define correctness with respect to the "inputs" $x_1, \ldots, x_n$ supplied to each player at the start of the protocol. Unfortunately, an adversary who corrupts a player at the start may simulate that player behaving as though it were given a value x_i' instead of x_i.

There is no immediate way to tell the difference between a reliable player and a corrupted player behaving correctly according to a different value. This problem is not often addressed directly, though usually there are assumptions or techniques that address it indirectly. For instance, some protocols assume the intractability of problems such as factoring large integers; by assuming that the adversary is computationally limited, they force the corrupted players to commit to input values or to use values already "committed" by some external, benign party who supplies the inputs. The correctness of the results is defined with respect to the values thus committed.

Noncryptographic protocols (i.e., protocols not based on unproven assumptions) often follow the three-stage paradigm, "Share Inputs; Compute New Secrets; Reconstruct Results," requiring each player to share his input secretly among the network at the start. (Threshold schemes such as secret-sharing **[Sha79]** form the basis for many such protocols.) The correctness of the protocol is defined with respect to the value thus committed.

Though these approaches do allow the protocols in question to be proven correct in a reasonably satisfactory manner, they leave a lot to be desired. They depend on specific intractability assumptions, or require that *all* protocols be based on a specific initial protocol like secret-sharing.

We adopt an approach that is similar in flavor to defining correctness with respect to committed inputs, yet allows protocols to be designed in the most general fashion. In other words, we do not assume that each protocol begins with an initialization phase in which each player secretly shares his input. Nor do we make unproven assumptions, or require the use of special devices for committing values.

Correctness is defined with respect to the input and output functions mentioned in §3.3 but yet to be described. The output functions $O_i : Q_i \to Y_i$ are intuitively clear: they map the (final) state of player i to an output value in Y_i.

The input functions $I_i : \text{EXEC} \to X_i$ map an execution of the protocol to the effective input held by each player. The key point here is that the input function I_i is defined not on the input of player i, on his initial state, or on the set of messages sent by player i, but on the global history at the end of the protocol. In order to satisfy our intuitive requirements for the specification of an input, we require that the effective input computed for each reliable player is, in fact, his original input x_i. In order to treat the subtle problem of a corrupted player who behaves indistinguishably from a reliable player having a different input from that which the corrupted player was given, we do not require that the input function match the original input under those circumstances.

A protocol Π for F is $(1-\varepsilon)$-*correct* if, for all t-adversaries A with auxiliary input a_A, for all inputs $\vec{x}$ and auxiliary inputs $\vec{a}$, for all reliable players $i \notin T(q_A^f)$, the probability of the following is at least $(1-\varepsilon)$:

- $I_i(\text{VIEW}) = x_i$
- $O_i(q_i^f) = F_i(I_1(\text{VIEW}), \ldots, I_n(\text{VIEW}))$

Methods such as broadcasting an encryption of x_i or secretly sharing x_i serve the purpose of allowing an input to be defined uniquely from the global history of the protocol, but are by no means comprehensive. Notice that there need not be a party who can compute everyone's effective inputs, nor does the computation of effective inputs from the global history need to be efficient; what is important is that the design of the protocol ensure that a unique set of inputs is defined for any execution.

Using our definition, we need not categorize the various sorts of solutions and compare them in their separate categories, but instead consider them as different ways to achieve the same purpose. Our definition adopts the philosophical approach that a player's input is defined, in a sense, according to his behavior. If one wishes to ensure that a *given* set of inputs is used (as, for instance, when encryptions or commitments of inputs have already been distributed, by a benevolent source or from a previous protocol), then the encryptions of x_i seen by other players are included in their inputs or auxiliary inputs, and the protocol is designed accordingly. In other words, the protocol designer may create a protocol to compute an extended function that computes the original function F when the extended inputs (basic inputs along with the encryptions) are consistent, and computes the original function applied to default values if player i behaves according to an x_i that is inconsistent with the encryptions that are part of the other players' inputs.

Thus it is up to the protocol designer to determine what arguments are used for corrupted players, i.e., to specify the input functions (whether they be default values, or values computed by the remaining reliable players). The protocol designer is not free, however, to change the inputs of reliable players; the input functions I_i must agree with the actual inputs of nonfaulty players.

4.1. Privacy. The notion of privacy has many flavors. Some approaches consider just the privacy of the inputs, requiring that whatever the protocol computes, it should not reveal any information about the inputs other than what the final results alone would reveal. This leaves the privacy of unrelated information open to attack. In other words, the protocol could reveal information unrelated to the current computation, such as the private information of a separate protocol. Though many of the definitions of privacy that concern just the inputs appear in works that also satisfy a stronger privacy property, it is important to distinguish the two situations.

A protocol that protects the privacy of its inputs may not be compatible with any other protocol, since it is guaranteed only to keep the current inputs private. In order to develop a more robust approach and to support the design of modular protocols that can be run sequentially or simultaneously, we propose a definition more along the lines of zero-knowledge proof systems **[GMR89]**.

Intuitively, a protocol reveals nothing but the output to a coalition of players if that coalition could simulate the history of the protocol given only their inputs and their outputs. The idea of simulation is the backbone of zero-knowledge proof systems **[GMR89]**. In the case of players who are computationally restricted (see §5), simulation results show intuitively that the adversary learns nothing it could not compute efficiently on its own. In general, even with computationally unbounded players, we would like to ensure that the adversary can simulate its portion of the history of the protocol using only the information that it is entitled to learn. In this case, there must be a *function* that maps the inputs and outputs of corrupted players to a distribution on protocol executions matching the distribution induced by actual runs of the protocol. Modelling the players and adversaries as "automata" with unrestricted (possibly nonrecursive) transition functions, as we have chosen to do for full generality, provides the strongest, information-theoretic notion of security.

A related idea that avoids the computational orientation of simulation says that the distribution on views seen by the adversary is *independent* of the reliable players' information, or more generally that the distribution depends *only* on the final output and the inputs of the corrupted players. This sort of approach forms the basis for the instance-hiding schemes of **[AFK89**, **BF90]**. When the players are not computationally bounded, defining privacy according to independence of variables is often a cleaner approach.

In general, if a distribution is independent of certain variables, then it can be simulated without the knowledge of those variables (though, of course, there is no guarantee that the simulated distribution is easy to compute). With this in mind, we shall adopt the simulation approach, since it covers both computationally-unbounded and computationally-bounded models for the participants.

Specific definitions of a simulator for a dynamic adversary against a multiparty protocol to compute a function resiliently are not common or evident in the literature. Here we define a simulator for a multiparty protocol and give a rigorous and strong definition of privacy, also referred to as zero-knowledge or minimum-disclosure.

Fix an arbitrary adversary A. When a protocol is executed with initial inputs $\vec{x}$ and auxiliary inputs $\vec{a}$, denote the resulting distribution on final adversarial views by

$$\mathscr{A}_{n,m,k}^{\vec{x},\vec{a}}(q_A^0).$$

The distribution on global views is denoted

$$\Pi(\vec{x}, \vec{a}, q_A^0).$$

4.1.1. *Fault oracles and simulators.* We would like to show that A learns only the function values and inputs corresponding to the coalition it corrupts. In the case of a static adversary, this means that there exists a simulator that, given the function values and inputs for players of its choice, produces an adversarial view VIEW_A^f of the protocol according to a distribution that cannot be distinguished from $\mathscr{A}_{n,m,k}^{\vec{x},\vec{a}}(q_A^0)$. When a dynamic adversary is involved, however, the adversary's choice of players to corrupt may depend on the progress of the protocol. A simulator cannot be expected to decide in advance the coalition that the adversary will choose; in fact, the adversary may corrupt later players based on the inputs it learns for players corrupted earlier.

We therefore introduce the idea of a *fault oracle*, which supplies the simulator with the inputs of players chosen by the simulator, and later supplies the simulator with the function values as well.

Essentially, the simulator S has access to an oracle that is given the initial states $\vec{q}$ and is willing to reveal some of them (dynamically), and to make a single computation of F at a set of arguments that is partially chosen by the simulator.

A *simulator* S is an oracle machine that generates queries of two types. The first type of query requests the inputs $\vec{x}_T$ and auxiliary inputs $\vec{a}_T$ for some coalition T. The second type of query requests the inputs, auxiliary inputs, and the outputs $\{ F_i \mid i \in T \}$ for a sample of F computed according to inputs $\vec{x}_T^{\star}$ chosen by the simulator (while the remaining inputs are determined by the oracle). Simulator S is given $n, m, k,$ and an adversary state q_A as input. It outputs an adversary state from Q_A.

An *admissible* simulator is one that requests F exactly once, and for which there exists a $T \in \mathscr{T}$ such that every query made by the simulator specifies a coalition $T(q) \subseteq T$. Note that the query about F need not be the final query; the adversary, and hence the simulator, is free to corrupt additional players after the value of the function has been revealed. Note also that the case of privacy against a static adversary is a simple special case of this definition.

A *fault oracle* $\mathscr{O}(\vec{x}, \vec{a})$ for F answers queries of two types:

- on input T, it returns $\vec{x}_T$ and $\vec{a}_T$, the inputs of players in T;
- on input $< T, \vec{x}_T^{\star} >$, it returns the value of $F(x_1', \ldots, x_n')$, where

$$x_i' = \begin{cases} x_i^{\star} & i \in T \\ x_i & i \notin T. \end{cases}$$

In order to show that the protocol discloses nothing but F, we allow an admissible simulator to query an oracle for F. We denote the ensemble of views produced by the simulator on input $n, m, k,$ and $q_A^0 \in Q_A$, and with access to an oracle $\mathscr{O}(\vec{x}, \vec{a})$, by

$$\mathscr{S}^{\mathscr{O}(\vec{x},\vec{a})}_{n,m,k}(q_A^0).$$

A protocol Π for F is perfectly (statistically) *t-private* if for any t-adversary A, there exists an admissible simulator S such that, for any initial adversary state $q_A^0 \in Q_A$, for all tuples of inputs $\vec{x}$ and auxiliary inputs $\vec{a}$, the ensembles $\mathscr{S}^{\mathscr{O}(\vec{x},\vec{a})}_{n,m,k}(q_A^0)$ and $\mathscr{A}^{\vec{x},\vec{a}}_{n,m,k}(q_A^0)$ are indistinguishable (statistically).

Let G be a function that, like F, maps n inputs to a distribution on n outputs, and let $\mathscr{O}_{FG}$ be a fault oracle for the pair of functions (F, G). We model the following definition after [**AFK89**, **BF90**]. A protocol Π for F is perfectly (statistically) *t-private leaking* G if for any t-adversary A, there exists an admissible simulator S such that, for any initial adversary state $q_A^0 \in Q_A$, for all tuples of inputs $\vec{x}$ and auxiliary inputs $\vec{a}$, the ensembles $\mathscr{S}^{\mathscr{O}_{FG}(\vec{x},\vec{a})}_{n,m,k}(q_A^0)$ and $\mathscr{A}^{\vec{x},\vec{a}}_{n,m,k}(q_A^0)$ are indistinguishable (statistically).

4.2. Independence. Since we have defined inputs in terms of behavior during the protocol, we have made no restrictions on the choices an adversary may make for the inputs of the faulty players. We would like the adversary not to be able to direct the computation toward its own purposes by choosing the faulty players' inputs in a manner that is dependent on the choices made by reliable players. The set of effective inputs for unreliable players should be distributed in the same manner regardless of the reliable players' inputs.

A protocol satisfies the property of *independence of inputs* if the following holds. For any t-adversary A, for any T of size $\leq t$, for any q_A^0, for all assignments $(\vec{x}_T, \vec{a}_T)$ to players in T, for all pairs of assignments $(\vec{x}_1, \vec{a}_1)$ and $(\vec{x}_2, \vec{a}_2)$ to players not in T, the induced distributions

$$I^1 = \{ \text{VIEW} \leftarrow \Pi(\vec{x}_1 \cup \vec{x}_T, \vec{a}_1 \cup \vec{a}_T, q_A^0) : \vec{I}_T(\text{VIEW}) \}$$

and

$$I^2 = \{ \text{VIEW} \leftarrow \Pi(\vec{x}_2 \cup \vec{x}_T, \vec{a}_2 \cup \vec{a}_T, q_A^0) : \vec{I}_T(\text{VIEW}) \}$$

are statistically indistinguishable. Here, $\vec{I}_T(\text{VIEW}) = \{ I_i(\text{VIEW}) \mid i \in T \}$, the set of effective inputs for faulty players.

4.3. Fairness. For completeness we touch briefly upon the issue of fairness. We desire that the adversary cannot learn the output of the function while preventing the reliable players from learning their outputs. The issue of fairness arises only in protocols where the fault-tolerance parameter t exceeds half the network, namely in two-party protocols and in n-party protocols with $2t \geq n$. Protocols with a reliable majority are usually not concerned with fairness since it is easily ensured by the power of the majority.

In a certain sense, the definition of correctness implies fairness; that is, each player must finish with its appropriate output. A weaker definition must be made for protocols allowing a faulty majority, since a faulty majority can provably prevent a correct output from being achieved. That is, correctness is not achievable in general when more than half the players are faulty. Usually, a default output instead of the "right" output is considered a correct one when too many faults occur. In that case, the "right" output of the function is revealed only when sufficiently few faults occur. In order to maintain parity in the knowledge among the adversary and the reliable players, methods for gradual disclosure of the results are employed [**LMR83**, **Yao86**, **Cle86**, **GHY87**, **BG89**]. There are two primary approaches to dealing with large numbers of faults occurring after some information about the results has been revealed. One approach allows the reliable players to run a recovery algorithm based on the program used by the adversary when large numbers of faults have occurred [**Yao86**, **GHY87**]. A stronger definition in which the reliable players do not have access to the program of the adversary, which therefore allows the adversary to depend on the programs of the reliable players, is presented and achieved in [**BG89**].

5. Interactive turing machines

Protocols fall into one of two categories, based on whether the participants have bounded or unbounded (even nonrecursive) computational resources. The protocol definitions given above are easily applied to modelling computations in a network of interactive, probabilistic Turing machines. The state set of each player includes the finite state of the Turing machine and the contents of its infinite work tape. The transition function is defined naturally according to the transition function of the Turing machine and the contents of its work tape and a tape of uniformly random bits. The distribution on the messages sent by each player must be computable given a random tape.

The complexity-based model for multiparty protocols assumes that each player, including the adversary, is a Turing machine which runs in probabilistic polynomial time. The definition of privacy is restricted so that the adversary is restricted to polynomial times in its malicious machinations; similarly, the simulator also has only polynomial time to complete its computations. The output of the simulator, of course, need only be computationally indistinguishable from views generated by actual executions of the protocol.

Independence also need not have such a strong definition; instead of requiring that the distributions on effective inputs of faulty players be identical, they need only be computationally indistinguishable (cf. [**BG89**]).

Because the simulator has restricted resources, one must be very careful to specify whether the protocol is resilient against static or dynamic adversaries. Simulation results may be possible when a static adversary is involved but impossible when a dynamic adversary is involved, even though the protocol in question seems intuitively secure against dynamic adversaries. For instance, when a dynamic adversary corrupts a new player, it may learn the decryption keys to all the messages previously encrypted by that player. If a simulator does not know the key and the decrypted messages in advance, it will be infeasible for it to construct a consistent history of the protocol up to that point.

The precise specification of a fault oracle also prevents the simulator from "backing up" the adversary to a point where it can proceed with a new choice of corrupted players in an attempt to generate an execution that the simulator does happen to have the information to simulate. A naive approach to simulation might allow this in order that the simulation be feasible. Upon more careful inspection, if the simulator *needs* to have access to arbitrary sets of inputs, this would imply that the protocol leaks information. The definitions of admissible simulators and fault oracles prevent such an error.

Thus, the definitions given for players with unbounded resources are easily modified to describe resource-bounded computations and to support the computational complexity-based approach to security.

6. Conclusions

We have listed many formal definitions for players, protocols, protocol executions, and protocol properties, in order to bring together a diverse and scattered set of ideas and intuitions about multiparty computations, and in the hope that, given these definitions, actual proofs of claimed properties may be written. We have introduced the idea of a fault oracle in order to describe resilience against dynamic adversaries, giving a concise means to analyze dynamic adversaries and support proofs of privacy and correctness.

References

[AFK89] M. Abadi, J. Feigenbaum, and J. Kilian. *On hiding information from an oracle*, J. Comput. System Sci. **39** (1989), 21–50.

[Bea88] D. Beaver, *Secure multiparty protocols tolerating half faulty processors*, J. Cryptology, to appear. Extended abstract in Proc. of 9th CRYPTO (1989), Springer-Verlag, to appear.

[BF90] D. Beaver and J. Feigenbaum, *Hiding instances in multioracle queries*, Proc. of 7th STACS (1990), Springer-Verlag, 37–48.

[BG89] D. Beaver and S. Goldwasser, *Multiparty computation with faulty majority*, Proc. of 30th FOCS (1989), IEEE, 468–473.

[BHY89] D. Beaver, S. Haber, and M. Yung, private communication.

[BGW88] M. Ben-Or, S. Goldwasser, and A. Wigderson, *Completeness theorems for noncryptographic fault-tolerant distributed computation*, Proc. of 20th STOC (1988), ACM, 1–10.

[Bla81] R. Blakley, *Security proofs for information protection systems*, Proc. of 1980 Symposium on Security and Privacy, IEEE Computer Society Press, New York, 1981, 79–88.

[BCC89] G. Brassard, D. Chaum, and C. Crépeau, *Minimum disclosure proofs of knowledge*, J. Comput. System Sci. **37** (1988), 156–189.

[CCD88] D. Chaum, C. Crépeau, and I. Damgård, *Multiparty unconditionally secure protocols*, Proc. of 20th STOC (1988), ACM, 11–19.

[CGMA85] B. Chor, S. Goldwasser, S. Micali, and B. Awerbuch, *Verifiable secret-sharing and achieving simultaneity in the presence of faults*, Proc. of 17th STOC (1985), ACM, 383–395.

[Cle86] R. Cleve, *Limits on the security of coin flips when half the processors are faulty*, Proc. of 18th STOC (1986), ACM, 364–370.

[GHY87] Z. Galil, S. Haber, and M. Yung, *Cryptographic computation: Secure fault-tolerant protocols and the public key model*, Proc. of 7th CRYPTO (1987), Springer-Verlag, 135–155.

[GMR89] S. Goldwasser, S. Micali, and C. Rackoff, *The knowledge complexity of interactive proof systems*, SIAM J. Comput. **18** (1989), 186–208.

[GMW86] O. Goldreich, S. Micali, and A. Wigderson, *Proofs that yield nothing but their validity and a methodology of cryptographic protocol design*, Proc. of 27th FOCS (1986), IEEE, 174–187.

[GMW87] ———, *How to play ANY mental game, or a completeness theorem for protocols with honest majority*, Proc. of 19th STOC (1987), ACM, 218–229.

[Hab88] S. Haber, *Multi-party cryptographic computation: techniques and applications*, Ph.D. thesis, Columbia University, 1988.

[Kil88] J. Kilian, *Founding cryptography on oblivious transfer*, Proc. of 20th STOC (1988), ACM, 20–29.

[LMR83] M. Luby, S. Micali, and C. Rackoff, *How to simultaneously exchange a secret bit by flipping a symmetrically biased coin*, Proc. of 24th FOCS (1983), IEEE, 11–22.

[Rab88] T. Rabin, *Robust sharing of secrets when the dealer is honest or cheating*, masters thesis, Hebrew University, 1988.

[RB89] T. Rabin and M. Ben-Or, *Verifiable secret sharing and multiparty protocols with honest majority*, Proc. of 21st STOC (1989), ACM, 73–85.

[Sha79] A. Shamir, *How to share a secret*, Commun. of the Assoc. Comput. Mach. **22** (1979), 612–613.

[Yao86] A. Yao, *How to generate and exchange secrets*, Proc. of 27th FOCS (1986), IEEE, 162–167.

AIKEN COMPUTATION LABORATORY, HARVARD UNIVERSITY

E-mail address: BEAVER@RESEARCH.ATT.COM

DIMACS Series in Discrete Mathematics
and Theoretical Computer Science
Volume 2, 1991

Perfect Privacy for Two-Party Protocols

Extended Abstract

DONALD BEAVER

ABSTRACT. We examine the problem of computing functions in a distributed manner based on private inputs, revealing the value of a function without revealing any additional information about the inputs. A function $f(x_1, \ldots, x_n)$ is t-private if there is a protocol whereby n parties, each holding an input value, can compute f, and no subset of t or fewer parties gains any information other than what is computable from $f(x_1, \ldots, x_n)$. The class of t-private *boolean* functions for $t \geq \lceil \frac{n}{2} \rceil$ was described in **[CK89]**. We give a characterization of 1-private functions for two parties, without the restriction to the boolean case. Incorrect proofs of this characterization appeared in **[Kus89, Bea89]**; we present a different proof. We also examine a restricted form of private computation in the n-party case, and show that addition is the only t-privately computable function in that model.

1. Introduction

Consider the following problem: n parties want to compute the value of a function $f(x_1, \ldots, x_n)$ without revealing additional information about the inputs. In particular, if a coalition of up to t parties pools their information after a run of the protocol, then they should not be able to obtain any information that they could not compute strictly from their input values and the value of $f(x_1, \ldots, x_n)$.

When the bound t on the number of curious parties satisfies $t < \lceil \frac{n}{2} \rceil$, any function can be computed privately **[BGW88, CCD88]**.

When $t \geq \lceil \frac{n}{2} \rceil$, the class of privately computable functions is restricted. Chor and Kushilevitz **[CK89]** characterized the set of *boolean* functions that

---

1980 *Mathematics Subject Classification* (1985 *Revision*). Primary 68-06, 68M10, 68Q75, 68Q99, 94A05, 94A60.

This research was supported in part under NSF grant CCR-870-4513.

1052-1798/91 $1.00 + $.25 per page

can be computed privately for $t \geq \lceil \frac{n}{2} \rceil$ as those of the form

$$f(x_1, x_2, \ldots, x_n) = f_1(x_1) \oplus f_2(x_2) \oplus \cdots \oplus f_n(x_n).$$

In other words, for the boolean case, the only functions privately computable when a majority of the parties are curious are exclusive-or's of n functions, each depending on one input.

The results of **[Yao86, GMW87, GHY87]** demonstrate that when the participants are computationally bounded but still only curious, *any* function can be privately computed for $t \leq n-1$. Furthermore, even functions that have non-boolean outputs are privately computable. In an information-theoretic sense, however, coalitions of curious parties do hold more information than that to which they are entitled.

The complete characterization of privately computable functions when the participants are not bounded remains an open question:

> What *general* functions (say from n inputs to n-bit outputs) can be computed privately by n parties, allowing $t \geq \lceil \frac{n}{2} \rceil$, and maintaining privacy in an *information-theoretic* sense?

In this paper, we take the penultimate step toward a complete characterization, by solving the following problem:

> What *general* functions can be computed privately by *two* parties?

We give a characterization of functions that are privately computable by two parties, based on a simple property of the table for the functions. Specifically, any function whose table can be *partitioned* in a certain manner can be privately computed by two parties; and any function that can be privately computed by two parties has a table which can be partitioned. (See §3.4 for a statement of the main theorem.)

In preliminary papers, Kushilevitz **[Kus89]** and Beaver **[Bea89]** independently obtained this characterization, but the proofs appearing in those papers contain a subtle flaw for which there does not appear to be an easy, direct fix. We present here a different proof, which uses a different approach. (See §3.2.)

Our characterization bears on the n-party problem in that any n-party protocol that allows $t \geq \lceil \frac{n}{2} \rceil$ can be adapted to a two-party protocol. Thus, functions that are privately computable in the n-party case must satisfy certain properties satisfied by functions that are private in the two-party case.

We also address a different version of the n-party problem, in which the output of the function is not revealed. Instead, it is maintained in a distributed form, such that the parties determine the value together, but small coalitions of parties have no information. In view of the recent development of multiparty computation protocols based on threshold schemes (cf. **[BGW88, CCD88]**), all of which allow the output to be maintained in a shared form, a characterization of the functions that can be computed secretly is needed. We show a strongly negative result: the only functions that can be computed secretly, maintaining the result as a secret (for use in further protocols), are additive functions. This result fits nicely with that of **[CK89]** showing that privately computable boolean functions are addition functions (mod 2).

2. Definitions

For the two-party case, we assume that the two parties communicate using finite strings and for a finite number of exchanges. Neither party is computationally bounded; the privacy of the protocols is based on information-theoretic bounds.

A party is simply a family of distributions on strings, parametrized by the input and the current transcript of the protocol. That is, party 1 is a family of distributions $\{ D^1_{x,t} \mid x \in X, t \in \Sigma^\star \}$, where $\Sigma = \{0, 1\}$, and each $D^1_{x,t}$ is a distribution on $\Sigma^\star$. The message that party 1 sends after round r is a finite string selected at random according to distribution D^1_{x,t_r}, where x is its input and t_r is the transcript of messages through round r. Party 2 is defined similarly. We assume that the transcripts are delimited so that the messages are uniquely decodable from the transcripts.

Let the domain of f be $X \times Y = \{1, \dots, \alpha\} \times \{1, \dots, \beta\}$. Let T be a random variable that describes the transcript of message exchanges between parties 1 and 2. We say that f is *private* if there is a protocol such that the following hold, when party 1 holds $x \in X$ and party 2 holds $y \in Y$:

- After any run of the protocol, each party knows $f(x, y)$.
- **(Privacy for party 1)** For any x' such that $f(x', y) = f(x, y)$ and for any transcript t:

$$\Pr[t \mid x', y] = \Pr[t \mid x, y].$$

- **(Privacy for party 2)** For any y' such that $f(x, y') = f(x, y)$ and for any transcript t:

$$\Pr[t \mid x, y'] = \Pr[t \mid x, y].$$

We shall also denote the prefix of a transcript t after the ith round by t_i, and the corresponding random variable by T_i.

3. Two-party privacy

3.1. Partitions. For any $x \in X$ and any subset $P \subseteq Y$, we define the *row set* for row x and columns in P to be the range of values that f takes over that row of its table:

$$R(x, P) = \{ f(x, y) \mid y \in P \}.$$

Similarly, we define the *column set* for $y \in Y$ and a subset of values $P \subseteq X$:

$$C(P, y) = \{ f(x, y) \mid x \in P \}.$$

We say that f is *column-partitionable* into f_P and f_Q if there exists a nontrivial partition of Y into blocks P and Q such that

$$(\forall x \in X) R(x, P) \cap R(x, Q) = \emptyset,$$

and f_P and f_Q are the restriction of f to the sets P and Q. In other words, if we look at a particular row in the table for f and consider the range of values that f takes on for $y \in P$, then no such value will appear as the output of f for $y \in Q$. Similarly, f is *row-partitionable* if there exists a nontrivial partition of X into blocks P and Q such that

$$(\forall y \in Y) R(P, y) \cap R(Q, y) = \emptyset,$$

and f_P and f_Q are the restriction of f to the sets P and Q.

Partitionability is recursively defined as follows. We say that f is *partitionable* if:

(i) f is constant; or
(ii) f is column-partitionable or row-partitionable into f_P and f_Q, each of which are themselves partitionable.

For example, the AND function is not partitionable, while the function $f(x, y) = x + y \bmod 7$ is partitionable. Functions that are not partitionable need not be based on AND or OR, as demonstrated by the following table, which cannot be partitioned by rows or by columns:

$f(x, y)$	0	1	2
0	0	0	1
1	3	4	1
2	3	2	2

It is easy to see that any function that is insensitive to x or to y is partitionable.

It is also straightforward to determine from an $n \times n$ table for f whether f is partitionable, by using a transitive-closure algorithm that runs in time polynomial in n, to determine the columns or rows that must fall in the same blocks of any allowable partition.

3.2. Two parties cannot compute unpartitionable functions. We show the following result:

LEMMA 1. *If f is not partitionable, then f cannot be computed privately by two parties.*

Before proceeding to the proof, let us expose the flaw in the earlier proofs of Kushilevitz [**Kus89**] and Beaver [**Bea89**].

Without loss of generality, let party 1 send messages m_r to party 2 during odd-numbered rounds r; let party 2 send messages during even-numbered rounds. This does not restrict who "speaks" first, since null or completely random messages are allowed. We expand the probability of a transcript t given x and y according to its prefixes $t_1, t_2, \ldots,$ where $t_i = m_1 \circ m_2 \circ \cdots \circ m_i$:

$$\begin{aligned}\Pr[t \mid x, y] &= \prod_r \Pr[t_r \mid x, y, t_{r-1}] \\ &= \left(\prod_j \Pr[t_{2j+1} \mid x, y, t_{2j}]\right)\left(\prod_j \Pr[t_{2j} \mid x, y, t_{2j-1}]\right) \\ &= P_1(t, x) P_2(t, y)\end{aligned}$$

where P_1 and P_2 are defined as the parenthesized expressions. (This notation appears literally as $P_1(s \mid x)$, $P_2(s \mid y)$ in [**Kus89**], and as $\gamma_t(x)$, $\delta_t(y)$ in [**Bea89**].)

The faulty proof appearing in [**Kus89**, **Bea89**] runs along the following lines. Using the privacy of f, it is shown by induction that $\Pr[t \mid x, y]$ is constant over all x. The induction step fails, however, since it is based on the following statement, which intends to show that P_1 is insensitive to x: If $\Pr[t \mid x_1, y] = \Pr[t \mid x_2, y]$ then $P_1(t, x_1) = P_1(t, x_2)$. Unfortunately, if $P_2(t, y) = 0$, this does not necessarily hold.

For example, consider the function described by

$f(x, y)$	y_1	y_2
x_1	1	2
x_2	1	3

and the 4-round deterministic protocol where party 1 starts, and each party sends 1 bit, described by the table of transcripts:

	y_1	y_2
x_1	0000	0100
x_2	0000	0110

Then $\Pr[0000 \mid x_1, y_1] = P_1(0000, x_1)P_2(0000, y_1) = \Pr[0000 \mid x_2, y_1] = P_1(0000, x_2)P_2(0000, y_1)$, and we have $P_2(0000, y_1) = 1$ and $P_1(0000, x_1) = P_1(0000, x_2) = 1$. The "claim" that P_1 is insensitive to x is satisfied for this particular transcript. On the other hand, $\Pr[0100 \mid x_1, y_1] =$

$\Pr[0100 \mid x_2, y_1] = 0$, but $P_1(0100, x_1) = 1$ while $P_1(0100, x_2) = 0$. Informally, transcript 0100 is impossible given y_1, but it may or may not be possible for different x, a fact that cannot be determined simply by looking at the column corresponding to y_1. The claim that P_1 is insensitive to x fails.

It turns out that P_1 is indeed insensitive to x when f cannot be partitioned into columns, but this is not a trivial observation, and the proof must use the unpartitionability of f by columns. The earlier proofs did not use this property, and thereby fail on a counterexample like the one presented above. (Note that f is not partitionable by rows, but it is partitionable by columns.) Introducing the property of unpartitionability by columns into the earlier proof techniques seems to be an unwieldy approach, without an easy fix; instead, we present an alternative proof.

PROOF OF LEMMA 1. Since $t_{2j+1} = t_{2j} \circ m_{2j+1}$, and m_{2j+1} is selected by party 1 according to distribution $D^1_{x, t_{2j}}$, we may write:

$$\Pr[t_{2j+1} \mid x, y] = \Pr[t_{2j+1} \mid x, t_{2j}] \Pr[t_{2j} \mid x, y].$$

Similarly,

$$\Pr[t_{2j} \mid x, y] = \Pr[t_{2j} \mid y, t_{2j-1}] \Pr[t_{2j-1} \mid x, y].$$

First we shall show that if f is privately computable but not partitionable, then party 1 "never speaks first." In other words, all conversations are independent of x until party 2 gives away some information depending on y. Then we shall show that party 2 never speaks first, leading to a contradiction.

In order to formalize the notion of not speaking first, consider the following notations. Let $D \subseteq X \times Y$, and let $\tau(x, y) = \{ t \mid \Pr[t \mid x, y] \neq 0 \}$. Given a transcript t and two pairs of inputs (x, y) and (u, v), let $\theta(t, x, y, u, v)$ be the value r such that

$$\Pr[t_r \mid x, y] \neq \Pr[t_r \mid u, v] \quad \text{and} \quad (\forall \rho < r) \Pr[t_\rho \mid x, y] = \Pr[t_\rho \mid u, v].$$

Clearly, such an r is unique if it exists. If no such r exists, let $\theta(t, x, y, u, v) = \infty$. The earliest round at which the probabilities of conversations on (x, y) differ from those for *some* other input (u, v) is denoted

$$\phi(t, D, x, y) = \min_{(u, v) \in D} \theta(t, x, y, u, v).$$

Now let

$$\psi(D) = \{ \phi(t, D, x, y) \mid (x, y) \in D, t \in \tau(x, y) \}.$$

We say that party 1 *does not speak first on* D if $\psi(D) \subset \{ 2j \mid j \in \mathbf{N} \} \cup \{ \infty \}$, that is, if the earliest times at which conversations differ are always even-numbered rounds, corresponding to party 2 sending a message to party 1.

First, let us show an easy lemma:

LEMMA 2 (ROW LEMMA). *For any* $x \in X$ *and* $y_1, y_2 \in Y$, *and for any possible transcript* $t \in \tau(x, y_1)$, *if*

$$\Pr[t_r \mid x, y_1] \neq \Pr[t_r \mid x, y_2] \quad \textit{and} \quad (\forall \rho < r)\Pr[t_\rho \mid x, y_1] = \Pr[t_\rho \mid x, y_2],$$

then r *is not odd.*

PROOF. If r is odd, party 1 sends the message at round r:

$$\begin{aligned}\Pr[t_r \mid x, y_1] &= \Pr[t_r \mid x, t_{r-1}]\Pr[t_{r-1} \mid x, y_1] \\ &= \Pr[t_r \mid x, t_{r-1}]\Pr[t_{r-1} \mid x, y_2] \\ &= \Pr[t_r \mid x, y_2],\end{aligned}$$

which is a contradiction. □

The crucial lemma we need is the following:

LEMMA 3. *If* f *is privately computable but not partitionable, then party* 1 *does not speak first on* $X \times Y$.

PROOF. We show by induction that there exist $P_1 \subset P_2 \subset \cdots \subset P_{|X|} = X$ such that party 2 speaks first on each $P_i \times Y$.

Using Lemma 2, we see that party 1 does not speak first on $P_1 \times Y$, where $P_1 = \{a_1\}$ and $a_1 \in X$ is arbitrary. Since party 1 only has one argument in P_1, this is intuitively clear.

Assume by way of induction that party 1 does not speak first on $P_i \times Y$. We must demonstrate a P_{i+1} such that $P_i \subset P_{i+1}$ and party 1 does not speak first on P_{i+1}.

Since f is not partitionable, there exist values $x_1 \in P_i$, $x_2 \in \overline{P}_i$, and $y_1 \in Y$ so that $f(x_1, y_1) = f(x_2, y_1)$. Let $P_{i+1} = P_i \cup \{x_2\}$. To show that party 2 speaks first on $P_{i+1} \times Y$, it suffices to show that for each $y \in Y$, $\phi(t, \{x_2\} \times Y, x_2, y)$ is never odd and $\phi(t, P_i \times Y, x_2, y)$ is never odd. In other words, we consider the earliest times that a meaningful message is sent for the new inputs in $\{x_2\} \times Y$ relative to the original set $P_i \times Y$ and relative to the new input set itself.

Lemma 2 shows that $\phi(t, \{x_2\} \times Y, x_2, y)$ is never odd.

To obtain the claim that $\phi(t, P_i \times Y, x_2, y)$ is never odd, let us divide the row $\{x_2\} \times Y$ into three sets,

$$\begin{aligned}A &= \{(x_2, y_1)\}, \\ B &= \{(x_2, y) \mid (\exists a \in P_i) f(a, y) = f(x_2, y)\} \backslash A,\end{aligned}$$

and

$$C = \{(x_2, y) \mid (\forall a \in P_i) f(a, y) \neq f(x_2, y)\}.$$

First, we show that $\phi(t, P_i \times Y, x_2, y_1)$ is even for any possible transcript $t \in \tau(x_2, y_1)$. If $t \in \tau(x_2, y_1)$ then by the privacy of f,

$$(\forall r) \Pr[t_r \mid x_1, y_1] = \Pr[t_r \mid x_2, y_1].$$

Then it follows easily that $\phi(t, P_i \times Y, x_2, y_1) = \phi(t, P_i \times Y, x_1, y_1)$, and our first claim follows.

By a similar argument, $\phi(t, P_i \times Y, x_2, y)$ is never odd for any $y \in B$.

Thirdly, for any $(x_2, y) \in C$, we show $\phi(t, P_i \times Y, x_2, y)$ is never odd. We have two cases to consider: $\theta(t, x_2, y, x_1, y_1)$ is minimal or it is not. Say it is minimal. Again, by the privacy of f we have that

$$(\forall r) \Pr[t_r \mid x_1, y_1] = \Pr[t_r \mid x_2, y_1],$$

and the smallest r at which $\Pr[t_r \mid x_1, y_1] \neq \Pr[t_r \mid x_2, y]$ is identical to that for which $\Pr[t_r \mid x_2, y_1] \neq \Pr[t_r \mid x_2, y]$. Since (x_2, y_1) and (x_2, y) are in the same row, r must be even.

If $\theta(t, x_2, y, x_1, y_1)$ is not minimal, let (u, v) be such that $\theta(t, x_2, y, u, v)$ is minimal. For a given transcript t, consider the probabilities $\Pr[t_r \mid u, v]$, $\Pr[t_r \mid x_1, y_1]$, and $\Pr[t_r \mid x_2, y]$. At some earliest round r, two or three of these differ. Since (u, v) gave the minimal value with respect to (x_2, y) we see that $\Pr[t_r \mid x_2, y] \neq \Pr[t_r \mid u, v]$. Since (x_1, y_1) did not give the minimal value, $\Pr[t_r \mid x_2, y] = \Pr[t_r \mid x_1, y_1]$. Therefore $\Pr[t_r \mid x_1, y_1] \neq \Pr[t_r \mid u, v]$. By the induction hypothesis, since (x_1, y_1) and (u, v) are in $P_i \times Y$, we deduce r is even. □

A symmetric argument gives the corresponding lemma:

LEMMA 4. *If f is privately computable but not partitionable, then party 2 does not speak first on $X \times Y$.*

Combining Lemmas 3 and 4, we see that neither party speaks first on $X \times Y$, implying that $\psi(X \times Y) = \{\infty\}$. Let $a \in X$ and $b \in Y$ be arbitrary, and let $t \in \tau(a, b)$. Then for every $x \in X$ and $y \in Y$, we have $\theta(t, a, b, x, y) = \infty$, implying $\Pr[t \mid a, b] = \Pr[t \mid x, y]$. Since $f(x, y)$ is determined by the transcript t, f must be constant and hence partitionable, giving a contradiction. □

REMARKS. The proof of Lemma 1 does not assume that the protocol is deterministic. In the next section we observe that a deterministic protocol suffices to compute any partitionable function. Furthermore, even if the protocol is only correct with probability exceeding $\frac{1}{2}$, the argument shows that the distributions on transcripts are identical regardless of the inputs, so that f must be constant, giving a contradiction.

3.3. Two parties can compute partitionable functions. We now show a converse result:

LEMMA 5. *If f is partitionable, then there is a (deterministic) protocol whereby f can be computed privately by two parties.*

PROOF. By induction on $\alpha = |X|$.
(Base Case.) If $X = \{x_1\}$, then party 2 simply announces $f(x_1, y)$. This protocol is trivially private for party 1, and since for all $y, y' \in Y$ such that $f(x_1, y) = f(x_1, y')$ the transcript consists exactly of $f(x_1, y)$, the protocol is private for party 2.
(Inductive Hypothesis.) If $|X| \leq \alpha$, then if f is partitionable then there is a deterministic protocol Π_f to compute f.
(Inductive Step.) Let $|X| = \alpha + 1$. Say that f is partitionable. If f is constant there is a trivial private protocol. Otherwise, f is row-partitionable or column-partitionable.

If f is row-partitionable into f_P and f_Q, then by the induction hypothesis there exist private protocols Π_{f_P} and Π_{f_Q} for f_P and f_Q. Define the protocol Π_f as follows. If $x \in P$, party 1 sends a 0; then the parties execute the protocol for Π_{f_P}. Otherwise, if $x \in Q$, party 1 sends a 1, and the parties execute the protocol for Π_{f_Q}.

Since the protocols are deterministic, let $\Pi(x, y)$ denote the transcript of protocol Π on inputs x and y.

Protocol Π_f is private with respect to party 1. If $f(x, y) = f(x', y)$, then either $x, x' \in P$ or $x, x' \in Q$; otherwise f would not be row-partitionable. If $x, x' \in P$, then

$$\Pi_f(x, y) = 0 \circ \Pi_{f_P}(x, y) = 0 \circ \Pi_{f_P}(x', y) = \Pi_f(x', y).$$

Similarly, if $x, x' \in Q$, then $\Pi_f(x, y) = \Pi_f(x', y)$.

Protocol Π_f is also private with respect to party 2. If $f(x, y) = f(x, y')$, then either $x \in P$, in which case

$$\Pi_f(x, y) = 0 \circ \Pi_{f_P}(x, y) = 0 \circ \Pi_{f_P}(x, y') = \Pi_f(x, y');$$

or $x \in Q$, which likewise gives $\Pi_f(x, y) = \Pi_f(x, y')$.

Now, if f is not row-partitionable then it must be column-partitionable into P and Q. We now prove by induction on $\beta = |Y|$ that f is private. Say $\beta = 1$; then f is trivially private. Now, assume that the hypothesis holds for $|Y| \leq \beta$. Consider $|Y| = \beta + 1$. Then f is partitionable into f_P and f_Q, where $|P|, |Q| \leq \beta$. Hence there exist private protocols Π_{f_P} and Π_{f_Q} for f_P and f_Q. The protocol for f is straightforward: If $y \in P$, party 2 sends a 0; then the parties execute the protocol for Π_{f_P}. Otherwise, if $y \in Q$, party 2 sends a 1, and the parties execute the protocol for Π_{f_Q}. The proof that this Π_f is private follows the same lines as above. □

3.4. Main result. We can summarize the main result of this paper in the following theorem:

THEOREM 6. *A finite function $f(x, y)$ is 1-private if and only if it is partitionable.*

PROOF. Follows from Lemmas 1 and 5. □

4. Multiparty privacy for modular protocols

Many of the methods for performing arbitrary secret computations follow the method of constructing a modular library of protocols that can be selected and combined to construct new protocols. These methods develop basic protocols to evaluate simple gates and from there to evaluate a circuit applied to the inputs (cf. **[GMW87, BGW88, CCD88, Kil88]**). A general library based on threshold (secret sharing) methods allows the output of one protocol to be maintained in a secret format suitable for input to another protocol, so that intermediate computations are not revealed.

In this section we consider what functions can be computed given an arbitrary threshold scheme which allows addition of secrets over the field used for sharing, when we also require that the output of the function be retained as a secretly shared value for potential use in further computations.

Let E be a field and let L_0 be a set of functions mapping E^n to E. Let L be the closure of functions that can be written as a finite composition of functions in L_0. For example, with $g, f_1, \ldots, f_n \in L$, the following function is in L:

$$g(f_1(x_1, \ldots, x_n), \ldots, f_n(x_1, \ldots, x_n)).$$

A t-private *library* $\mathscr{L}$ for L is a set of protocols satisfying:

- Each protocol $\Pi \in \mathscr{L}$ computes a function $f \in L$, t-privately.
- For every $f \in L$ there is a protocol $\Pi \in \mathscr{L}$ that computes it.

The protocols for multiplication and addition given in **[BGW88, CCD88]** satisfy these properties and in fact are complete for any finite function when $t < \lceil \frac{n}{2} \rceil$. In other words, they form a $\lceil \frac{n}{2} \rceil$-private library for the class of all finite functions.

For $t \geq \lceil \frac{n}{2} \rceil$, however, the situation is less optimistic:

THEOREM 7. *If $\mathscr{L}$ is a t-private library of protocols that includes all affine functions over the field E, and if $t \geq \lceil \frac{n}{2} \rceil$, then any function $f(x_1, \ldots, x_n) \in L$ can be written*

$$f(x_1, \ldots, x_n) = f_1(x_1) + f_2(x_2) + \cdots + f_n(x_n).$$

PROOF. Let $f(x_1, \ldots, x_n)$ be t-private for some $t \geq \lceil \frac{n}{2} \rceil$, and let f depend on k variables, $1 \leq k \leq n$. That is, for some $j_1, \ldots, j_k$ and $\hat{f}$,

$$f(x_1, \ldots, x_n) = \hat{f}(x_{j_1}, \ldots, x_{j_k}).$$

Then we show by induction on k that

$$(\exists f_1, \ldots, f_n, \hat{f}) \;\; f(x_1, \ldots, x_n) = \sum_{i=1}^{n} f_i(x_i).$$

The statement is trivially true for $k = 1$. Assume that it holds for k. Let f be t-private and let f depend on $k+1$ variables:

$$(\exists j_1, \ldots, j_{k+1}) \;\; f(x_1, \ldots, x_n) = \hat{f}(x_{j_1}, \ldots, x_{j_{k+1}}).$$

Without loss of generality let $j_1 = 1, j_2 = 2, \ldots, j_{k+1} = k+1$. Fix arbitrary arguments $a_1, \ldots, a_{k+1}$, and let $l = \lceil \frac{k}{2} \rceil$. Suppose there exist $b_1, \ldots, b_{k+1}$ such that

$$\begin{aligned}(1)\;\; &\hat{f}(b_1, \ldots, b_l, b_{l+1}, \ldots, b_{k+1}) + \hat{f}(a_1, \ldots, a_l, a_{l+1}, \ldots, a_{k+1}) \\ &\neq \hat{f}(a_1, \ldots, a_l, b_{l+1}, \ldots, b_{k+1}) + \hat{f}(b_1, \ldots, b_l, a_{l+1}, \ldots, a_{k+1}).\end{aligned}$$

It is not hard to see that there exist r and s, with $r \neq s$, such that $a_r \neq b_r$ and $a_s \neq b_s$.

Define the linear functions p_r and p_s as

$$\begin{aligned} p_r(x_1, \ldots, x_{k+1}) = (x_r - a_r)(b_r - a_r)^{-1}(&\hat{f}(b_1, \ldots, b_l, a_{l+1}, \ldots, a_{k+1}) \\ &-\hat{f}(a_1, \ldots, a_l, a_{l+1}, \ldots, a_{k+1})) \\ &+\hat{f}(a_1, \ldots, a_l, a_{l+1}, \ldots, a_{k+1}), \\ p_s(x_1, \ldots, x_{k+1}) = (x_s - a_s)(b_s - a_s)^{-1}(&\hat{f}(a_1, \ldots, a_l, b_{l+1}, \ldots, b_{k+1}) \\ &-\hat{f}(a_1, \ldots, a_l, a_{l+1}, \ldots, a_{k+1})) \\ &+\hat{f}(a_1, \ldots, a_l, a_{l+1}, \ldots, a_{k+1}). \end{aligned}$$

Using the assumption that the library contains all affine functions, the function G defined as follows is t-private:

$$\begin{aligned} G(x_1, \ldots, x_n) = f(x_1, \ldots, x_n) &- p_r(x_1, \ldots, x_{k+1}) \\ &- p_s(x_1, \ldots, x_{k+1}) + \hat{f}(a_1, \ldots, a_{k+1}). \end{aligned}$$

Clearly,

$$\begin{aligned} G(a_1, \ldots, a_l, a_{l+1}, \ldots, a_{k+1}, 0, 0, \ldots, 0) &= 0, \\ G(a_1, \ldots, a_l, b_{l+1}, \ldots, b_{k+1}, 0, 0, \ldots, 0) &= 0, \\ G(b_1, \ldots, b_l, a_{l+1}, \ldots, a_{k+1}, 0, 0, \ldots, 0) &= 0, \\ G(b_1, \ldots, b_l, b_{l+1}, \ldots, b_{k+1}, 0, 0, \ldots, 0) &\neq 0. \end{aligned}$$

Let Π_G be a t-private protocol for G. We use Π_G to construct a 1-private protocol for two parties to compute AND(x,y), by having party 1 simulate half the parties and party 2 simulate the other half. Party 1 holds an input $x \in \{0, 1\}$, and party 2 holds an input $y \in \{0, 1\}$, though when they simulate Π_G they will "pretend" to hold general arguments instead. Let $m = \lfloor \frac{n-k-1}{2} \rfloor$. Party 1 follows Π_G, simulating the parties holding inputs $x_1, \ldots, x_l; x_{k+2}, \ldots, x_{k+1+m}$. Party 2 follows Π_G, simulating the parties holding inputs $x_{l+1}, \ldots, x_{k+1}; x_{k+m+2}, \ldots, x_n$. Notice that neither party 1 nor party 2 simulates more than t parties.

If party 1 holds input $x = 0$, it selects $x_1 = a_1, \ldots, x_l = a_l$. If party 1 holds input $x = 1$, it selects $x_1 = b_1, \ldots, x_l = b_l$. It sets all other variables to 0. Similarly, if party 2 holds input $y = 0$, it selects $x_{l+1} = a_{l+1}, \ldots, x_{k+1} = a_{k+1}$. If party 2 holds input $y = 1$, it selects $x_{l+1} = b_{l+1}, \ldots, x_{k+1} = b_{k+1}$. It sets all other variables to 0.

Together, party 1 and party 2 simulate Π_G, sending messages to one another when Π_G specifies that a player from the group simulated by party 1 interact with a player from the group simulated by party 2. Both party 1 and party 2 learn the value of G from the simulated protocol. If $G = 0$, each outputs AND(x,y) $= 0$; if $G \neq 0$, each outputs AND(x,y) $= 1$. It is easy to see that their outputs are correct.

Since Π_G is t-private, where $t \geq \lceil \frac{n}{2} \rceil$, this two-party protocol is also 1-private. But Theorem 6 implies that there is no two-party 1-private protocol for AND; hence supposition (1) is false. Thus,

$$\begin{aligned} f(x_1, \ldots, x_n) = f(a_1, \ldots, a_l, x_{l+1}, \ldots, x_{k+1}, 0, \ldots, 0) \\ +f(x_1, \ldots, x_l, a_{l+1}, \ldots, a_{k+1}, 0, \ldots, 0) \\ -f(a_1, \ldots, a_l, a_{l+1}, \ldots, a_{k+1}, 0, \ldots, 0). \end{aligned}$$

Define

$$\begin{aligned} g(x_1, \ldots, x_n) &= f(a_1, \ldots, a_l, x_{l+1}, \ldots, x_{k+1}, 0, \ldots, 0), \\ h(x_1, \ldots, x_n) &= f(x_1, \ldots, x_l, a_{l+1}, \ldots, a_{k+1}, 0, \ldots, 0). \end{aligned}$$

Since f is t-private, so are g and h. But g and h each depend on at most k variables. By the induction hypothesis, there are $g_1, \ldots, g_n$, $h_1, \ldots, h_n$ such that

$$\begin{aligned} g(x_1, \ldots, x_n) &= g_1(x_1) + \cdots + g_n(x_n), \\ h(x_1, \ldots, x_n) &= h_1(x_1) + \cdots + h_n(x_n). \end{aligned}$$

Let $d = f(a_1, \ldots, a_l, a_{l+1}, \ldots, a_{k+1}, 0, \ldots, 0)$. Then we have

$$\begin{aligned} f(x_1, \ldots, x_n) &= g(x_1, \ldots, x_n) + h(x_1, \ldots, x_n) - d \\ &= g_1(x_1) + \cdots + g_n(x_n) + h_1(x_1) + \cdots + h_n(x_n) - d \\ &= f_1(x_1) + \cdots + f_n(x_n), \end{aligned}$$

where we define $f_1(x_1) = g_1(x_1) + h_1(x_1) - d$ and $f_i(x_i) = g_i(x_i) + h_i(x_i)$ for $i \geq 2$. This completes the induction step.

Applying the result for $k = n$, we conclude that for an arbitrary t-private function f there exist $f_1, \ldots, f_n$ such that

$$f(x_1, \ldots, x_n) = f_1(x_1) + \cdots + f_n(x_n),$$

completing the proof of Theorem 7. □

5. Conclusions

This paper presents work in progress and gives solutions to two problems:

- The set of finite functions that can be computed privately in an information-theoretic sense by two parties is exactly the set of partitionable functions.
- Any library of protocols, for $\lceil \frac{n}{2} \rceil$-privately computing functions of n inputs over a field E, that is powerful enough to privately compute linear combinations of inputs, is *only* powerful enough to compute linear combinations of inputs.

We leave open the question of characterizing which general functions can be computed privately by n processors when half of them can be curious.

References

[Bea89] D. Beaver, *Perfect privacy for two-party protocols*, TR-11-89, Harvard University, May, 1989.

[BGW88] M. Ben-Or, S. Goldwasser, and A. Wigderson, *Completeness theorems for non-cryptographic fault-tolerant distributed computation*, Proc. of 20th STOC (1988), ACM, 1–10.

[CCD88] D. Chaum, C. Crépeau, and I. Damgård, *Multiparty unconditionally secure protocols*, Proc. of 20th STOC (1988), ACM, 11–19.

[CK89] B. Chor and E. Kushilevitz, *A zero-one law for Boolean privacy*, Proc. of 21st STOC (1989), ACM, 62–72.

[GHY87] Z. Galil, S. Haber, and M. Yung, *Cryptographic computation: Secure fault-tolerant protocols and the public-key model*, Proc. of 7th CRYPTO (1987), Springer-Verlag, 135–155.

[GMW87] O. Goldreich, S. Micali, and A. Wigderson, *How to play any mental game, or a completeness theorem for protocols with honest majority*, Proc. of 19th STOC (1987), ACM, 218–229.

[Kil88] J. Kilian, *Founding cryptography on oblivious transfer*, Proc. of 20th STOC (1988), ACM, 20–29.

[Kus89] E. Kushilevitz, *Privacy and communication complexity*, Proc. of 30th FOCS (1989), IEEE, 416–421.

[Yao86] A. Yao, *How to generate and exchange secrets*, Proc. of 27th FOCS (1986), IEEE, 162–167.

Aiken Computation Laboratory, Harvard University

E-mail address: beaver@research.att.com

DIMACS Series in Discrete Mathematics
and Theoretical Computer Science
Volume 2, 1991

On the Structure of Secret Key Exchange Protocols

MIHIR BELLARE, LENORE COWEN, AND SHAFI GOLDWASSER

ABSTRACT. A Secret Key Exchange protocol, which enables two parties to establish a common and secret key over public channels, is a fundamental primitive for private communication. We show here that any Secret Key Exchange protocol has strong structural properties. Our results imply that one-way functions are necessary for Secret Key Exchange. As a corollary we obtain that one-way functions are also necessary for oblivious transfer.

Our results also imply that the existence of a Secret Key Exchange protocol implies the existence of strong bit commitment schemes, where the prover has probability 0 of cheating.

1. Introduction

Modern cryptography is fundamentally concerned with the problem of secure private communication. Suppose two parties, Alice and Bob, wish to communicate privately over a public channel (for instance, a telephone line with an eavesdropper). If Alice and Bob are able to meet, privately, beforehand, and agree on some common secret key, then it becomes easy for them to achieve such private communication. But Alice and Bob might not be able to meet first in private and agree on a key. In this case, we ask under what assumptions they can still agree on a common secret key, where their conversation is conducted entirely in public.

A Secret Key Exchange is a protocol where Alice and Bob, having no secret information in common to start, are able to agree on a common secret key, conversing over a public channel. The notion of a Secret Key Exchange protocol was first introduced in the seminal paper of Diffie and Hellman [DH]. [DH] presented a concrete implementation of a Secret Key Exchange protocol, dependent on a specific assumption (a variant on the discrete log), specially tailored to yield Secret Key Exchange. Secret Key Exchange is of

Supported in part by NSF grant CCR-87-19689 and DARPA Contract N00014-89-J-1988.
Supported in part by NSF grant CCR-86-57527 and DARPA Contract N00014-89-J-1988.
Supported in part by NSF grant CCR-86-57527 and DARPA Contract N00014-89-J-1988.

course trivial if trapdoor permutations exist. However, there is no known implementation based on a weaker general assumption.

Recently Impagliazzo and Rudich [**IR**] showed that any "natural" proof that Secret Key Exchange was possible with one way permutations would imply a proof that $P \neq NP$. We can look at the Impagliazzo and Rudich result as a negative one. It is hard to prove that the existence of a one-way permutation is sufficient to implement a Secret Key Exchange protocol.

In this paper we look at the other side of the coin. We ask, what can one say about the conditions necessary for Secret Key Exchange, and what is its power to yield other important primitives? We show that any Secret Key Exchange protocol has strong structural properties. We define the *Matrix of Conversations* for any Secret Key Exchange protocol, and the results we obtain follow directly from our anaylsis of monochromatic blocks of this matrix. We show the following.

(1) The existence of a Secret Key Exchange protocol implies the existence of a one-way function. As a corollary, we immediately get that oblivious transfer implies one-way functions. Coupled with results of [**ILL**] and [**GGM**], our results also imply that Secret Key Exchange is by itself enough to obtain pseudorandom bit generation, and private key encryption secure against chosen ciphertext attack. We obtain these theorems in both the uniform and nonuniform models, under two slightly different definitions of Secret Key Exchange. [**IL**] can independently obtain our result that Secret Key Exchange implies the existence of a one-way function in the nonuniform model (Theorem 4.4 in our paper), by viewing Secret Key Exchange as an "Identification Scheme."

(2) The existence of a Secret Key Exchange protocol is enough to obtain bit commitment, in a setting where the player who commits to the bit need not be computationally bounded and will have probability 0 of cheating. This is of separate interest, because we do not know that bit commitment follows from a one-way function with uniform security assumptions. This implies that we need only assume the existence of a Secret Key Exchange protocol to create envelopes, and hence carry out zero knowledge proofs.

2. Definitions

A Secret Key Exchange protocol involves two probabilistic polynomial-time interactive Turing machines, Alice and Bob. Each machine has its own (private) worktape and a private random tape (this last to model the fact that Alice and Bob can flip coins in private). In addition there is a common, public, tape on which both Alice and Bob can read and write; Eve, a probabilistic polynomial-time Turing machine eavesdropping on their conversation, can read this tape as well.

If our probabilistic polynomial-time Turing machines are A and B, we let R_A and R_B denote their respective random tapes. For notational convenience, we assume that the protocol has the following form: in round i, A "speaks" first, by writing some string α_i on the shared conversation tape, and then B_i speaks. (Here, α_i is some function of R_A and the earlier portion of the conversation; A performs any necessary computation before she writes, and similarly for B.) Then if we let $\mathrm{conv}(R_A, R_B)$ denote the conversation between A and B when their random tapes are R_A and R_B, we have that $\mathrm{conv}(R_A, R_B) = (\alpha_1, \beta_1, \ldots, \alpha_t, \beta_t)$ where

$$A(R_A, \alpha_1\beta_1 \cdots \alpha_{i-1}\beta_{i-1}) = \alpha_i,$$
$$B(R_B, \alpha_1\beta_1 \cdots \alpha_{i-1}\beta_{i-1}\alpha_i) = \beta_i.$$

There is a security parameter k, and for convenience we assume that $|R_A| = |R_B| = k$.

Each of A and B has a *key-obtaining algorithm* (respectively denoted K_A and K_B). These are polynomial-time functions that each party can compute on the conversation and his own coin tosses to yield his estimate of the key. For any instance (i.e., fixed choice of R_A, R_B) of the protocol we say that A and B have *agreed* on a key if

$$K_A(R_A, \mathrm{conv}(R_A, R_B)) = K_B(R_B, \mathrm{conv}(R_A, R_B)) \;;$$

this common value is the key they have agreed on. The probability of agreement is thus $P_{\mathrm{agree}} =$

$$\boldsymbol{P}\,(K_A(R_A, C) = K_B(R_B, C) : R_A, R_B \leftarrow \{0, 1\}^k ; C \leftarrow \mathrm{conv}(R_A, R_B)).$$

(For those unfamiliar with this notation, please see the appendix.) We are now ready to define Secret Key Exchange.

DEFINITION 2.1. A protocol constitutes a *Secret Key Exchange* (SKE) if there is an $\alpha > 0$ such that we have

- **Agreement:** $P_{\mathrm{agree}} \geq \alpha$, and on each instance, A and B *know* whether or not they agreed.
- **Secrecy:** For all probabilistic polynomial-time algorithms E, for all $d > 0$, and all sufficiently large k,

$$\boldsymbol{P}(E(C) = K_A(R_A, C) = K_B(R_B, C) : R_A, R_B \leftarrow \{0, 1\}^k ; \; C \leftarrow \mathrm{conv}(R_A, R_B)) \leq k^{-d}.$$

A few words of explanation and justification are needed for our requirement that A and B know whether or not they have agreed at the end of the SKE protocol. This requirement is left out of the definition of SKE given in **[IR]**, which we will call Weak Secret Key Exchange.

DEFINITION 2.2. A protocol constitutes a *Weak Secret Key Exchange* (Weak SKE) if there is an $\alpha > 0$ such that we have

- **Agreement:** $P_{\text{agree}} \geq \alpha$.
- **Secrecy:** For all probabilistic polynomial-time algorithms E, for all $d > 0$, and all sufficiently large k,

$$\boldsymbol{P}(E(C) = K_A(R_A, C) = K_B(R_B, C) : R_A, R_B \leftarrow \{0, 1\}^k; \\ C \leftarrow \text{conv}(R_A, R_B)) \leq k^{-d}.$$

Weak SKE, though, is quickly seen to be too weak to capture any real notion of Secret Key Exchange. (We remark that since **[IR]** prove that it is hard to prove the existence of even a Weak SKE protocol from one-way permutations, using this weaker definition only strengthens their results.) To see the problems with this definition, look at what happens in a Weak SKE protocol when A and B disagree. They may not even know that they have done so and, attempting to communicate based on different keys, would be unable to understand each other. One way to avoid this is through redundancy: perform many key exchanges and then use all keys to send duplicate copies of messages simultaneously. But although the communication will now succeed with high probability because there will probably be a common key amongst the many keys used, the eavesdropper might be able to understand the messages based on keys other than the one agreed on. A related problem is that one usually wants, from the key, to extract a single hard bit since the eavesdropper might, for example, know a few bits of the key; but in this case even the redundancy approach will fail to supply a common key.

One might imagine from this discussion that a much stronger notion of key exchange is required to attain anything reasonable. However, the condition we added to Weak SKE, that A and B know whether or not they agree, will suffice, since A and B only take action (communication, extracting a hard bit) when they do agree. Since this is after all what "agreement" means, this is only the natural definition.

Nevertheless, we show that even the assumption that Weak SKE protocols exist implies that one-way functions exist, but, for this weak case, we need nonuniform security assumptions. In fact, we present most of the structural results in Section 3 in terms of Weak SKE, since the existence of a Weak SKE protocol is already enough to guarantee the strong structural properties that we are interested in.

Finally, in our definition of (strong) SKE the following theorem shows that just assuming that A and B know when they agree means that an even stronger property holds. Namely, we may assume the ideal case, that A and B *always* agree.

THEOREM 2.1. *Suppose we have an SKE protocol. Then there is another SKE protocol in which A and B agree with probability* 1.

PROOF. A and B can execute the original SKE

$$\frac{k}{\lg(1/(1-\alpha))}$$

times. If any of these runs yields agreement, they take as their key the one from the first agreeing run. If all runs yield disagreement, they agree on some default value (say 0^k) as their key. Eve can certainly find the key in the latter case, but the probability that this case occurs is $\leq 2^{-k}$. On the other hand, the agreement probability is 1. □

These definitions are in the uniform setting; in the corresponding nonuniform setting, Alice, Bob, and Eve would all be polynomial-size circuits.

3. Structure of SKE

We show here that certain structural properties are inherent in a Secret Key Exchange protocol.

Fix any Weak SKE protocol. Since any SKE protocol is also automatically a Weak SKE protocol, our lemmas in this section apply to both SKE and Weak SKE protocols alike.

3.1. Terminology. The *matrix of conversations* of the SKE is the 2^k by 2^k matrix whose row i column j entry is $\text{conv}(i, j)$. (Here $0 \leq i, j < 2^k$ are identified with the corresponding binary strings of length k.) This represents a convenient way to summarize the information as to the conversations taking place.

We say that $R_A R_B$ is an *agreement point* if $K_A(R_A, \text{conv}(R_A, R_B)) = K_B(R_B, \text{conv}(R_A, R_B))$; otherwise it is a *disagreement point.* It is an agreement/disagreement point of C if $\text{conv}(R_A, R_B) = C$. If $R_A R_B$ is an agreement point we denote the agreed-on key by $K(R_A, R_B)$.

3.2. Basic "rectangle" lemmas. The following "rectangle" property is a well-known fact about protocols.

LEMMA 3.1. *Suppose* $R_A^1, R_A^2, R_B^1, R_B^2$ *are such that* $\text{conv}(R_A^1, R_B^1) = \text{conv}(R_A^2, R_B^2)$. *Then in fact* $\text{conv}(R_A^1, R_B^1) = \text{conv}(R_A^1, R_B^2) = \text{conv}(R_A^2, R_B^2) = \text{conv}(R_A^2, R_B^1)$.

PROOF. Suppose $\text{conv}(R_A^1, R_B^1) = \text{conv}(R_A^2, R_B^2) = (\alpha_1, \beta_1, \dots, \alpha_t, \beta_t)$. It follows that

$$\begin{aligned}
A(R_A^1, \varepsilon) &= A(R_A^2, \varepsilon) = \alpha_1, \\
B(R_B^1, \alpha_1) &= B(R_B^2, \alpha_1) = \beta_1, \\
A(R_A^1, \alpha_1\beta_1) &= A(R_A^2, \alpha_1\beta_1) = \alpha_2, \\
B(R_B^1, \alpha_1\beta_1\alpha_2) &= B(R_B^2, \alpha_1\beta_1\alpha_2) = \beta_2, \\
&\vdots \\
A(R_A^1, \alpha_1\beta_1\cdots\alpha_{t-1}\beta_{t-1}) &= A(R_A^2, \alpha_1\beta_1\cdots\alpha_{t-1}\beta_{t-1}) = \alpha_t, \\
B(R_B^1, \alpha_1\beta_1\cdots\alpha_{i-1}\beta_{t-1}\alpha_t) &= B(R_B^2, \alpha_1\beta_1\cdots\alpha_{i-1}\beta_{t-1}\alpha_t) = \beta_t.
\end{aligned}$$

Now consider the point $R_A^1R_B^2$. The first message sent by A at this point is $A(R_A^1, \varepsilon)$, which by the above is α_1. The message sent by B in response is $B(R_B^2, \alpha_1)$, which by the above is β_1. A now sends $A(R_A^1, \alpha_1\beta_1)$, which by the above is α_2. Continuing in this manner, it is easy to see that the conversation at this point is $(\alpha_1, \beta_1, \dots, \alpha_t, \beta_t)$. The same argument applies to the point $R_A^2R_B^1$. □

This enables us to show that the set of entries in the matrix of conversations that are equal to a fixed conversation C form a submatrix.

LEMMA 3.2. *Let C be a conversation, and let*

$$\mathcal{R}(C) = \{(R_A, R_B) : \text{conv}(R_A, R_B) = C\}.$$

Then there exist sets $\mathcal{R}_A(C), \mathcal{R}_B(C) \subseteq \{0, 1\}^k$ such that $\mathcal{R}(C) = \mathcal{R}_A(C) \times \mathcal{R}_B(C)$.

PROOF. Let

$$\begin{aligned}
\mathcal{R}_A(C) &= \{R_A : \text{ there exists } R_B \text{ such that conv}(R_A, R_B) = C\}, \\
\mathcal{R}_B(C) &= \{R_B : \text{ there exists } R_A \text{ such that conv}(R_A, R_B) = C\}.
\end{aligned}$$

Clearly $\mathcal{R}(C) \subseteq \mathcal{R}_A(C) \times \mathcal{R}_B(C)$. So it suffices to show that $\mathcal{R}_A(C) \times \mathcal{R}_B(C) \subseteq \mathcal{R}(C)$. So suppose $R_A^1 \in \mathcal{R}_A(C)$ and $R_B^2 \in \mathcal{R}_B(C)$. Thus there exists R_B^1 such that $\text{conv}(R_A^1, R_B^1) = C$ and R_A^2 such that $\text{conv}(R_A^2, R_B^2) = C$. Hence by Lemma 3.1 we get $\text{conv}(R_A^1, R_B^2) = C$. Thus $(R_A^1, R_B^2) \in \mathcal{R}(C)$. □

We now proceed to examine in more detail this submatrix of points with the same conversation.

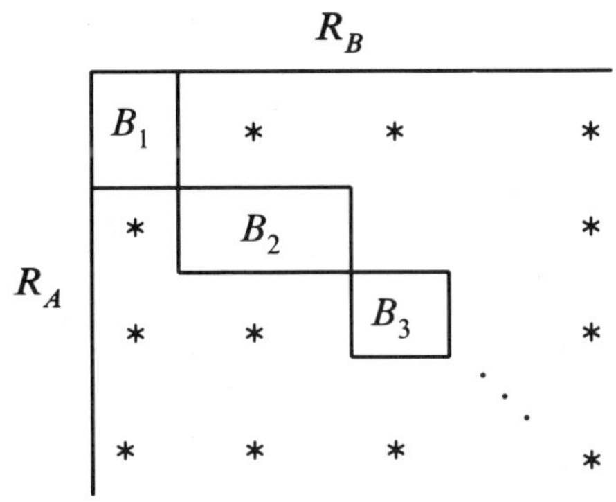

FIGURE 1. $M(C)$ in normal form: each block B_i is the set of all points at which agreement is on a particular key κ_i.

3.3. Agreement matrix of a conversation. The *agreement matrix* of the conversation C, denoted by $M(C)$, is an $m \times n$ matrix where $m = |\mathcal{R}_A(C)|$ and $n = |\mathcal{R}_B(C)|$. The rows represent elements of $\mathcal{R}_A(C)$, whereas the columns represent elements of $\mathcal{R}_B(C)$. The row R_A column R_B entry of $M(C)$ is $K(R_A, R_B)$ in the case that $K_A(R_A, C) = K_B(R_B, C)$, and is the special symbol $*$ otherwise; that is, this entry is the agreed-on key in the case that agreement is reached, and is $*$ in the case of disagreement. The agreement matrix of C captures all the information about what happens when the conversation is C.

We examine the structure of $M(C)$ in the case that C has many agreement points. We begin with a lemma about points of $M(C)$ where key agreement is reached, but the agreement is on *different* keys. We can conclude that this implies the existence of disagreement points for this conversation.

LEMMA 3.3. *Suppose* $R_A^1, R_A^2, R_B^1, R_B^2$ *are such that*

- $\mathrm{conv}(R_A^1, R_B^1) = \mathrm{conv}(R_A^2, R_B^2) = C$,
- $K_A(R_A^1, C) = K_B(R_B^1, C) = \kappa_1$,
- $K_A(R_A^2, C) = K_B(R_B^2, C) = \kappa_2$,
- $\kappa_1 \neq \kappa_2$.

Then $R_A^1 R_B^2$ *and* $R_A^2 R_B^1$ *are disagreement points of* C.

PROOF. Suppose A has R_A^1 and B has R_B^2. By Lemma 3.1 we have $C = \mathrm{conv}(R_A^1, R_B^2)$. So A will get $\kappa_1 = K_A(R_A^1, C)$ and B will get $\kappa_2 = K_B(R_B^2, C)$. Similarly, if A has R_A^2 and B has R_B^1 then A will get κ_2 and B will get κ_1. The lemma follows from the fact that $\kappa_1 \neq \kappa_2$. □

This enables us to show that if C has no disagreement points then the structure of this matrix is exceedingly simple: all its entries are the same.

LEMMA 3.4. *Suppose C has no disagreement points. Then there exists a single key κ such that the key agreed on when the conversation is C is always κ.*

PROOF. If there were R_A^1, R_B^1, R_A^2, R_B^2 such that

$$K_A(R_A^1, C) = K_B(R_B^1, C) \neq K_B(R_B^2, C) = K_A(R_A^2, C) \ ,$$

then (by Lemma 3.3) C would have disagreement points: namely $R_A^1 R_B^2$ and $R_A^2 R_B^1$. □
Another useful fact to note is

LEMMA 3.5. *Let κ be a key. The set of entries of $M(C)$ equal to κ forms a submatrix of $M(C)$.*

PROOF. Clear. □
Even if there are some disagreement points, we can show that a fair number of agreement points still do have the same key.

LEMMA 3.6. *Suppose that the number of agreement points in $M(C)$ is $\geq mn\alpha/2$. Then there exists a single key κ such that $\geq mn\alpha^2/16$ entries of $M(C)$ are equal to κ.*

PROOF. We first put $M(C)$ into a normal form. We pick a key κ_1 that occurs in the matrix, and, by permuting rows and columns, we move the submatrix (Lemma 3.5) of entries equal to this key to the upper-left corner to get a block we call B_1. We are then assured that points directly to the right of this block as well as points directly below this block are all $*$. We then take another key κ_2 and move it as far up and left as possible in the remaining matrix (the one with the rows and columns of B_1 removed). Continuing in this way we obtain the structure of Figure 1. □

We let x_i and y_i denote the length and breadth, respectively, of block B_i:

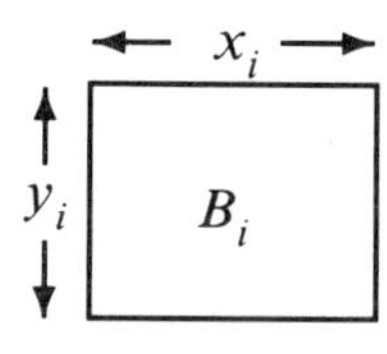

We wish to show that there is an i with $x_i y_i \geq mn\alpha^2/16$. We visualize this geometrically: we have a set of rectangles in the plane, laid out in the particular pattern of Figure 1, and we know that they cover a total area of $mn\alpha/2$. We have to show that there is a single rectangle of large enough area.

We claim that we can assume, without loss of generality, that $m = n$. For if this is not the case then we can apply a linear transformation of the plane (say $(x, y) \mapsto (\sqrt{mn}x/n, \sqrt{mn}y/m)$) via which the $m \times n$ rectangle is turned into a $\sqrt{mn} \times \sqrt{mn}$ square, and then use the fact that linear transformations preserve ratios of areas.

Now let $N = m = n$. Assume towards a contradiction that $x_i y_i < N^2\alpha^2/16$ for all i. Let $M_i = \max(x_i, y_i)$ and $m_i = \min(x_i, y_i)$. Then $m_i < \sqrt{N^2\alpha^2/16}$ for all i. So

$$\begin{aligned}\sum_i x_i y_i &= \sum_i M_i m_i \\ &< \sqrt{\frac{N^2\alpha^2}{16}} \sum_i M_i \\ &\le \sqrt{\frac{N^2\alpha^2}{16}}(2N) \\ &= \frac{N^2\alpha}{2},\end{aligned}$$

contradicting the fact that by assumption

$$\sum_i x_i y_i \ge \frac{N^2\alpha}{2}.$$

3.4. Distribution of "good" conversations. Since, by definition of a (Weak) SKE protocol, agreement occurs with $\ge \alpha$ probability over all possible runs of the protocol, there must be a set of conversations on which, when A and B have one of these conversations, then it is fairly likely they will reach agreement. We call these conversations "good."

DEFINITION 3.1. A conversation C is *good* if $M(C)$ has $\ge mn\alpha/2$ agreement points.

LEMMA 3.7. *The probability of a good conversation is* $\ge \alpha/2$.

PROOF. Apply the pigeonhole principle. □

4. Applications

4.1. One-way functions.

DEFINITION 4.1. A polynomial-time computable function $f = \{f_k\}$ (where $f_k : \{0, 1\}^k \to \{0, 1\}^k$) is *one way* if for all probabilistic polynomial-time algorithms I, for all $c > 0$, and sufficiently large k,

$$\boldsymbol{P}(f(y) = f(x) : x \leftarrow \{0, 1\}^k ; y \leftarrow I(f(x))) < k^{-c}.$$

This is the uniform definition; for the nonuniform one, change everything to polysized circuits.

The concept of an informationally one-way function was introduced in [ILL]. We give only an informal definition here.

DEFINITION 4.2. A polynomial-time computable function $f = \{f_k\}$ is informationally one way if there is no probabilistic polynomial-time algorithm that (with probability of the form $1 - k^{-e}$ for some $e > 0$) returns on input $y \in \{0, 1\}^k$ a random element of $f^{-1}(y)$.

In the nonuniform setting **[ILL]** show that these are not weaker than one-way functions.

THEOREM 4.1 **[ILL]** (nonuniform). *The existence of informationally one-way functions implies the existence of one-way functions.*

We will stick to the convention introduced above of saying "nonuniform" before the theorem statement when the theorem makes use of nonuniformity. It should be understood that if nothing is said then the result holds for both the uniform and the nonuniform models.

We now have

THEOREM 4.2. *SKE implies the existence of a one-way function.*

PROOF. By Theorem 2.1 we may assume that we have an SKE protocol in which A and B always agree. We now show that the function $f(R_A R_B) = \text{conv}(R_A, R_B)$ is one way. Assume not. We thus have an inverting algorithm I for f. We use this to construct an eavesdropper E who breaks the secrecy of the SKE. E works exactly as expected: on input a random conversation C she evaluates $I(C) = R_A R_B$ and then outputs $K(R_A, R_B)$ as her estimate of the key. Lemma 3.4 (which applies since the agreement probability is 1) now provides the crucial step: it says that this is indeed the key that A and B agreed on. The eavesdropper is thus succeeding with exactly the same probability that I is inverting f, contradicting the secrecy of the SKE. □

If we allow nonuniformity we can prove that even Weak SKE implies the existence of one-way functions. First, via Lemma 3.6, we get informationally one-way functions:

THEOREM 4.3. *Weak SKE implies the existence of an informationally one-way function.*

PROOF. The idea of the proof is to show that the function $f(R_A R_B) = \text{conv}(R_A, R_B)$ is informationally one way. Suppose not. Let I be an algorithm that on input C returns a random element of $f^{-1}(C)$ with probability $\geq 1 - k^{-e}$. This algorithm is thus sampling the agreement matrix $M(C)$. Since good conversations have a fairly large probability (Lemma 3.7) we hit them fairly often. Whenever we do, Lemma 3.6 says that we break the key exchange with probability $\geq \alpha^2/16$. Putting all this together, we get a contradiction to the secrecy of the key exchange. □

It now follows from Theorem 4.1 **[ILL]** that

THEOREM 4.4 (NONUNIFORM). *Weak SKE implies the existence of a one-way function.*

4.2. Bit commitment. We show that SKE implies strong committer bit commitment (bit commitment where the committer cannot cheat on the decommittals even if he is not computationally bounded).

A *bit commitment* protocol involves two parties: D (the committer) and R (the receiver). The protocol has two stages:

- **Stage 1 (Commitment):** D has a bit b that she wishes to commit. She and the receiver exchange messages. At the end of the conversation R has some information that represents the bit b.
- **Stage 2 (Decommitment):** D gives R some additional information that reveals b to R.

The protocol must obey the following, for all $c > 0$ and large enough security parameter k:

- After the commitment stage, R cannot guess b with probability greater than $\frac{1}{2} + k^{-c}$.
- In the decommitment stage, D can only reveal one value. If she tries to reveal a different value she is caught with probability at least $1 - k^{-c}$.

We say that the protocol is a *strong committer* bit commitment if the property that the committer can reveal only one value holds regardless of the computational power of the committer.

In the bit commitment protocol we will now construct, the committer, D, will simulate a key exchange between A and B. In some sense, R, the receiver, will be in the position of the eavesdropper. First, however, we need the following generalization of the theorem of Goldreich and Levin [GL]:

THEOREM 4.5. *Suppose $f = \{f_k\}$, $g = \{g_k\}$ are polynomial-time computable functions, where $f_k, g_k : \{0,1\}^k \to \{0,1\}^k$. Suppose that for all PPT algorithms I, all $c > 0$, and sufficiently large k,*

$$\boldsymbol{P}(y = g(x) : x \leftarrow \{0,1\}^k \; ; \; y \leftarrow I(f(x))) < k^{-c}.$$

Then for all PPT algorithms I, all $c > 0$, and sufficiently large k,

$$\boldsymbol{P}(b = \mathscr{B}(g(x), r) : x, r \leftarrow \{0,1\}^k \; ; \; b \leftarrow I(f(x), r)) < \frac{1}{2} + k^{-c},$$

where $\mathscr{B}(g(x), r)$ is the inner product mod 2 of $g(x)$ and r.

PROOF. The proof of [GL] extends. □

THEOREM 4.6. *SKE implies (strong committer) bit commitment.*

PROOF. By Theorem 2.1 we may assume that the agreement probability of the SKE protocol is 1. If the committer D wishes to commit to bit b she picks $x = R_A R_B$ at random and computes

$$f(x) = \mathrm{conv}(R_A, R_B) = C,$$
$$g(x) = K(R_A, R_B) = \kappa.$$

She then picks r at random and sends $(\mathscr{B}(\kappa, r) \oplus b, C, r)$ to the receiver R. To decommit she reveals x. □

The fact that this is an SKE protocol implies that $g(x)$ is hard to compute in probabilistic polynomial time given $f(x)$. Theorem 4.5 thus implies that R has no advantage in predicting b as long as he is PPT.

On the other hand, κ is uniquely determined given C (Lemma 3.4) so the probability that D can cheat and later reveal $\bar{b}$ is 0.

Naor [N] has shown that pseudorandom generators can be used for bit commitment, and hence if we have nonuniform security assumptions one-way functions suffice [ILL]. The above is stronger in that

- it does not require nonuniformity,
- the probability of cheating on the part of the committer is zero rather than just exponentially small as in Naor's scheme,
- the scheme is *noninteractive*; that is, the receiver does not have to talk in the commitment stage.

4.3. Other implications. Clearly, anything that yields Secret Key Exchange must imply the existence of one-way functions. Of particular interest is oblivious transfer:

COROLLARY 4.1. *Oblivious transfer implies the existence of a one-way function.*

PROOF. Oblivious transfer implies SKE. (Note: Earlier reductions may not have had the property that the parties know whether or not they have agreed, but we can get that.) □

On the other hand, the fact that the Secret Key Exchange yields one-way functions and bit commitment implies that various much more powerful cryptographic primitives are possible given the existence of Secret Key Exchange alone. Combining with results of [ILL] and [GGM] we get

COROLLARY 4.2 (NONUNIFORM). *(Weak) SKE implies pseudorandom bit generators and private key encryption are secure against chosen message attack. Bit commitment suffices for zero knowledge proofs* [GMW] *so*

COROLLARY 4.3. *SKE implies the ability to give zero knowledge proofs for any language in NP.*

4.4. Agreement in SKE. We can show a 0-1 law for agreement in any SKE protocol:

THEOREM 4.7. *For any conversation in an SKE protocol, the probability of agreement on this conversation is either* 0 *or* 1.

PROOF. If there is one agreement point then the fact that A and B know whether or not they agree means that the row and column of this point also consist of agreement points. Applying the argument to these points, we see that the whole matrix consists of agreement points. □

4.5. Perfect Secret Key Exchange. Secret Key Exchange can also be defined in the "information theoretic" sense. That is, we allow A, B, and E to be infinitely powerful. We call this Perfect SKE. Recently Yung **[Y]** showed that perfect oblivious transfer is impossible. The same holds for Secret Key Exchange, and this has been known; one proof is due to Kilian **[K]**. We note that we can prove the impossibility of Perfect SKE directly from our definition of the Matrix of Conversations.

THEOREM 4.8. *Perfect (Weak) SKE is impossible.*

PROOF. E knows the agreement matrix of the conversation. For SKE this means, by Lemma 3.4, that she gets the key with the same probability that A and B agree on it. For Weak SKE we use Lemma 3.6; E gets the key with probability $\alpha^2/16$. □

Acknowledgments

The first author thanks John Rompel and Su-Ming Wu for helpful discussions.

Appendix. Notation and conventions

We take these notations and conventions for probabilistic algorithms from **[GMR]**.

We emphasize the number of inputs received by an algorithm as follows. If algorithm A receives only one input we write "$A(\cdot)$"; if it receives two we write "$A(\cdot, \cdot)$", and so on.

If A is a probabilistic algorithm, then, for any input i, the notation $A(i)$ refers to the probability space that to the string σ assigns the probability that A, on input i, outputs σ. We point out the special case in which A takes no inputs; in this case A refers to the algorithm itself, whereas the notation $A(\,)$ refers to the probability space obtained by running A on no input.

If S is a probability space we denote by $\boldsymbol{P}_S(e)$ the probability that S associates with element e. We denote by $[S]$ the set of elements to which S assigns positive probability.

If $f(\cdot)$ and $g(\cdot, \cdots)$ are probabilistic algorithms, then $f(g(\cdot, \cdots))$ is the probabilistic algorithm obtained by composing f and g (i.e., running

f on g's output). For any inputs $x, y, \ldots$ the associated probability space is denoted $f(g(x, y, \cdots))$.

If S is a probability space, then $x \leftarrow S$ denotes the algorithm that assigns to x an element randomly selected according to S. (That is, x is assigned the value e with probability $\boldsymbol{P}_S(e)$.) If S is a finite set, $x \leftarrow S$ denotes the operation of selecting an element of S uniformly at random. (In the case that the set is of only one element e we write $x \leftarrow e$ rather than $x \leftarrow \{e\}$.)

For probability spaces $S, T, \ldots$, the notation

$$\boldsymbol{P}(p(x, y, \ldots) : x \leftarrow S; y \leftarrow T; \ldots)$$

denotes the probability that the predicate $p(x, y, \ldots)$ is true after the (ordered) execution of the algorithms $x \leftarrow S$, $y \leftarrow T$, etc. The notation

$$\{ f(x, y, \ldots) : x \leftarrow S; y \leftarrow T; \ldots \}$$

denotes the probability space that to the string σ assigns the probability

$$\boldsymbol{P}(\sigma = f(x, y, \ldots) : x \leftarrow S; y \leftarrow T; \ldots),$$

f being some function.

We let PPT denote the set of probabilistic (expected) polynomial-time algorithms.

References

[DH] W. Diffie and E. Hellman, *New directions in cryptography*, IEEE Trans. Inform. Theory, Vol. 22, No. 5 (November 1976), 644–654.

[GGM] O. Goldreich, S. Goldwasser, and S. Micali, *How to construct random functions*, J. Assoc. Comput. Mach., Vol. 33, No. 4 (October 1986), 792–807.

[GL] O. Goldreich and L. Levin, *A hardcore predicate for any one-way function*, Proc. of 21st STOC (1989), ACM, 25–32.

[GMR] S. Goldwasser, S. Micali, and R. Rivest, *A digital signature scheme secure against adaptive chosen-message attacks*, SIAM J. Comput., Vol. 17, No. 2 (April 1988), 281–308.

[GMW] O. Goldreich, S. Micali, and A. Wigderson, *Proofs that yield nothing but their validity and a methodology of cryptographic protocol design*, Proc. of 27th FOCS (1986), IEEE, 174–187.

[IL] R. Impagliazzo and M. Luby, *One-way functions are essential for complexity based cryptography*, Proc. of 30th FOCS (1989), IEEE, 230–235.

[ILL] R. Impagliazzo, L. Levin, and M. Luby, *Pseudorandom generation from one-way functions*, Proc. of 21st STOC (1989), ACM, 12–24.

[IR] R. Impagliazzo and S. Rudich, *Limits on the provable consequences of one-way permutations*, Proc. of 21st STOC (1989), ACM, 44–61.

[K] J. Kilian, private communication.

[N] M. Naor, *Bit commitment using pseudo randomness*, Lecture Notes in Computer Science **435**, Advances in Cryptology—Crypto '89 Proceedings, Springer-Verlag, 128–136.

[Y] M. Yung, *On the impossibility of oblivious transfer*, these proceedings.

Massachusetts Institute of Technology, Laboratory for Computer Science, 545 Technology Square, Cambridge, Massachusetts 02139

E-mail address: bellare@theory.lcs.mit.edu

E-mail address: lenore@theory.lcs.mit.edu

E-mail address: shafi@theory.lcs.mit.edu

DIMACS Series in Discrete Mathematics
and Theoretical Computer Science
Volume 2, 1991

Privacy-Enhanced Electronic Mail*

MATT BISHOP

ABSTRACT. The security of electronic mail sent through the Internet may be described in exactly three words: there is none. A proposal designed to provide security enhancements has recently been released. The mechanisms provide authentication, integrity checking, and privacy. This paper describes the proposal, as well as an associated certificate-based key management scheme.

1. Introduction

Probably the best-known use of computer networks is for the transmission of electronic mail. The software used to transmit these messages may be represented as a *Message Handling System* composed of a number of connected *Message Transport Agents* and corresponding *User Agents* (see, for example, [**1**], section 2.2.1). A *sender* or an *originator* creates an electronic message using the user agent, which—on behalf of the user—submits that message to a message transport agent. This agent passes the message along to message transport agents on other hosts until it reaches the message transport agent at the destination host. This agent passes the message on to a user agent, which saves the message until the recipient requests it. The *recipient* may then invoke the user agent to read the message, and perform other functions such as save it or reply to it.

Most message transport agents expect a message to have a specific format which varies from network to network. When networks connect, either the format must be translated or it must be known to agents on both networks. For example, the largest set of connected networks (called the Internet) re-

1980 *Mathematics Subject Classification* (1985 *Revision*). Primary 68M10; Secondary 68N99.

* This paper describes the state of the privacy-enhanced electronic mail proposals as of October, 1989.

† UNIX is a trademark of Bell Laboratories.

The author's participation in this work was supported by grant NCC2-387 from the National Aeronautics and Space Administration to the Research Institute for Advanced Computer Science, by grants NAG29-480 and NAG2-628 from the National Aeronautics and Space Administration to Dartmouth College, and by a Burke Award from Dartmouth College.

quires messages to be in a format described in RFC-822 [2], which consists of a set of *header fields* followed by a blank line, and then the body of the message. The information in the header lines is used to forward the message from one message transfer agent to another using the Simple Mail Transfer Protocol described in RFC-821 [3]. Another very large network is that of UNIX-based† systems, which often use an alternate transfer protocol called UUCP [4] when transmitting mail messages by telephone. A major problem with these, and most other, protocols for transferring electronic mail is that those protocols guarantee little if any security and privacy, and especially when the mail must cross from one network to another. Mail messages can be forged, altered, or any party impersonated undetectably. This paper describes a protocol to remedy this.

The existence of these numerous message transport agents and protocols imposes a number of constraints upon any protocol designed to enhance the security and privacy of electronic mail. First, existing mail systems and protocols must not be redesigned. Otherwise many sites would simply refuse to integrate the changes into their message transport system, on the theory that what exists now at least functions, whereas adding the enhancements might break it. Better not to improve something and be sure it works (even minimally) than to try to enhance it and risk breaking it.

Given this, the enhancements must *not* reside at the transport level, but instead must be at the user agent level. This means that whatever is proposed will be invisible to the message transport agent, and therefore the mail systems will be able to send both privacy-enhanced messages and regular messages. In short, the security enhancements will be available separately; one need not use them to send electronic mail from a host on which they are available.

The set of services provided cannot rely on trusted software over which the user has no control; he or she must have some means of verifying that information received is correct. This means that the enhancements may assume the local software will not compromise the message † but cannot make any such assumption about the message transport agents. This again suggests putting the enhancements *above* the transport level at the end systems. Note too that this suggests the use of cryptography to protect the messages [5], since any controls built into the message transport agents can be subverted.

Finally, the mechanism must be flexible enough to work in a number of environments; for this reason, the key management scheme should be separate from the message encoding scheme. This way, users who had an environment where they could trust a central server to manage session keys could do so, whereas users in an environment without such a server could use a certificate-based key distribution mechanism.

---

† Strictly speaking, this is a poor assumption; however, it separates the issues of the security of a computer and attendant software from the security enhancements necessary to protect and authenticate a message in transit. Since the security of end hosts is an extremely complex issue, it is better left unaddressed in this discussion.

These considerations suggest that protection of privacy, sender authenticity, and message integrity are all possible. In what follows we shall discuss the two proposals made in RFC-1113 [**6**], RFC-1114 [**7**], and RFC-1115 [**8**], which address these issues. The first simply describes how a privacy-enhanced message is generated, formatted, and sent; the second part discusses the key management scheme.

2. Sending a privacy-enhanced mail message

The interoperability constraints described in the Introduction suggest encapsulating the header fields related to the enhancements and the privacy-enhanced body of the message. The delimiter

```
-----PRIVACY-ENHANCED MESSAGE BOUNDARY-----
```

is placed both before and after the privacy-enhanced portion of the message. Figures 1 and 2 show examples of this. Note that if the entire message is protected, a blank line must separate the delimiter from the headers; this is required by RFC-822.

```
-----PRIVACY-ENHANCED MESSAGE BOUNDARY-----
X-Proc-Type:  3,ENCRYPTED
X-DEK-Info:  DES-CBC,F8143EDE5960C597
X-Sender-ID: linn@ccy.bbn.com::
X-Recipient-ID: linn@ccy.bbn.com:ptf-kmc:3
X-Key-Info:  DES-ECB,RSA-MD2,9FD3AAD2F2691B9A,
  B70665BB9BF7CBCDA60195DB94F727D3
X-Recipient-ID: privacy-tf@venera.isi.edu:ptf-kmc:4
X-Key-Info:  DES-ECB,RSA-MD2,161A3F75DC82EF26,
  E2EF532C65CBCFF79F83A2658132DB47

LLrHB0eJzyhP+/fSStdW8okeEnv47jxe7SJ/iN72ohNcUk2jHEUSoH1nvNSIWL9M
8tEjmF/zxB+bATMtPjCUWbz8Lr9wloXIkjHUlBLpvXR0UrUzYbkNpk0agV2IzUpk
J6UiRRGcDSvzrsoK+oNvqu6z7Xs5Xfz5rDqUcMlK1Z6720dcBWGGsDLpTpSCnpot
dXd/H5LMDWnonNvPCwQUHt==
-----PRIVACY-ENHANCED MESSAGE BOUNDARY-----
```

FIGURE 1. Sample encapsulated message (from [**6**, p. 19])

The body of the message undergoes a three-step transformation: first it is put into a machine-independent character-oriented format, then an integrity check is generated and (if required) the message is encrypted, and finally the resulting bit stream is converted to printable characters suitable for processing by any (reasonable) message transport agent. Initially, of course, the message text is entered into the system, for example with a text editor; the representation of the characters is that used by the local computer system and so is called the *local form*. The local form is then altered as follows:

1. *Canonicalization*: The characters in the message are transformed into their ASCII representations, with the parity (high-order) bit cleared. Line (record) delimiters are changed to ⟨CR⟩⟨LF⟩ . This ensures that encryption, decryption, and integrity checking all are done on a consistent representation of the message.

```
 -----PRIVACY-ENHANCED MESSAGE BOUNDARY-----
X-Proc-Type:  3,ENCRYPTED
X-DEK-Info:  DES-CBC,F8143EDE5960C597
X-Sender-ID: linn@ccy.bbn.com::
X-Certificate:  jHUlBLpvXR0UrUzYbkNpk0agV2IzUpk8tEjmF/zxB
  +bATMtPjCUWbz8Lr9wloXIkYbkNpk0agV2IzUpk8tEjmF/zxB
+bATMtPjCUWbz8Lr9wloXIkjHUlBLpvXR0UrUzagV2IzUpk8tEjmFjHUlBLpv
  XR0UrUz/zxB+bATMtPjCUWbz8Lr9wloXIkYbkNpk0
X-Issuer-Certificate:
   TMtPjCUWbz8Lr9wloXIkYbkNpk0agV2IzUpk8tEjmFjHUlBLpvXR0UrUz/zxB+bA
   IkjHUlBLpvXR0UrUzYbkNpk0agV2IzUpk8tEjmF/zxB+bATMtPjCUWbz8Lr9wloX
   vXR0UrUzYbkNpk0agV2IzUpk8tEjmF/zxB+bATMtPjCUWbz8Lr9wloXIkjHUlBLp
X-MIC-Info:  RSA-MD2,RSA,
   5rDqUcMlK1Z6720dcBWGGsDLpTpSCnpotJ6UiRRGcDSvzrsoK+oNvqu6z7Xs5Xfz
X-Recipient-ID: linn@ccy.bbn.com:RSADSI:3
X-Key-Info:  RSA,
   lBLpvXR0UrUzYbkNpk0agV2IzUpk8tEjmF/zxB+bATMtPjCUWbz8Lr9wloXIkjHU
X-Recipient-ID: privacy-tf@venera.isi.edu:RSADSI:4
X-Key-Info:  RSA,
   NcUk2jHEUSoH1nvNSIWL9MLLrHB0eJzyhP+/fSStdW8okeEnv47jxe7SJ/iN72oh

LLrHB0eJzyhP+/fSStdW8okeEnv47jxe7SJ/iN72ohNcUk2jHEUSoH1nvNSIWL9M
8tEjmF/zxB+bATMtPjCUWbz8Lr9wloXIkjHUlBLpvXR0UrUzYbkNpk0agV2IzUpk
J6UiRRGcDSvzrsoK+oNvqu6z7Xs5Xfz5rDqUcMlK1Z6720dcBWGGsDLpTpSCnpot
dXd/H5LMDWnonNvPCwQUHt==
-----PRIVACY-ENHANCED MESSAGE BOUNDARY-----
```

FIGURE 2. Another sample encapsulated message (from [**6**, pp. 19–20])

2. *Authentication and Encipherment*: An integrity check is computed on the canonical representation of the message. Currently two algorithms are defined for use: the DEA-1 algorithm [**9**] and the RSA-MD2 Message Digest Algorithm [**8**]. If privacy is required, the message will then be enciphered using a per-message *data encryption key*. The encryption algorithm is the DES in cipher block chaining mode; any needed padding is supplied by appending octets with all bits set.

Note that the entire message need not be encrypted, even if integrity checking is being done. In this case, the message consists of regions to be encrypted (call them *ciphertext regions*) and regions to be unencrypted (*cleartext regions*). The position at which each cleartext region begins and ends is remembered (for the next step), and the initialization vector and sets of characters are accumulated across these ciphertext regions. Hence the encrypted portion of the message may be split up by the cleartext regions.

Several encapsulated header fields are set to convey the information needed to decrypt, and check the integrity of, the message. All privacy-enhanced messages contain the encapsulated header field

X-Proc-Type: *protocol,proc_type*

which indicates the type of processing done. Its first subfield, *protocol*, is the number of the protocol used; that corresponding to the current proposal is `3`. Its second subfield, *proc_type*, is `MIC-ONLY` if *no* part of the message is encrypted; otherwise it is `ENCRYPTED`. A second header field, required only for encrypted messages, conveys the message encryption algorithm and initialization vector:

X-DEK-Info: *encrypt_alg, init_vector*

The first subfield is a string indicating how the message was encrypted; as only the DES in cipher block chaining mode [**10**, **11**] is defined for use, this string must be `DES-CBC`. The second subfield is the initialization vector represented as a string of 16 hexadecimal digits. The integrity check, data encryption key, and the initialization vector will be transmitted after being encrypted with the interchange key, and we shall defer the details until the next section.

3. *Printable Encoding*: After the second step, the message text should be thought of as a sequence of bit streams, each associated with a cleartext or ciphertext region. (The encapsulated headers are not part of this stream unless they are replicated within the message text for integrity checking purposes.) Note that the number of bits in each bit stream is a multiple of 8. As many message transport agents allow only a limited line length and only 7 bits per character, the bit streams in this sequence must be converted into a printable form with limited line length. First, each bit stream is grouped into sets of 6 bits, each of which is mapped into a character in the alphabet shown in Table 3.

   The final set of bits in each stream may contain 2 or 4 bits rather than 6. In the former case, the two meaningful bits are padded with four cleared bits, and two "=" characters are appended to indicate the last 4 bits are padding. In the latter case, the pad is two cleared bits,

TABLE 3. Printable Encoding Characters

0 A	8 I	16 Q	24 Y	32 g	40 o	48 w	56 4
1 B	9 J	17 R	25 Z	33 h	41 p	49 x	57 5
2 C	10 K	18 S	26 a	34 i	42 q	50 y	58 6
3 D	11 L	19 T	27 b	35 j	43 r	51 z	59 7
4 E	12 M	20 U	28 c	36 k	44 s	52 0	60 8
5 F	13 N	21 V	29 d	37 l	45 t	53 1	61 9
6 G	14 O	22 W	30 e	38 m	46 u	54 2	62 +
7 H	15 P	23 X	31 f	39 n	47 v	55 3	63 /

and one "=" is appended to the printably encoded character. Finally, an asterisk "*" is placed before and after the character sequences corresponding to cleartext regions, and the resulting character stream is split into lines of 64 printable characters (except, possibly, for the last line, which may contain fewer). This form is suitable for transmission by any reasonable message transport agent.

2.1. Transmission of integrity check and data encryption key. We now turn to the transmission of the data encryption key and the message integrity check. The former must be encrypted using an interchange key to protect the privacy of the message, that latter to ensure authenticity. The mechanism used to do this depends on whether the interchange key is used with a classical cryptosystem or with a public key cryptosystem. In either case, the interchange key depends upon proper identification of the sender and recipient.

2.1.1. *Sender, recipient, and interchange key information.* The sender and recipient of each message are identified in the following encapsulated header fields, which also are to be replicated in the encapsulated text to ensure integrity:

X-Sender-ID: *entity_id* : *issuing_authority* : *version*

X-Recipient-ID: *entity_id* : *issuing_authority* : *version*

These fields specify which interchange key was used. The first subfield contains the identity of the sender or receiver, the second the identity of the authority issuing the interchange key, and the third an indicator of the specific interchange key being used. Since interchange keys depend on both the sender and the recipient, each **X-Recipient-ID** is associated with the last preceding **X-Sender-ID** line.

The first subfield is mandatory; it also requires that each sender be uniquely identifiable. Hence it assumes the form *user@host*, where *user* is unique to *host* and *host* is unique throughout the set of hosts using electronic mail. Any scheme guaranteeing this will work, but those sites which transmit into the Internet should use the fully qualified domain name for *host*.

The second subfield contains the unique name of the authority that issued the interchange key; it need not be unique among all entities, but must be unique over all issuing authorities.

The third subfield is some number or string selected by the issuing authority to disambiguate among the interchange keys issued by that authority to the sender/recipient pair. The proposal recommends the use of timestamps; not only does this provide uniqueness but it also allows an expiration date to be prescribed (for example, two years after issue).

If the subfields contain redundant information, they may be omitted; for example, if the interchange key is used in a classical cryptosystem, the contents of the last two subfields of both **X-Sender-ID** and **X-Recipient-ID** fields will be the same for each sender/recipient pair, and so these subfields are normally omitted from the **X-Sender-ID** field. Similarly, if the sender's public key is sent in the message as a certificate containing both the version number and issuing authority (using the certificates and the **X-Certificate** header field described below), the last two subfields in the **X-Sender-ID** field may be omitted. The illustrations in Figures 1 and 2 reflect this; in both, the field

```
X-Sender-ID: linn@ccy.bbn.com::
```

identifies the sender as user *linn* at host *ccy.bbn.com*, but leaves the issuing authority and version subfields blank. In Figure 1 the relevant information is in the associated **X-Recipient-ID** lines;

```
X-Recipient-ID: linn@ccy.bbn.com:ptf-kmc:3
```

means that the recipient is *linn@ccy.bbn.com*, that the interchange authority named *ptf-kmc* (most likely standing for "*p*rivacy *t*ask *f*orce *k*ey *m*anagement *c*enter") has issued an interchange key for *linn* to use when he sends messages to himself (since the last preceding **X-Sender-ID** field identified *linn@ccy.bbn.com* as the sender), and that this key can be identified uniquely by the string 3. The second such field,

```
X-Recipient-ID: privacy-tf@venera.isi.edu:ptf-kmc:4
```

means that *ptf-kmc* has also issued an interchange key for *linn@ccy.bbn.com* to use when sending messages to *privacy-tf@venera.isi.edu*, and that this key can be identified uniquely by the string 4. In Figure 2, the certificate in the **X-Certificate** line is that of the sender in the preceding **X-Sender-ID** line, so again the latter two subfields of that field are omitted.

2.1.2. *Symmetric interchange keys.* With classical cryptosystems, the encryption key is either the same as, or easily derivable from, the decryption key. For this reason, the *interchange key* is defined as the single key associated with both the sender and the recipient, and the message integrity check and data encryption key follow the identification of each sender and recipient.

The message integrity check and data encryption key for each sender and recipient pair are given on lines of the form

X-Key-Info: *ik_use,mic_algorithm,dek,mic*

One such line normally follows each recipient name, and uses the interchange key associated with the sender and that recipient. The first subfield identifies the algorithm which was used to encrypt the data exchange key; the proposal requires using either the DES in electronic code book mode [**11**] (indicated by `DES-ECB`) or the DES in encrypt-decrypt-encrypt mode [**12**, §7.2] (indicated by `DES-EDE`). The second subfield identifies the algorithm used to generate the message integrity check; this subfield must be either `MAC` (for the DEA-1) or `RSA-MD2` (for the RSA-MD2 Message Digest Algorithm). The third and fourth subfields are the data exchange key and the message integrity check encrypted using the algorithm given by the first subfield with the interchange key. Both are represented as strings of hexadecimal digits. For example, in Figure 1, the line

```
X-Key-Info:  DES-ECB,RSA-MD2,
             9FD3AAD2F2691B9A,B70665BB9BF7CBCDA60195DB94F727D3
```

indicates that the message integrity check was computed using the RSA-MD2 Message Digest Algorithm, and both it and the data exchange key were encrypted using the interchange key and the DES algorithm in electronic code book form. The second **X-Key-Info** line in that figure indicates the same thing, but since another **X-Recipient-ID** line has occurred since the last **X-Key-Info** line, the data encryption key and message integrity check were encrypted with the interchange key for the sender/recipient pair *linn@ccy.bbn.com* and *privacy-tf@venera.isi.edu* (and hence look quite different than in the preceding line).

2.1.3. *Asymmetric interchange keys.* With public key cryptosystems, encryption and decryption keys are different, and neither can be derived merely by knowing the other. This allows authentication and encryption to be done with two different keys, and so the *interchange key* is both the recipient's public key and the sender's private key, the former being used to encrypt the data exchange key (privacy), and the latter being used to encrypt the message integrity check (integrity/authenticity). With this interchange key, the message integrity check and data encryption keys are given by two different header fields because the parts of the interchange key differ. The message integrity check is given in header fields of the form

X-Key-Info: *ik_use,dek*

The first subfield is the name of the algorithm used to encrypt the data encryption key; since only one algorithm is currently defined for this purpose, the first subfield will always be `RSA`. The second subfield is the data exchange key, encrypted using the recipient's public key and represented as a string of printable encoding characters using the encoding transformation. For example, the first recipient (*linn@ccy.bbn.com*) has the data encryption key encrypted using RSA and *linn@ccy.bbn.com*'s public key, and the second again using RSA and *privacy-tf@venera.isi.edu*'s public key.

The message integrity check is transmitted similarly, in a header field of the form

X-MIC-Info: *ik_use,mic_algorithm,mic*

The first subfield identifies the algorithm used to compute the integrity check, and so must be either `MAC` (if DEA-1 was used) or `RSA-MD2` (if the `RSA` Message Digest Algorithm was used). The second subfield identifies the algorithm used to encrypt the integrity check; again, currently this must be RSA. The final subfield is the message integrity check encrypted using the recipient's public key and represented as a string of printable encoding characters using the encoding transformation. Note that the information is associated with the sender and not the recipient, so this line should only occur after the **X-Sender-ID** field. For example, the message in Figure 2 has its message integrity check computed using the RSA-MD2 Message Digest Algorithm, and is encrypted using the RSA algorithm and *linn@ccy.bbn.com*'s private key.

3. Certificate based key management

If asymmetric interchange keys are used, a method for ensuring that correct public keys are made available must be provided; without such assurance, an active wiretapper could spoof the intended recipient and read the sender's supposedly private message. The privacy-enhanced mail proposal suggests using certificates containing an entity name, a public key, an issuer name, and a digital signature created by the issuer based on its public key and the information in the certificate. This section presents the proposal for managing those certificates.

3.1. Overview of proposal. The proposal envisions a set of trees with the inner nodes being organizations entitled to issue certificates. The root of each tree will be a *top-level certification authority*; each of the inner nodes will be a *certification authority.* (This hierarchy is expected to be shallow—usually two-tiered.) The leaves are subjects to whom certificates are issued, and who are not authorized to issue certificates themselves. The next tier is composed of organizations who may certify users; the next tier is composed of organizations who may certify other organizations, and so forth. In all cases a certifying authority may only certify those entities directly beneath it. The top-level certifying authority (or any certifying authority, for that matter) establishes its own procedures for and rules for determining what entities it will certify, how those entities request certification, and how the certification is done. An example of how such a certifying authority might work is given in the next section.

The hierarchical arrangement of certifying authorities within each tree allows a simple checking of certificate validity. As noted above, each certificate contains an entity name, a public key, an issuer name, and a digital signature created by the issuer based on its public key and the information in the certificate. To validate that the certificate has not been altered, one need only obtain the issuer's certificate, extract the public key, and use that to compute the digital signature of the certificate in question. If this differs from the signature on the certificate in question, that certificate is bogus. The certificate of the issuer may be checked in a similar fashion, all the way up the hierarchy, until the top-level certification authority is reached; the public key of this authority will be widely publicized and available in ways other than certificates, as well as in a certificate.

The problem of transmitting and obtaining certificates for use with privacy-enhanced electronic mail in the absence of ubiquitous directory servers is solved by including two optional encapsulated header fields in the privacy-enhanced mail message. The encapsulated header field

X-Certificate: *encoded_certificate*

contains the sender's certificate as a bit stream represented as a string of printable encoding characters using the encoding transformation. Similarly, the encapsulated header field

X-Issuer-Certificate: *encoded_certificate*

is like the **X-Certificate** field, except that it contains the certificate of the issuer of a certificate. It may be used to validate the certificate in either the **X-Certificate** or in another **X-Issuer-Certificate** header field. Examples of both these fields are given in Figure 2.

A second problem arises across hierarchies: if two users are in different hierarchies, how can they validate each others' certificates? Either the top-level certifying authorities may issue certificates for each other, or one of the two users may obtain certificates from both certifying authorities and use the appropriate one.

A third issue is the revocation question. Each certificate is issued for a limited period of time, and—more importantly—may be compromised in a number of (out-of-band) methods. For example, the entity name might change, or the private key associated with the public key in the certificate may be revealed. In this case, the serial number of the certificate is added to a revoked certificate list maintained by the certifying authority issuing the certificate. This list is publicly available, is signed by the private key of the certifying authority, is dated, and contains the date at which the next revoked certificate list will be issued. Note that this requires a new list to be issued at the stated time even if no certificates have been revoked; however, it also allows a site to determine if the list is out of date.

3.2. Certificate definition and use. A *certificate* binds a public key to an issuing authority, subject (which may be a user or some other entity), and other information. Each contains a version number (currently 0), a subject identity, an issuer name, a serial number defined by the issuer and unique to that issuer, a validity period after which the certificate expires, the subject's public key, and a hash binding all the above information together.

In addition to the subject's identity, the subject name must contain an organizational affiliation and country name; this composes a *Distinguished Name.* A typical Distinguished Name would look like:

Matt Bishop, Dept. of Math & CS, Dartmouth College, US

where "Matt Bishop" is the subject's personal name, "Dept. of Math & CS" is the organizational unit name, "Dartmouth College" the organizational name, and "US" the country name in ISO-3166 encoding. For compatibility with the U. S. Government Open Systems Interconnection Profile, Version 2, this proposal limits the number and length of each field in the Distinguished Name; the country name may be at most 3 characters, the personal name at most 64, the organizational name 64, and there may be at most four organizational unit names of maximum length 32 characters each. As another example, the Distinguished Name

Matt Bishop, Network Systems Division, RIACS, USRA, US

contains two hierarchical organizational unit names ("Network Systems Division" is a branch of "RIACS" which is in turn a research laboratory of "USRA"). If multiple organizational unit names are present, they are taken hierarchically, with the lowest unit first.

We now give an example of a certification hierarchy in which certificates are issued and validated.

3.3. Example of a certifying authority hierarchy: RSA data security inc. Since this certificate management proposal currently presupposes the use of the RSA cryptosystem for encrypting data exchange keys and message integrity checks, the public keys in the certificates will be public keys for RSA; this cryptosystem was selected because it is the primary algorithm identified in international standards for use where asymmetric algorithms are required,† is relatively efficient to implement, and has not yet been broken. Outside the United States, or for the United States Government, this poses no problems. Within the United States, RSA Data Security, Inc. has patented the RSA cryptosystem, and hence it may not be used except under license. RSA Data Security, Inc. has agreed to issue certificates for a biennial fee of $25.00, and that the user identified in the certificate will have a license to use the RSA algorithm for certificate validation and encryption and decryption operations to send privacy-enhanced electronic mail.

RSA Data Security Inc. has established a set of procedures for obtaining and validating certificates; as this is currently the only top-level certifying authority, its procedures may serve as an example of how a certifying authority issues certificates. Of course, certifying authorities are not constrained to follow these procedures; they may use others.

† The international standard (X.509, Annex C) does not mandate a key length but recommends that "a value ... of 512 bits be adopted initially, but subject to *further study*" (emphasis in original). This standard is explicitly referenced by the proposal [**8**, p. 3].

To obtain a certificate from RSA Data Security Inc., a user must first generate a public key and private key pair, possibly by using special-purpose software. She then creates an order on paper containing her Distinguished Name elements, a postal address, an electronic mail address, and a message hash computed on the public component and the other information. (Note that the public component is not sent on paper; since such a component should consist of over 150 digits, errors copying that component will be too common.) This order must be submitted directly to RSA Data Security Inc. If the user is not obtaining the certificate through an organization, she must have a Notary Public notarize it and must include a check or money order for $25.00; however, organizations may make their own billing arrangements. The same information, but with the public key, must also be sent electronically either to RSA Data Security Inc. or to the user's organization if it is authorized to issue certificates.

If the organization is authorized to issue certificates, the user submits her electronic message to an *organizational notary.* The organizational notary is a clearinghouse for certificate orders within an administrative domain such as an organization or organizational unit, and is assumed to be somewhat independent of the users in that administrative domain. Only those users in the domain may order certificates through that organizational notary, who accepts and validates the information in the electronic letter. The organizational notary then forwards the electronic message to RSA Data Security, Inc. by privacy-enhanced electronic mail; this letter must vouch for the correctness and integrity of the information, and authorizes RSA Data Security Inc. to issue a certificate on behalf of the organization. †

When RSA Data Security Inc. receives both the electronic and paper letters, and is convinced all is in order, it issues a certificate. If the certificate is being issued on behalf of an organization, the certificate will be signed with the private key of the organization; if the user is not associated with an organization, RSA Data Security Inc. will sign with its own private key, but will make the issuer name be the special string `Notary`. It then sends to the user an electronic letter containing a copy of the certificate, a copy of the certificate of the organization in the issuer field, and the public component of RSA Data Security Inc. used to validate the certificates it issues. It also sends a paper letter containing the response to the user's request, a hash computed on the user's Distinguished Name and public component as sent to RSA Data Security Inc., and a hash computed on the public key of RSA Data Security Inc. used to validate the certificates it issues.

When the user receives both letters, she must validate her certificate before she uses it. First, she extracts the RSA Data Security Inc. public component,

† The organizational notary could issue the certificate at this point, but RSA Data Security Incorporated would then require special safeguards and legal agreements to ensure proper accounting of the number of certificates issued, and adequate protection of the special-purpose software used to generate those certificates.

the issuer certificate, and her certificate. She then checks RSA Data Security Inc.'s public key as sent electronically using the hash in her paper letter. If this is correct, she then validates the signature on the certificate of the issuing organization. If that is correct, she then uses the public key from that certificate to validate her own certificate. Finally, she obtains her Distinguished Name and public key from her certificate, computes the hash, and checks that against the hash in her paper letter. If this matches, the certificate is valid, and she has the public key of the top-level certifying organization for use in checking correspondents' certificates should she so desire.

4. Conclusion

The first proposal provides the three most important services for security-enhanced electronic mail, namely privacy of the message, authenticity of the sender, and message integrity. Mail sent using it cannot be altered undetectably, and if encrypted cannot be read in transit. Further, the recipient can confirm the identity of the sender. The second proposal provides a mechanism integrating key management and distribution in support of the first, thereby making it viable.

Problems arise in connection with the second proposal. The most serious is the cost of the certificates; while $12.50 per user per year seems small, if a computer installation has several thousand users and wishes to obtain certificates for all, the cost grows rather quickly. Possible solutions include having the users buy their own certificates (which is reasonable since those who do not can still use regular electronic mail), or buying certificates only for those for whom the installation deems them a necessity. An even better solution is to use some other public key cryptosystem to generate keys; however, factors such as ciphertext expansion (if the size of the interchange key or the size of the encrypted data encryption key becomes several thousand bits, the overhead would become prohibitive) and the need for software may constrain this option.

That these two proposals are distinct must be emphasized; one is free to adopt the first without using the second. Indeed, RFC-1113 specifically describes protocols to be used with key management schemes other than certificate-based schemes, and hence the second proposal merely supports the first. Organizations that decide not to use the public key approach may substitute their own key management scheme; however, all implementations of privacy-enhanced electronic mail should support the certificate-based approach as well as any other for compatibility reasons.

More research in cryptography would aid in the maturation of this proposal. Specifically, message digest functions such as RSA-MD2 that can be used to compute a message integrity check are very few; more are needed, as is an understanding of how to develop them and prove that they are in fact good. A public key cryptosystem as strong as RSA would allow the use of interchange keys not encumbered by licensing. If such a cryptosystem could be implemented as efficiently as the DES, it could be used to encrypt the message as well.

Finally, this proposal does not address issues in network and system security, such as the development of trusted software, routing controls, replays, and access controls. While all are important to the sending of electronic mail, they have much wider applications, and provide a fertile field for research and development.

ACKNOWLEDGMENTS: This paper presents a set of proposals developed during a series of meetings of the IAB's Privacy and Security Task Force, and stated in a series of RFCs. Thanks are due to David Balenson, Curt Barker, Jim Bidzos, Danny Cohen, Tom Daniel, Charles Fox, Morrie Gasser, Stephen Kent, John Laws, John Linn, Steve Lipner, Dan Nessett, Mike Padlipsky, Rob Shirey, Miles Smid, Steve Walker, and Steve Wilbur.

REFERENCES

1. CCITT Recommendation X.400, *Message handling system model* 1988.
2. D. Crocker, *Standard for the format of ARPA Internet text messages*, RFC-822, August 1982.
3. J. Postel, *Simple mail transfer protocol*, RFC-821, August 1982.
4. D. Nowitz and M. Lesk, *A dial-up network of UNIX systems*, document SMM:21 in UNIX System Manager's Manual, Computer Systems Research Group, University of California, Berkeley, CA 94720, April 1986.
5. V. Voydock and S. Kent, *Security mechanisms in high-level network protocols*, Computing Surveys **15** (2) (June 1983), 135–171.
6. J. Linn, *Privacy enhancement for Internet electronic mail: Part I—Message encipherment and authentication procedures*, RFC-1113, August 1989.
7. S. Kent and J. Linn, *Privacy enhancement for Internet electronic mail: Part II—Certificate-based key management*, RFC-1114, August 1989.
8. J. Linn, *Privacy enhancement for Internet electronic mail: Part III—Algorithms, modes, and identifiers*, RFC-1115, August 1989.
9. Federal Information Processing Standards Publication 113, Computer Data Authentication, May 1985.
10. Federal Information Processing Standards Publication 46, Data Encryption Standard, January 1977.
11. Federal Information Processing Standards Publication 81, DES Modes of Operation, December 1980.
12. ANSI X9.17-1985, *American National Standard, Financial Institution Key Management* (*Wholesale*), American Bankers Association, April 1985.

DEPARTMENT OF MATHEMATICS AND COMPUTER SCIENCE, DARTMOUTH COLLEGE, HANOVER, NH 03755

E-mail address: Matt.Bishop@dartmouth.edu

DIMACS Series in Discrete Mathematics
and Theoretical Computer Science
Volume 2, 1991

Program Result Checking against Adaptive Programs and in Cryptographic Settings

MANUEL BLUM*, MICHAEL LUBY, AND RONITT RUBINFELD**

ABSTRACT. The theory of program result checking introduced in [**Bl**] allows one to check that a program P correctly computes the function f on input x. The checker may use P's outputs on other inputs to help it check that $P(x) = f(x)$. In this setting, P is always assumed to be a fixed program, whose output on input x is a function $P(x)$. We extend the theory to check a program P that returns a result on input x that may depend on previous questions asked of P. We call a checker that works for such a program an *adaptive checker.* We consider the case in which there is an adaptive program that supposedly computes f running on each of several noninteracting machines. We design adaptive checkers that work for a constant number of independent and noninteracting programs.

We also consider the following cryptographic scenario: A user wants to evaluate function f on input x using program P running on another machine. As in checking, the user does not trust the program to be correct. The additional requirement is that the user wants to let the other machine know as little information as possible about x from the questions asked of the program P (for example, the user may want the program to be able to learn at most the input size) as in [**AFK**], [**BF**]. We call a program that satisfies the above constraints a *private checker.* As is the case for adaptive checking, we consider the case where there is a program that supposedly computes f on each of several noninteracting machines. We design private checkers that work for a constant number of independent and noninteracting programs.

The adaptive and private checkers given are general techniques that work for a variety of numerical problems, including integer multiplication, modular multiplication, matrix multiplication, the mod function, integer division, modular exponentiation, and polynomial multiplication.

1. Introduction

Consider the task of writing a program P to evaluate a function f. One of the main difficulties of this task is that when P is implemented, it is

*Supported by NSF Grant No. CCR 88-13632.
**Supported by an IBM Graduate Fellowship and NSF Grant No. CCR 88-13632.

1052-1798/91 $1.00 + $.25 per page

difficult to verify that $P(x) = f(x)$ for all inputs x. The theory of program result checking, introduced by **[Bl]**, provides a way of doing this. Intuitively, a checker C for f makes calls to a program P that supposedly computes f. C is a program that is much "different" from any correct program for computing f. On input x and β, C outputs $P(x)$ and either "FAULTY" or "PASS". C always outputs "PASS" if P is a correct program for f *on all inputs*, whereas if $P(x) \neq f(x)$ then C outputs "FAULTY" with probability $\geq 1 - \beta$.

We want to ensure that the checker is in some way different from the program being checked, so that bugs in the checker are not the same as bugs in the program. This can be done in several ways. The way that we use here is to require that the running time of the checker, not including the time required by calls to the program, be asymptotically faster than the running time of any known correct program that computes $f(x)$. We call a checker that has this property *different.*

Since the checker is run each time that the program is used, it is also important that the total running time, including calls to the program, be efficient. We say a checker is *efficient* if the total running time is a constant multiplicative factor times the running time of the program. We say a checker is $f(n)$*-efficient* if the total running time is $f(n)$ multiplied by the running time of the program.

The definition of a checker assumes that the program P is static; i.e., it computes some function, though not necessarily the function f. (P can be a probabilistic program in this definition, as long as the output of P on input x only depends on x, and not other inputs.) This is not always the case, as there are programs whose behavior changes as they run, even though the functions that they supposedly compute remain fixed. For example, hardware errors may evolve over time depending on the previous inputs that the program has been run on, or the software may be written such that running the program on certain inputs may have unintended side effects on the program's future behavior. This could occur in a program that stores tables of previously computed information in a permanent file to make subsequent processing more efficient. We call such a program that can modify itself and its subsequent computation an *adaptive program.* In this model, we assume that the program is an adversary that can give answers depending on all the previous questions asked of it by the checker. This is a restriction of the model used in interactive proof systems, in which the role of the verifier is played by the checker and the role of the prover is played by the program P. The restriction is that the verifier may only ask questions of the form "What is the value of $f(x)$?". All checkers extract an interactive proof of correctness from the program P. Since we do not always know how to extract such an interactive proof from a single program P running on one machine, we allow one program that supposedly computes f on each of k noninteracting machines, where k is a parameter that we would like to minimize. This corresponds to a restriction of multi-prover interactive proof systems where k is the number of provers.

DEFINITION 1.1. Program C is an *adaptive checker* for f if C is a checker for f that also works with respect to adaptive programs that supposedly compute f.

DEFINITION 1.2. Program C is a *k-adaptive checker* if C is a checker for k adaptive programs that do not communicate among themselves.

An adaptive checker is automatically a k-adaptive checker, and a k-adaptive checker is automatically a (nonadaptive) checker.

Many checkers that have been found are also adaptive checkers. For example, it can easily be seen that the GCD checker in [**AHK**] and all of the checkers given in [**BK**] are adaptive. Other checkers do not work for an adaptive program. Examples of such checkers are the ones in [**BLR**], where adaptive programs can easily fool the checkers. At the present time we see no way to convert such a checker into an adaptive checker. However, if more than one copy of the program exists, we show that a checker based on the methods in [**BLR**] can work for adaptive programs.

Next suppose we are in the following cryptographic situation: A user wants to evaluate function f on input x using program P running on another machine. As in checking, the user does not trust the program to be correct. The additional requirement is that the user wants to let the other machine know as little information as possible about x from the questions asked of the program P. (For example, the user may want the program to be able to learn at most the input size.) This is similar to the model introduced in [**AFK**] and later extended in [**BF**], where several noncommunicating programs compute the same function, except that here we do not trust the program to return correct answers. In addition, we only allow protocols that are restricted versions of [**AFK**], [**BF**]; in our protocols, the checker may only ask the program questions of the form, "What is the value of $f(x)$?".

We introduce some notation in order to define a private checker:

Let k be the number of programs purporting to compute f, such that none of these programs can communicate with any other program, and let P_i be the program on the ith machine for $1 \leq i \leq k$.

As in [**AFK**], we define L to be a function that we call the *leak function*. Intuitively, $L(x)$ is the amount of information leaked by the checker to the programs on input x. An example is $L(x) = |x|$; i.e., the checker leaks the length of x to the programs, but nothing more.

Let $\mathrm{CONV}_i[x]$ denote the probability distribution of the variable representing the concatenation of the questions that C asks of P_i on input x and let $\Pr_{\mathrm{CONV}_i[x]}(y)$ denote the probability of the string y according to the distribution.

DEFINITION 1.3. A program C is (k, L)-*private* if for all k-tuples of programs $(P_1, \ldots, P_k)$, for all v, w such that $L(v) = L(w)$, for all $1 \le i \le k$ and all y, $\Pr_{\mathrm{CONV}_i[v]}(y) = \Pr_{\mathrm{CONV}_i[w]}(y)$.

If a checker C is (k, L)-private where L leaks a very small amount of information about x (e.g., the length of x), then with high probability, C does not ask any of the programs $P_1, \ldots, P_k$ to evaluate input x. This means that the usual way of defining a checker to output "FAULTY" on input x if $P(x) \neq f(x)$ is insufficient. We define a private checker as follows:

DEFINITION 1.4. A program C is a (k, L)-*private checker* if C is (k, L)-private and, on input x and β, outputs $C(x)$ satisfying the following conditions: (1) if $P_1, \ldots, P_k$ answer correctly on all inputs, $C(x) = f(x)$; (2) $\Pr[C(x) = f(x)$ or $C(x) = \text{"FAULTY"}] \ge 1 - \beta$.

Thus, C outputs the correct answer if all programs always compute f as they should, but on the other hand it is unlikely that they can fool C into outputting the wrong answer (with probability at most β).

DEFINITION 1.5. A program C is a (k, L)-*private/adaptive checker* if it is a k-adaptive checker and a (k, L)-private checker.

We ask that the adaptive and private checkers be *different*, and as efficient as possible. A (k, L)-private checker or a k-adaptive checker is $f(n)$-efficient if the total work done *by all* k *programs* and the checker is $f(n)$ multiplied by the running time of the program.

2. Description of results and related work

We present general techniques for constructing simple-to-program and efficient (k, L)-private and k-adaptive checkers, for a constant k and where L is a function that does not leak much about the input (for example, only the size of the input), for a variety of numerical problems. The techniques given in this paper are all based on the algorithms given in **[BLR]**, though the proofs are different. The techniques apply to integer multiplication, the mod function, modular multiplication, modular exponentiation, integer division, and polynomial and matrix multiplication over finite fields. For all problems, the checker algorithms are both efficient and different. Furthermore, the checker algorithms consist of the execution of the following basic operations, at most a logarithmic number of times in a prescribed order: (1) calls to P on random instances of the problem; (2) additions; (3) comparisons.

[AFK] show that there is not likely to be a $(1, |x|)$-private checker for SAT that runs in polynomial time (not including the time required by the oracle). **[BF]** describe how to compute any function privately with $O(|x|)$ oracles that are trusted not to err; however, the oracles are not restricted to answer questions of the form, "What is the value of $f(x)$?". **[BFKR]** later improved this result to show that it can be done with $O(|x|/\log|x|)$ oracles.

The notion of random self-reducibility, as defined in **[FKN]**, is related to private checking, because it is possible to compute random self-reducible functions privately in polynomial time. Recently, [**FKN**] have shown that random Boolean functions are not k-random self-reducible for any polynomial k, and that if a function is 2-random self-reducible, then the function can be computed nonuniformly in nondeterministic polynomial time.

[**BF**] and [**Li**] show that any function that is a polynomial of degree d over a finite field is d-random self-reducible. Thus, one can get a $(O(d), L)$-private checker for the function, where L is the description of the finite field, under the following conditions: (1) the program is not adaptive, and (2) the program is already known to be correct on a large fraction of inputs in the finite field.

In [**FRS**], there is a general technique for turning any checker into a 2-adaptive checker. This technique can actually be used for many of the checkers. However, it requires a quadratic blowup in the number of calls made. Thus, if the number of calls made to the program is not constant, the extra work done by their technique is not of the same time order. For example, we give a way of converting one of the checking techniques in [**BLR**], which makes $O(\log n)$ calls to the program, into an adaptive checker of the same efficiency as the original checker. The techniques of [**FRS**] yield an adaptive checker that is slower than the original checker by a multiplicative factor of $O(\log n)$.

Previous to our work, [**Ka**] introduced a result checker for integer and polynomial multiplication based on computing the result of the program mod small special numbers. This checker trivially works for an adaptive program as well, because it makes no extra calls to the program. Independently of our work, [**AHK**] describe a result checker for multiplication in the same spirit as, but different from, that of [**Ka**]. Also previous to our work, [**Fr**] introduced a result checker for matrix multiplication that does not call the program.

3. Three properties of functions

The three properties described in this section are also described in [**BLR**], and for completeness we include them here. We build checkers for functions that have these properties. We include the running example of multiplication in order to show how the definitions are applied to a specific problem.

Let $\hat{U}$ denote the domain of f and let $\hat{x} \in \hat{U}$ be an input to f. Let $\hat{I}^1, \hat{I}^2, \ldots$ be a sequence of subsets of $\hat{U}$ such that $\hat{U} = \bigcup_{n \in \mathcal{N}} \hat{I}^n$. The superscript n indicates the *size* of the problem. Let $\mathcal{D} = \{D_n | n \in \mathcal{N}\}$ be a collection of probability distributions such that D_n is a distribution on $\hat{I}^n$. Let P be a program that supposedly computes f.

In the case of integer multiplication, $\hat{U} = \mathcal{N} \times \mathcal{N}$ *is the set of pairs of natural numbers and* $\hat{x} = (x_1, x_2) \in \hat{U}$ *where* $f(\hat{x}) = x_1 \cdot x_2$. $\hat{I}^n$ *is the set of pairs of numbers of length at most* n $(\{x | 0 \leq x \leq 2^n\} \times \{x | 0 \leq x \leq 2^n\})$.

3.1. Computability by random inputs. The first property that we are interested in is that any particular instance of the problem can be expressed as the solution to a few random instances of the same size:

Let $\hat{x} \in \hat{I}^n$ be an instance of the problem. Let $c_1(n)$ be an easily computable function of n. (In the following we use c_1 in place of $c_1(n)$ for brevity and because, in most cases, $c_1(n)$ is a constant.) Informally, the property is that $f(\hat{x})$ can be expressed as an easily computable function of $f(\hat{a}_1), \dots, f(\hat{a}_{c_1})$, where $\hat{a}_1, \dots, \hat{a}_{c_1}$ are each randomly distributed in $\hat{I}^n$ according to D_n.[1] More formally, there is a generation procedure G and a computation F, both easily computable, that interact as follows. For all n and for all $\hat{x} \in \hat{I}^n$:

- $G(n, \hat{x}, R) = \hat{a}_1, \dots, \hat{a}_{c_1}, A$, where R is the bit string used as a random source of bits. When R is randomly and uniformly distributed then, for each $k = 1, \dots, c_1$, $\hat{a}_k$ is randomly distributed in $\hat{I}^n$ according to D_n. A is auxiliary information generated in the process that is used in Part (2).
- $F(n, \hat{x}, G(n, \hat{x}, R), \alpha_1, \dots, \alpha_{c_1})$ evaluates to a possible output of an input in $\hat{I}^n$. Intuitively, $\alpha_1, \dots, \alpha_{c_1}$ are the answers that the program being checked produces on inputs $\hat{a}_1, \dots, \hat{a}_{c_1}$, respectively. We require that:
- If, for all $k = 1, \dots, c_1$, $\alpha_k = f(\hat{a}_k)$ then

$$F(n, \hat{x}, G(n, \hat{x}, R), \alpha_1, \dots, \alpha_{c_1}) = f(\hat{x}).$$

For integer multiplication, the conditions are fulfilled as follows:

- *First, generate two truly random and independent bit strings* r_1 *and* r_2, *each of length* n, *using a random bit string* R *of length* $2n$. *Then, compute* δ_1 *and* δ_2, *where* $\delta_1 = 1$ *if* $r_1 > x_1$ *and* $\delta_1 = 0$ *otherwise and* δ_2 *is calculated analogously with respect to* r_2 *and* x_2. *Let* $s_1 = \delta_1 2^n + x - r_1$ *and* $s_2 = \delta_2 2^n + x_2 - r_2$. *It can easily be verified that each of the pairs* $\hat{a}_1 = (r_1, r_2)$, $\hat{a}_2 = (r_1, s_2)$, $\hat{a}_3 = (s_1, r_2)$, *and* $\hat{a}_4 = (s_1, s_2)$ *are randomly and uniformly distributed in* $\{0, 1\}^n \times \{0, 1\}^n$. *Then,* $G(i, \hat{x}, R) = \hat{a}_1, \hat{a}_2, \hat{a}_3, \hat{a}_4, I$ *where* $I = (r_1, r_2, s_1, s_2, \delta_1, \delta_2)$.
- *Define* $F(n, \hat{x}, G(n, \hat{x}, R), \alpha_1, \dots, \alpha_4) = \alpha_1 + \alpha_2 + \alpha_3 + \alpha_4 - (r_1 + s_1)\delta_2 2^n - (r_2 + s_2)\delta_1 2^n + \delta_1 \delta_2 2^{2n}$. *It is easy to verify that* F *satisfies the requirements stated above.*

The generation and computation steps require the checker to perform a constant number of shifts, comparisons, and additions on numbers of length n.

[1] However, no independence between these random variables is needed; e.g., given the value of $\hat{a}_1$ it is not necessary that $\hat{a}_2$ be randomly distributed in $\hat{I}^n$ according to D_n.

3.2. Computability by smaller inputs. Informally, the property is that there is a constant c_2 such that for all $\hat{x} \in \hat{I}^n$, $f(\hat{x})$ can be expressed as an easily computable function of $f(\hat{a}_1), \dots, f(\hat{a}_{c_2})$, where $\hat{a}_1, \dots, \hat{a}_{c_2}$ are each in $\hat{I}^{n-1}$. More formally, there is a generation procedure G' and a computation F', both easily computable, that interact as follows. For all $n > 1$ and for all $\hat{x} \in \hat{I}^n$:

- $G'(n, \hat{x}) = \hat{a}_1, \dots, \hat{a}_{c_2}, I$ where for each $k = 1, \dots, c_2$, $\hat{a}_k \in \hat{I}^{n-1}$. I is auxiliary information generated in the process that is used in Part (2).
- $F'(n, \hat{x}, G'(n, \hat{x}), \alpha_1, \dots, \alpha_{c_2})$ evaluates to a possible output of an input in $\hat{I}^n$. Intuitively, $\alpha_1, \dots, \alpha_{c_2}, \beta$ are the answers that the program being checked produces on inputs $\hat{a}_1, \dots, \hat{a}_{c_2}, \hat{x}$, respectively. We require that:
- If, for all $k = 1, \dots, c_2$, $\alpha_k = f(\hat{a}_k)$ then

$$F'(n, \hat{x}, G'(n, \hat{x}), \alpha_1, \dots, \alpha_{c_2}) = f(\hat{x}).$$

For example, for integer multiplication this condition is fulfilled as follows. In fact, instead of reducing to inputs one bit smaller we reduce to half the number of bits. Assume n is even.

- Let x_1^L be the most significant $n/2$ bits of x_1 and let x_1^R be the least significant $n/2$ bits of x_1. Define x_2^L and x_2^R analogously with respect to x_2. Let $\hat{a}_1 = (x_1^R, x_2^R)$, $\hat{a}_2 = (x_1^L, x_2^R)$, $\hat{a}_3 = (x_1^R, x_2^L)$, and $\hat{a}_4 = (x_1^L, x_2^L)$. Then, $G'(n, \hat{x}) = \hat{a}_1, \hat{a}_2, \hat{a}_3, \hat{a}_4$.
- Define $F'(n, \hat{x}, G'(n, \hat{x}), \alpha_1, \dots, \alpha_4) = \alpha_1 + (\alpha_2 + \alpha_3) \cdot 2^{n/2} + \alpha_4 \cdot 2^n$. It is easy to verify that F' satisfies the requirements stated above.

3.3. Computability by random homomorphisms. Let G be a finite group with group operation $\circ$ and with generators $g_1, \dots, g_{c_3}$ and identity element 0. For $y \in G$, let y^{-1} denote the inverse of y. Let G' be a (finite or countable) group with group operation $\circ'$ and identity element $0'$. For $\alpha \in G'$, let α^{-1} denote the inverse of α. Let $f : G \to G'$ be a function. Intuitively, f is relatively hard to compute compared to either $\circ$ or $\circ'$.

Let $\mathcal{U}_G$ be the uniform probability distribution on G. We say that f has the *computability by random homomorphisms* property if:

- It is easy to choose random elements of G according to $\mathcal{U}_G$.
- F is an easily computable function with the property that, for any pair $x_1, x_2 \in G$, $F(x_1, x_2) \in G'$ and furthermore $f(x_1 \circ x_2) = f(x_1) \circ' f(x_2) \circ' F(x_1, x_2)$. We call this property *linear consistency*. In all of our applications except for integer multiplication,

$F(x_1, x_2) = 0'$ for all inputs x_1, x_2, in which case f is a group homomorphism.
- For each generator $g_i \in G$, F_i is an easily computable function with the property that, for any $z \in G$, $F_i(z) \in G'$ and furthermore $f(z \circ g_i) = f(z) \circ' F_i(z)$. We call this property *neighbor consistency.* This property is not needed for integer multiplication. For all of the other applications, both G and G' are generated by a single element denoted 1 and $1'$, respectively (i.e., they are both cyclic groups), and for all $z \in G$, $f(z \circ 1) = f(z) \circ' 1'$.

The computability by random homomorphisms property is a special case of the computability by random inputs property. The name comes from the fact that f is a group homomorphism in all of our applications except for integer multiplication, in which case f exhibits properties similar to a group homomorphism.

4. Main theorems

We first show how to construct a checker that is both adaptive *and* private for any function computable by random inputs and computable by smaller inputs. The checker is an adaptation of the self-testing/correcting pair using the method based on reduction to smaller sized inputs given in [**BLR**].

ALGORITHM 4.1. *The algorithm is designed to run asking questions of programs $P_1, \ldots, P_{c_1}$ running on noncommunicating machines. We describe the algorithm as if the questions are asked and immediately answered. However, the actual order of the questions is as follows: Let Q_i be the set of questions asked of P_i. The questions in Q_i are asked in a randomly permuted order, and then the verifications are done once all of the answers have been given. This can be done because none of the questions asked depends on results of previous questions.*

We make the convention that if any call to one of the subroutines returns "FAULTY" then the entire checker program outputs "FAULTY" and halts immediately.

Program $Check[l, \hat{x}]$: The inputs are $l \in \mathcal{N}$, $\hat{x} \in \hat{I}^l$.

For $i = 1, \ldots, l$, call $Random\_test[i]$.
$answer = Random\_Compute[l, \hat{x}]$
Output ($answer$,"PASS")

Subroutine $Random\_Test[n]$:

Choose $\hat{x}$ at random from $\hat{I}^n$.
If $n = 1$ then compute $f(\hat{x})$ directly
For $1 \le i \le c_1$, $y_i \leftarrow P_i(\hat{x})$.
If there is an i s.t. $f(\hat{x}) \ne y_i$ then output "FAULTY"

Else if $n > 1$ then:
Use computability by smaller inputs to generate $G'(i, \hat{x}) = \hat{a}_1, \dots, \hat{a}_{c_2}, I$.
For all $k = 1, \dots, c_2$ let $y_k \leftarrow Random\_compute[n-1, \hat{a}_k]$.
For $1 \le i \le c_1$, $z_i \leftarrow P_i(\hat{x})$.
If there is an i such that $F'(n, \hat{x}, G'(n, \hat{x}), y_1, \dots, y_{c_2}) \neq z_i$ then output "FAULTY"

Subroutine $Random\_Compute(n, \hat{x})$:
Use computability by random inputs to generate $G(n, \hat{x}, R) = \hat{a}_1, \dots, \hat{a}_{c_1}, I$,
where R is a random, independent, and uniformly distributed bit string.
For $i = 1, \dots, c_1$, $\alpha_i \leftarrow P_i(\hat{a}_i)$.
$answer \leftarrow F(n, \hat{x}, G(n, \hat{x}, R), \alpha_1, \dots, \alpha_{c_1})$

This checker is based on the checker in **[BLR]** that tests the program on successively larger ranges, bootstrapping on the fact that the smaller ranges have already been tested. Since testing has no meaning for an adaptive program, the proofs in **[BLR]** do not work in this setting. In fact, a naive implementation of the protocol described in **[BLR]** can be fooled by c_1 adaptive programs, because the adaptive program can figure out where the checker is in the computation by the questions asked of it, and lie accordingly. The above protocol overcomes this by asking the questions on each machine in a random order. Using the techniques of **[FRS]**, one can simply transform the checker in **[BLR]** into a 2-adaptive checker, with an additional cost of $O(\log n)$ multiplicative overhead in the running time over the original checker. On the other hand, the adaptive checker presented here is as efficient as the original checker of **[BLR]**.

THEOREM 4.1. *Any function that is computable by random inputs and computable by smaller inputs has a different and $T(x)$-efficient (c_1, L)-private/adaptive checker, where $T(x) = L(x)$ is the* size *of x.*

PROOF OF THEOREM 4.1. The intuition behind why this checker works in the adaptive setting is that the questions are being sent to c_1 adaptive programs in such a way that the programs do not know whether the question was generated at random in the first line of Random-Test or whether the question was generated at random within Random-Compute. We show that this is enough to get a c_1-adaptive checker. Let m be the total number of questions asked of program P_i and let $q_1, \dots, q_m$ be the questions asked of P_i. Each program receives a random permutation of the questions $(q_1, q_2, \dots, q_m)$. One can easily verify that the distribution of the questions is the same for all inputs of the same size, showing that the checker is (c_1, L)-private. One can also easily verify that $q_1, \ldots, q_m$ are independently and uniformly distributed (but not identically distributed; there are a subset of questions that are uniformly distributed in $\hat{I}^r$ for each $r = 1, \ldots, l$). Some of the questions are generated in Random-Test, and some of the questions are generated in Random-Compute in order to verify the questions in Random-Test. Notice that the questions asked in Random-Test are verified by computing them from questions that are of a smaller size. Let r be the smallest-sized question on which *any* program errs and let P_i be a program that errs on an input of size r. Since the questions are asked in a randomly permuted order, with probability p where $1/(c_2+2) \leq p \leq 1/(c_2+1)$, the question was generated in Random-Test rather than Random-Compute. This is because Random-Test only makes one call to P_i on inputs of size r, whereas Random-Compute is called c_2 times on inputs of size r (c_2+1 times on inputs of size l) and makes one call to P_i on an input of size r each time that it is called. The program P_i cannot tell which subroutine generated the questions of size r because they are asked in a random order. If P_i errs on a question generated by Random-Test, then if $r > 1$, since the question is being verified with smaller inputs, all of which are correct (by choice of r), the mistake is caught. Otherwise, if $r = 1$, the question is being verified by computation done by the checker, and the mistake is caught.

To decrease the probability of error to $\leq \beta$, run the protocol $O(\log 1/\beta)$ times sequentially. If *answer* is always the same, output *answer*, otherwise output "FAULTY". □

This outline can be used to develop an adaptive and private checker for the following problems:

COROLLARY 4.1. *There is a* $(4, L)$*-private/adaptive checker for integer multiplication, where* $L(x) = |x|$. *The checker is both different and efficient.*

COROLLARY 4.2. *There is a* $(2, L)$*-private/adaptive checker for integer division* $f(a, b) = (a \operatorname{div} b, a \bmod b)$, *where* $L(a, b) = \{|a|, b\}$. *The checker is both different and* $(\log n)$*-efficient.*

COROLLARY 4.3. *There is a* $(4, L)$*-private/adaptive checker for modular exponentiation* $f(a, x, q) = a^x \bmod q$, *where* $L(a, x, q) = \{|a|, |x|, q\}$. *The checker is both different and* $(\log^2 n)$*-efficient.*

COROLLARY 4.4. *There is a* $(4, L)$*-private/adaptive checker for matrix multiplication over a finite field* $f(A, B) = A \cdot B$, *where* $L(A, B) = \{|A|, |B|\}$. *The checker is both different and efficient.*

COROLLARY 4.5. *There is a* $(4, L)$*-private/adaptive checker for polynomial multiplication over a finite field* $f(a(x), b(x)) = a(x) \times b(x)$, *where* $L(a, b) = \{\text{degree}(a), \text{degree}(b)\}$. *The checker is both different and efficient.*

It is also possible to construct an adaptive and private checker for any function computable by random homomorphisms. The checker is an adaptation of the self-testing/correcting pair using the method based on computability by random homomorphisms given in [**BLR**].

THEOREM 4.2. *Any function that is computable by random homomorphisms has efficient and different 2-adaptive and* (k, L)*-private/adaptive checkers, for constant* $k = \max\{4, c_1 + 1\}$, *where* $L(x) = G$. *(*G *is the underlying group.)*

PROOF IDEA OF THEOREM 2. [**FRS**] show how to transform any checker into a 2-adaptive checker by simply running the original checking protocol with the first program. If the original checker would have accepted, a random question asked of the first program is chosen, and is also asked of the second program. If the second program gives the same answer as the first program, then the adaptive checker returns "PASS". Otherwise, if the original checker would have returned "FAULTY", or if the second program answers differently from the first, the adaptive checker returns "FAULTY". An adaptation of the algorithm for self-testing/correcting based on computability by random homomorphisms in [**BLR**] combined with the technique of [**FRS**] proves Theorem 2. □

COROLLARY 4.6. *There is a 2-adaptive and* $(5, L)$*-private/adaptive checker for modular multiplication* $f(a, b, q) = a \times b \bmod q$, *where* $L(a, b, q) = \{|a|, |b|, q\}$. *The checkers are both different and efficient.*

COROLLARY 4.7. *There is a 2-adaptive and* $(4, L)$*-private/adaptive checker for the mod function* $f(a, q) = a \bmod q$, *where* $L(a, q) = \{|a|, q\}$. *The checkers are both different and efficient.*

COROLLARY 4.8. *There is a 2-adaptive and* $(4, L)$*-private/adaptive checker for the exponentiation mod a prime function* $f(a, x, p) = a^x \bmod p$, *where* $L(a, x, p) = \{a, |x|, p\}$. *The checkers are both different and efficient.*

5. Open questions

By the results of [**FRS**], any checker can be converted into a 2-adaptive checker. A question that arises naturally is whether a checker can in general be converted into a 1-adaptive checker, as opposed to 2-adaptive. Since there is a complete language in NEXPTIME that has a checker [**BFL**], there is no general technique that converts any checker into a 1-adaptive checker unless NEXPTIME=PSPACE. To see this, suppose there is such a general technique and consider the checker for the complete language in NEXPTIME. Now, because we can supposedly convert this checker into a 1-adaptive checker, there is an interactive proof for the language. Then by the result of [**Fe**], the language must be in PSPACE.

Since there is probably no general technique for converting a checker into a 1-adaptive checker, it would be interesting to characterize which problems do have adaptive checkers.

Another interesting question is, "Under what conditions on L is it true that a $(1, L)$-private checker is always a 1-adaptive checker?".

[FRS] have shown a technique by which any checker can be made into a 2-adaptive checker. Is there a more efficient technique that does the same thing?

6. Acknowledgments

We thank Oded Goldreich, Sampath Kannan, Joan Feigenbaum, Silvio Micali, and Shafi Goldwasser for many enlightening discussions and for technical suggestions.

References

[AFK] M. Abadi, J. Feigenbaum, and J. Kilian, *On hiding information from an oracle*, J. Comput. System Sci. **39** (1) (1989), 29–50.

[AHK] L. Adleman, M. Huang, and K. Kompella, Personal communication through L. Adleman.

[BFL] L. Babai, L. Fortnow, and C. Lund, *Non-deterministic exponential time has two-prover interactive protocols*, Technical Report 90-03, University of Chicago, Dept. of Computer Science, Proc. of FOCS (1990).

[BF] D. Beaver and J. Feigenbaum, *Hiding instances in multioracle queries*, Proc. of the 7th STACS (1990), Springer-Verlag LNCS 415, 37–48.

[BFKR] D. Beaver, J. Feigenbaum, J. Kilian, and P. Rogaway, *Cryptographic applications of locally random reductions*, AT&T Bell Laboratories Technical Memorandum, November, 1989.

[Bl] M. Blum, *Designing programs to check their work*, submitted to Comm. Assoc. Comput. Mach.

[BK] M. Blum and S. Kannan, *Program correctness checking ... and the design of programs that check their work*, Proc. of the 21st STOC (1989), ACM, 86–97.

[BLR] M. Blum, M. Luby, and R. Rubinfeld, *Program result checking against adaptive programs and in cryptographic settings*, Proc. of the 22nd STOC (1990), ACM, 73–83.

[FKN] J. Feigenbaum, S. Kannan, and N. Nisan, *Lower bounds on random-self-reducibility*, Proc. of the 5th Structure in Complexity Theory Conference (1990), IEEE, to appear.

[Fe] P. Feldman, *The Optimum Prover lives in PSPACE*, manuscript, 1986.

[Fo] L. Fortnow, *Complexity-theoretic aspects of interactive proof systems*, Tech. Report MIT/LCS/TR-447, Ph.D. Thesis, May, 1989.

[FRS] L. Fortnow, J. Rompel, and M. Sipser, *On the power of multi-prover interactive protocols*, Proc. of the 3rd Structure in Complexity Theory Conference (1988), IEEE, 156–161.

[Fr] R. Freivalds, *Fast probabilistic algorithms*, Proc. of Mathematical Foundations of CS, Springer-Verlag LNCS **74** (1979), 57–69.

[Ka] M. Kaminski, *A note on probabilistically verifying integer and polynomial products*, J. Assoc. Comput. Mach. **36** (1) (1989), 142–149.

[Li] R. Lipton, *New directions in testing*, manuscript, October, 1989.

[LFKN] C. Lund, L. Fortnow, H. Karloff, and N. Nisan, *The polynomial time hierarchy has interactive proofs*, Proc. of FOCS (1990).

[Ru] R. Rubinfeld, *Designing checkers for programs that run in parallel*, manuscript, 1989.

[Sh] A. Shamir, IP=PSPACE, Proc. of FOCS (1990).

Computer Science Division, University of California, Berkeley, California 94720

International Computer Science Institute, Berkeley, California 94704

Computer Science Division, University of California, Berkeley, California 94720
E-mail address: luby@icsi.berkeley.edu
E-mail address: ronitt@ernie.berkeley.edu

DIMACS Series in Discrete Mathematics
and Theoretical Computer Science
Volume 2, 1991

The Scope of a Logic of Authentication

MICHAEL BURROWS, MARTÍN ABADI,
AND ROGER NEEDHAM

1. A logic of authentication

Authentication protocols are both essential to security in distributed systems and notoriously obscure. A typical authentication protocol involves only two or three parties (called principals) and a few messages between them. (See [**2**, **11**, **14**, **15**, **16**, **17**, **20**], for example.) The intended outcome is that the parties obtain a guarantee that they are dealing with each other. In addition, the parties sometimes acquire a new shared secret, such as a session key. The exchanges are brief, but many of the authentication protocols found in the literature contain serious security flaws ([**2**, **11**, **15**, **20**], for example).

A logic of authentication has helped us in analyzing certain aspects of authentication protocols [**1**]. Our logic consists of a simple set of inference rules, in a notation designed specifically for the study of authentication protocols.[1] The goal of the logic is to describe the beliefs of trustworthy parties involved in authentication, and the evolution of these beliefs while the principals communicate. This approach has proved useful. We have met with some success in explaining protocols and in uncovering subtle assumptions and dangerous bugs. On occasion, we have also found redundancies, such as unnecessary message parts and unnecessary encryption. More recently, others have used the logic, sometimes with a similar result [**5**, **18**].

The logic does not attempt to answer every important question about every conceivable authentication protocol. In this note, we wish to clarify what the logic captures and what it does not capture, and where there is room for other formal or informal techniques. We introduce and discuss the logic through an example that relies on public-key cryptography [**19**].

1980 *Mathematics Subject Classification* (1985 *Revision*). Primary 03B70, 68M10, 68P25, 68Q60, 94A60.

[1] We use slightly different notation in other works on the logic. The notation here is more verbose, but more readable.

In our example, a principal A obtains the public key of another principal B from a server S. First, A requests a certificate containing B's public key, from a trusted server S. In an informal notation, this message might be written:

$$A \rightarrow S: \; A, B.$$

The server replies with the desired certificate, which includes B's name, a key K_b, a timestamp T, and which is encrypted under the server's secret key K_s^{-1}:

$$S \rightarrow A: \; S, \{K_b, B, T\}_{K_s^{-1}}.$$

The analysis of a protocol consists of three phases:

- reformulating the protocol in our notation;
- spelling out the implicit assumptions;
- applying the inference rules of the logic to the assumptions and to the messages.

We will go through these phases in our example.

First, we transform the protocol into an idealized form, where each message becomes an expression in the logic. Intuitively, the expression reflects the logical meaning of the message. For example, S says that K_b is B's public key (written $\overset{K_b}{\mapsto} B$) in the second message, and hence the second message becomes

$$S \rightarrow A: \; \{\overset{K_b}{\mapsto} B, T\}_{K_s^{-1}}.$$

We have removed a cleartext field from the second message. Similarly, the first message, from A to S, can be omitted altogether from the idealized form of the exchange. Unencrypted parts are simply "hints" designed to help with the timely progress of the protocol, and would not contribute to our proofs. Therefore, the idealized protocol proceeds as if S sends B's public key to A spontaneously.

The transformation from an informal description of a protocol to a description in our notation is carried out by hand, but we have found that it is usually straightforward. Nevertheless, this transformation is not always possible: some protocols rely on techniques that cannot be represented adequately in the logic. However, the class of protocols treated is large enough to be useful.

We have not yet been able to make rigorous the correspondence between formulas in idealized protocols and bits transmitted. Hence, our derivations provide no guarantees about actual implementations of the protocols. It might be desirable and possible (at least in principle) to prove properties of authentication protocols expressed in conventional programming languages.

In the second phase of the analysis, we write assumptions. The assumptions that underly this message exchange are fairly obvious.

- The server's public key must be known to A, otherwise the message is of no use to A. We say that A believes that K_s is S's public key, and write it A *believes* $\stackrel{K_s}{\mapsto} S$.
- A must believe that the timestamp is a recent one if it is to accept S's message as timely (and not a replay by an intruder). In this case we say that A believes that T is fresh, and write it A *believes* $fresh(T)$. What it is about T that causes A to believe it fresh is outside the province of the logic.

  We divide time into two epochs, the present (the current run) and the past; a fresh expression is one that was never uttered in the past. The distinction of present and past suffices for our purposes.
- S must believe that K_b really is B's public key, for S's message to be honest and not a deliberate lie. Although we allow for the possibility of attackers, we take all the principals mentioned in the protocol to be honest.
- Finally, A must trust S to provide B's key. More precisely, if A believes that S believes that K_b is B's key, then A believes that K_b is B's key. We say that A believes that S has jurisdiction over $\stackrel{K_b}{\mapsto} B$, and write A *believes* S *controls* $\stackrel{K_b}{\mapsto} B$.

Once the protocol is idealized and the assumptions are made explicit, we check that all the principals communicate honestly in the course of the exchange. This means that the sender of each message believes in the truth of its contents, either on the basis of initial assumptions or as a result of valid inference from previously received messages. In the example, the honesty of S follows from the assumption that S *believes* $\stackrel{K_b}{\mapsto} B$.

We also use the assumptions and the messages to reason about the final state achieved by the protocol. We consider only stable formulas, those that once true remain true for the duration of a protocol run. Therefore, all the assumptions about the initial state still hold as post-conditions to the messages. (The manipulation of pre-conditions and post-conditions is inspired by Hoare logic [**8**].) In addition, it also holds as a post-condition that A sees S's message, which we write A *sees* $\{\stackrel{K_b}{\mapsto} B, T\}_{K_s^{-1}}$.

Hence we proceed to apply the rules of inference of the logic to the assumptions and to the post-condition A *sees* $\{\stackrel{K_b}{\mapsto} B, T\}_{K_s^{-1}}$. These rules simply account for how A ascertains that K_b is B's public key.

The first relevant rule is

$$\frac{P \textit{ believes } \stackrel{K}{\mapsto} Q, \quad P \textit{ sees } \{X\}_{K^{-1}}}{P \textit{ believes } Q \textit{ said } X}$$

which expresses that if P believes that K is Q's public key and it receives a message $\{X\}_{K^{-1}}$ under the inverse of K, then P believes that Q once said the contents of the message. We derive $A\ believes\ S\ said\ (\overset{K_b}{\mapsto} B, T)$.

Another rule enables us to deduce $A\ believes\ fresh(\overset{K_b}{\mapsto} B, T)$ from the assumption $A\ believes\ fresh(T)$:

$$\frac{P\ believes\ fresh(Y)}{P\ believes\ fresh(X, Y)}.$$

A third rule,

$$\frac{P\ believes\ fresh(X), \quad P\ believes\ Q\ said\ X}{P\ believes\ Q\ believes\ X},$$

then yields that $A\ believes\ S\ believes\ (\overset{K_b}{\mapsto} B, T)$. This rule expresses the check that a message belongs to the current run of the protocol. If P believes that X is fresh and Q has once said X, then P believes that Q has said X during the current run, and hence that Q believes X at present.

Immediately, we can derive $A\ believes\ S\ believes\ \overset{K_b}{\mapsto} B$. Notice a formal oddity here: We can also derive $A\ believes\ S\ believes\ T$, where a timestamp is treated as a statement—a "believable" expression. This seems less odd if we view T as a statement such as "it is 5 P.M.," rather than as the corresponding term "5 P.M." A reformulation of the syntax of the logic could avoid the oddity altogether.

We complete the proof with the rule

$$\frac{P\ believes\ Q\ controls\ X, \quad P\ believes\ Q\ believes\ X}{P\ believes\ X}$$

which expresses that if P believes that Q believes X and P trusts Q on X then P believes X as well. Immediately, we obtain $A\ believes\ \overset{K_b}{\mapsto} B$.

Thus, we have followed the process of obtaining a public key step by step. The derivation may have seemed particularly trivial, but in fact similar derivations, with the same rules, do account for many of the authentication protocols found in the literature.

2. The scope of the logic

The purpose of the logic is to describe the beliefs of principals in the course of authentication, and this purpose affects our choice of constructs and rules. For example, the logic has a notation for saying that K_b is a public key for B, but there is no rule for checking that K_b is long enough, as this sort of check does not typically happen in the course of authentication. Nor is there a way to show that a cryptosystem is secure and that it is used properly. (Moore **[12]** and Voydock and Kent **[21]** discuss inappropriate use of cryptosystems.)

Nevertheless, a few basic assumptions about encryption and how it is used underlie the rules of the logic, and they are worth keeping in mind.

- Each encrypted unit is integral; it cannot be altered or adapted by a principal not knowing the appropriate key(s), without the encrypted part being reduced to nonsense. For example, an encrypted message $\{S, T\}_K$ may not be fabricated from $\{S\}_K$, $\{T\}_K$, $\{S, U\}_K$, and $\{V, T\}_K$ except by decryption and re-encryption, with knowledge of K.
- An encrypted message is verifiable. That is, when a principal applies a decryption algorithm D to a ciphertext C using key K, it will be able to judge whether the result is or is not the plaintext used to generate C in the first place, and thus whether it has been decrypted using the "right" key. The decision will necessarily be based on prior knowledge, total or partial, of the expected plaintext.

  Gong, Needham, and Yahalom [7] have recently proposed a way of bringing verifiability within the scope of the logic. This may be useful, since it is not always obvious whether an author has overlooked the question of verifiability or has assumed it is handled at a lower level.
- A principal can recognize his own encrypted messages, and will not mistakenly attribute them to another principal. This is easily achieved through direction bits, for example. In the logic, we make $\{X\}_K$ an abbreviation for the longer expression $\{X\}_K$ *from* P; we use the "from" field in side conditions to some rules.

  The assumption is more important in the shared-key world than in the public-key world, because it is uncommon for a principal to encrypt with his own public key in authentication protocols.

The foregoing are assumed properties of encryption. Another issue concerns the purposes of encryption. Encryption may be used to preserve secrecy, to maintain the integrity of a compound message, or simply to demonstrate knowledge of a key by using it. Our logic does not capture these distinctions.

A great deal of what is interesting in an authentication protocol does not depend on the cryptosystem chosen, but rather on the structure of the message exchange. Many of the bugs in published authentication protocols do not come from a poor cryptosystem, but rather from mistakes in the higher-level design. Often the formal analysis of a protocol has suggested the existence of these high-level bugs, and how to construct attacks. In order to illustrate how some bugs manifest themselves in proofs, let us consider a few flawed variants of our example:

- B's name is omitted: If B's name is not mentioned in the encrypted message from S, there is nothing to tie B to this message, and there is a danger of misinterpreting a message about some other principal C (perhaps an adversary) as a message about B. Notice that it does not suffice to include B's name in clear next to the encrypted packet, as cleartext can be modified by adversaries. In our analysis, we would not be entitled to idealize S's message as we have, since we cannot argue that S believes that K_b is B's key when S sends $\{K_b, T\}_{K_s^{-1}}$.

- S is not an authority: If it is not assumed that A trusts S to provide B's public key, the formal analysis would proceed exactly as above, but the last step would be blocked, as the last rule of inference would not be applicable. Thus, under the weaker assumptions, the protocol yields only A *believes* S *believes* $\stackrel{K_b}{\mapsto} B$.
- A has no key for S: If A does not know that K_s is S's public key, the protocol is totally useless, as A cannot read the message, or cannot recognize it as coming from S. We obtain A *sees* $\{\stackrel{K_b}{\mapsto} B, T\}_{K_s^{-1}}$, but cannot proceed further.
- S's secret key can be discovered: For the protocol to work, it is essential that S's secret key remain secret. Otherwise, A has no reason to trust a message signed with S's secret key, and in fact the message could come from an attacker. If we add a step where S broadcasts his secret key, the formal analysis still goes through, and we obtain that A believes that K_b is B's public key. When we trace the origin of this ridiculous conclusion, we find that the protocol no longer justifies the assumption A *believes* $\stackrel{K_s}{\mapsto} S$. The bad assumption naturally leads to a vacuous proof. Once this assumption is removed, the analysis becomes correct again, though quite uninteresting.

  We make no formal attempt to detect incongruities between assumptions and messages. This might be possible, using existing tools to guard against release of secrets. (See [**3**, **6**, **10**, **11**, **13**], for example.)
- T is not fresh: If the message includes an old timestamp, A should not accept the message as fresh. Old messages can be replays, and could provide A with a compromised key for B [**4**]. In the formal analysis, the proof would be blocked at A *believes* S *said* $(\stackrel{K_b}{\mapsto} B, T)$.
- T is omitted: The danger is exactly the same as when T is not fresh. In the formal analysis, the idealized protocol would not include T, and the proof would finish with A *believes* S *said* $\stackrel{K_b}{\mapsto} B$.

If no bug becomes apparent, then the protocol is correct, in the sense that if all initial assumptions are justified then all conclusions are justified as well. More precisely, define knowledge as truth in all possible states (as in [**9**]); our notion of belief is a rudimentary approximation to knowledge, and it is simple to show that if all initial beliefs are knowledge then all final beliefs are knowledge and, in particular, they are true.

There is much room for improvement here. For example, we do not take into account complexity-theoretic assumptions or provide probabilistic guarantees. A strong semantics for the logic might remedy this, and at the same time it should provide a more compelling and robust notion of belief than those we have considered.

Finally, we should point out that knowledge and belief must not be confused, and that the usual semantics of knowledge is not adequate for the belief operator. As knowledge is often defined, principals can know only true facts. It follows that if P knows that Q knows X, then P knows X. In contrast, one of our rules says that if P believes that Q believes X, then P believes X, but only under an additional hypothesis: P must believe that Q has jurisdiction over X. The additional hypothesis expresses the trust that P puts in Q, and should not be suppressed. The delegations in a distributed system are often founded on subtle trust relations, which it is fruitful to make explicit.

References

1. M. Burrows, M. Abadi, and R. M. Needham, *A logic of authentication*, Proc. of the Royal Society of London A **426** (1989), 233–271. (A preliminary version appeared as Digital Equipment Corporation Systems Research Center Report No. 39, February 1989.)
2. CCITT, CCITT Blue Book, Recommendation X.509 and ISO 9594-8: The Directory-Authentication Framework, Geneva, March 1988.
3. R. A. DeMillo, N. A. Lynch, and M. J. Merritt, *Cryptographic protocols*, Proc. of the Fourteenth ACM Symposium on the Theory of Computing (1982), 383–400.
4. D. E. Denning and G. M. Sacco, *Timestamps in key distribution protocols*, CACM **24** (1981), 533–536.
5. D. Davis and R. Swick, *Workstation services and Kerberos authentication at Project Athena*, M.I.T. LCS Technical Memorandum **424**, February 1990.
6. D. Dolev and A. C. Yao, *On the security of public key protocols*, IEEE Trans. Inform. Theory **29** (1983), 198–208.
7. L. Gong, R. M. Needham, and R. Yahalom, *Reasoning about belief in cryptographic protocols*, manuscript, 1989.
8. C. A. R. Hoare, *An axiomatic basis for computer programming*, CACM **12** (1969), 576–580.
9. J. Y. Halpern and Y. O. Moses, *Knowledge and common knowledge in a distributed environment*, Proc. of the Third ACM Conference on the Principles of Distributed Computing, (1984), 480–490.
10. R. A. Kemmerer, *Analyzing encryption protocols using formal verification techniques*, IEEE Journal on Selected Areas in Communications **7** (1989), 448–457.
11. W. P. Lu and M. K. Sundareshan, *Secure communication in Internet environments: A hierarchical key management scheme for end-to-end encryption*, IEEE Trans. Comm. **37** (1989), 1014–1023.
12. J. H. Moore, *Protocol failures in cryptosystems*, Proc. IEEE **76** (1988), 594–602.
13. J. K. Millen, S. C. Clark, and S. B. Freedman, *The Interrogator: protocol security analysis*, IEEE Trans. Software Engrg. **13** (1987), 274–288.
14. S. P. Miller, C. Neuman, J. I. Schiller, and J. H. Saltzer, *Kerberos authentication and authorization system*, Project Athena Technical Plan, Section E.2.1, MIT, July 1987.
15. R. M. Needham and M. D. Schroeder, *Using encryption for authentication in large networks of computers*, CACM **21** (1978), 993–999.
16. R. M. Needham and M. D. Schroeder, *Authentication revisited*, Operating Systems Review **21** (1987), 7.
17. D. Otway and O. Rees, *Efficient and timely mutual authentication*, Operating Systems Review **21** (1987), 8–10.
18. Racal Research Ltd, private communication to R. M. Needham, 1989.
19. R. L. Rivest, A. Shamir, and L. Adleman, *A method for obtaining digital signatures and public-key cryptosystems*, Comm. ACM **21** (1978), 120–126.

20. M. Satyanarayanan, *Integrating security in a large distributed system*, ACM Trans. Computer Systems **15** (1989), 247–280.
21. V. L. Voydock and S. T. Kent, *Security mechanisms in high-level network protocols*, Comput. Surveys **15** (1983), 135–171.

Digital Equipment Corporation, Systems Research Center
E-mail address: burrows@src.dec.com

Digital Equipment Corporation, Systems Research Center

Computer Laboratory, University of Cambridge

DIMACS Series in Discrete Mathematics
and Theoretical Computer Science
Volume 2, 1991

Secure Policy Enforcement in Internetworks

DEBORAH ESTRIN AND GENE TSUDIK

ABSTRACT. In an environment of interconnected autonomous networks, network usage policies are expressed by each participant organization. In order to apply policy enforcement to internetwork packet traffic, controls must be added to internetwork protocols. Since neither traditional network access control methods nor current internetwork routing protocols are well suited for the enforcement of organizational network policies, a new generation of *policy-sensitive* protocols is currently under development. While these protocols are designed to enforce network policies, they raise new security-related concerns.

This paper discusses internetwork policy enforcement, identifies associated security issues and threats, and addresses the design and performance of policy enforcement protocols that support secure control of internetwork traffic.

1. Introduction

In recent years, interconnection of administratively autonomous networks has become commonplace. Using current internetworking protocols (e.g., IP [**8**]), a collection of interconnected autonomous networks forms a single internetwork where information can flow transparently across autonomous network boundaries. Despite the interconnection, organizations would like to maintain their autonomy by independently expressing and enforcing network usage policies. In order to do so, internetwork routing decisions must be made according to policy-related parameters such as access rights and cost, in addition to the traditional parameters of connectivity and delay ([**7**, **5**]).

Network access control methods that restrict the information flow between end-systems on individual networks have been demonstrated ([**13**, **21**, **25**]).

1980 *Mathematics Subject Classification* (1985 *Revision*). Primary 68M10, 68M20, 94A60.

This research was supported in part by the National Science Foundation Presidential Young Investigator award and matching funds from ATT, GTE, and NCR.

This paper was presented at the DIMACS Workshop on Connections between Distributed Computing and Cryptography, October 1989, Princeton, NJ.

1052-1798/91 $1.00 + $.25 per page

Moreover, end-systems employ a range of operating-system and application-level mechanisms that restrict access to data and resources. However, controlling access to transit network resources such as gateways and links requires additional protocol support because of the need to coordinate routing decisions among all intervening networks. As a result, organizations cannot simply enforce policy restrictions on a unilateral basis at packet-forwarding time. Instead, policies pertaining to network resources must either be implicit in the topology of an internetwork, or advertised to the anticipated resource users. Only then can entities throughout the internetwork determine the logical, *policy-based* connectivity of the internetwork and synthesize valid routes.

This paper addresses the design of *secure* protocols for controlling transit traffic on an internetwork. This topic is fundamentally of interest to the security community because it concerns issues of resource control and accounting. Moreover, transit control protocols can be designed with varying levels of security. In some environments, relatively vulnerable protocols may be used in conjunction with *post facto* detection mechanisms. Most of the work in policy-based protocol development is being conducted with such environments in mind ([**7**, **5**, **19**, **6**]). This paper addresses environments where *post facto* detection is not adequate or possible in a timely manner. In particular, we address the costs and implications (i.e., performance and manageability) of incorporating more defensive, *preventative* security measures into the protocols for controlling internetwork traffic.[1]

This paper is organized as follows. As further introduction, Section 2 discusses the interconnection of autonomous networks. Section 3 begins by considering the extension of network access control methods to control transit internetwork traffic. In response to some fundamental deficiencies, the remainder of Section 3 describes the role of the so-called Policy Routing protocols in providing transit control. Next, Section 4 outlines the security concerns particular to the Policy Routing protocols. The discussion of security is continued in the remaining sections on secure protocol design (Section 5) and cost assessment (Section 6). Section 7 summarizes our discussion and proposes areas for future work.

2. Interconnection of autonomous networks

In order to provide appropriate background for the subsequent discussion, this section defines our terminology and assumptions regarding internetwork environments, policies, and protocol design principles.

2.1. Administrative domains. An internetwork is composed of a number of Administrative Domains, or ADs. An AD is defined as a collection of network resources under control of a single administrative entity [**14**]. It is important to distinguish between two dominant types of ADs: *stub* and

[1] Portions of this paper first appeared in [**12**].

transit. *Stub* ADs are interested mainly in communication with other stub ADs, i.e., providing communication for their constituent end-systems. A campus network is an example of a stub AD. *Transit* ADs are involved in providing transit service for traffic between stub ADs. NSFNET is an example of a transit AD [**14**]. Finally, there are also hybrid ADs that combine transit service with end-point communication (e.g., UC Berkeley).

One of our central goals is not to place restrictions on allowed internet scale and topology. Any inter-AD routing protocol should have the potential of supporting very large scale internetworking. We anticipate on the order of 10^5 ADs.[2] In an internet of such enormous size it would be unwise to design a protocol that relied on topological restrictions; enforcement would be nearly impossible. Consequently, one of our design goals is to allow for maximum degree of flexibility in regard to the configuration of the internetwork. The protocols discussed below do not place restrictions on the internetwork topology at the granularity of ADs.

2.2. Policies. As frequently happens with a new concept, an analogy can lead to better understanding of the problem at hand. One interesting analogy is to view ADs as sovereign countries, each with a specific set of foreign policy statements regarding interaction with foreign entities (other ADs). For example, a country may have policies restricting foreign visitors to specific areas or restricting travel privileges of the local populace when visiting foreign countries. Countries may also have specific policies pertaining to transit travelers, e.g., restricting entry on the basis of the traveler's itinerary. Security policies regarding international travel can express policy as to passport and visa requirements, length of stay, etc. Accounting or billing policies may concern, for example, visa fees or departure taxes.

ADs can express similar policies regarding communication with external entities, e.g., restrict internal systems available for external access or restrict external systems available for internal access. Transit traffic may or may not be allowed at all, or it may be restricted to specific source and/or destination ADs or hosts. Policies can also embody security requirements, e.g., authentication and authorization for inter-AD traffic as well as accounting and billing conditions.

2.2.1. *Stub and transit policies.* Due largely to the nature of service provided, stub and transit ADs tend to express different policies. Policies expressed by stub ADs, for the most part, serve to protect internal resources from external access, while those expressed by transit ADs are often cost-related. Another way of making this distinction is to observe that transit ADs, by virtue of providing transit service, are inherently more *open* than their stub counterparts. Furthermore, subversion of transit ADs' policies

[2]Although the majority will be stub ADs, our model assumes a large number of transit and hybrid ADs as well.

will, in the worst case, result in denial of service, whereas subversion of stub network policies can potentially disrupt the end-systems themselves. Another reason for separating the respective policies is the difference in accounting and billing requirements. Stub ADs are more likely to bundle communication costs into billing for end services, if any such billing occurs. Transit ADs are more likely to charge for the communication itself. We refer to policies that pertain to end-system traffic as *stub* policies, and, to those that pertain to transit traffic as *transit* policies.

In some respects, the requirements for transit policy enforcement are simpler than those for stub policy enforcement. However, several factors complicate the implementation of the latter. First, in an internetwork, a packet may travel through a number of transit ADs on its way to the destination. Consequently, applicable policies from all transit ADs must be considered when a packet is being sent; whereas for stub control, only the policies of the two end-point ADs have to be taken into account. In addition, transit control has to be reconciled with topology changes (gateways or links going down). If in the middle of a connection any component of the route becomes disabled, entirely different policies may come into effect. Also, when a transit AD decides to account and/or bill for resource usage, coordination is required to pass charges back to the end points. These factors add to the complexity of potential enforcement mechanisms. Based in part on the difference in policies, and in part on the functionality required in any routing (i.e., transit) mechanism, transit and stub AD *mechanisms* also differ. By analogy with international travel, in most countries transit travelers are set apart from other visitors. They are issued special *transit* visas and are restricted in movement and length of stay. We discuss this further in later sections.

2.2.2. *Policy attributes.* Policies can be based upon a number of attributes:

- **Endpoint**
  Policies can place restrictions on the source and/or destination of traffic. The policy may apply to an entire AD or it may apply to some particular network, host, or class of users in an AD. The travel analogy is refusing entry to citizens of a particular country, or to convicted felons of a particular country.
- **Path**
  Policies can place restrictions on other components of the path in addition to source and destination. For example, an AD may have a policy not to send traffic through a particular AD even if it is not destined for that AD. This is similar to a country disallowing transit through another country even if the traveler does not remain in the forbidden country. Another example of path control is if a destination or transit AD refuses to accept traffic that passed through a particular AD earlierin the path. In the case of international travel this

is enforced by refusing entry to persons who have passports stamped by forbidden countries.[3]

- **Security**
  This attribute can express requirements for authentication, data integrity, temporal integrity, and privacy. For example, a policy requiring all network layer headers to be signed is analogous to the requirement to carry a passport at all times.
- **Application Protocols**
  Higher-level applications (protocols) may also be restricted. For example, an AD can limit all incoming traffic to electronic mail. This is similar to permitting only business-related travel.
- **Temporal Parameters**
  This includes restrictions on usage based on time of day, day of the week, or other time-related parameters. This is analogous to allowing travel, for example, only in the summer months.
- **Accounting/Billing Conditions**
  Policies can be used to express conditions related to charging and accounting. In particular, how charges are accrued (e.g., per packet, per connection, or per Kbyte), what kind of charging is acceptable (i.e., collect, source, or neighboring AD), who must keep accounting records, etc. Similarly, tourists are charged visa fees, departure fees, and road usage dues.

A typical policy statement can be based upon several policy attributes. For example, the policy statement

transit voice traffic from AD_a *is accepted between 2 and 6 A.M. with a per-packet charge*

applies to transit traffic and combines application protocol, temporal, and accounting/billing attributes. Further examples of policy types can be found in **[14]**.

2.3. Design goals. The key design goals for the secure control of internetwork traffic are (i) security, i.e., resistance to identified threats, and (ii) performance, i.e., ability to maintain acceptable delays and throughput.

Security and performance requirements are almost always at odds. Consequently, one of our design goals is to develop flexible protocols that allow individual participating ADs to select their ownsecurity-performance trade-

[3]This particular example turns out to be very difficult (i.e., costly) to enforce reliably. By analogy with international travel, enforcing path restriction policies based on the previous stamps on a person's passport is very unreliable since the person can always ask the forbidden country not to stamp the passport. Since there is little trust between the countries in this scenario, it is difficult to control or predict what the forbidden country may do.

offs. In other words, one AD should be able to compromise throughput in order to obtain more security against identified threats, while a second AD may choose to accept additional vulnerability in order to achieve improved throughput. Furthermore, the more security-conscious AD should be able to choose the extent to which it relies on the less secure AD.

Similarly, we would like our protocol to allow some flexibility in addressing other trade-offs. In particular, some designs are more suited to stub network access controls and others to transit controls. Likewise, some designs are more suited to connection-oriented protocols and others to connectionless protocols. A final requirement is that the family of protocols and mechanisms be manageable. This requirement will hold in check our attempts at flexibility by avoiding excessively complex protocols. Manageability also impacts our assumptions about feasible key distribution and management.

3. Controlling transit internetwork traffic

There are two basic approaches to transit control. In the first part of this section, we discuss an approach based on network access control mechanisms and identify its limitations. Next, we discuss three approaches to policy-based routing.

3.1. Extending network access controls. One potential method of enforcing transit policy enforcement is to extend existing stub network access control mechanisms to the generalized internetwork model. In this section, we discuss an extension of visa protocols **[13]** that incorporates support for transit policy enforcement. Other network access control schemes are discussed briefly at the end of this section.

Visa protocols were originally developed to provide datagram-level control at AD boundaries. Conceptually, a secret key is used by the communicating host to compute an unforgeable stamp. This stamp is placed in the datagram's header to assure the border-gateway that the transmission of this datagram across AD boundaries is authorized. The stamp is called a *visa*, by analogy with the stamp on a passport that allows a tourist to cross international borders. A unique visa is bound to each datagram in order to guarantee the authenticity and the integrity of the data.

A host on a visa-controlled network that wants to communicate across the AD boundary is initially required to engage in a high-level authorization/authentication dialogue with an Access Control Server (ACS) on both local and destination ADs. The need for and particulars of this dialogue are determined independently by the administration of each AD involved. When and if the communication is approved, the respective ACSs issue *visa-keys* to the requesting host. The host proceeds to use these keys to generate stamps, which it places on each outbound datagram. Thus, each datagram carries two stamps: one which allows it to exit the local AD, and, the other, which allows it to enter the destination AD. Border gateways of end-point ADs proceed to verify the validity of their respective visas and pass datagrams until a visa expires or is otherwise revoked. If the communication is two-way, visa-keys are issued to the destination host as well, and the authorization procedure is symmetric. For further details of the visa protocol see [**13**].

The process of establishing authorization in visa-controlled, transit ADs is essentially the same as for stub ADs in the visa protocol. The major difference is that the source host must obtain a transit visa for each transit AD that requires one, in addition to obtaining a usual pair of exit/entry visas from AD_{src} and AD_{dst}. In the worst case, each transit AD's ACS will conduct an authorization and authentication procedure before issuing a transit visa, and each packet will have to carry a separate visa for each intervening AD. Of course, transit ADs may choose to issue visas automatically, or not require any visas at all where transit traffic is concerned. Furthermore, ADs could program their ACSs to obtain and issue transit visa-keys in advance of the actual communication. This would reduce the setup delay at connection-establishment time. On the other hand, such mechanisms increase the problems associated with visas expiring before, or while, they are in use.[4]

The use of visa for transit control may be appropriate if (i) transit policies are as diverse as stub network policies, and (ii) policies change frequently. The former limits the practicality of expressing policies in a simple universal syntax. The second assumption also makes it impractical to distribute policies in the way that we distribute connectivity information, for the fear of using stale route information or incurring excessive overhead due to frequent information updates. These assumptions result in several interesting features of transit visa. First, organizational policies are embodied in ACSs and are not propagated outside; hence, a wide range of policy statements can be accommodated. Moreover, very little coordination among ADs (beyond that in visa protocols for stub networks) is required to implement this protocol.

Although the extension of the visa concept to transit control is rather straightforward, the approach does not scale well to an internetwork where many ADs, both stub and transit, want to control traffic flows. For example, visa acquisition and route setup must be repeated (or adapted) each time an involved visa-gateway goes down. Moreover, a source AD has no way of determining if it will be issued a visa without incurring the overhead of contacting the particular ACS in question. *The essence of the problem is that transit control is related to packet routing. Therefore, controls for transit should be incorporated into the route calculation itself, not only into the packet-forwarding function.*

[4]More aggressive policies could also be implemented such as applying for group visas in advance of use to accommodate a collection of hosts that have a need for communication. However, these may imply significantly more trust among the ADs and require more careful consideration.

Other network access control schemes such as SDNS [**30**] and gateway-packet filters [**21**] face the same limitation when it comes to controlling transit traffic; i.e., these schemes enforce controls on packet forwarding and do not include any route-synthesis functions.[5]

In summary, visa protocols and other network-access control mechanisms are best suited for stub network control. Transit-network control for large internetworks is more efficiently achieved by integrating policy considerations into the route-synthesis process. After discussing policy-routing approaches in the next section we return to the problem of secure control of transit internetwork traffic.

3.2. Policy-based routing. As discussed earlier, the central goal of transit traffic control is to allow ADs to independently express and enforce policies regarding transit traffic. Our discussion in the previous section demonstrates that transit control is intimately related to Inter-Administrative Domain routing. There are currently three different approaches to policy-based routing:

- Border Gateway Protocol (BGP)[**6**] is implemented in parts of the Research Internet and is intended to support a limited notion of policy.
- European Computer Manufacturers' Association (ECMA)[**19**] Inter-Domain Intermediate Systems Routing proposal addresses primarily the issues associated with route synthesis.
- RFC 1102 Policy Routing proposal [**7**] describes an entire Policy Routing architecture for the Research Internet.

Of the above, the RFC 1102 proposal is the most general and flexible, and yet, it provides the finest-grained control over the internetwork traffic and resources. This is not to imply that the other two are without merit; a thorough discussion of all three methods appears in [**1**]. In the remainder of this paper we use the RFC 1102 as the springboard for our discussion of security issues in policy-based routing. The key features of RFC 1102 are described in the next section.

3.2.1. *RFC 1102 policy routing proposal.* RFC 1102 Policy Routing proposal allows stub and transit ADs to express and exchange packet-routing and forwarding policies [**7**]. The most distinguishing feature of this approach is the use of AD-level source routing. It uses a Link State algorithm [**29**] to compute source Policy Routes (PRs). Each AD expresses its policies in a *standard* form, so-called Policy Terms (PTs), and distributes them to other ADs. Each AD designates special Policy Servers (PSs) to collect PTs and synthesize policy routes for constituent users. The base assumptions of this

---

[5]SDNS's access control policy, in particular, is endpoint-oriented. It is concerned mainly with determining whether or not two peers may communicate and what type of information they may exchange.

model are:

(i) most policies can be classified and expressed in a standard notation;
(ii) policies change relatively slowly;
(iii) current routing protocols that were not designed with explicit support for policy enforcement are not sufficient.

The two major components in this proposal are *Policy Routes (PRs)* and *Policy Terms (PTs)*. A PR is a series of ADs. It can be viewed as an AD-level source-route. In other words, there may be multiple physical realizations of a PR given multiple physical connections between ADs and multiple intra-AD routes. The actual selection of a particular physical path is done at packet-forwarding time by each intervening AD, rather than by the source AD at route-synthesis or route-selection time. This *lazy evaluation* provides for a more adaptive protocol and unrestricted AD interconnection. Policy Terms (PTs) are the units of routing information exchanged by communicating ADs. Each PT represents a distinct policy of the AD that synthesized it. The format of a PT is:

$$[(H_{src}, AD_{src}, AD_{ent}), (H_{dst}, AD_{dst}, AD_{exit}), \text{UCI}, \text{Conditions}].$$

The purpose of a PT is to specify that packets from some host, H_{src}, (or a group of hosts) in a source AD, AD_{src}, are allowed to enter the AD in question via some directly connected AD, AD_{ent}, and exit through another directly connected AD, AD_{exit}, on its way to a host, H_{dst}, (or a group of hosts) in some destination AD, AD_{dst}. User Class Identifier (UCI) allows for distinguishing between various user classes, e.g., Government, Research, Commercial, Contract. Conditions represent billing and other variables and can reflect the agreements between neighboring ADs.

Policies are expressed by source, destination, and all intervening ADs. The source AD may select all transit ADs while transit and destination ADs control only which source and destination ADs can communicate via which directly connected ADs. In other words, transit and destination ADs do not exert control over the entire PR. ADs run routing algorithms (similar to link-state algorithms) to maintain their respective tables of PRs. There may be multiple PRs listed for a single destination, each with a different set of conditions associated with its use.

Each AD has one or more Policy Server (PS), an entity that collects Policy Routing information from other ADs, distributes local policy information to other ADs, and synthesizes, as well as issues, PRs to local hosts. Actual policy enforcement is done at a Policy Gateway (PG), which, in addition to the usual task of forwarding packets, handles validation and verification of the PRs attached to the incoming packets.

A connection or a stream begins with the first packet carrying the full PR containing a sequence of ADs in the route and applicable PT identifiers. Policy Gateways along the way make sure that the PR agrees with the local PTs (through use of templates, for example). The result is cached so that a specified handle can be used in the future to refer to the cached entry. A PR handle is treated much like a virtual circuit number. Successive packets carry a PR handle to a cache entry, not a full PR. Policy Gateways use these handles in the packets to check for cache entries. Policy Gateways also may relate return-flow packets with forward flow. This aspect of Policy Routing makes use of what is referred to as *soft state* in Policy Gateways. Given information about the next AD for a particular packet, each Policy Gateway selects the next PG based on information exchanged in a traditional up-down protocol.

3.3. Discussion. One essential difference between visa and the PR-based approaches is the per-session setup overhead. Transit visa requires that a dialogue transpire between the source and each transit-visa networks' ACS, and that corresponding keys be distributed. Consequently, the initial setup delay grows in proportion to the number of transit networks. For short transactions such overhead is not acceptable. A PR-based approach such as that in RFC 1102 avoids this setup dialogue through background distribution of policy term information that is used in route synthesis. The work that the Policy Routing protocols do to distribute policy terms and synthesize authorized routes must be done at the time of the session setup in visa. In particular, with visa protocol this translates into a reject packet, ACS dialogue, and visa-key grant message for each AD in the path. Moreover, this assumes that the source attempts communication over a path for which it has authorization. If there is a conflict with even one transit AD's policy, the process must begin again. Policy Routing incorporates policy into the route-computation process in advance of the actual communication, thereby avoiding this problem.

On the other hand, the PR schemes, as described, rely on after-the-fact detection of abuse, and are, in that sense, less secure than the network-access control schemes discussed, e.g., visa protocols. The remainder of this paper addresses the integration of preventative mechanisms into policy routing to achieve secure control of transit traffic.

4. Security issues in policy routing

In this section we identify potential security threats faced by the three PR schemes described above. In the subsequent section we design a secure version of one of the three schemes described.

The two basic threats to the security of PR protocols are falsification of routing information and falsification of data packets.

(i) An intruder may distribute false routing information in order to (i) disrupt communication, e.g., create routing loops, or (ii) eavesdrop on communication, e.g., reroute traffic to a specific location. In BGP and ECMA this can take the form of distributing falsified or prerecorded routing updates. In RFC 1102, falsified Policy Terms can be similarly distributed causing invalid PRs to be synthesized.

(ii) If routing protocols protect themselves by prescribing some kind of authentication mechanism for validating routing information, an intruder can turn to falsifying data packets. This kind of attack can lead to unauthorized resource usage, unauthorized communication, and inappropriate accrual of charges. Three subthreats are identified:

(a) Falsification of control information
In addition to the usual network-layer information (source and destination addresses, data size, etc.), control information includes the route-setup and packet-forwarding parameters. In ECMA, the direction tag can be modified and data packets can be made to loop or violate the two-phase rule. In RFC 1102, an intruder can steal a PR header created by an authorized PS and substitute an invalid Charge Code.

(b) Falsification of data segments
In all three protocols, the data portion of a packet can be modified or replaced by an intruder.

(c) Replay
Previously-recorded legitimate packets can be replayed by an intruder. Two sources of replay are of equal concern: accidental replay due to the *stuttering* of a misbehaving machine, and malicious replay due to a misbehaving person attempting a denial of service attack.

In the remainder of this paper we describe and analyze mechanisms to resist these threats. As mentioned before, the RFC 1102 PR proposal provides the finest-grained control through the use of AD-level source routes. At the same time, this greater control provides a wider range of opportunities for an intruder. Our approach is not inconsistent with the original proposal in RFC 1102, although we use *prevention-*, as opposed to detection-based, measures to combat the above security threats.

5. Secure policy routing

In this section we detail the steps needed in a secure PR protocol and discuss issues dealing with data integrity checking and replay prevention.

5.1. Terminology. The following terminology is used throughout the remainder of the paper:

- $||$ is the concatenation operator, e.g., $X||Y$.
- N denotes the length of a PR, i.e., the number of ADs in a PR.
- AD_i $(0 < i < N)$ denotes the ith AD in a PR ($AD_1 = AD_{\mathrm{src}}$ and $AD_N = AD_{\mathrm{dst}}$).
- K_i^j denotes a secret key shared by AD_i and AD_j.
- K_{dsig} denotes a secret key used for computing data signatures.

- EK_i, DK_i denote public (encryption) and private (decryption) keys of AD_i.
- $E(Data)^K$ and $D(Data)^K$ denote encryption and decryption, respectively, of $Data$ with key K.
- $F_{\text{char}}(Data)$ is a characteristic function of $Data$, e.g., DES-based MAC.

In the next three sections we consider separately security issues pertaining to different phases of Policy Routing: distribution of PTs, PR setup, and packet forwarding. The secure PR protocol is described in Section 5.7, and the remainder of Section 5 deals with data integrity and replay prevention.

5.2. Distribution of policy terms. In order to provide for secure distribution of Policy Term updates, each AD must be able to sign its own, and authenticate incoming PTs. Because of the Link State nature of the protocol, PT updates must be flooded to ADs throughout the internetwork so that all participant ADs can use them in their PR synthesis. Before using a new PT, each AD needs to authenticate its contents. This is difficult to achieve in a Secret Key environment, as the number of potential recipients of a PT update is quite large. In general, Secret Key encryption is not well suited for an environment such as Link State routing where routing updates are broadcasted to a large number of recipients.

One obvious alternative is to use Public Key encryption for the distribution of PTs. At first glance, this is problematic because current Public Key technology is still inferior in terms of performance. Nonetheless, one of the central assumptions in the RFC 1102 proposal is that policies change relatively slowly. Therefore, since PTs are distributed infrequently (e.g., once a day) and data sizes involved are relatively small, the added complexity of Public Key encryption is counter-balanced by the ubiquity and efficiency of being able to generate a single unforgeable packet signature that can be authenticated by any recipient.[6] An example of a Link State routing protocol that uses Public Key encryption for routing update distribution is presented in [**27**].

Although the distribution of PTs raises a number of interesting issues, the underlying concept of broadcasting signed messages is not unique to Policy Routing.[7] Other aspects of secure Policy Routing, such as PR setup and packet forwarding, require more careful protocol design because of the associated costs and threats.

[6] It is also possible to speed up the Public Key encryption somewhat. One such method is specified in CCITT X.509 document [**34**]. It uses the RSA [**35**] encryption method in a manner such that message decryption (verification) is significantly faster than encryption.

[7] The exception is that routing updates are infrequent, thus favoring the use of Public Key encryption.

5.3. Route setup. The route setup phase requires that each intervening AD have means to forward subsequent data packets along a specific Policy Route. As described in Section 3.2.1, each AD along the route must be supplied with the next hop AD at PR setup time. The purpose of PR setup is to establish state in all intervening ADs so that Policy Routing decisions can be made in advance of the actual communication, and subsequent data packets can carry a minimum of PR-related information, thus reducing the overhead and latency. In addition, in a secure PR scheme, each AD must be able to authenticate and authorize a PR. Authentication means verifying that a PR was issued by a recognized entity, and was not tampered with. Authorization entails making sure that a PR conforms to local policy. (The latter is beyond the scope of this paper.)

More specifically, Secure PR setup needs to address two types of threats:

> **Type 1.** *Creating, or tampering with existing, PRs by an intruder.* In order to defend against this threat, each PR must be traceable to the issuing AD. In other words, it must be signed with an unforgeable signature, so that all intervening ADs can verify the PR's authenticity.
> **Type 2.** *Replay of previously issued (and signed) PR setup packets.* This can be prevented if we include a unique identifier within each PR. This would make PR signatures dependent on this identifier, and, provided that ADs keep track of these identifiers, would make replay detection possible.

Unlike PT updates, PRs are set up frequently, which makes the Public Key encryption less practical. However, Secret Key encryption implies a significant key management burden, since an AD has to share a secret key with every other AD that it ever communicates with. Moreover, it entails computing a PR signature for every AD involved, whereas a single PR signature verifiable by all intervening ADs is sufficient in Public Key encryption. On the other hand, a typical PR traverses a relatively small number of ADs (N is much less than the diameter of the internetwork). This makes Secret Key encryption a viable choice since a PR would only have to be signed N times. Nevertheless, while it may be cheaper to compute a number of Secret Key signatures than one Public Key signature, the latter certainly utilizes band width more efficiently. Furthermore, because PRs are frequently precomputed, it is possible to reduce the overhead by pre-encrypting partial PR signatures as well.

The above discussion is a standard Public Key *versus* Secret Key debate. Both methods have beneficial as well as burdensome features. We begin with a setup protocol based upon Secret Key encryption; the changes necessary for a Public Key-based variation are outlined in Section 5.7.2.

5.4. Packet forwarding. After a PR has been set up, subsequent data packets can take advantage of the PR state in intermediate ADs. Instead of carrying a full PR in each data packet, only an abbreviated version is needed. This abbreviated PR is referred to as the *PR header.* It must contain the information necessary to identify the appropriate state in intervening ADs. Its exact contents are described in the next section.

Assuming appropriate security measures to prevent PR setup threats above, there remain means of malicious attack at packet-forwarding time:

> **Type 3.** *An intruder located at some point along a PR can copy a valid PR header from a legitimate packet, attach its own data, and send it along a PR, thus obtaining service.*
> This attack can be remedied if each data packet (or some portion thereof) is signed by the source. The overhead incurred by signing each data packet in its entirety can be prohibitively high. A less expensive solution is to sign only those network layer (e.g., IP) header fields that do not change on a per packet basis. An intruder can still tamper with packets' data segment; however, it will not be able to alter addressing information. For some environments, this may be an acceptable risk. Other data signature scenarios varying in cost and complexity are discussed in Section 5.5.
> **Type 4.** *Finally, an intruder can replay previously recorded data packets, which can potentially lead to unjustified charging and/or denial of service.*[8]
> Replay of data packets can be avoided by using packet identifiers, similar to PR setup replay prevention above. Prevention of this type of replay attack is addressed in Section 5.6.[9]

5.5. Variations on data integrity checking. A critical dimension of secure PR protocol design is the nature of data integrity checking. In conjunction with the protocol to follow, several variations are possible. The performance and cost of each variation is discussed in Section 6.

5.5.1. *Full transit.* In network environments where data integrity and security concerns outweigh the overhead of extra processing, the data portion of every packet is subject to forgery and must be authenticated at each hop on its way to the destination, i.e., the data packet is signed. The protocol for this class of environment has the highest overhead, commensurate with security requirements. Note that the per-packet processing in this scheme is similar to transit visa.[10]

---

[8]There are other, more serious threats posed by malicious replay. However, we are concerned primarily with protecting network layer resources; other replay attacks are assumed to be handled by the end-points.

[9]Note that we only need to protect against replayed packets within the life span of the associated PR.

[10]However, the Full Transit approach avoids the per-session setup dialogue associated with visa.

5.5.2. *Endpoint.* If authenticating data in each packet at every hop is prohibitively expensive, end-to-end data integrity similar to that in endpoint *visa* protocols may be appropriate. This approach has limitations, most notably the fact that an intruder located at some point along the route can modify data in each packet, and the forgery will not be detected until the packet reaches the destination, AD. This can result in inappropriate billing of the source. On the other hand, this approach benefits from lower per-packet overhead, which is independent of the PR's length. Basically, this approach provides preventative control for stub ADs, but only detection-based control for transit ADs.

5.5.3. *Designated transit.* If Endpoint provides less than adequate security, yet Full Transit is too expensive, the source AD can designate a specific transit AD to perform data integrity checks. The positioning of the designated AD in the PR is important: having it too close to AD_{src} is almost equivalent to no checking at all, whereas having it too close to AD_{dst} is equivalent to the Endpoint variant. The designated AD can be reassigned from time to time in order to reduce the chance of its exploitation by an intruder. However, this variant provides relatively light protection.

5.5.4. *Patterned.* Instead of each transit AD having to authenticate each packet, it may suffice to authenticate every mth packet. In the simplest version of this patterned authentication scheme, AD_{src} would choose m at random from a locally defined range of values and then specify m during route setup. Transit ADs would either accept or reject the proposed m. If all ADs accept the proposed value for m, then every AD will check data integrity of every mth packet. If any AD does not accept m (if it is considered too large or too small) then the source and all other ADs must choose a different m. In return for reduced overhead, if the value for m is discovered by an intruder then $(m-1)/m$ of the PR's band width can be abused. Moreover, the synchronization inherent to this protocol implies that care must be taken to recover from lost and out-of-order packets. Similar to Designated Transit, this method provides a lighter form of protection.

Alternatively, instead of the source choosing m (as in Patterned variation above), transit AD_is can choose their own m_is and may elect not to disclose them. In yet another variation, transit AD_is can choose to authenticate each packet with probability p_i. This method has the advantage of being flexible and robust in that synchronization becomes a nonissue.

5.5.5. *Round robin.* This scheme achieves constant per-packet overhead by using *round-robin* data authentication. Transit ADs take turns authenticating packets. In general, packet number K is authenticated by a PG in $AD_{[K \bmod M]}$ where M is the number of ADs in the PR. The overhead is reduced to just two encryptions per packet (regardless of the route). End-to-end checking can be added for extra assurance at the cost of a single additional decryption by the destination. Moreover, unlike Source Patterned variant, lost and out-of-order packets can be accommodated easily. On the other hand, AD independence must be sacrificed due to the coordination required to set up the round-robin arrangement. While this approach benefits from fair sharing of encryption costs among transit ADs, it is only worth considering in cases when the number of transit ADs is large, i.e., the PR is long.

5.5.6. *Coverage of data signatures.* It is possible to use any of the above variations without signing entire data packets. For example, it may suffice to compute signatures over network layer packet headers, or, say, first K bytes in each packet to reduce to size of the channel usable by an intruder.

5.6. Preventing replay. Replay of data packets (**Type 4** attack) is of concern because it can lead to unjustified charges and denial of service. Two sources of replay deserve equal consideration. The first is accidental replay due to a misbehaving machine stuttering and generating replayed packets. The second is malicious replay due to an intruder intentionally replaying prerecorded packets in order to deny resources (or inflate costs) to the rightful owner. Neither kind of replay should be handled on a strictly end-to-end basis because by the time the duplicate packet is discovered, the resources are consumed and associated charges are incurred; e.g., the bill reflects the replayed packets, and the rightful user of the afflicted charge code can no longer obtain service due to an overdrawn account.

In some circumstances, the *post facto* approach of replay detection and cost recovery may be adequate. This includes auditing packet counts, setting a limit on the number of packets that can use a PR and other *ad hoc* methods. However, in sensitive environments, more aggressive prevention is required, albeit at significant cost. Since this paper is analyzing the implications of PR in sensitive environments, we discuss the design of a protocol for preventing replay.

Replay of data packets can result in inappropriate charges and denial of service. Data packets, due to their density, cannot be easily accommodated by *coarse* identifiers, e.g., timestamps. Therefore, a nonce identifier must be present in each packet [3]. A secret sequence number is an example of a nonce. Consider the following protocol steps:

(i) When a PR is issued, AD_{src} generates a random number. This number, hereafter referred to as a *seed*, will serve as the initial sequence number for the PR.

(ii) The seed is then distributed in a secure fashion (as a part of the encrypted PR) to all intervening PGs in transit ADs. If the seed is not available to a potential intruder, chosen plaintext attacks can be avoided.

(iii) When the source has a packet to send, it modifies the seed and includes it in the (encrypted) PR header in each packet.

(iv) When the packet reaches a policy gateway, the PR header is decrypted and the sequence number found in it is compared to the expected sequence number found in the gateway's cache. Three outcomes are possible:
   (a) Sequence numbers match. The packet is forwarded, and the expected sequence number is incremented.
   (b) The sequence number is greater than expected. The difference between the two numbers must be examined. If the difference is small, i.e., less than some (locally defined) threshold, T_i, the packet can be forwarded. Otherwise the gateway may suspect foul play and request an update of the sequence number from the issuing AD.
   (c) The sequence number is less than the threshold T_i. The packet is dropped.

   Case (c) is quite *unforgiving* if T_i is small. However, mechanisms to support out-of-order packets are complicated and costly. If out-of-order arrivals are to be supported, the mechanism of choice would be a sliding-window scheme. The biggest problem is selecting an optimal window size that is acceptable to all intervening ADs. In this situation, robustness of end-to-end connectivity across ADs is traded off for security and performance of individual ADs.

An intruder's chances for subverting the protocol are further reduced if, in addition, packet data integrity is verified at each intervening AD in the PR.

An important drawback in the above protocol is the fundamental difficulty in synchronizing sequence numbers when there are multiple Policy Gateways providing redundant connectivity between a pair of neighboring ADs. However, it is up to the individual ADs whether or not to implement this protocol. In other words, in environments where such redundant connectivity exists, replay prevention may be too cumbersome, whereas ADs with single entry points (for a given PR) can implement it.

5.7. Protocol description. We can now combine the PR setup and packet-forwarding mechanisms into a common protocol. For the purpose of the following protocol description, a PR is composed of:

$$(1)\quad [AD_1, JUSTIFY_1, CU_1], [AD_2, JUSTIFY_2, CU_2], \ldots, [AD_N, JUSTIFY_N, CU_N]$$

where $JUSTIFY_i$ is the information that AD_i can use to validate a PR (e.g., a list of applicable Policy Terms), and CU_i reflects the conditions of usage, such as UCIs and/or Charge Codes. Typically, a PR will contain no secret information; thus, it can travel in the clear.

Note that a PR contains no additional information regarding individual host pairs. This is because all PRs are initially validated on a $[AD_{src}, AD_{dst}]$

basis. If a transit AD's policy terms are host-specific, that AD needs to verify host addresses at the time of packet forwarding.

5.7.1. *Secret Key version.* The Secret Key-based version of the secure PR setup protocol is as follows: We assume out-of-band distribution of K_i^j.

(i) Upon issuing a PR, AD_{src} generates a new key, K_{dsig}. This key is to be used subsequently for computing packet data signatures. Next, AD_{src} computes N PR signatures (one for each AD_i):

$$(2) \qquad SIG_i = F_{char}(E[PR||K_{dsig}||SEQ_i^{src}]^{K_i^{src}})$$

where SEQ_i^{src} is a unique identifier, such as a monotonically increasing sequence number with a large period, which is used to number PRs. This sequence number must be maintained on a per AD-pair basis. This requirement is reasonable because of the previous assumption that secret keys are maintained on the same basis.

The goal of secure PR setup is to deliver in a secure fashion to each AD_i the following: PR, SEQ_i^{src}, and K_{dsig}. The PR signatures provide defense against **Type 1** attacks, while SEQ_i^{src}s provide defense against **Type 2** attacks. As mentioned before, PR can travel in the clear since it is protected by SIG_i. The same is true for SEQ_i^{src}. K_{dsig}, on the other hand, is secret and, thus, has to be encrypted individually for each AD_i. The resulting PR setup packet is depicted in Figure 1(a).

(ii) Next, the PR setup packet is sent along the route. Each participating AD_i obtains K_{dsig} by decrypting $E(K_{dsig})^{K_i^{src}}$, recomputes and verifies SIG_i and SEQ_i^{src}, and then authorizes the PR by checking it against local policy constraints. Finally, it caches $[PR, SIG_i, SIG_{i+1}, K_{dsig}]$.

At this point, each AD_i is assured that (i) the PR is valid, i.e., does not violate local policy, (ii) the PR is authentic, i.e., issued by a recognized entity; and (iii) the PR is *fresh*, i.e., issued recently. In other words, each AD_i is protected against attacks of **Type 1** and **Type 2**.

(iii) In order to take advantage of an existing PR, the source of communication must be able to supply information necessary to associate each data packet with a specific PR.[11] This information is placed in the *PR header* mentioned in Section 5.4. Contents of a secure *PR Header* must include the PR signatures. However, attaching N PR signatures to each packet wastes a lot of band width. We observe that, since PR signatures are independent of individual data packets,

[11] The term *source* is used loosely here; it can mean a source host as well as a designated router acting on behalf of a source host.

PR Handle		
PR		
SIG_1	SEQ_1^{src}	$E(K_{\text{dsig}})^{K_1^{\text{src}}}$
SIG_2	SEQ_2^{src}	$E(K_{\text{dsig}})^{K_2^{\text{src}}}$
.	.	.
.	.	.
.	.	.
SIG_N	SEQ_N^{src}	$E(K_{\text{dsig}})^{K_N^{\text{src}}}$

(a) Secret Key version

PR Handle	
PR	
SIG_{src}	
SEQ_1^{src}	$E(K_{\text{dsig}})^{EK_1}$
SEQ_2^{src}	$E(K_{\text{dsig}})^{EK_2}$
.	.
.	.
.	.
SEQ_N^{src}	$E(K_{\text{dsig}})^{EK_N}$

(b) Public Key version

FIGURE 1. PR Setup Packets

it is not necessary for the source to include all N signatures of each packet. If PR signatures are distributed during setup such that each AD_i caches not only SIG_i, but SIG_{i+1} as well, then upon receiving a data packet and verifying SIG_i, AD_i can replace it with SIG_{i+1}. This means that the source only needs to include SIG_1.

Also, if packet or network header authentication is desired, the source must be able to compute packet signatures with K_{dsig} in order to defend against **Type 3** attacks. Therefore, in order to utilize an existing PR, the Policy Server in AD_{src} needs to supply the source with SIG_1 and K_{dsig}.

(iv) When the source is ready to send a data packet, P, it first needs to compute a packet signature:

$$DSIG = F_{\text{char}}(E[Packet]^{K_{\text{dsig}}}). \tag{3}$$

The details of this process depend on the variation of data integrity checking used (as described in Section 5.5). Then, the source attaches $[SIG_1, DSIG]$ to the packet and sends it along. The exit gateway uses SIG_1 to look up the corresponding cache entry, verifies $DSIG$, and replaces SIG_1 with SIG_2. In general, an entry gateway of AD_i verifies $DSIG$ and replaces SIG_i with SIG_{i+1}. It is quite possible that some ADs choose not to verify PR and/or packet signatures. Such an AD is only required to replace its (possibly dummy) SIG_i with SIG_{i+1}.

It should be noted that this entire step is optional and can be omitted altogether if **Type 3** attacks do not pose a threat. Alternatively, one of the variations on data integrity checking (see Section 5.5) can be used. Irrespective of the particular method, packet signatures are not necessarily computed over an entire packet. Instead, one may choose to sign only the control information, e.g., network layer headers.

5.7.2. *Public Key version.* In this section we present a version of the secure PR setup protocol based on Public Key encryption. For the most part, it mimics its Secret Key counterpart, though it differs in a few details:

(i) As before, the issuing AD_{src} generates a new data signature key, K_{dsig}. Then, instead of computing N distinct PR signatures, only one signature is computed:

$$(4) \qquad SIG_{src} = F_{char}(D(PR||K_{dsig}||SEQ_1^{src}||\ldots||SEQ_N^{src})^{DK_{src}})$$

where DK_i is the private (signature) key of AD_{src}. This signature is sufficient to maintain the integrity of the PR setup packet. However, K_{dsig} must be communicated in secret to each AD_i. This requires that AD_{src} encrypt K_{dsig} N times, i.e., compute $E(K_{dsig})^{EK_i}$ for all AD_i. The resulting PR setup packet is depicted in Figure 1(b).

(ii) When the PR setup packet propagates along the route, each AD_i obtains K_{dsig} by decrypting $E(K_{dsig})^{EK_i}$, recomputes and verifies SIG_{src} and SEQ_i^{src} as before, and authorizes the PR. The cache entry differs from that in Section 5.7.1. Because there is but a single PR signature, only $[PR, SIG_{src}, K_{dsig}]$ is cached.

The remainder of the protocol is the same as the Secret Key variant.

5.8. Applicability to other PR approaches. In the previous sections, we concentrated on a more secure version of the RFC 1102 PR proposal. It is also of interest to examine the applicability of the methods discussed to other PR approaches such as BGP and ECMA.

- Distribution of Policy Terms
  Policy Terms are a feature unique to RFC 1102. In BGP and ECMA,

policy is embodied in the internetwork topology. However, paths and distance metrics are exchanged among neighboring ADs. In order to make these exchanges secure, it is sufficient to use a Secret Key cryptosystem as the number of message recipients is always limited by the number of AD's neighbors.

- Route Setup and Packet Forwarding
  Route setup is not done in BGP and ECMA as described in ([**6, 19**]). This means that Policy Routes must be authorized/authenticated at packet-forwarding time. However, nothing precludes PR setup from being implemented on a network that uses protocols. In that case, the discussion in Sections 5.3, 5.4, and 5.7 will be applicable.
- Data Integrity Checking
  Of the five variants discussed, only Endpoint-AD and Transit-AD data integrity checking apply to all three PR approaches. Other variants require coordination among ADs beyond that provided in BGP and ECMA models as they are currently specified.

6. Assessment and cost of security

Our purpose in this section is to investigate bounds on achievable data rates with the security schemes described above. Previous work in the area of performance and cost evaluation of secure protocols (e.g., *visa* protocols [**13**]) identifies four important overhead contributors (in this order of magnitude):

(i) per-packet encryption,
(ii) increased packet length,
(iii) setup overhead,
(iv) other additional per-packet processing.

Experimental results show that overhead due to encryption constitutes the majority of the total overhead. In the remainder of this section we analyze each of the above contributing factors in several variations of the general scheme.

6.1. Per-packet encryption costs. Per-packet encryption costs are largely dependent upon the particular variation of data integrity checking. These costs are summarized in Figure 2. N refers to the PR length including AD_{src} and AD_{dst}, and m refers to the index agreed to in the Source Patterned scheme.

If we consider, for example, an encryption speed of 1.0 Mbyte/sec,[12] the encryption overhead for a typical packet size of, say, 500 bytes will amount to 1 ms for either Endpoint-AD or Round Robin data integrity checking. The same packet size will incur the overhead of N ms for the Full Transit variant (where N is the PR length). These numbers should be considered relative to the usual packet processing, transmission, and propagation delays

[12] 1.0 Mbyte/sec is a readily attainable speed for current state-of-the-art encryption hardware.

Variation	Cost in # of encryptions
Endpoint	2
Full Transit	N
Designated Transit	2
Source Patterned	N/m
Round Robin	2

FIGURE 2. Encryption Operations

encountered in transiting a wide-area network. Replay prevention can be used independently of the data authentication method. The cost of replay prevention amounts to one additional small (PR-header) encryption for the source host and all intervening ADs that choose to implement it.

6.2. Costs due to increased packet length. Increased packet length is incurred by the PR signature carried in every data packet. It is anticipated that the length of this header will be on the order of 24-30 bytes. Previous measurements of *visa* protocols [**13**] show that this overhead ranges from 20% for small packets (e.g., 16 bytes of user data) to less than 4% for larger packets (e.g., 1 Kbyte); the length of a *visa* header is roughly the same as that of a PR header. Roughly, the header overhead amounts to about 1 ms per packet per hop.

6.3. Setup overhead. PR setup is accomplished by sending a packet containing the entire PR and its signatures as described in Section 5.7.1. The length of this packet is proportional to N (the length of a PR). The encryption costs include N encryption operations to compute PR signatures for all intervening AD_is by the issuing AD and another N encryptions to verify these signatures during actual setup. This is, of course, the worst-case scenario. Some AD_is may not care to authenticate PRs upon setup. Furthermore, if PR authentication requirements (or lack thereof) are expressed in AD_i's PTs, AD_{src} can avoid unnecessary signature computation and reduce the setup overhead.

Cache sizes and cache replacement algorithms used in Policy Gateways can influence the overhead as well. When a cache miss occurs at an intermediate PG, it must be supplied with a fresh copy of a relevant PR. This requires that another PR setup packet be sent to the PG in question by the issuing PS. If the number of active PRs in a PS measures in hundreds, cache sizes and look-up costs can be kept small. If an LRU cache replacement algorithm is used, hit ratios in the 90% range can be achieved.

6.4. Other per-packet processing costs. Additional (other than encryption) processing costs are incurred mainly by the added logic in gateways for processing of PR-based packets, in particular, cache look-ups. As discussed above, cache sizes are expected to measure in hundreds of entries. Similar experiments show that time spent on cache look-ups is overshadowed by encryption costs [**13**].

6.5. Summary. As demonstrated in the preceding sections, secure Policy Routing takes its toll in performance. This is largely due to the encryption overhead incurred in maintaining the authenticity of PRs and the integrity of data. Because of the high degree of autonomy enjoyed by the ADs, it is unreasonable to expect all ADs to adhere to the same set of security mechanisms. While this makes it difficult to put a price tag on the security of Policy Routing, it allows us to design flexible protocols that can be adapted to suit any environment with regard to the security concerns. In this section we describe an example usage scenario and attempt to evaluate its costs.

Suppose that a pair of hosts communicate across an internetwork along the following PR of length six:

$$[AD_{\text{src}}, AD_2, AD_3, AD_4, AD_5, AD_{\text{dst}}].$$

In order to setup state in intervening ADs, the setup procedure (as described in Section 5.7) must take place. Assuming that the PR and its signatures have been precomputed, the setup overhead is equal to the packet travel time from AD_{src} to AD_{dst} plus setup costs incurred by each of the six ADs. As discussed earlier, these setup costs are comprised largely of the verification of PR signatures (SIG_is). If we assume the length of the PR to be 1 Kbyte (most PRs will be much shorter) and the average encryption rate to be a reasonable 1.0 Mbyte/sec, then the encryption overhead will amount to 6 ms. This results in a total overhead of one packet travel time plus 6 ms of encryption overhead.

The overhead experienced by data packets depends on whether or not data integrity checking and replay prevention is performed (assuming no cache misses). Aside from that, the only PR-related operations are (i) look-up of a PR handle, and (ii) verification of SIG_i, which is a constant value and does not change from packet to packet. There is, of course, the overhead due to increased packet length, but it is expected to be minimal since, in the worst case, the PR header will be around 24 bytes (4 byte PR handle, 8 byte SIG_i, 8 byte $DSIG$ and 4 byte sequence number). Using the approximate figure of 1 ms per hop (see Section 6.2), PR header overhead is around 6 ms per data packet.

If we assume that *Designated Transit* data integrity checking variation is used, then for each data packet the source computes $DSIG$, which is subsequently verified by the designated AD. This amounts to two encryptions per data packet. For 1 Kbyte packets the encryption cost is 2 ms (with the encryption rate of 1.0 Mbyte/sec). The total overhead is then 8 ms per data packet.

These *ad hoc* estimates, although somewhat liberal, show that with reasonable encryption rates the cost of security is not prohibitively high. Moreover, the flexibility of the secure Policy Routing permits individual ADs to independently select their own trade-off between security and performance.

7. Conclusions and future work

Transit control mechanisms are needed by interconnected ADs to retain their autonomy in setting and enforcing policy while still achieving desired connectivity. This problem of interconnecting and navigating across Administrative Domains is of inherent interest to the security community because the policies in question concern control of resource access and usage. Moreover, the security of the transit control mechanisms themselves must be considered if they are to be applicable in sensitive environments. On the other hand, the security mechanisms, as usual, take a toll in overall system complexity and performance. The purpose of this paper is to explore the design of transit control mechanisms for sensitive environments and to investigate the performance overhead of the proposed mechanisms. After evaluating the application of stub-network access control techniques, we described and evaluated a secure protocol design for transit ADs.

Our proposed mechanisms were designed to support interoperability across ADs with heterogeneous policies to the extent that their combined policies allow. Moreover, these *preventative* PR schemes can interoperate with *detection*-based PR schemes.[13]

There remains much work to be done in several areas: simulating and experimenting with implementations of Policy Routing protocols, speeding up available signature mechanisms, experimenting with the data integrity alternatives proposed here for more detailed understanding of their behavior, integrating Policy Routing with end-to-end mechanisms (e.g., *visa*), and developing formal tools to verify the Policy Terms and Policy Routes synthesized by ADs. Perhaps of utmost importance is to study techniques for streamlining packet processing in gateways, in general, and with respect to validation issues in particular. Some of the more interesting techniques may be implemented at the expense of security.

- One such technique is to check the signature *after* a packet is forwarded and then treat the *next* packet in the session/from that source according to the result of the previous check. This technique has the attractive characteristic that an individual AD can implement this short cut unilaterally and thereby select its own point on the security performance curve. Cheriton [23] calls this approach *optimistic authentication.*

---

[13] In order to accomplish this, PR headers must encode the flavor of data integrity, replay prevention mechanisms must be employed for packets belonging to a stream, and each AD's Policy Term Conditions must contain details as to data integrity checking and replay prevention requirements.

- A similar idea at a lower level is to compute and append the signature at the *end* of each packet so that it can be done in parallel with other packet-processing tasks. This technique is described by Cheriton and Kanakia for transport protocols [**26**].
- Tasks such as the PR setup can be performed more efficiently with multicasting support. Methods for delivery of signed multi-destination messages are the subject of future work ([**31, 32**]).
- A higher-level issue is to integrate the support of connection- and transaction-oriented traffic. Schemes such as RFC 1102 PR and secure PR, in particular, require significant state to be set up and maintained in the gateways. Such overhead makes sense for connections but may be excessive for transactions. It is worth investigating a scheme that would allow the source to flag transaction traffic and have policy gateways handle the traffic differently (more efficiently) if their respective ADs are so willing.
- This brings us to the more general issue of managing the state in gateways. Management issues include route setup and tear-down, cache management, and state reestablishment in case of a failure or cache overflow. For example, while the protocols allow for state reestablishment without breaking the higher-level connection by repeating route setup, there may be techniques to obtain recently lost state information from neighboring ADs. Such protocols are worth investigating to support route-state management. Moreover, such a requirement is not unique to PR, it is shared by other schemes involving setup such as resource reservation protocols.
- Charging for services, i.e., accounting and billing, is going to play a major role in Policy Routing protocols. When charges are incurred, service providers (e.g., a transit AD) need to bill the subscribers for usage. Doing so in a secure manner is not a trivial problem. For example, if users are charged on a per-connection basis, records must be kept to serve as proof of usage (much like credit card slips). Exactly what such records may need to contain is subject for further investigation.

Consideration of techniques such as these highlights the need for tools to systematically identify, evaluate, and express security risks. Without such tools it is difficult to identify the security risks that are introduced when we attempt to improve performance.

In conclusion, this paper presents the design of preventative security mechanisms and an analysis of their performance implications. We conducted our analysis in the context of a specific PR protocol in order to provide a concrete basis for the evaluation of performance and implementation overhead.

REFERENCES

1. D. Estrin and G. Tsudik, *Secure control of transit internetwork traffic*, University of Southern California TR-89-15, December 1989.
2. D. Clark, *Design philosophy of the DARPA internet protocols*, Proc. of 1988 ACM SIGCOMM Symposium, August 1988.
3. R. Needham and M. Schroeder, *Using encryption for authentication in large networks of computers*, Communications of the ACM, December 1978.
4. D. Estrin and G. Tsudik, *Visa scheme for inter-organization network security*, Proc. of 1987 IEEE Symposium on Security and Privacy, April 1987.
5. H. Braun, *Models of policy routing*, RFC 1104, SRI Network Information Center, June 1989.
6. K. Lougheed and Y. Rekhter, *Border gateway protocol*, RFC 1105, SRI Network Information Center, June 1989.
7. D. Clark, *Policy routing in internet protocols*, RFC 1102, SRI Network Information Center, May 1989.
8. J. Postel, *Internet protocol*, RFC 791, SRI Network Information Center, September 1981.
9. E. Rosen, *Exterior gateway protocol (EGP)*, RFC 827, SRI Network Information Center, October 1982.
10. *Federal information processing standards*, National Bureau of Standards, Publication 46, 1977.
11. D. Estrin, J. Mogul, G. Tsudik, and K. Anand, *Visa protocols for controlling inter-organizational datagram flow: Extended description*, University of Southern California TR-88-50. Also, DEC TR 88/5, December 1988.
12. D. Estrin and G. Tsudik, *Security issues in policy routing*, Proc. of 1989 IEEE Symposium on Security and Privacy, May 1989.
13. D. Estrin, J. Mogul, and G. Tsudik, *Visa protocols for controlling inter-organizational datagram flow*, IEEE Journal on Selected Areas in Communications, May 1989.
14. D. Estrin, *Policy requirements for resource control in the research internet*, RFC 1121, SRI Network Information Center, December 1989.
15. *Advanced micro devices MOS microprocessors and peripherals data book*, Advanced Micro Devices, Inc., Sunnyvale, CA., 1987.
16. W. Diffie, *The first ten years of public-key cryptography*, Proc. of the IEEE, May 1988.
17. D. Davies and W. Price, *Security for computer networks*, Wiley, New York, NY, 1984.
18. C. Meyer and S. Matyas, *Cryptography: a new dimension in computer data security*, Wiley, New York, NY, 1982.
19. European Computer Manufacturers Association, *Interdomain intermediate systems routing*, Technical Report ECMA/TC32-TG10/89/56, May 1989.
20. R. Merkle, *A software encryption function*, Working Paper, Xerox PARC, Palo Alto, CA, February 1989.
21. J. Mogul, *Simple and flexible datagram access controls for unix-based gateways*, Proc. of Summer 1989 USENIX Technical Conference, August 1987.
22. J. Steiner, *The Kerberos network authentication service overview*, MIT Project Athena RFC, Draft 1, April 1989.
23. D. Cheriton, *SIRPENT: a high-performance internetworking approach*, Proc. of 1989 ACM SIGCOMM Symposium, September 1989.
24. M. Merritt and W. Griffieth, *Authentication protocols*, Working Paper, AT&T Laboratories, May 1989.
25. *Blacker front end interface control document*, DDN Protocol Handbook, Volume 1, DDN Network Information Center, SRI International, 1985.
26. H. Kanakia and D. Cheriton, *The VMP network adapter board NAB: high-performance network communication for multiprocessors*, Proc. of 1988 ACM SIGCOMM Symposium, August 1988.
27. R. Perlman, *Network layer protocols with byzantine robustness*, MIT LCS TR-429, Ph.D. Dissertation, October 1988.
28. J. McQuillan, *Adaptive routing algorithms for distributed computer networks*, BBN Report 2831, May 1984.

29. J. McQuillan, I. Richer, and E. Rosen, *The new routing algorithm for the ARPANET*, IEEE Transaction on Communications, May 1980.
30. SDNS Protocol and Signaling Working Group, SP3 Subgroup, *SDNS Secure Data Network System Security Protocol 3 (SP3)*, SDN.301 Revision 1.5 1989-05-15.
31. J. Linn, *Privacy enhancement for internet electronic mail. Part I: Message encipherment and authentication procedures*, RFC 1113, SRI Network Information Center, January 1989.
32. J. Linn, *Privacy enhancement for internet electronic mail. Part II: Algorithms, modes and identifiers*, RFC 1115, SRI Network Information Center, January 1989.
33. J. Moy, *The open shortest path first (OSPF) specification*, RFC 1131, SRI Network Information Center, October 1989.
34. *The directory authentication framework*, CCITT Recommendation X.509, 1988.
35. R. Rivest, A. Shamir, and L. Adelman, *A method for obtaining digital signatures and public key cryptosystems*, Communications of the ACM, February 1978.

Computer Networks and Systems Distributed Laboratory, Computer Science Department, University of Southern California, Los Angeles, California 90089-0782

E-mail address: estrin@lono.usc.edu

E-mail address: tsudik@jerico.usc.edu

DIMACS Series in Discrete Mathematics
and Theoretical Computer Science
Volume 2, 1991

On Expected Polynomial Time Simulation of Zero Knowledge Protocols

URIEL FEIGE AND ADI SHAMIR

ABSTRACT. The standard definition of the zero knowledge concept allows for expected polynomial time simulation. This seems like a necessity for many zero knowledge protocols. We argue that some more conceptual work must be done before we accept such a definition as satisfactory.

1. Introduction

The concept of zero knowledge (ZK) [**9**] is very appealing because of its paradoxical philosophical interpretation. The verifier receiving a ZK proof has no idea why the statement being proven is correct, yet he is convinced "beyond any reasonable doubt" that the statement is indeed correct. As is well established, zero knowledge protocols are central building blocks in many cryptographic applications ([**7**, **4**, **8**, **2**], and others).

The formal definition of zero knowledge involves a simulator that works in *expected* polynomial time, rather than strictly polynomial time. In this paper we study the effect of this definition. We argue that the verifier in these systems should also be modeled as an expected polynomial time machine. We then show that for this class of verifiers, the proposed simulation of known *computational* zero knowledge protocols (e.g., [**7**, **1**, **3**]) cannot be carried out even in expected polynomial time.

Related work. There is strong and justified criticism raised by Levin [**10**] and explained by Goldreich [**6**] on the way "average" computer scientists define the concept of expected polynomial time. Levin suggests an alternative definition for the concept *polynomial on the average*. Our claims are independent of the way expected polynomial time computation is defined, and they continue to hold even if the simulator runs in time *polynomial on the average*, as in Levin's [**10**] definition.

1980 *Mathematics Subject Classification* (1985 *Revision*). Primary 68P25, 68Q15.

2. The attack

The following two definitions are given in **[9]**.

DEFINITION 1 (ZERO KNOWLEDGE). Let $L \subset \{0, 1\}^*$ be a language and (A, B) a protocol. (A, B) is *perfectly (statistically) (computationally) zero knowledge on* L if for any probabilistic polynomial time B' the family of random variables $View_{A,B'}$ is perfectly (statistically) (computationally) approximable on

$$L' = \{(x, H) \mid x \in L \text{ and } |H| = |x|^c\}.$$

H is the auxiliary input for B' and represents knowledge B' has before the protocol begins.

DEFINITION 2 (APPROXIMABILITY OF RANDOM VARIABLES). Let $L \subset \{0, 1\}^*$ be a language and $U = \{U(x)\}$ a family of random variables. U is *perfectly (statistically) (computationally) approximable on* L if there exists a probabilistic Turing machine M, running in expected polynomial time, such that the families of random variables $\{M(x)\}$ and $\{U(x)\}$ are perfectly (statistically) (computationally) indistinguishable on L.

It is important to notice that M is expected polynomial time. As remarked in **[9]**, this appears to be necessary for some zero knowledge proof systems.

We now make some philosophical claims. These are not mathematical theorems.

CLAIM 1. The simulator M should do only things that B' can do by himself.

JUSTIFICATION. This is the essence of the idea of zero knowledge. B' does not learn anything from A, because he himself can simulate the whole protocol.

CLAIM 2. M must not be of a complexity class higher than the complexity class B' is in.

JUSTIFICATION. Otherwise, M does things that B' cannot do. If M does not use his extra power, then there is no point in having him in a higher complexity class in the first place.

CLAIM 3. B' must be allowed to run for expected polynomial time (and not just worst case polynomial time).

JUSTIFICATION. The simulator in zero knowledge protocols is allowed to run for expected polynomial time (see Definition 2). Thus Claim 3 follows from Claim 2.

To continue our argument, we pause to inspect the nature of the simulator M. In virtually all zero knowledge protocols, the proof that the protocol is zero knowledge involves *blackbox simulation* **[11]**. In this case, we have one simulator M that can be used for any B', and this M uses B' as a blackbox subroutine. On common input x and auxiliary input H, M supplies the blackbox B' with x, H, and a random string r. If B' is polynomial time, then there is one polynomial bounding the number of random bits B' can use, and M can supply all these bits in advance. But since we allow B' to be expected polynomial time, then M does not know in advance how many random bits to supply. Thus we have to modify the process of the simulation, and have M supply the random bits to B' upon demand.

Now we reach the heart of our argument. We show that for *computationally* zero knowledge protocols, there exists a verifier B', such that the following two conditions hold:

(1) When interacting with the real prover A, the interactive proof (A, B') always terminates in polynomial time.
(2) The blackbox simulation $M_{B'}$ does not end even in expected polynomial time.

We do not prove this statement for all computational zero knowledge protocols and for all possible simulators $M_{B'}$. We only demonstrate this phenomenon on one simplified example, derived from Blum's **[1]** zero knowledge interactive proof for the directed Hamiltonian cycle problem. However, the same argument applies equally well to all proposed simulations of all published computationally zero knowledge protocols.

PROTOCOL 1. *Common input: a Hamiltonian graph G with n nodes. The basic step of Blum's protocol is composed of three moves:*

(i) *A secretly chooses a random permutation π and permutes the nodes of G. A secretly constructs the adjacency matrix of $\pi(G)$ and encrypts each entry* ('1' *if an edge exists,* '0' *otherwise*) *independently, using a secure probabilistic encryption scheme.*
(ii) *B randomly selects a bit* '0' *or* '1' *as a challenge and sends it to A.*
(iii) *If A receives* '0', *A reveals π and all the encrypted bits. B can check that the edges revealed indeed correspond to the graph $\pi(G)$. If A receives* '1', *A decrypts only n edges, comprising a Hamiltonian cycle in $\pi(G)$. B can easily check that this is the case from the structure of the adjacency matrix. If A receives a message different from* '0' *or* '1', *she interprets the message as* '0'.

The standard simulation of this protocol is based on the following procedure:

(1) M randomly guesses B''s future reply, '0' or '1'.
(2) If M guesses '0' it follows A's prespecified protocol. It can complete this protocol provided B' does not send '1' in Step 2.
(3) If M guesses '1', it encrypts an n node clique. If B' sends '1' in Step 2, M opens a random Hamiltonian cycle in the clique.

For any x, let $D(x)$ be a distribution on strings of length $|x|$. Assume that the family $\{D(x)\}$ of random variables can be approximated in expected polynomial time, but not in polynomial time. (Throughout this paper we assume that there exist families of random variables that can be approximated in expected polynomial time, but that cannot be approximated in polynomial time. This assumption is also implicit in Definition 2, as otherwise there would be no reason to let M run for expected polynomial time.)

Consider now the following cheating B'. B' always replies '1' in Step 2 of the protocol, forcing the simulator always to encrypt the n node clique. When the protocol ends, B' looks at the transcript of the protocol and tries to guess an NP witness that proves that he was interacting with a simulator. (Such a witness is composed of valid decryptions of all encrypted messages that B' received in Step 1 and a check that the graph encrypted was a clique.) Because the encryption scheme is secure, B' has only negligible probability of exposing M, denoted by $\nu(n)$. If B' succeeds, he generates infinitely many random bits and never stops. If B' fails, he outputs a random element $d \in D(x)$, which he generates in expected polynomial time.

When B' interacts with the real prover, the whole protocol takes expected polynomial time, because A never encrypts the n node clique. But when B' interacts with the simulator, then if the simulator is exposed, M is required to supply B' with infinitely many random bits. The expected running time of the system $M_{B'}$ is thus

$$\text{poly}(n) + \nu(n)\infty = \infty > \text{poly}(n).$$

We note that two simple attempts to patch the simulation process in order to make it expected polynomial time do not work.

(1) M cannot restrict B' to some prespecified polynomial number of random bits, because as far as M knows, B' may well be trying to generate an element in $D(x)$, and this process cannot be approximated in strictly polynomial time.

(2) M cannot supply an element of $D(x)$ by itself, because this would not be blackbox simulation. When M receives the blackbox B', it does not know what the distribution $D(x)$ is, and so it has no choice but to use B' in order to generate elements of $D(x)$.

The example demonstrates what we consider to be our most disturbing claim:

CLAIM 4. For computational zero knowledge protocols in general, known simulation procedures are not guaranteed to end in expected polynomial time.

3. The defense

One may counter Claim 4 by the following argument: The event that B' exposes M has negligible probability. Hence the problem presented has no real practical significance. We wholly agree with this argument. We present our claims only as a stimulation for conceptual and philosophical discussion. In this section we discuss possible ways of answering the claims of the previous section.

Improve the simulation process. Devise a new simulation procedure for computationally zero knowledge protocols that ends in expected polynomial time. Alternatively, prove the existence of such a simulation, without giving an explicit construction. Note that we require the simulation to work with any possible cheating verifier, and not just with the particular B' we presented.

Require M to run in worst case polynomial time. In this case, the problem of expected polynomial time verifiers (Claim 3) does not arise. We can still retain expected polynomial time simulation for *perfectly* zero knowledge protocols, since Claim 4 does not apply to these protocols.

This solution is good for any zero knowledge protocol that does not require expected polynomial time simulation (including Protocol 1, as pointed out to us by Goldreich [**5**]). But many interesting zero knowledge protocols do require expected polynomial time simulation (e.g., quadratic nonresiduosity [**9**], graph nonisomorphism [**7**], and constant round zero knowledge protocols [**3**]). These protocols incorporate subprotocols in which B gives *proofs of knowledge.* The concept of proof of knowledge involves a knowledge extractor ([**4**, **12**]), which runs in *expected polynomial time.* In the zero knowledge protocols cited above, the simulator must be allowed to run for expected polynomial time, because in part it does the work of a knowledge extractor.

Define expected polynomial time interactive Turing machines as those that run for expected polynomial time with *any* partner. In this case, B' must run for expected polynomial time with M as well, and Claim 4 does not hold.

This solution does not meet the following argument. Let (A, B) be a zero knowledge protocol. Assume you found a blackbox B' that is not restricted to expected polynomial time. Further assume that whenever B' interacts with the real prover A, B' happens to run in expected polynomial time, and manages to extract secret information from A. Such a blackbox may be very useful in practice. The restrictive definition of zero knowledge that tells B' in advance that its interaction with M must not exceed expected polynomial time is unapplicable to this type of blackbox.

Introduce a new complexity class. One may try to characterize a complexity class that is somewhat higher than expected polynomial time, in which both B' and M can reside with no contradiction. Other than complicating matters, this solution still leaves open the question of what can be said about verifiers that belong to existing complexity classes.

Change the interpretation of zero knowledge. The problems arise not because of a mathematical flaw in the combination of polynomial time verifiers and expected polynomial time simulators, but because this seems to violate the intended philosophical interpretation of the zero knowledge concept. A solution would be to retain the mathematical definition, but to give it a less ambitious interpretation. One such interpretation can be that if polynomial time B' can use A to do some difficult computation, the same computation is *expected* to take B' polynomial time even without the help of A.

One should check that such an interpretation is strong enough for all the intended uses of the zero knowledge concept.

Acknowledgments. We would like to thank Mihir Bellare, Manuel Blum, Joan Feigenbaum, Lance Fortnow, Oded Goldreich, Shafi Goldwasser, and Rafail Ostrovsky for helpful discussions.

REFERENCES

1. M. Blum, *How to prove a theorem so no one else can claim it*, Proc. of the International Congress of Mathematicians, Berkeley, California (1986), 1444–1451.
2. M. Bellare and S. Goldwasser, *New paradigms for digital signatures and message authentication based on noninteractive zero knowledge proofs*, Lecture Notes in Computer Science **435**, G. Brassard, Ed., Advances in Cryptology—Crypto '89 Proceedings, Springer-Verlag, 194–211.
3. U. Feige and A. Shamir, *Zero knowledge proofs of knowledge in two rounds*, Lecture Notes in Computer Science **435**, G. Brassard, Ed., Advances in Cryptology—Crypto '89 Proceedings, Springer-Verlag, 526–544.
4. U. Feige, A. Fiat, and A. Shamir, *Zero knowledge proofs of identity*, J. Cryptology, Vol. 1 (1988), 77–94.
5. O. Goldreich, Private communication.
6. ——, *Towards a theory of average case complexity (a survey)*, Technion, Computer Science Department, Technical Report 531, December 1988.
7. O. Goldreich, S. Micali, and A. Wigderson, *Proofs that yield nothing but their validity and a methodology of cryptographic protocol design*, Proc. of 27th FOCS (1986), IEEE, 174–187.
8. ——, *How to play any mental game*, Proc. of 19th STOC (1987), ACM, 218–229.
9. S. Goldwasser, S. Micali, and C. Rackoff, *The knowledge complexity of interactive proof systems*, SIAM J. Comput., Vol. 18, No. 1 (1989), 186–208.
10. L. Levin, *Average case complete problems*, SIAM J. Comput., Vol. 15 (1986), 285–286.
11. Y. Oren, *On the cunning power of cheating verifiers: Some observations about zero knowledge proofs*, Proc. of 28th FOCS (1987), IEEE, 462–471.
12. M. Tompa and H. Woll, *Random self-reducibility and zero knowledge interactive proofs of possession of information*, Proc. of 28th FOCS (1987), IEEE, 472–482.

THE WEIZMANN INSTITUTE OF SCIENCE, REHOVOT 76100, ISRAEL

DIMACS Series in Discrete Mathematics
and Theoretical Computer Science
Volume 2, 1991

Cryptographic Protection of Databases and Software

JOAN FEIGENBAUM, MARK Y. LIBERMAN, REBECCA N. WRIGHT

ABSTRACT. We describe experimental work on *cryptographic protection* of databases and software. The database in our experiment is a *natural language dictionary* of over 4000 Spanish verbs. Our tentative conclusion is that the overhead cost of computing with encrypted data is fairly small.

1. Introduction

It is often desirable to allow a user to access a database D via some program P while preventing her from obtaining a copy of the entire contents of the database. For example, let D be a table of pairs (l_i, r_i), $1 \leq i \leq n$, where each l_i is the name of a person and $P(l_i, D) = r_i$ is the phone number of l_i. A typical user of D should be able to obtain the number r_i if she knows l_i but should not be able to obtain the names and numbers of the people she does not know.

More formally, given a database D and program P that accesses it, we wish to construct an encrypted database D' and a corresponding program P' with the following properties:

- for any query q, $P(q, D) = P'(q, D')$;
- given P' and D', it is computationally infeasible to reconstruct D.

This report describes:

- a simple cryptographic solution for protecting table-structured databases;
- experimental work applying this technique to certain natural-language databases and the automata-based programs that access them;
- potential alternative approaches and open questions.

Various theoretical problems concerning computation with encrypted data have appeared in the cryptologic literature. We mention two of them and then explain how they differ from the problem that we study here.

1980 *Mathematics Subject Classification* (1985 *Revision*). Primary 68P25, 68S15.

Yao [**30**] posed the problem of which distributed computation problems have *secure multiparty protocols*. That is, when is it possible for equally powerful parties P_i, $1 \leq i \leq n$, each holding a private input x_i, to cooperate in the computation of $y = f(x_1, \ldots, x_n)$ in such a way that each P_i learns y and no P_i learns anything about x_j, $j \neq i$, except what is implied by y and x_i? Secure multiparty protocols in which all of the parties are limited to polynomial-time computation are discussed in [**10**, **13**]. Those in which all of the parties are computationally unlimited are discussed in [**3**, **4**].

Abadi, Feigenbaum, and Kilian [**1**] posed the problem of which functions have *instance-hiding schemes*. In their scenario, one party, say P_0, has a private input x, but lacks the computational resources to compute f. Party P_1 has the power to compute f but cannot guarantee the privacy of inputs it receives. For which functions f can P_0 cooperate with P_1 to obtain $f(x)$ without revealing x? Instance-hiding schemes in which P_0 cooperates with multiple powerful parties $P_1, \ldots, P_m$ are discussed in [**2**].

In this paper, we take an experimental approach to computing with encrypted data, and we set a more modest goal than that of the previous authors. We wish to allow users to learn the answers $P(q, D)$ to specific queries q, but we wish to make it difficult for them to incorporate the entire database D into another program of their own design. We do this by providing only an encrypted database D'. The "information content" of D is certainly present in D', but we can make it difficult to extract by using a good encryption function. Note that access to D' via the program P' *does* allow a user to recover the input-output relation of P by computing $P'(q, D')$ for all possible queries q. This does not mean that we have not gained anything in encrypting D. First, the value of D may be in the way it is structured, not in the "raw data" that it contains; indeed, the raw data of the input-output relation is often publicly available and is, in fact, the starting point for both the database designer and the potential thief. If the user were willing to structure D from the raw data, then he would not need D' at all. Second, the set of all *syntactically valid* queries is usually a proper superset of the set of queries that yield meaningful output, and it may be far too large to generate by exhaustive search.

The natural-language software that we seek to protect is a good example of *leaky technology*, as defined by Ouchi [**27**]. Once developed and sold by one vendor, it can easily be modified and resold by someone who has not borne any of the development costs. Traditional patent and copyright laws may not be applicable, and litigation is a costly and cumbersome source of protection in any case. Ouchi suggests joint research and development by large companies, all of whom stand to gain from the advancement of a leaky technology. Clearly a technical solution to the problem of leakage would be more satisfying, and, in the software industry, where there are many potential vendors, most of whom have no research and development efforts, it may be the only possible type of solution.

The rest of this paper is organized as follows. Section 2 describes a method of encrypting table-structured databases such as the phone database described above. Section 3 gives the structure of the natural-language databases that we seek to protect and describes our experiment with the Spanish-verb dictionary. Finally, Section 4 states our conclusions and open questions.

2. A method for encrypting tables

Suppose that D consists of a table of pairs (l_i, r_i), $1 \le i \le n$, and that P is a simple lookup program. That is, for any l that is equal to l_i, for some $1 \le i \le n$, $P(l, D) = r_i$, and, for any other l, $P(l, D) = \mathrm{NIL}$. The l_i's are referred to as *keys* and the r_i's as *values*. We construct the corresponding D' and P' as follows.

Let L be the set of all syntactically valid keys; in particular, $L_{in} \subseteq L$, where $L_{in} = \{l_1, \dots, l_n\}$. Let h be a one-way hash function whose domain is L. Ideally, such a function h would be a polynomial-time computable, one-to-one mapping from L onto the integers 1 through $|L|$ with the property that, given $j \in \{1, \dots, |L|\}$, it is computationally infeasible to find $h^{-1}(j) \in L$. For a more thorough discussion of one-way hash functions, refer to [**24**, **25**].

Let *Enc* and *Dec* be encryption and decryption functions such that, for all x and k, $Dec(Enc(x, k), k) = x$. Then the encrypted database D' is derived from D as follows: For every (l_i, r_i) pair in D, a pair $(h(l_i), Enc(r_i, l_i))$ is inserted into D'. The modified lookup program P' uses the algorithm:

$P'(l, D')$:

```
{
l' ← h(l)
r' ← P(l', D')
if r' = NIL, return(NIL).
else return(Dec(r', l)).
}
```

This table-encryption scheme is an enhancement of a standard password-storage technique first developed by Needham. (See Denning's book [7, Section 3.6] for a thorough discussion.) Normally such a scheme is used only when $|L|$ is too large for h to be inverted by brute force and L_{in} is a subset that is infeasible to generate.

3. An application to dictionaries

3.1. Why natural languages? Natural-language dictionaries as used by computer programs are good candidates for the kind of protection discussed in this paper. Information about the form and usage of words is not inherently secret—thus the fact that *conozcamos* is the **first person plural present subjunctive** form of the Spanish verb *conocer* (to know) is public knowledge. Such facts certainly cannot be patented, and copyright can only protect the form of their expression, which can easily be changed without altering the content. Nevertheless, a significant investment of skilled labor goes into arranging such facts for computer applications—for instance, it takes a good fraction of a year's work to create a database that correctly relates all possible Spanish orthographic forms with their dictionary head-words and inflectional categories.

There are many other types of information that might be contained in such linguistic databases: the pronunciation of English words, the relationship between words and probability distributions over grammatical categories, the relationship between Japanese and English terms of art in electrical engineering, and so forth. These databases may have hundreds of thousands or even millions of entries, which usually have to be created or checked by human labor. For convenience in exposition, we will use the word "dictionary" to mean natural-language databases that require skilled labor and linguistic knowledge to design and assemble from the raw data.

Anyone who creates software that includes such a dictionary must face the fact that its information content is likely to be stolen if it is not somehow protected. That is, dictionary software is leaky. Our aim in this section is to present a general method for protecting dictionaries, along with an experimental implementation.

3.2. Structuring and storing the cleartext dictionary. Sometimes a dictionary is naturally expressed as a simple key-value table, and in this case, the method sketched in Section 2 can be applied directly. Often, however, the forms to which the dictionary applies arise from the rule-governed combination of parts, and the resulting relation may be large enough that we would rather generate it on-line than store it. Thus regular plural and possessive forms in English would triple the size of the noun list in a pronouncing dictionary, but can be derived in a simple way from the singular forms. For each Spanish verb stem, regular inflection and the attachment of enclitic pronouns can produce almost 100 forms. In some cases, such as the treatment of compound words in German, the full table is not bounded in any nonarbitrary way, and a decomposition in terms of simpler parts is forced.

One simple but useful way to treat such computations is as **transductions**, that is, n-ary word relations definable by the component-wise concatenation of n-tuple labels along paths in a finite directed labeled graph.[1] Define an

[1] See Rabin-Scott [**28**] and Elgot-Mezei [**8**].

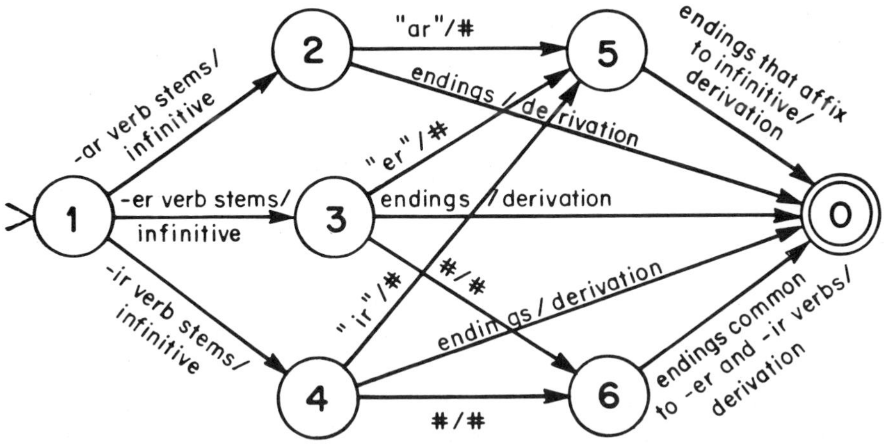

FIGURE 1. Spanish regular verb inflection

n-ary nondeterministic finite automaton as a 5-tuple

$$\mathscr{A} = (Q, q_1, F, \Sigma, H)$$

where Q is a finite nonempty set of states, q_1 is a designated start state, F is a set of designated final states, Σ is a finite nonempty alphabet, and H is a finite subset of $\{Q \times (\Sigma^*)^n \times Q\}$, where $(\Sigma^*)^n$ is the set of n-tuples of (possibly empty) words over Σ. Thus $\mathscr{A}$ defines a labeled directed graph, whose nodes are elements of Q, and whose edges are elements of H. Each edge is labeled with an n-tuple of (possibly empty) words. The componentwise concatenation of labels along every path that begins in q_1 and ends in an element of F defines a set of n-tuples, $R \subseteq (\Sigma^*)^n$, which is the relation transduced by $\mathscr{A}$.

The information content of most dictionaries (in the sense in which we are using that term) can be comfortably expressed by such a graph.[2] To use the dictionary, we need to run a program that searches this graph in order to find all the n-tuples in R meeting some condition, say those for which the "spelling" component of the relation is the string w.

Figure 1 shows a sample graph, labeled by pairs of strings, which expresses the regular aspects of Spanish verb inflection. As a cleartext database D we represent such a graph by an *arcfile* as follows. We assume, without loss of generality, that the start state has a designated name $START$ and that there is a single final state with the designated name $FINAL$. Every other node in the graph is assigned some unique string as an identifier. Then the

[2]Many researchers have based dictionary-access programs on nondeterministic finite transducers, although little of this work has been documented (see [**15**, **16**, **17**, **20**, **21**]). Previous work of this type is based on architectures in which the relations defined by multiple automata are intersected or composed, with an implementation that either simulates the multiple automata directly or (where this is possible) first constructs an equivalent single automaton.

information content of the graph is given by a set of 4-tuples of strings:

```
OriginState DestinationState InString OutString.
```

3.3. A program for accessing the cleartext dictionary. The lookup program P searches the graph represented by such an arcfile for all paths consistent with a given input string; that is, for all paths such that the input string matches the concatenation of *InStrings* along the path. Obviously, the labeling of tuple components as input and output is arbitrary—the same arclist can be used for computations in either direction. In the Spanish verb dictionary described in Section 3.5 below, this means that the same graph can be used to map verbs to morphological descriptions (e.g., *conozcamos* to **first person plural present subjunctive** of *conocer*) and to map morphological descriptions to verbs (e.g., **first person plural present subjunctive** of *conocer* to *conozcamos*); for the first mapping, we search the graph in one direction, and for the second, we search it in the opposite direction.

A recursive algorithm for P running on a given user input w is shown below. It assumes a function $find(D, OriginState, InString)$ that returns the (possibly null) list of $(DestinationState, OutString)$ pairs from all the arcs in D with that OriginState and InString. The notation `string1 - string2`, where string2 is an initial substring of string1, denotes the remaining characters of string1 if string2 is removed from its beginning. The notation `string1 + string2`, where string1 and string2 are arbitrary strings, denotes concatenation. `NULL` denotes the null string. *Process* uses the Boolean variable *accept* to keep track of whether there has been any accepting path.

```
P(w, D) :
    Initialize:
            {
            state ← START           /* current state */
            in ← w                  /* input not yet used up */
            out ← NULL              /* output seen so far */
            accept ← FALSE
            accept ← process(state, in, out, accept)
            if accept = FALSE, print(NIL)
            }
    process(state, in, out, accept):
        {
            if state = FINAL and in = NULL {
                print(out)
                accept ← TRUE
                return(accept)
            }
            /* otherwise continue */
            for i ← 0 to length(in) {
```

```
            s ← initial substring of in of length i
            for (dstate, outstr) in find(D, state, s) {
                accept ← process(dstate, in-s,
                                        out+outstr, accept)
            }
        }
    return(accept)
    }
```

3.4. The encrypted dictionary and modified lookup program. In order to create the corresponding encrypted database D', the arcfile can be treated as a table D of pairs (l_i, r_i), $1 \leq i \leq n$, by taking, for each arc, the concatenation of the OriginState and InString as l_i, and the concatenation of the DestinationState and OutString as r_i. Additional complexity can be given to D' by renaming the states to long random strings before encryption.

The program P' will then search the graph encrypted as D'. The algorithm is similar to P, with additional steps to deal with the encryption. It assumes a program *xfind*(*D'*, *hashvalue*), which returns the (possibly null) list of encrypted r values corresponding to arcs with that specified hash-value in D', and a program *separate*(*string*), which determines whether its input string is a valid DestinationState-OutString concatenation, returns the separated DestinationState and OutString if valid, and returns FALSE if its input is not valid.[3] As before, `string1 - string2` denotes the remaining characters of string1 after removing string2 from the beginning, `string1 + string2` denotes concatenation, and `NULL` denotes the null string.

$P'(w, D')$:

```
    Initialize:
        {
            state ← START           /* current state */
            in ← w                  /* input not yet used up */
            out ← NULL              /* output seen so far */
            accept ← FALSE
            accept ← process(state, in, out, accept)
            if accept = FALSE, print(NIL)
        }
    process(state, in, out, accept):
        {
            if state = FINAL and in = NULL {
                print(out)
                accept ← TRUE
```

[3]If we could guarantee the absence of hash collisions, this check on the validity of the encrypted form of r given l would not be necessary.

```
            exit
        }
        /* otherwise continue */
        for i ← 0 to length(in) {
            s ← initial substring of in of length i
            for enctext in xfind(DB, hash(state+s)) {
                dectext ← Dec(enctext, state+s)
                if separate(dectext) = NIL, return(accept)
                /* otherwise continue */
                (dstate, outstr) ← separate(dectext)
                accept ← process(dstate, in-s,
                                      out+outstr, accept)
            }
        }
        return(accept)
    }
```

As noted in Section 1, the complete input/output relation of a program accessing the database does not always provide enough information to reconstruct the database. In the case of an automaton simulator, for example, reconstructing the sequential transducer would require an exhaustive search of the space of possible Origin-Instring pairs.

3.5. Our implementation and the Spanish-verb analyzer. In the implementation described in this section, the hash function $hash(x)$ was a modified version of the hash function used by the UNIX spelling checker *spell* [**23**]. For the encryption-decryption pair $Enc(x, k)$ and $Dec(y, k)$, a modification of Don Mitchell's DES implementation was used.

The programs are called *dictionary*, *datacrypt*, and *lookup*. As a test case, the Spanish regular verb analyzer shown in Figure 1 was used.[4] It contains 4417 regular Spanish verbs and recognizes 48 of the inflected forms of each verb: the infinitive, the present and past participles, the imperatives, the indicative present, imperfect, preterite, future and conditional, and the subjunctive present and imperfect of each verb for all applicable combinations of person and number. The size in bytes of the cleartext arcfile and the encrypted files are as follows:

cleartext arcfile	94,704
encrypted arcfile	108,682
encrypted reverse arcfile	95,057

[4]Following this experiment, the same framework was applied to a complete implementation of the large Collins Spanish/English dictionary [**6**]. This database covers 55,000 base forms and the full set of their inflections and regular derivations.

Thus the space overhead for encryption was not very great. Of course, the cleartext arcfile is quite redundant and could be represented much more compactly. Significant compression (e.g., by a factor of 3 to 4) could also easily be achieved in the encrypted version, although some techniques (such as those that use shared structure) would not work, and it would therefore be hard to match the ultimate level of compression achievable in the clear. Still, the size of dictionary databases encrypted by this method would be acceptable for many applications.

We implemented both P and P', as described above, in C, aiming more at clarity and simplicity than at optimal performance. Our implementation of the P algorithm runs about twice as fast as our implementation of the P' algorithm, which nevertheless is able to process more than 100 words per second on a 10-MIP machine. The P' implementation spends a good deal of its time on a rather inefficient conversion of character strings into DES keys, and caching of previously obtained results would give a big performance boost given the usual Zipf's-law distribution of input forms. Even without any tuning, however, the performance is acceptable for many applications.

We should note that there are some efficient implementation techniques that would not be usable with this approach to database protection. An example is the use of a letter trie[5] associated with each state to encode the set of *instrings* that can be matched at that state, thus avoiding the need to test all possible substrings.

4. Conclusion and open questions

Our tentative conclusion is that it is feasible, both in terms of storage-space overhead and in terms of running-time overhead, to compute with encrypted versions of natural-language databases encoded as automata. Two types of open questions remain and invite further work.

First, there are open questions about our implementation. How close to one-way is the *spell* hash function? Our software can be modified easily to use any hash function that is fast enough to render the resulting *lookup* program practical. In our implementation of *lookup*, the following "false" matches are detected: $h(OriginState + InString)$, for some invalid available substring, matches the key of an entry in the encrypted automaton, but the decrypted value of the same entry is not a valid $h(destination - state + outstring)$ pair. The applicable notion of "validity" need not require the algorithm to know the set of possible state names, but could (for instance) be determined by a redundancy check character inserted into the decrypted string after the character that delimits the boundary between *destination-state* and *outstring*. It seems unlikely, but is obviously not impossible, that an undetectable false match could occur; i.e., an invalid *instring* choice could cause the automaton to "hit" a valid $h(destination - state + outstring)$ pair and to continue

[5]Refer to Knuth [19] for a detailed description of tries and their use in data retrieval.

through an erroneous path of the simulation. Is this really unlikely enough in practice to be ignored? Note that for output actually to be produced in such a case, the nonsensical instring would have to produce false matches along an entire path from start state to final state.

Next, we mention two open questions about the relationship of this work to more general questions in software protection and software engineering.

If the hashing, encryption, and decryption algorithms used in our scheme are good enough, then a computationally-bounded adversary cannot compute D given P' and D'. However, a trace of the execution of P' on a particular input would allow an adversary to learn one path through the automaton D. To recover the entire automaton, the adversary would have to generate inputs that "cover" all of D. The following observation is due to R. J. Lipton: the consensus in the program-testing community is that "coverage," i.e., generating a set of test inputs that cause every statement in a program to be executed, is very hard to achieve. Is it possible to formalize the apparent "reduction" from coverage to decryption? That is, can we say precisely that, to recover D, or even a significant portion of it, the adversary would have to generate a covering set of inputs, which appears to be hard in practice?

Finally, we draw the reader's attention to the Goldreich software protection model [**12**]; see also the recent work of Ostrovsky ([**26**]; abstract in these proceedings [**9**]). We do not review the details of the model here, but merely point out that our database protection goal is a special case of the goal of the software vendor in the Goldreich model. In [**12**], the end user feeds an encrypted program π' and a cleartext input x to a computer that contains a nonstandard piece of hardware, called a "cryptographic cpu." The software vendor wants the user not to be able to infer *anything* significant about the original program π from the memory-access pattern of the computer running π' on input x. In our case, the original program is the pair P, D, and the input is the query q. When we feed the encrypted pair P', D' to the computer, we do not care whether the user learns P. For the automaton case that we have already implemented, P is just a certain kind of graph search program, which the user could presumably construct on his own, and in general, P is some sort of database lookup program; all of the valuable information is in the encrypted data D'. Are there inexpensive versions of the solutions of Goldreich or Ostrovsky that work for the type of programs that we are interested in but that may not work in general?

5. Acknowledgments

It is a pleasure to acknowledge the help of Doug Blewett and Don Mitchell.

References

1. M. Abadi, J. Feigenbaum, and J. Kilian, *On hiding information from an oracle*, J. Comput. and System Sci. **39**(1) (1989), 21–50.

2. D. Beaver and J. Feigenbaum, *Hiding instances in multioracle queries*, Proc. of the 7th STACS (1990), Springer-Verlag, 37–48.
3. M. Ben-Or, S. Goldwasser, and A. Wigderson, *Completeness theorems for noncryptographic fault-tolerant distributed computation*, Proc. of the 20th STOC (1988), ACM, 1–10.
4. D. Chaum, C. Crépeau, and I. Damgård, *Multiparty unconditionally secure protocols*, Proc. of the 20th STOC (1988), ACM, 11–19.
5. N. Chomsky, *Context-free grammars and pushdown storage*, MIT Research Lab of Electronics Quarterly Progress Report, 1962.
6. *Collins Spanish Dictionary: Spanish-English*, Collins Publishers, Glasgow, 1989.
7. D. Denning, *Cryptography and data security*, Addison-Wesley, Reading, MA, 1982.
8. C. C. Elgot and J. E. Mezei, *On relations defined by generalized finite automata*, IBM J. Res. **9**(1965), 47–68.
9. J. Feigenbaum and M. Merritt, *Open Questions, Talk Abstracts, and Summary of Discussions*, these proceedings.
10. Z. Galil, S. Haber, and M. Yung, *Cryptographic computation: Secure fault-tolerant protocols and the public-key model*, Proc. of the 7th CRYPTO (1987), Springer-Verlag, 135–155.
11. S. Ginsburg, *An introduction to mathematical machine theory*, Addison-Wesley, Reading, MA, 1966.
12. O. Goldreich, *Towards a theory of software protection and simulation by oblivious RAMs*, Proc. of the 19th STOC (1987), ACM, 182–194.
13. O. Goldreich, S. Micali, and A. Wigderson, *How to play ANY mental game*, Proc. of the 19th STOC (1987), ACM, 218–229.
14. J. E. Hopcroft and J. D. Ullman, *Introduction to automata theory, languages and computation*, Addison-Wesley, Reading, MA, 1979.
15. M. Kay, "When meta-rules are not meta-rules", in *Automatic natural language processing*, Spark-Jones and Wilks (eds.), University of Essex, Cognitive Studies Center (CSM-10), 1982.
16. L. Kartunnen, *KIMMO: A general morphological processor*, Texas Linguistic Forum **22** (1983), 165–186.
17. L. Kartunnen, K. Koskenniemi, and R. Kaplan, *A compiler for two-level phonological rules*, manuscript, Xerox Palo Alto Research Center, 1987.
18. R. Khan, *A two-level morphological analysis of Roumanian*, Texas Linguistic Forum **22** (1983), 253–270.
19. D. Knuth, *The art of computer programming – Vol. 3: Searching and sorting*, Addison-Wesley, Reading, MA, 1973.
20. K. Koskenniemi, *Two-level morphology: A general computational model for word-form recognition and production*, University of Helsinki, Dept. of General Linguistics, Publications No. 11, 1983.
21. K. Koskenniemi and K. W. Church, *Complexity, two-level morphology, and Finnish*, Proc. of the 12th International Conference on Computational Linguistics, Budapest, Hungary, 1988.
22. S. Lun, *A two-level morphological analysis of French*, Texas Linguistic Forum **22** (1983), 271–277.
23. M. D. McIlroy, *Development of a spelling list*, IEEE Trans. Comm. COM-**30**(1) (1982), 91–99.
24. R. Merkle, *One-way hash functions and DES*, Proc. of the 9th CRYPTO (1989), Springer-Verlag, 428–446.
25. M. Naor and M. Yung, *Universal one-way hash functions and their cryptographic applications*, Proc. of the 21st STOC (1989), ACM, 33–43.
26. R. Ostrovsky, *Efficient computation on oblivious RAMs*, Proc. of the 22nd STOC (1990), ACM, 514–523.
27. W. G. Ouchi, *The new joint R&D*, Proc. of the IEEE, **77** (1989), 1318–1326.
28. M. O. Rabin and D. Scott, *Finite automata and their decision problems*, IBM J. Res. **3** (1959), 114–125.

29. M. P. Schützenberger, *A remark on finite transducers*, Information and Control **4** (1961), 185–196.
30. A. C. Yao, *Protocols for secure computations*, Proc. of the 23rd FOCS (1982), IEEE, 160–164.

AT&T Bell Laboratories, Room 2C473, Murray Hill, NJ 07974 USA
E-mail address: jf@research.att.com.

AT&T Bell Laboratories, Room 2D446, Murray Hill, NJ 07974 USA
E-mail address: myl@research.att.com.

Yale University, Comp. Sci. Dept., New Haven, CT 06520 USA
E-mail address: wright-rebecca@cs.yale.edu.

DIMACS Series in Discrete Mathematics
and Theoretical Computer Science
Volume 2, 1991

Secret Bit Transmission Using a Random Deal of Cards

Extended Abstract

MICHAEL J. FISCHER
MICHAEL S. PATERSON
CHARLES RACKOFF

ABSTRACT. Protocols are developed and analyzed for transmitting a secret bit between a sender and a receiver process using only the information contained in a random deal of hands of specified sizes from a deck of n distinct cards. The sender's and receiver's algorithms are known in advance, and all conversation between sender and receiver is public and is heard by all. A correct protocol always succeeds in transmitting the secret bit, and the other player(s), who receive the remaining cards and are assumed to have unlimited computing power, gain no information whatsoever about the value of the secret bit. In other words, their probability of correctly guessing the secret bit is exactly the same after listening to a run of the protocol as it was before. Both randomized and deterministic protocols are considered. A randomized protocol is described that works whenever the sender's and receiver's hands comprise a constant fraction of the deck, for all sufficiently large decks. A deterministic protocol is also described, but it requires the sender and receiver to each have approximately 43% of the cards. A general condition is presented that provides a lower bound on sizes of the sender's and receiver's hands in order for a protocol to exist. There is still a considerable gap between the upper and lower bounds, and improving the bounds remains an open problem.

1. Introduction

In the game of bridge, partners exchange public bids in order to arrive at a contract before playing the cards. In the course of bidding, partners gain information about each other's hands, and indeed, considerable effort has

---

1980 *Mathematics Subject Classification* (1985 *Revision*). Primary 94A60; Secondary 68P25.
This work was supported in part by the National Science Foundation under grant number DCR-8405478 and by the Office of Naval Research under contract numbers N00014-82-K-0154 and N00014-89-J-1980. We are grateful to the Sonderforschungsbereich 124 of the Universität des Saarlandes for partial support of this research.

been put into designing bidding conventions (protocols in our terminology) for maximizing the amount of useful information conveyed to the partner. It is of course desirable that the opponents obtain as little useful information as possible from the bidding.

It is considered dishonest for partners to use secret conventions, and the laws of bridge require that a partnership make public their conventions prior to play. Nevertheless, one partner may well learn more from her partner's bid than do the opponents. For example, a partner responding to the Blackwood convention makes a bid whose meaning is the number of aces held. While all players thereby learn that number, the initiating partner will learn by inference *which* aces the responding partner holds if the initiator happens to hold all of the remaining aces.

Peter Winkler carried this idea further and developed bidding conventions whereby one player could send her partner secret information about her hand that was totally unrelated to the actual bid and completely undecipherable to the opponents, even though the protocol was known to them [**1**, **2**, **3**, **4**]. While one such convention was turned down in Great Britain for use in tournament play, the idea that card games could be used to achieve perfect cryptography without further assumptions remains intriguing and led to this paper.

2. Secret bit transmission

The secret bit transmission problem that we study is the classical problem of cryptography. An agent, Alice, has a secret bit s, which she wishes to send to another agent, Bob. All communication is via an insecure channel, so we must proceed under the assumption that an eavesdropper, Eve, overhears all communication between Alice and Bob. The goal of the protocol is for Bob to learn s but for Eve to gain no information about s. In other words, Eve's probability of correctly guessing s is unchanged after listening to the run of the protocol between Alice and Bob. Since Eve is assumed to have unlimited computing power, cryptographic systems based on computational difficulty are not applicable, and we seek instead a perfect scheme in the information-theoretic sense.

We are interested only in protocols that *always* work, as opposed to protocols that only sometimes work or that have a probability of error. Thus, we say that a protocol solves the *secret bit transmission problem* if in *every* run, Bob learns s and Eve gains no information about s.

Of course, if Alice and Bob share a random secret bit r that is not known to Eve, then it suffices for Alice to send the message $m = r \oplus s$ (the exclusive "or" of r with s). Bob computes $s = m \oplus r$, and Eve learns nothing about s, since the possibility that $s = 0$ and $r = m$ and the possibility that $s = 1$ and

$r = 1 \oplus m$ are equally likely, given knowledge only of m. r is called a "one-time pad" (since it cannot safely be used again to send another message), and this scheme is an example of a secure private-key cryptosystem for sending a single secret bit.

A generalization of the one-time pad is important when we consider deterministic protocols. Suppose that Alice and Bob share a random value $r \in \{0, \ldots, d-1\}$. When d is odd, r cannot be mapped to a random fair bit, but it can still be used to send s secretly; namely, Alice sends the message $m = (r+s) \bmod d$. As in the binary case, Eve learns nothing about s since all values m are equally likely, regardless of the value of s. We call such an r a *d-generalized one-time pad.*

We rule out private-key cryptography by assuming that Alice and Bob have no prior secret information between themselves. Both the protocols and initial state of Alice and Bob are known to Eve. The only information that Eve does not know in advance is the value of the secret bit s, which we can regard as a private input to Alice.

It is easily shown that without any further assumptions, secret bit transmission is impossible, for Eve can simulate Bob and reach the same conclusion as to the value of s that Bob does. In case Bob is a deterministic algorithm, the simulation is obvious. If Bob is a randomized algorithm (i.e., can flip private fair coins), then Eve simulates Bob on all possible coin-toss sequences, discarding those simulated runs in which the simulated behavior deviates from Bob's actual observed behavior. Any remaining simulated runs are *possible* runs for Bob, and thus any such run that determines a value for s must determine the correct value. In this way, Eve learns s.

Henceforth, we assume that the three players have available randomly dealt hands from a deck of n distinct totally ordered cards. In an (a, b, c) deal, Alice gets a cards, Bob gets b cards, and Eve gets $c = n - a - b$ cards. The size of the deck, the values of the cards in the deck, and the total ordering on the cards are common knowledge among all players, as are the cardinalities of each player's hands. Only the identities of the particular cards in each player's hand are private to that player. Unlike a deal in a real card game, we assume that each player's hand is sorted by the dealer, so that no random information is contained in the order in which the cards are presented to the player. This assumption is significant when we discuss deterministic protocols.

In carrying out a secret bit transmission using a deal of cards, players are allowed to say anything they want and to reveal as much information as they like about their hands. The only requirement is that Bob eventually learns s and Eve remains completely in the dark about s. A protocol that, given a random (a, b, c) deal, succeeds in transmitting s secretly is called an (a, b, c) *secret bit transmission protocol.*

3. A simple randomized protocol

To illustrate some of the basic ideas underlying this problem, we first consider a simple randomized protocol and prove that it works whenever $a, b \geq 1$ and $a+b \geq c+2$.

A *key set* K consists of any two cards, one from Alice's hand and one from Bob's hand. We say that $K = \{x, y\}$ is *hidden* if the two situations, that Alice holds x and Bob holds y or that Alice holds y and Bob holds x, are equally likely, given the information available to Eve. Note that by this definition, K can be hidden even though Eve knows which two cards are in K.

Assuming Alice and Bob can somehow identify a hidden key set $K = \{x, y\}$, they can then obtain from it a one-time pad r. Namely, they agree that $r = 0$ if Alice holds the smaller card in K and $r = 1$ if she holds the larger. Since Alice and Bob each know which card of K they hold, they each also know r. Eve on the other hand has no information about which card which partner holds, so r looks completely random to her. Alice can then use r to send s to Bob as described above.

The following protocol allows Alice and Bob to determine a key set:

(i) Alice chooses a random card x contained in her hand and a random card y not in her hand and proposes $K = \{x, y\}$ as a key set to Bob.[1]

(ii) If Bob holds y (i.e., holds a card in K), he knows that K is a key set, so he *accepts* K and announces that fact to Alice, who then also knows that K is a key set. K is hidden since it is equally likely to be proposed by Alice in the symmetric deal in which everything is the same except that Alice holds y and Bob holds x. K is the desired key set, and the protocol terminates.

(iii) If Bob does not hold y, he *rejects* K and announces this fact to Alice. In this case, the facts that Alice holds x and Eve holds y are common knowledge between Alice and Eve, so Alice tells these facts to Bob as well, making the locations of x and y public. Alice and Bob then discard x and y from the deck and go back to step 1 of the protocol, pretending that the cards remaining in their hands came from a $(a-1, b, c-1)$ deal from an $n-2$ card deck. Eve has no information about how the remaining cards not in her hand are divided up between Alice and Bob, so the remaining hands indeed look random to her. Alice and Bob keep repeating the protocol in this way until they find a key set or until Alice is unable to complete step 1 (because either her hand is empty or she holds all of the cards in the deck).

---

[1]To keep from revealing information about which of the two cards she holds, she sorts K into increasing order before sending it to Bob.

If $a > c$, then Eve runs out of cards before Alice does, since both Alice and Eve lose one card on each iteration where Alice proposes a set K that is rejected by Bob. If also $b \geq 1$, then when c becomes 0, the next proposed key set is guaranteed to be accepted by Bob and the protocol terminates.

By modifying this protocol so that on each iteration, Alice and Bob switch roles if Bob holds more cards than Alice, we obtain:

THEOREM 1. *Let $a, b \geq 1$ and $a + b \geq c + 2$. Then there is a randomized (a, b, c) secret bit transmission protocol.*

4. A solution requiring only a fraction of the cards

The protocol of Section 3 requires that Alice and Bob jointly are dealt more than half the cards. We next sketch a protocol in which Alice and Bob each receive only $\lfloor \alpha n \rfloor$ of the cards, where α is an arbitrary positive constant.

The idea here is to generalize the notion of a key set. Call a set K an *i-set* if the cardinality of K is i and K contains exactly one card from each of Alice's and Bob's hands (and the remaining $i - 2$ cards belong to Eve's hand). By this definition, a key set as previously defined is the same as a 2-set.

The protocol operates in two phases. The first phase produces a large collection of disjoint m-sets and $(m-1)$-sets, where $m = \lceil n/a \rceil$. A reduction phase then transforms this collection into a single 2-set. The reduction phase operates iteratively, at each stage replacing two sets in the collection by a new set. An entropy argument is used to show that the reduction process eventually terminates in a 2-set, assuming the initial collection of sets was sufficiently large.

In slightly more detail, Alice initially partitions the deck into a sets, each of which contains one card from her hand and either $m - 1$ or $m - 2$ cards not in her hand. Bob accepts a proposed set if he holds one or more cards in it; otherwise he rejects it. In the worst case, he will accept at least $b/(m-1)$ sets since all of his cards lie in the various proposed sets. By making n sufficiently large, the number of accepted sets can be made arbitrarily large.

If Bob holds more than one card in an accepted set, he randomly chooses one such card to keep and he discards the rest. The result is an m'-set for some $m' \leq m$. Hence, the first phase yields at least $b/(m-1)$ m'-sets of various sizes $m' \leq m$.

In the reduction phase, Alice chooses two sets R, S of maximal size from the collection. For definiteness, say R is an i-set and S is a j-set ($2 < i, j \leq m$). She then chooses one of the two sets at random, say R. Let x be the (unique) card in R that Alice holds. Let y be chosen randomly from among the cards of S that Alice does *not* hold. Alice then proposes $T = \{x, y\}$ as a key set, and Bob accepts or rejects it according to whether he holds y or not. If he accepts it, then T is a 2-set, and the reduction phase succeeds. If not, then Alice announces the locations of the cards in $R \cup \{x, y\}$, which are then discarded. She removes R and S from her collection of sets and puts the new set $S' = S - \{y\}$, which is a $(j-1)$-set, back into the collection. This process is repeated until either a key set is obtained or until only one set remains in the collection. A simple inductive proof shows that if the collection originally contains at least 2^{m-2} sets, then the reduction process eventually yields a key set.

The above establishes:

THEOREM 2. *Let α be an arbitrary positive real number. There exists n_0 such that for all $n \geq n_0$, if $a = b = \lfloor \alpha n \rfloor$ and $c = n - a - b$, then there is a randomized (a, b, c) secret bit transmission protocol.*

For the above protocol, n_0 is $O(m^2 2^m)$. The protocol can be improved to yield a much smaller bound, which we currently believe will work out to about $O(m^{d \log m / \log\log m})$ for some constant d. The protocol improvements involve both phases. In phase 1, if Bob holds more than $k > 1$ cards in a proposed m'-set then, rather than discard the extras, he can partition the set into k sets each of size about m'/k such that he holds a card in each. One of them will contain Alice's card and hence be an m''-set for $m'' \approx m'/k$. In phasc 2, instead of choosing two sets R and S and forming a trial 2-set T, it is better to choose r sets $R_1, \ldots, R_r$ from the collection and to form a trial r-set T by choosing one card from each R_i such that T has exactly one card from Alice's hand and $r-1$ cards not in her hand. If Bob accepts T, then T is an r-set and replaces $R_1, \ldots, R_r$ in the collection. Otherwise, the cards in T are discarded, leaving r sets $R_i' = R_i - T$, $1 \leq i \leq r$. Since T contained one card from Alice's hand, one of the R_i' sets has an empty intersection with Alice's hand, and it too is discarded. The remaining R_j' sets are returned to the collection. r is chosen at each stage to optimize the progress made. Our improved bound results from taking r approximately equal to $m \log\log m / \log m$.

5. A lower-bound theorem

The above protocols establish triples (a, b, c) for which an (a, b, c) secret bit transmission protocol exists. We now present a lower bound on the sizes of Alice's and Bob's hands for such a protocol to exist.

THEOREM 3. *Let $n = a + b + c$. Let γ be the probability that a pair of random hands A (for Alice) and B (for Bob) intersect when dealt from* different *decks, where as usual, $|A| = a$ and $|B| = b$. If $\gamma < 1/2$, then there is no (a, b, c) secret bit transmission protocol, even if Eve is not allowed to look at her hand.*

The idea behind the proof is to look at runs of the protocol according to the transcript (conversation) τ that Eve hears. Assume for the moment that Alice and Bob are deterministic protocols, so τ is a function of s, A, and B. Call the triple (s, A, B) a *situation.* The secrecy condition implies that the number of situations giving rise to τ with $s = 0$ is the same as the number with $s = 1$. Now suppose $(0, A_0, B_0)$ and $(1, A_1, B_1)$ are two situations both giving rise to τ. Then an easy inductive argument shows that the situations $(0, A_0, B_1)$ and $(1, A_1, B_0)$ also give rise to τ. Moreover, since Bob outputs 0 in $(0, A_0, B_0)$ and outputs 1 in $(1, A_1, B_1)$, then he outputs 0 in $(1, A_1, B_0)$ and outputs 1 in $(0, A_0, B_1)$. Since his answers in these latter two situations are both incorrect and we assume a correct protocol, it must be the case that these situations cannot occur in a proper deal; i.e., $A_0 \cap B_1 \neq \emptyset$ and $A_1 \cap B_0 \neq \emptyset$. Thus, corresponding to legal pairs (A_0, B_0) and (A_1, B_1) (i.e., pairs dealt from the same deck) are illegal pairs (A_0, B_1) and (A_1, B_0). A counting argument shows that # legal pairs $\leq$ # illegal pairs, from which it follows that $\gamma \geq 1/2$. Hence, if $\gamma < 1/2$, then no protocol exists.

When Alice and Bob are randomized algorithms, the transcript τ depends on Alice's and Bob's random choice sequences as well as on s, A, and B, so the definition of a situation must be extended to include the choice sequences, and one must sum over all choice sequences at the end. Details are given in the full paper.

COROLLARY 1. *There is no* $(1, 1, 1)$ *secret bit transmission protocol.*

PROOF. For this case, $\gamma = 1/3 < 1/2$. □

6. Deterministic protocols

The protocols given so far in this paper heavily exploit randomization by the players. Moreover, it is not at all clear how to get rid of randomization. For example, if Alice proposes a key set $\{x, y\}$ by picking the *smallest* card in her hand for x and the *smallest* card not in her hand for y, then she may be revealing her entire hand by announcing the set $\{x, y\}$. For example, if $a < n/2$ and the set she announces contains card number $n - a + 1$, that card must be x, and Alice's hand is $\{n - a + 1, n - a + 2, \ldots, n\}$, where as usual, $n = a + b + c$, and we assume the cards of the deck are numbered $1, 2, \ldots, n$. Nevertheless, deterministic protocols are possible, at least for some triples of hand sizes. We describe a recursive protocol below.

The protocol proceeds as follows on an (a, b, c) deal:

(i) If $a, b \geq 1$ and $c = 0$, then there are $d = \binom{n}{a}$ possible $(a, b, 0)$ deals. Index them from 0 to $d - 1$ in some predetermined way, and let r be the index of the actual deal. Both Alice and Bob know the exact placement of every card (since $c = 0$), so both can compute r. Eve however has no information about r. Alice sends s to Bob using r as a d-generalized one-time pad as described in Section 1, and the protocol succeeds.

(ii) If $a = 0$ or $b = 0$, there is nothing Alice or Bob can do and the protocol fails.

(iii) If n is odd, Alice and Bob determine the location of card n by each announcing whether or not they hold the card, and that card is discarded from further play. This leaves the three players with a random deal from a deck of $n - 1$ cards and hands of sizes $(a-1, b, c)$, $(a, b-1, c)$, or $(a, b, c-1)$, depending on which of the three players originally held card n. Alice and Bob know which of these three situations they are in, and they play accordingly by using this protocol recursively.

(iv) If n is even, Alice and Bob regard the deck as consisting of $n/2$ *suits* of two cards each by mapping card $2k$ to suit k, rank 0, and card $2k+1$ to suit k, rank 1. Alice and Bob then name all of their singleton suits. If they both name the same singleton suit, then the two cards of that suit form a key set and the protocol succeeds. If not, then Eve holds the other card of each singleton suit named by either Alice or Bob. Alice and Bob now select a subset of the deck for which they have a random deal and they use this protocol recursively on the subset. The subset consists of all cards of rank 0 and all suits k such that k is *not* one of the singleton suits named by either Alice or Bob. Let (a', b', c') be the numbers of cards in the subset held by Alice, Bob, and Eve, respectively. If Alice previously named p singleton suits and Bob named q, then $a' = (a-p)/2$, $b' = (b-q)/2$, and $c' = (c-p-q)/2$. This is because after all of the cards of singleton suits have been discarded, then every player that holds the rank 0 card of a suit also holds the rank 1 card of the same suit.

This protocol always succeeds for (a, b, c) if either $a, b \geq 1$ and $c = 0$, or if it always succeeds on all of the smaller deals that might be produced by the above rules. The recurrence relation that results is not particularly well behaved, but we can prove the following:

THEOREM 4. *There exists a deterministic* (a, b, c) *protocol for secret bit transmission if* $a, b \geq 1$ *and* $c \leq \min(a, b)/3$.

7. Conclusion and open problems

This work is a first step at trying to understand the notion of the shared secret random information contained in a deal of cards and to find protocols to make use of such shared information. It also gives further insight into the power of private coins and multiround interaction.

An obvious direction for further investigation is to find tighter bounds on triples (a, b, c) for which randomized and deterministic (a, b, c) protocols do and do not exist. An obvious extension is to consider the problem of sending more than one secret bit with a single deal of cards and/or to relax some of the requirements we have imposed on a solution. For example, one might allow a small probability of error in the protocol so that Bob sometimes fails to learn the secret, or Eve sometimes does learn the secret, or Eve's probability of correctly guessing the secret increases by a small positive ε.

Another direction for further research, suggested by Peter Winkler, is to replace probabilistic statements by knowledge statements. Thus, the problem becomes one of finding an (a, b, c) protocol such that after running it, Bob knows the secret value but Eve does not. Every secret bit transmission protocol satisfies these conditions, but the converse does not hold, for even when Eve does not learn the secret bit for sure, she may nevertheless have acquired partial information about it. Our lower bound theorem does not seem to apply to this case, and it appears that a detailed analysis of the knowledge structure will be necessary.

A final avenue for further research is to look at even more restricted protocols. For example, a *one-way deterministic protocol* is one in which Alice sends only a single message to Bob, who then, on the basis of his hand, can figure out Alice's secret but Eve learns nothing about it. Andrew Berman has shown that such protocols can exist by exhibiting one for a $(5, 4, 1)$ deal. It is an open problem to find other nontrivial triples for which such one-way protocols exist.

Acknowledgment

We are grateful to Andrew Berman and Peter Winkler for helpful discussions.

References

1. Jeremy Flint, "Cheating by degrees," *The Times Saturday Review*, May 1981.
2. Peter Winkler, "Cryptologic techniques in bidding and defense," parts i, ii, iii, and iv, *Bridge Magazine*, April: 148–149, May: 186–187, June: 226–227, and July: 12–13, 1981.
3. Peter Winkler, "My night at the cryppie club," *Bridge Magazine*, pages 60–63, August 1981.
4. Peter Winkler, *The advent of cryptology in the game of bridge*, Cryptologia 7 (1983), 327–332.

YALE UNIVERSITY

UNIVERSITY OF WARWICK

UNIVERSITY OF TORONTO

DIMACS Series in Discrete Mathematics
and Theoretical Computer Science
Volume 2, 1991

Security against Replay Chosen-Ciphertext Attack

ZVI GALIL, STUART HABER, AND MOTI YUNG

ABSTRACT. Since zero-knowledge proofs were proposed, they have had several different uses in cryptography. In a number of extended abstracts published in conference proceedings, zero-knowledge proofs have been used in one or another way in order to specify a public-key cryptosystem that achieves one or another sort of security against chosen-ciphertext attack. (For example, the authors did this in Crypto '85 [2].) None of these published claims included a precise definition of the security achieved, let alone a proof.

In this note we would like to suggest a formal definition for chosen-ciphertext security, hoping to elicit comment and criticism. We are able to use the properties of zero-knowledge proofs of knowledge (as formalized by Feige, Fiat, and Shamir [1] and by Tompa and Woll [8]) in order to prove that the interactive cryptosystem we proposed at Crypto '85 in fact satisfies our definition.

Following a suggestion of Michael Fischer offered at this workshop, we propose a definition of a stronger sort of security against "replay chosen-ciphertext attack." Our Crypto '85 scheme also satisfies this more stringent definition of cryptographic security.

1. Introduction

The designer of a multi-user cryptosystem must be concerned not only with passive attacks or unauthenticated messages sent by impersonators but also with attacks carried on by active participants. One or more malicious users may take advantage of their user privileges, sending and receiving specially computed plaintext and ciphertext messages, or deviating from the system's message-sending protocols in some other manner, in order to attack a legitimate user's security. In this note we offer complexity-theoretic definitions of security against such attacks.

1980 *Mathematics Subject Classification* (1985 *Revision*). Primary 68P25, 94A60.

A preliminary announcement of part of this work will appear as "A secure public-key authentication scheme" in *Advances in Cryptology: Proceedings of Eurocrypt '89*, Springer-Verlag (forthcoming). The full paper is available in [3] and has been submitted for publication.

We use the following notation. Our public-key setting includes a *security parameter* k, a sequence of *message spaces* $\{M_k\}$ (probability distributions on strings of a fixed length polynomial in k), a probabilistic *key-generator* G, a *public-key encryption-decryption algorithm pair* (E, D), and one or more "message-sending protocols." In general, E may be a probabilistic algorithm. We use (e, d) to denote a typical output of G, consisting of a public and a private key. A message-sending protocol is a pair of interacting probabilistic Turing machines (S, R), a *sender* and a *receiver.* Each machine takes as input a pair of public keys (e_S, e_R) (belonging to S and R, respectively) as well as its own private key d_S or d_R (respectively). The sender receives as additional input a message chosen according to the message space M_k. The machines proceed with their computation. At any point, either party may *reject* the execution. Otherwise, when they halt, the receiver writes out, as a private output, the cleartext message m that it has *accepted.* Observe that the transcript of communications in a particular execution may be regarded as an encryption of the message m. Note also that a public-key pair (E, D) may be regarded as special message-sending protocol in which there is only one communication between the sender E and the receiver D.

The participants' attack on a cryptosystem may include two sorts of activity: participation stages during which the attackers take part in protocol executions and interact with other users, gaining information about ciphertext strings of their choice, and an extraction stage during which the attackers try to infer additional information about legitimate users' messages or private keys. As in the definitions of Goldwasser and Micali **[5]**, which we generalize here, we will call an attack successful if the extraction stage results in a very weak sort of cryptanalytic ability, namely the ability to distinguish which of two cleartext messages, chosen by the adversary, has been encrypted by a given ciphertext.

In these definitions, we model the adversary as a suite of computational devices with polynomially bounded resources: polynomial-time probabilistic interactive Turing machines and polynomial-size families of probabilistic circuits. The Turing machines model the participation stages of an attack. We speak of two circuit families, a *message-finder* $F = \{F_k\}$ and a *message-distinguisher* $T = \{T_k\}$, using the kth member of each family as a component of the attack on keys with security parameter k. Given one or two public keys—the target of the attack—and some information gleaned from the participation stage, the finder circuit F_k produces as output two messages $m_0, m_1 \in M_k$. One of these messages is chosen at random and encrypted or sent using the target key(s). Given this encryption, as well as all the information gathered during the participation stage(s) of the attack, the task of the distinguisher circuit T_k is to guess whether m_0 or m_1 was chosen.

For a fuller discussion of these definitions, see **[5, 6, 9]**, as well as our complete version of this paper **[3]**.

2. Chosen-ciphertext attack, noninteractive setting

It may be helpful formally to define a chosen-ciphertext attack on a public-key encryption-decryption algorithm pair (E, D) before defining the attack on a more general message-sending protocol. This definition is an adaptation of Goldwasser and Micali's definition of the "polynomial security" of a probabilistic public-key encryption-decryption pair [5]. The Goldwasser-Micali definition is the appropriate version, in this context, of security against chosen-message attack.

A *chosen-ciphertext attack* on (E, D) consists of an interactive Turing machine $\mathscr{A}$, a message-finder $F = \{F_k\}$, and a message-distinguisher $T = \{T_k\}$, as follows. The input to $\mathscr{A}$ consists of a security parameter k and a public key e; this key is the target of $\mathscr{A}$'s attack. Several times during the course of its computation, $\mathscr{A}$ interacts with D by requesting that a ciphertext string c of its choice be decrypted using the private key d that corresponds to e. (More precisely, $\mathscr{A}$ writes c on one of its communication tapes, and then reads $D(c, d)$ from its other communication tape.) The message-finder circuit F_k takes as input the target key e along with the contents of $\mathscr{A}$'s history tape, and computes as output two messages $m_0, m_1 \in M_k$. The message-distinguisher T_k takes as input a public key, the contents of an interactive Turing machine's history tape, a pair of messages in M_k, and an encryption produced by E, and produces a single bit as output.

Consider the following experiment. Run G on 1^k to get (e, d). Run $\mathscr{A}$ with input e, using D (and the private key d) to decrypt the requested strings; this computation is the participation stage of the attack. Next, in the extraction stage, give e and $\mathscr{A}$'s history tape h to F_k to obtain a pair of messages $m_0, m_1 \in M_k$. Choose one of these at random, m_b say, and give (m_b, e) to E to produce an encryption α; finally, give (e, h, m_0, m_1, α) as input to T_k to obtain the bit b'—its guess as to whether the message sent was m_0 or m_1. The experiment is a success if $b = b'$. We say that (E, D) is *polynomially secure against chosen-ciphertext attack* if for any interactive Turing machine $\mathscr{A}$, for any message-finder F, for any message-distinguisher T, and for any constant c, the probability of success is less than $\frac{1}{2} + \frac{1}{k^c}$ for sufficiently large k.

3. Chosen-ciphertext attack, interactive setting

Next, we generalize the above definition to deal with the more general setting of interactive protocols. Suppose that we are given a message-sending protocol (S, R). A *chosen-ciphertext attack* on the protocol consists of an interactive Turing machine $\mathscr{A}$, a message-finder $F = \{F_k\}$, and a message-distinguisher $T = \{T_k\}$, as follows. The input to $\mathscr{A}$ consists of a security parameter k and two public keys e_0 and e_1; these keys are the targets of $\mathscr{A}$'s attack. After performing several executions of the message-sending protocol, as described below, $\mathscr{A}$ writes out its view of these executions. The k th message-finding circuit F_k takes as input the target keys e_0, e_1 along with $\mathscr{A}$'s execution views, and computes as output two messages $m_0, m_1 \in M_k$, as well as a *choice* of either 0 or 1. The message-distinguisher is as above, except that T_k 's inputs include a pair of public keys with security parameter k instead of a single public key, the machine $\mathscr{A}$'s history string, and the transcript of a protocol execution instead of an output of the encryption algorithm.

The attacking machine $\mathscr{A}$ is meant to model a coalition of several malicious users; it operates as follows. Several (polynomially many) times, $\mathscr{A}$ chooses to participate in the given message-sending protocol, each time choosing either to send or to receive a message, as well as choosing one of the two keys e_0 or e_1 to be used by the "legitimate" receiver or sender.

- If the choice is to send, then $\mathscr{A}$ takes the role of the sender in a protocol execution with R. In this execution, $\mathscr{A}$ may "send" a message from the message space M_k or a message chosen according to some other computation. R uses either (e_0, d_0) or (e_1, d_1) according to $\mathscr{A}$'s choice. At the end of the execution, $\mathscr{A}$ is given R's private output (the message that R accepted). For convenience, we may refer to $\mathscr{A}$'s computation during this execution as a "subroutine" $\tilde{S}$.
- If the choice is to receive, then $\mathscr{A}$ takes the role of the receiver in a protocol execution with S, in which S attempts to send a message chosen according to the distribution M_k. S uses either (e_0, d_0) or (e_1, d_1) according to $\mathscr{A}$'s choice. At the end of the execution, $\mathscr{A}$ is given S's private output (the message that S tried to send). Once again, we may refer to $\mathscr{A}$'s "subroutine" $\tilde{R}$.

In each execution, $\mathscr{A}$ may request a new public-key, private-key pair generated by G (with security parameter k), or may use a pair requested earlier. These pairs are generated independently of the target keys.

$\mathscr{A}$'s attack may be "adaptive": any of its computation steps may depend on previous steps. For instance, the sending (or receiving) subroutine $\tilde{S}$ (or $\tilde{R}$) invoked by $\mathscr{A}$ during a particular execution of the protocol may be different from the subroutine used by $\mathscr{A}$ in an earlier execution. Of course, the computation of R (or of S)—modeling the actions of a legitimate receiver (or sender)—is not adaptive; each step is an independent execution with a new sequence of random coin-flips. Without loss of generality we may require that the concatenation of $\mathscr{A}$'s execution views be a string v of length at most $l(k)$, where l is a polynomial.

Consider the following experiment. Run G twice on input 1^k to obtain (e_0, d_0) and (e_1, d_1). Run $\mathscr{A}$ with input (e_0, e_1) as described above to produce the execution history h; this computation is the participation stage of the attack. Next, in the extraction stage, give (e_0, e_1) and h to F_k to produce $m_0, m_1 \in M_k$ and a "choice" of 0 or 1; this is a choice as to whether to use the target keys e_0 and e_1 as the receiver's key and the sender's key or vice versa in the next run of the protocol. Next, choose one of the messages m_0, m_1 at random, m_b say, and run (S, R) to send m_b, using as keys either (e_0, d_0) and (e_1, d_1) or (e_1, d_1) and (e_0, d_0) according to F_k's choice of 0 or 1, respectively; let τ be the "public" transcript of this run. Finally, give the public keys e_0 and e_1, the pair of messages (m_0, m_1), the transcript τ, and the history string h as input to T_k to obtain the bit b'. The experiment is a success if $b = b'$. We say that the message-sending protocol is *polynomially secure against chosen-ciphertext attack* if for any interactive Turing machine $\mathscr{A}$, for any message-finder F, for any message-distinguisher T, and for any constant c, the probability of success is less than $\frac{1}{2} + \frac{1}{k^c}$ for sufficiently large k.

4. Replay chosen-ciphertext attack

Following a suggestion of Michael Fischer, we can strengthen the power of a chosen-ciphertext attack to allow what we may call a "replay chosen-ciphertext attack." This attack begins in the same way as the chosen-ciphertext attack: the adversary probes the cryptosystem, and chooses two messages m_0 and m_1, and then is challenged to guess which of the two has been sent in a particular execution of (S, R). Now, after being given the challenge, he is allowed to continue probing as before. If he wishes he can try to sample protocol executions for m_0 and for m_1, or he can try to replay the particular challenge execution he has seen. Even with this additional information, the adversary's distinguisher should not have any non-negligible advantage in guessing whether the challenge was an encryption of m_0 or of m_1.

More formally, we define a *replay chosen-ciphertext attack* on a message-sending protocol (S, R) to consist of message-finder and message-distinguisher circuits as before, along with two interactive Turing machines $\mathscr{A}_1$ and $\mathscr{A}_2$. The two Turing machines model the two parts of the participation stage of the attack, before and after the challenge. The first Turing machine $\mathscr{A}_1$ acts like the single machine $\mathscr{A}$ of the chosen-ciphertext attack defined above. After the message-finder F_k has computed two messages m_0, m_1, and one of them chosen at random has been sent from S to R, we now allow our adversary further to probe our cryptosystem, using $\mathscr{A}_2$, before challenging him to guess via T_k whether m_0 or m_1 was sent. That is, the second machine $\mathscr{A}_2$, which is allowed all the attacking capabilities of $\mathscr{A}_1$, is given as additional input the execution transcript of (S, R).

Thus, the experiment we consider is the following. Run G twice on input 1^k to obtain (e_0, d_0) and (e_1, d_1). In the initial participation stage of the attack, run $\mathscr{A}_1$ with input (e_0, e_1) as described above to produce the execution history h_1. Next, give (e_0, e_1) and h_1 to F_k to produce $m_0, m_1 \in M_k$ and a "choice" of 0 or 1. Choose one of the messages m_0, m_1 at random, m_b

say, and run (S, R) to send m_b, using as keys either (e_0, d_0) and (e_1, d_1) or (e_1, d_1) and (e_0, d_0) according to F_k's choice of 0 or 1, respectively; let τ be the transcript of this run. Give the parameter k, the public keys e_0 and e_1, the pair of messages (m_0, m_1), the transcript τ, and the history string h_1 as input to $\mathscr{A}_2$, and let h_2 be the execution history of this further participation stage. Finally, give $[(e_0, e_1), h_1, (m_0, m_1), \tau, h_2]$ as input to T_k to obtain the bit b'. The experiment is a success if $b = b'$. We say that the message-sending protocol is *polynomially secure against replay chosen-ciphertext attack* if for any interactive Turing machines $\mathscr{A}_1$ and $\mathscr{A}_2$, for any message-finder F, for any message-distinguisher T, and for any constant c, the probability of success is less than $\frac{1}{2} + \frac{1}{k^c}$ for sufficiently large k.

Under the assumption that there exist trapdoor functions—which is the minimum assumption under which public-key cryptography is known to be possible at all—in the full paper we propose an interactive message-sending protocol that we prove to be polynomially secure against replay chosen-ciphertext attack.

5. Remarks

Notc that, in its full generality, the definition of a replay chosen-ciphertext attack does not make sense for the noninteractive setting. If the adversary is allowed access to the decryption equipment *after* being given a ciphertext c, he may as well just use the equipment directly in order to decrypt c.

In place of the definitions in terms of (nonuniform) circuit families discussed above, the attacks can also be formulated as a uniform adversary (cf. [**4**]).

The definition of chosen-ciphertext attack suggested here is used in the noninteractive public-key setting in a forthcoming paper by Naor and Yung [7].

References

1. U. Feige, A. Fiat, and A. Shamir, *Zero knowledge proofs of identity*, J. Cryptology **1**(2) (1988), 77–94.
2. Z. Galil, S. Haber, and M. Yung, *Symmetric public-key encryption*, Proceedings of the 5th CRYPTO (1985), Springer-Verlag (1986), 128–137.
3. Z. Galil, S. Haber, and M. Yung, *Symmetric public-key cryptosystems*, Bellcore Technical Memorandum ARH-013-160 (1989).
4. O. Goldreich, *A uniform-complexity treatment of encryption and zero-knowledge*, Technical Report TR-568, Computer Science Department, Technion, 1989.
5. S. Goldwasser and S. Micali, *Probabilistic encryption*, J. Comput. System Sci. **28** (1984), 270–299.
6. S. Micali, C. Rackoff, and B. Sloan, *The notion of security for probabilistic cryptosystems*, SIAM J. Comput. **17**(2)(1988), 412–426.
7. M. Naor and M. Yung, *Public-key cryptosystems provably secure against chosen-ciphertext attacks*, Proc. of the 22nd STOC (1990), ACM, 427–437.
8. M. Tompa and H. Woll, *Random self-reducibility and zero knowledge interactive proofs of possession of information*, Proc. of the 28th FOCS (1987), IEEE, 472–482.

9. A. C. Yao, *Theory and applications of trapdoor functions*, Proc. of the 23rd FOCS (1982), IEEE, 80–91.

Tel Aviv University and Columbia University, Department of Computer Science, New York, N.Y. 10027
E-mail address: galil@cs.columbia.edu

Bellcore, 445 South Street, Morristown, N.J. 07960
E-mail address: stuart@bellcore.com

IBM Research Division, T. J. Watson Research Center, P.O. Box 218, Yorktown Heights, N.Y. 10598
E-mail address: moti@ibm.com

DIMACS Series in Discrete Mathematics
and Theoretical Computer Science
Volume 2, 1991

New Directions in Testing

RICHARD J. LIPTON

ABSTRACT. We present a new theory of randomly testable functions. This theory is distribution-free; i.e., it makes no assumption about the distribution of values used at run-time. It demonstrates that testing can "prove" that programs are correct.

1. Introduction

One of the most important problems in computer science is the *correctness* of computations. Currently, there are three major approaches to this problem. The first is the classical approach based on *testing* [**5**, **10**, **13**, **23**]. The second is based on *verification* [**8**]. Independently, Blum et al. have developed a formal theory of programs that "test and correct themselves" [**6**]. Almost all real computations use testing to insure their correctness. For example, it has been estimated that 50 to 80 percent of the cost of software development is directly related to testing. Today, little real software uses verification: for a recent discussion of the role of verification see [**3**].

The state of testing is mainly based on *ad hoc* techniques. There are many practical suggestions concerning how to test programs, but they are all "rules of thumb" at best [**12**]. Further, testing is usually viewed as a method of *discovering* errors, not as a method of *proving* the absence of errors. Indeed, the main appeal of verification is that it has the potential to yield "proofs" that software is error free. Clearly, testing would be more valuable if it led to provable statements about programs.

The main goal of this paper is to construct a theory of testing that leads to provable statements about programs. This theory shows that testing can "prove" that certain programs are error free. The class of programs that this theory applies to includes a number of important programs. However, the

---

Work supported by DARPA and ONR contracts N00014-85-C-0456 and N00014-85-K-0465, and by NSF Cooperative Agreement DCR-8420948 and NSF Grant CCR-90008247.

1052-1798/91 $1.00 + $.25 per page

theory does not provide absolute correctness. It does prove that a computation is correct with a certain probability. Since this probability can be made as close to 1 as desired, this suffices for practical purposes. It is important to note that this probability is *not* an empirical statement: it is a rigorous statement about mathematics.

Our approach is based on random testing. Now it is well known that random testing is a poor method for testing even the most trivial programs. Then, how can we show that random testing works? The key is to examine why random testing usually fails. The reason this method performs so poorly in practice is that the distribution used at test-time is often not the same as the one used at run-time. Our new approach solves this problem: we have a *distribution-free theory of random testing.* That is, our theory makes *no* assumption about the distribution used at run-time. The theory works whether the inputs to the program are random or not.

One further advantage of our theory is that it is based on "black-box" testing. We only execute programs; we never "look inside" them. The main advantage of black-box testing is that we can handle not only software correctness but also hardware correctness. Thus, if we say that a program is correct, with high probability we are including in the calculation not only the correctness of the software, but also the correctness of the actual hardware that is used to execute the program. This is especially interesting since simple functions are often implemented on complex hardware, i.e., on special-purpose or parallel machines.

2. A simple example

Before we present our model it may be helpful to consider a simple example. Suppose that we wish to compute the trivial function

$$f(x) = x$$

where x ranges over the values $0, 1, \ldots, 2^{32} - 1$. Of course this function is absolutely trivial; however, it will allow us to present our method without introducing extraneous complications. Now let $P(x)$ be a program that is supposed to compute $f(x)$. Consider the following strategy:

> randomly generate 100 x's in the given range and for each of them test whether or not $P(x)$ is equal to $f(x)$.

If any of the values show that P is incorrect, then clearly we have discovered an error. Otherwise, we will assert that P is "correct."

This is clearly the classic strategy of random testing. As we stated earlier, this strategy is well known to be a weak one. It is easy to see why. Let P be the following program:

> **if** $x = 0$ **then** 1 **else** x.

Then, P correctly computes $f(x)$ on all but one input; i.e., it is only incorrect when x is equal to 0. The probability that the random testing discovers this error is very small: it is several million to one that the 100 tests will *not* discover the error. However, since we wish to assume nothing about the distribution of inputs to P, the program could fail the first time it is used.

Thus, it seems hopeless to expect that a purely random testing strategy will discover this error in program P. Note, even if we add a few nonrandom points to the test set, there is another program that will pass the test and yet potentially fail.

However, we do know something precise about the program P. We know that it is "close" to the correct function. Thus, P can be used to compute the correct answer for "most" points. It just cannot be relied on to compute the correct answer for all points.

Our critical insight is the following: the program P *can* be used to compute the correct answer at *all* points. The idea is that we can construct from P another program Q with the property that it can compute $f(x)$ correctly on any point. Consider the following program $Q(x)$:

$$r := \textbf{random}();\ \textbf{return}\ P(x+r) - P(r).$$

Note: we perform all the arithmetic modulo 2^{32}; also random() returns a uniformly distributed point in the range $0, 1, \ldots, 2^{32} - 1$. Now Q is a probabilistic program with the following property:

> for any x, the program Q correctly computes $f(x)$ with probability at least $1 - 2^{-31}$.

In order to see this let x be an arbitrary point. Now let $\tilde{r}$ be the selected random value. Suppose that both $x + \tilde{r}$ and $\tilde{r}$ are not equal to 0. Then, $Q(x)$ is equal to $P(x + \tilde{r}) - P(\tilde{r})$, which is equal to $x + \tilde{r} - \tilde{r}$; thus, in this case $Q(x)$ is equal to x. It therefore remains to calculate the probability that both $x + \tilde{r}$ and $\tilde{r}$ are not equal to 0. The key point is the following: both $x + \tilde{r}$ and $\tilde{r}$ are *random* values in the range $0, 1, \ldots, 2^{32} - 1$. Thus, the probability that $x + \tilde{r}$ is equal to 0 is exactly 2^{-32}; the same is true for $\tilde{r}$. Therefore, the probability that one of these is equal to 0 is at most 2^{-31}. This shows that Q is correct at least $1 - 2^{-31}$ of the time.

Thus, the program Q computes the correct answer for any input x with very high probability: it has at most one chance in a billion of being incorrect. The key point is that this is *not* a probabilistic statement about the x values; instead it is about the behavior of the program Q. For each input x the program has at most a chance of 2^{-31} of failure.

Our method is a generalization of the above simple example. Suppose that P is a program that is supposed to compute a function $f(x)$. Then, our method operates as follows:

(i) Determine that P is correct on a substantial fraction of all possible inputs.

(ii) Then, construct a new program that calls P at a set of random points and "uses" these values to return the value of $f(x)$.

It is interesting to note that the idea of allowing multiple calls to increase the reliability of computations is already in the literature [**17**, **25**]. We will have more to say about this in the next section. In our simple example, we had to call the original program twice in order to compute the given function.

3. Randomly testable functions

In this section we present our basic model of distribution-free randomly testable functions. Let $\mathscr{C}$ be a class of functions. Typically, $\mathscr{C}$ will contain "easy" functions, i.e., functions whose correctness is not an issue. Then, a function $f(x)$ is *randomly testable of order k over the class* $\mathscr{C}$ provided there are functions φ, $\tilde{\alpha}_1, \ldots, \tilde{\alpha}_k$ in the class $\mathscr{C}$ so that for all x,

$$f(x) = \varphi(f(\tilde{\alpha}_1(x)), \ldots, f(\tilde{\alpha}_k(x))).$$

Moreover, for each input x and each i the value $\tilde{\alpha}_i(x)$ is a uniform random value.

A number of comments are in order concerning this definition. First, we do not assume that the values $\tilde{\alpha}_1(x), \ldots, \tilde{\alpha}_k(x)$ are independent: in general they cannot be. We only assume that each value is uniformly distributed. In our simple example from the last section, the values were $x + \tilde{r}$ and $\tilde{r}$. Actually, it is not necessary that these values are uniformly distributed; we only require that they be random elements from a known distribution. Second, roughly, our definition means that "one can easily compute $f(x)$ at an arbitrary point provided one can compute it at a number of random points." The class $\mathscr{C}$ plays the role of easy-to-compute functions. We will call it the *function basis*. Since we have to assume that the functions in this class are correct, it is important that the class contain only simple functions. For example, often $\mathscr{C}$ will only contain "addition," i.e., functions of the form $x_1 + \cdots + x_n$. Note that all methods of checking the correctness of programs assume something. Even verification assumes that the underlying hardware is correct. Our method makes this assumption explicit. Moreover, what we assume is usually very weak.

Third, there is the question of efficiency. We usually assume that the function basis is not only correct, but also that it takes less time to compute than the original function f. If this is true, then our method runs approximately k times slower. If k is small, then we claim that this added cost at run-time is a small price to pay to get "provable" correctness.

It is interesting to note that increasing execution time in order to enhance correctness has been suggested before. The method of *n-version* programming [**17**, **25**] runs n different versions of a program: it then uses these n values and "votes" to determine which value to use. The fundamental point is that our method is a kind of n-version programming. However, we have two major advantages. We do not require that the program be implemented in multiple ways. Instead, we just call it at different values, and use these values to compute the original answer. Also, we can *prove* that our method works. Normally, n-version programming relies on an empirical belief that at least half of the n versions will be correct on any given point. Since there is evidence that this is not true in practice [**17**], the provability of our method is a major advantage. Another method, called *data diversity* [**1**], is closer to our method. However, it too is an empirical method and cannot "prove" anything about its correctness.

In order to state our main theorems we need a definition. Say that the program P is *ε-correct* for the function f provided $P(x) = f(x)$ for at least $1 - \varepsilon$ of the inputs x. Note: we assume that we can check that a program has this property by some method other than the one outlined in this paper.

THEOREM 3.1. *Suppose that f is randomly testable of order k with respect to the functions φ, $\tilde{\alpha}_1, \ldots, \tilde{\alpha}_k$. Also assume that P is ε-correct for the function f. Consider the program $\widetilde{Q}(x)$:*

$$\textbf{\textit{return}}\ \varphi(P(\tilde{\alpha}_1(x)), \ldots, P(\tilde{\alpha}_k(x))).$$

Then, for any x, *$\widetilde{Q}(x)$ is equal to $f(x)$ with probability at least $1 - \varepsilon k$.*

PROOF. Fix an input x. Clearly, the probability that $\widetilde{Q}(x)$ is correct is at least the probability that for each i, $P(\tilde{\alpha}_i(x)) = f(\tilde{\alpha}_i(x))$. This follows since f is randomly testable of order k with respect to the given functions φ, $\tilde{\alpha}_1, \ldots, \tilde{\alpha}_k$. It therefore follows that $\widetilde{Q}$ is correct at least $1 - \varepsilon k$ of the time. □

Note that allowing the behavior of $\widetilde{Q}$ to be probabilistic and not deterministic is a powerful modern trend in computational complexity [**18**]. It is well known that allowing probabilistic behavior is very helpful in designing algorithms. It should, therefore, not be surprising that such behavior is also very helpful in developing a new approach to testing.

In the next section we will present a number of examples of randomly testable functions. They are all of quite small order; many have order at most 2. Thus, for these functions, Theorem 3.1 is very strong. For example, if k is 2 then for ε equal to $1/100$, the probability that $\widetilde{Q}$ is correct is at least 0.98.

There is an interesting problem that this example demonstrates. Suppose that we want to use Theorem 3.1 to get a program $\widetilde{Q}$ that fails to be correct with at most one chance in a trillion. Then, we must have at least a trillion tests. In most situations this is not practical. Tests are expensive to perform. Not only must we execute the program to run a test, but more importantly we must know the correct answer. This is one of the reasons that testing is believed to be incapable of demonstrating that a program is highly reliable.

However, we will now generalize Theorem 3.1 so that with few tests one will be able to get high probability of correctness.

THEOREM 3.2. *Suppose that* f *is randomly testable of order* k *with respect to the functions* φ, $\tilde{\alpha}_1, \ldots, \tilde{\alpha}_k$. *Also assume that* P *is* ε*-correct for the function* f *where* $1 - \varepsilon k > 2/3$. *Consider the program* $\tilde{Q}(x)$:

> ***for*** $i := 1, r$ ***do*** $y[i] := \varphi(P(\tilde{\alpha}_1(x)), \ldots, P(\tilde{\alpha}_k(x)))$; ***return*** *majority* $(y[1], \ldots, y[r])$.

Then, for any x, $\tilde{Q}(x)$ *is correct with probability at least* c^r, *where* $c < 1$ *is an absolute constant.*

Note that each time we call the function $\tilde{\alpha}_i(x)$ we get an independent random value with the same given distribution. Also, the function majority(...) selects the value that occurs most frequently; in case of a tie it selects the first such value. In practice, if the majority() function does not get all the same values, then it would at least "log" that some error has been detected. The point of the theorem, however, is that it is unlikely that the majority of the values are wrong.

PROOF. Fix an input x. Clearly, $\tilde{Q}$ is correct if a majority of the r blocks of k calls to P are correct. A simple calculation shows the claimed bound. □

Theorem 3.2 allows us to show that a long-standing "folk theorem" about testing is *false.* The folk theorem states that one cannot get very high reliability solely by testing. Another way to state it is this: in order to get a chance of error of $1/m$ we must do approximately m tests. Thus, if m is very large, say a trillion, we must do a hopeless number of tests. As we stated before, it is not just the computational cost in performing the tests that is the problem, but the fact that for each test we must know the correct answer.

Thus, we can make the probability that the program Q of Theorem 3.2 is correct exponentially close to 1. The critical point, however, is that *the probability of error goes to zero exponentially fast as r grows.*

4. Examples

In this section we present several examples of randomly testable functions. They include, for example, many functions from number theory and basic linear algebra. Indeed, the next section will demonstrate that this is no accident: a large collection of functions can be proved to be randomly testable.

We first state a basic but useful lemma:

LEMMA 4.1. *Let* G *be an abstract finite group under the operation* $\circ$, *and let* x *be an arbitrary value from the group. If* $\tilde{r}$ *is a uniform random value, then so is* $x \circ \tilde{r}$.

PROOF. Consider the function $f(z) = x \circ z$. Since G is a group this is a one-to-one onto function. Thus, if $\tilde{r}$ is selected randomly, then so is $f(\tilde{r})$. □

4.1. Signal processing. Our first examples are the transforms used in signal processing such as the Fast Fourier Transform (FFT). Consider such a transformation $T(x_1, \dots, x_n)$ where the values x_i are fixed point numbers, i.e., 2-complement's arithmetic of some fixed size. Then, this transformation is randomly testable of order 2. This follows since the transformation is *linear.* Thus,

$$T(x_1, \dots, x_n) = T(x_1 + \tilde{r}_1, \dots, x_n + \tilde{r}_n) - T(\tilde{r}_1, \dots, \tilde{r}_n).$$

The key point here is that since fixed-point values are a group under addition, the value $x_i + \tilde{r}_i$ is a uniform random value by Lemma 4.1. Note that the function basis consists of just addition. Also, since the order is just two, we lose a relatively small factor in performance.

One might feel that this class of examples is uninteresting since the algorithms for these problems are not that complex; i.e., perhaps they are not that hard to implement correctly. This, however, misses two points. First, many of these transforms have quite "tricky" algorithms based on clever attempts to minimize their computational cost. For example, there are whole monographs devoted to the study of such algorithms **[16]**. Second, many times these algorithms are implemented on special purpose or parallel machines. These implementations can be very complex. Thus, the correctness of the implementations may not be clear at all. For example, **[26]** contains a whole collection of complex implementations of the basic FFT algorithm on vector machines. Here is a typical fragment of such codes:

```
          IF(LS.LT.NS) GOTO 300
          DO 200 J=1,NS
          OMEGAK = 1.
          DO 200 I=1,LS
          WYK = OMEGAK*C(I,2,J)
          C(I,1,J) = C(I,1,J) + WYK
          C(I,2,J) = C(I,2,J) - WYK
          OMEGAK = OMEGAK*OMEGAK
200       CONTINUE
```

Note, that a three-dimensional array is used to make the code easier for the FORTRAN compiler to vectorize; however, this makes the code much harder to understand.

4.2. Number theory. Our second family of examples is from number theory. Consider, first, the multiplication function: $f(x, y) = xy \bmod n$ where

n is fixed. This function is randomly testable of order 4. This follows from the simple formula:

$$f(x, y) = f(x + \tilde{r}, y + \tilde{s}) - f(\tilde{r}, y + \tilde{s}) - f(x + \tilde{t}, \tilde{s}) + f(\tilde{t}, \tilde{s}).$$

Note that each call to the function f is on a pair of *independent* random values. Consider, for example, $f(\tilde{r}, y + \tilde{s})$. The values $\tilde{r}$ and $y + \tilde{s}$ are clearly independent random values: this follows since $\tilde{r}$ and $\tilde{s}$ are independent random values.

This example is interesting for several reasons. It is one of the common examples used in the verification literature **[8]**. Also, the implementation of large precision multiplication is not trivial: such large multiplications often use sophisticated techniques based on FFTs. Even low precision multiplications are sometimes implemented in complex ways. For instance, one method uses the Chinese Remainder Theorem and table-lookup into a read-only memory. It may be interesting to note that the verification literature always seems to consider trivial methods of implementing multiplication; i.e., they study simple shift and add algorithms. Our method, since it is a black-box method, is independent of how the algorithm is implemented. Thus, it can handle complex methods of implementation.

In a similar manner we can show that a variety of other functions from number theory are randomly testable. They include $x^{-1} \bmod n$, $x^d \bmod n$, and $a^x \bmod n$. In addition, many functions from linear algebra such as determinant and others are randomly testable. Rather than look at *ad hoc* examples we will now show that two large classes of functions are randomly testable.

5. Functions over finite fields

In this section we show that any function over a finite field with "small" degree is randomly testable. Finite fields are widely used in error-correcting codes **[22]**, digital signal processing **[21]**, random number generation **[14]**, and cryptography **[7]**.

LEMMA 5.1. *For any distinct nonzero numbers $a_1, \dots, a_{d+1}$, there are weights $w_1, \dots, w_{d+1}$ in a finite field of size $q > d + 1$ so that for any polynomial $f(x)$ of degree d,*

$$f(0) = \sum_{i=1}^{d+1} w_i f(a_i). \tag{1}$$

PROOF. We will show that it is possible to select the weights so that (1) is true for all monomials x^j with $0 \le j \le d$. Then, (1) follows by linearity.

The constraints on the weights are just that for $j = 0, \dots, d$,

$$\sum_{i=1}^{d+1} w_i a_i^j = \delta_j,$$

where $\delta_0 = 1$ and $\delta_j = 0$ for $j > 0$. This is a linear system of equations in the weights. The determinant of the system is nonzero. (It is a so-called "Vandermonde" determinant [**19**].) Since $d + 1 < q$, it follows that the determinant is not zero; hence, the system of equations has a solution. □

In the following theorem, we use a technique due to Beaver and Feigenbaum [**4**, Theorem 3.1].

THEOREM 5.1. *For any distinct nonzero numbers* $a_1, \dots, a_{d+1}$, *there are weights* $w_1, \dots, w_{d+1}$ *in a finite field of size* $q > d + 1$ *so that for any polynomial* $f(x_1, \dots, x_n)$ *of degree* d, $f(x_1, \dots, x_n)$ *is equal to*

$$\sum_{i=1}^{d+1} w_i f(\tilde{x}^{(i)}),$$

where $\tilde{x}^{(i)} = (x_1 + a_i\tilde{\alpha}_1, \dots, x_n + a_i\tilde{\alpha}_n)$ *and each* $\tilde{x}^{(i)}$ *is a uniform random element from the space of* n*-vectors.*

PROOF. Define $g(z) = f(x_1 + \alpha_1 z, \dots, x_n + \alpha_n z)$. Clearly, $\deg(g) \leq \deg(f) < q$. So by Lemma 5.1,

$$\sum_{i=1}^{d+1} w_i g(a_i) = g(0).$$

Thus, $f(x_1, \dots, x_n)$ is equal to

$$\sum_{i=1}^{d+1} w_i f(\tilde{x}^{(i)}).$$

If $\tilde{\alpha}_1, \dots, \tilde{\alpha}_n$ are random independent values, then so is the n-vector, $(x_1 + a_i\tilde{\alpha}_1, \dots, x_n + a_i\tilde{\alpha}_n)$, since a_i is nonzero. □

COROLLARY 5.1. *Suppose that* $f(x_1, \dots, x_n)$ *is a polynomial over a finite field of size* q *with* $q > \deg(f) + 1$. *Then,* f *is randomly testable of order* $\deg(f) + 1$ *over the function basis that includes just addition.*

This corollary is quite strong. For example, in the last section we proved that multiplication xy is randomly testable of order 4; however, the corollary shows that it has order 3. The corollary also shows that any bilinear function such as *convolution* is randomly testable of order 3 [**16**].

Another interesting example is the permanent function: perm (A) is defined to be equal to

$$\sum_{\pi} a_{1\pi(1)} \cdots a_{n\pi(n)}$$

where the summation is over all permutations π and A is an $n \times n$ matrix. Then, it follows that permanent is randomly testable of order $n+1$. This is interesting since permanent is an example of a function that is believed to be very difficult to compute. Thus, our theory does not just apply to easy-to-compute functions.

Our observation about the permanent has consequences way beyond the theory of testing. It was one of the crucial building blocks in the recent characterization of the power of interactive proof systems (cf. Lund-Fortnow-Karloff-Nisan [**20**] and Shamir [**24**]).

6. Functions over the rationals

One of the major reasons that we can show that any low-degree polynomial over a large enough finite field is randomly testable is Lemma 4.1. Thus, it is critical that in a finite field, if $\tilde{r}$ is random then so is $x + \tilde{r}$ for *any* x. If we allow $\tilde{r}$ to be selected from the rationals, then this lemma is no longer true: one way to think about this is that $x + \tilde{r}$ gives out "some" information about x even if $\tilde{r}$ is uniformly chosen from some large range. However, with care we can generalize our previous theorem to polynomials over the rationals. In order to do this we need to extend the definition of randomly testable as follows. Informal version: Suppose that S and T are finite sets of rationals. We will say that a polynomial $f(x_1, \dots, x_n)$ is *quasi-randomly testable of order* k with respect to S and T provided any program for f that works for "most" points of T^n can be converted to a program $\widetilde{Q}$ that calls P at most k times and works with high probability on any point of S^n.

Then we can prove the following theorem:

THEOREM 6.1. *Suppose that* S *is a set of rationals with at most* b *bits in their representation. Any polynomial function* $f(x_1, \dots, x_n)$ *of degree at most* d *is quasi-randomly testable of order* $d+1$ *over* S *and* T *where* T *consists of rationals of at most* $O(b + \log(n) + \log(d) \log\log(d))$ *bits.*

The proof is a generalization of the ones used in the last section. The critical new problem is that, as stated earlier, certain expressions are no longer uniform random values. Thus, one must carefully argue that certain random distributions do not "leak" much information. Note that the bound is quite practical; i.e., the implied constant is very small. Roughly, this theorem shows that if one can compute a polynomial at "most" "double" precision values, then one can compute it at an arbitrary "single" precision value.

7. Conclusions

There are a number of important open questions concerning our notion of randomly testable functions. First, there is the main question of exactly what functions are in this class. We have shown that many important functions are in this class. We as yet do not know how to exactly characterize these functions. We have shown that all functions of "small" degree are randomly testable; however, examples such as $a^x \bmod n$ show that some large degree functions are randomly testable. It is possible that the class of randomly testable functions, at least over finite fields, is very large.

Acknowledgment

I would like to thank Joan Feigenbaum for explaining her recent results on "hiding information from multiple oracles." Essentially, Theorem 5.1 is proved in the same way as her result with Donald Beaver. I would like to thank Leon Osterweil for kindly inviting me to the 1989 Workshop on Directions in Software Analysis and Testing. I would also like to thank Manuel Blum for a number of comments. I would also like to thank Jin-yi Cai for many helpful comments concerning this work. Finally, I would like to thank Rich DeMillo for many discussions about this work and for testing in general.

References

1. P. E. Ammann and J. C. Knight, *Data diversity: An approach to software fault tolerance*, The Seventeenth International Symposium on Fault-Tolerant Computing, pp.122–126, 1987.
2. E. Bach, *Number-theoretic algorithms*, Computer Sciences Technical Report 844, April 1989.
3. J. Barwise, *Mathematical proofs of computer system correctness*, Notices of the AMS, vol. 36, number 7, 1989.
4. D. Beaver and J. Feigenbaum, *Hiding instances in multioracle queries*, Proceedings of the 7th STACS, Springer-Verlag LNCS 415, 1990, pp. 37–48.
5. B. Beizer, *Software system testing and quality assurance*, Van Nostrand Reinhold Company, 1984.
6. M. Blum, M. Luby, and R. Rubinfeld, *Self-testing/correcting with applications to numerical problems*, Proceedings of the 22nd ACM STOC, 1990.
7. M. Blum and S. Micali, *How to generate cryptographically strong sequences of pseudo-random bits*, SIAM J. Computing **13** (1984).
8. R. S. Boyer and J. S. Moore, *The correctness problem in computer science*, Academic Press, 1981.
9. D. A. Buell and R. L. Ward, *A multiprecise integer arithmetic package*, J. Supercomputing **3** (1989), 89–107.
10. R. A. DeMillo, W. M. McCracken, R. J. Martin, and J. F. Passafiume, *Software testing and evaluation*, The Benjamin Cummings Publishing Company, 1987.
11. R. A. DeMillo and R. J. Lipton, *A probabilistic remark on algebraic program testing*, Information Processing Letters **7** (1978), 193–195.
12. R. A. DeMillo, R. J. Lipton, and F. G. Sayward, *Hints on test data selection: Help for the practicing programmer*, Computer **11** (1978), 34–41.
13. R. H. Dunn, *Software defect removal*, McGraw-Hill Book Company, 1984.
14. S. W. Golumb, *Shift register sequences*, Holden-Day, 1967.
15. M. Hall, Jr., *Combinatorial theory*, John Wiley & Sons, 1967.

16. M. T. Heideman, *Multiplicative complexity, convolution, and the DFT*, Springer-Verlag, 1988.
17. J. C. Knight and N. G. Leveson, *An experimental evaluation of the assumption of independence in multiversion programming*, IEEE Trans. Software Engineering **1** (1986), 96–109.
18. E. Kranakis, *Primality and cryptography*, John Wiley & Sons, 1986.
19. S. Lang, *Algebra*, Addison-Wesley Publishing Company, 1984.
20. C. Lund, L. Fortnow, H. Karloff, and N. Nisan, *The polynomial-time hierarchy has interactive proofs*, manuscript, December, 1989.
21. J. H. McCellan and C. M. Rader, *Number theory in digital signal processing*, Prentice-Hall, 1979.
22. F. J. McWilliams and N. J. A. Sloane, *The theory of error correcting codes*, North Holland, 1977.
23. G. J. Myers, *The art of software testing*, John Wiley & Sons, 1979.
24. A. Shamir, IP = PSPACE , manuscript, December, 1989.
25. S. K. Shrivastava, *Collected papers of the Newcastle Reliability Project*, Springer-Verlag, 1985.
26. P. N. Swarztrauber, *FFT algorithms for vector computers*, Parallel Computing **1** (1984), 45–63.

Department of Computer Science, Princeton University
E-mail address: rjl@princeton.edu

DIMACS Series in Discrete Mathematics
and Theoretical Computer Science
Volume 2, 1991

Towards a Theory of Cryptographic Systems: A Critique of Crypto-Complexity

MICHAEL MERRITT

1. Introduction

Some fourteen years ago Diffie, Hellman, and Merkle ushered in a new era with their *New Directions in Cryptography* **[DH76]** and *Secure Communication over Insecure Channels* **[Mer78]**. The result has been an explosion of interest, many new ideas, and a sizeable literature of the "new cryptography." This essay takes a critical look at some of this research, stressing three central themes arising from these seminal papers.

The first topic is asymptotic cryptography, here dubbed "crypto-complexity," which has been the focus of so much recent theoretical research. Researchers in this area are challenged to demonstrate that this work is not fundamentally irrelevant to the construction and validation of cryptographic systems. It is suggested that useful cryptographic complexity theory emphasizes the *concrete* complexity of defeating specific cryptographic primitives, over the *structural* relationships that hold between different intractability assumptions. Such a theory usefully combines modern algorithmic theory with the heuristic approaches advocated by Shannon **[Sha49]** and the traditional paradigm of certification via cryptanalysis invented by Kerckhoffs **[Kah67]**.

A second theme, and perhaps the real revolution that took place in the 1970s, was escape from the conceptual strictures of the classical crypto-channel formalized by Shannon **[Sha49]**. Shannon noted that information-theoretic security was inadequate to describe the practice of secure computation. But he failed to recognize that reliance on practical complexity over information-theoretic security allows the definition of alternative cryptographic paradigms that are ridiculous from an information-theoretic point of view. With the invention of public-key cryptography and digital signatures, Diffie, Hellman, and Merkle ushered in an unprecedented era of innovation and inventiveness, resulting in a veritable "crypto-menagerie" of

1980 *Mathematics Subject Classification* (1985 *Revision*). Primary 68, 94.

information-hiding primitives. While providing practitioners with a wealth of abstract tools for architecting systems, the focus on polynomial reducibilities masks practical implications. Which of these primitives have practical implementations? Which of the reductions are efficient in practice? Indeed, what characterizes an efficient reduction? What are the consequences of combining different primitives within a single system?

Finally, while the standard of mathematical proof has not yet been applied to certification of individual cryptosystems, that is not to say that formalism has no role in practical cryptography. Considering cryptographic primitives as individual components of complex cryptographic systems provides a perspective from which a host of formal tools may usefully be brought to bear. To this end, the high standards of rigor and subtle arguments of crypto-complexity set an important example for the designer of cryptographic systems. This essay concludes by suggesting that tools and techniques developed to investigate problems in distributed computing will be important in the development of a useful theory of cryptographic systems.

2. Asymptotics

"The development of computers has led for the first time to a mathematical theory of algorithms which can begin to approach the difficult problem of estimating the computational difficulty of breaking a cryptographic system. The position of mathematical proof may thus come full circle and be reestablished as the best method of certification." **[DH76]**

How far have we come in accomplishing this ambitious goal? Debate continues on the appropriate definitions of "secure" cryptographic systems, but the research community seems to have agreed that asymptotic definitions are the most appropriate. This decision has been made without emphasizing the inherent weaknesses of any such definition.

The most obvious weakness is that asymptotic theorems don't say anything about real cryptographic systems, in which the key size is fixed. Knowing that an adversary's attack must eventually falter is no consolation if it suffices to break the system at hand.

A second obvious weakness is that no specific problem is known to be intractable; moreover, it is not even known whether there exist intractable problems on which to base cryptographic systems. In recognition of this limitation, researchers have sought to base particular systems on the weakest possible assumption, such as the existence of appropriately-defined one-way functions.

The result is a literature defining various problems (e.g., oblivious transfer, bit commitment, one-way functions), and establishing relationships among them via polynomial reductions. The game is to build a family of protocols that will eventually defeat a polynomially-bounded adversary under the weakest possible asymptotic intractability assumption. Indeed, the equivalence of three such definitions has been postulated as "evidence that the right formalization of the notion of security has been reached" [**MRS88**], although such results seem to inflame rather than close debate on the "right" asymptotic definitions.

Though seldom concerned with languages *per se* or with classical complexity classes, the resulting literature seems to bear more on structural complexity than on cryptography.

Put another way, which of the following is the weaker assumption?

(i) Factoring 512-bit numbers will be infeasible for the next ten years.
(ii) One-way functions exist.

These statements are not simply incomparable, but are concerned with issues that appear completely unrelated. A case that the second is or ought to be relevant to the practice of cryptography has yet to be made.

What would be the consequences for practical cryptography of the resolution of item 2 or other major open problems in crypto-complexity theory? Ironically, it is possible that such theoretical results could have no real impact on the practice of secure information management, regardless of how the questions are resolved. A theory of cryptography with major open problems may be forgiven for not impacting practice, but it is legitimately criticized if resolution of those problems is irrelevant to practicing cryptographers.

It is an engineering principle, not a mathematical truth, that asymptotically good algorithms tend to be good in practice. But the modern theory of cryptography turns this principle on its head, postulating that all asymptotically bad algorithms for solving a given problem will be bad in practice. I challenge the research community with the following open question: What evidence or argument supports this claim?

3. Reductions

By focussing on the structural consequences of their results, theoretical researchers may be ignoring important practical consequences. Consider for example the RSA public-key cryptosystem [**RSA88**]. Factoring algorithms can be used to invert RSA, but RSA is not known to be as hard as factoring. The existence of a reduction from factoring to RSA has long been an open question in cryptography. Suppose such a polynomial-time reduction were found. What would be the practical consequences?

Suppose first that the reduction from factoring were not length-preserving: that it reduces factoring an n-bit number to inverting RSA over a modulus of n^3 bits. This would mean that inverting RSA with a 512-bit modulus would be as hard as factoring 8-bit integers, not a very reassuring result.

Suppose instead that the postulated reduction from factoring were length-preserving, invertible, and efficient in practice. Then an assumption that 512-bit numbers cannot be factored would justify the choice of an RSA modulus of length 512.

This example illustrates that important practical information may be lost in typical polynomial-time reduction arguments. Details of the reduction may have important implications to practice, and should not be lost completely in the emphasis on structural implications. When the research community focusses exclusively on the asymptotic properties of specific cryptographic primitives, it distracts itself from the fundamental problem of secure computing. When that community goes further and indulges in the rhetoric of "provable security" it may also distract implementers from attending to other security-critical aspects of the systems they construct.

4. Certification

In judging the security of a particular cryptosystem, have we escaped from the "paradigm of certification by cryptanalytic attack set down by Kerckhoffs in the last century" [**DH76**], replacing this *ad hoc* approach with the paradigm of mathematical proof?

I know of three modern cryptosystems that have actually been implemented: cryptographic knapsack systems, RSA, and exponential key exchange. All three problems have the distinction of being "similar" to problems presumed to be intractable. In particular, cryptographic knapsacks are special cases of an NP-complete problem, RSA is "related" to factoring, and exponential key exchange is similarly related to discrete logarithms.

The victim of a classical cryptanalytic attack, cryptographic knapsacks have been shown to be a tractable subproblem of general knapsacks and are no longer considered effective cryptographic tools. The RSA and exponential key exchange systems have withstood attack so far, although it is not clear how much effort has focussed on attacking these systems directly and how much focussed instead on the related problems of factoring and discrete logarithms.

Nevertheless, experimental work on both factoring such as [**Len89**, **LM89**], and in discrete logarithms (see, e.g., [**LO90**]) has profound practical implications for RSA and exponential key exchange. This and theoretical work on the concrete complexity of these problems provides invaluable information in guiding the cryptographer's choice of key size in implementing either of these systems. But this is cryptography in the purist classical mode—efforts and techniques of active cryptanalysts are extrapolated to guide best-guess engineering decisions!

Further, I will hazard to predict that this paradigm will continue to be the bread-and-butter of practical cryptographers. Not even a provably asymptotically unbreakable cryptosystem will be useful without extended practical experience in its cryptanalysis to guide an implementor in the choice of key size. Moreover, savvy cryptographers should prefer such classical certification over asymptotic proofs of difficulty.

Of course, this is not to say that cryptographic systems cannot in principle be proven secure in meaningful ways. Shamir's secret-sharing algorithm is an example of a novel information-theoretically secure cryptographic system **[Sha79]**. Perhaps we will invent a finite complexity theory that will allow us to bound the minimum circuit required to break DES **[NBS77]**. Neither do I mean to suggest that asymptotic results are necessarily meaningless to practitioners. But certainly we can be clearer as to the practical implications of such work, and perhaps we should be less eager to describe asymptotic intractability theorems as "proofs of security."

5. Novel cryptographic primitives

A second seminal contribution of Diffie and Hellman's *New Directions* paper was to recognize and popularize "the need for new types of cryptographic systems" **[DH76]**. Concurrently, Merkle recognized a similar need **[Mer78]**. The novel systems they introduced were public-key cryptosystems, digital signatures, and one-way authentication. Their specific example of exponential key exchange and the later invention of the RSA system **[RSA88]** together have had important practical impact. Perhaps even more important, however, was the resulting revolution in thinking about cryptographic primitives, freeing the community from the constraints of the classical private key crypto-channel.

Currently, the menagerie of cryptographic primitives is quite large, and includes the following:

authentication,
bit commitment,
blobs,
claw-free one-way permutations,
coherence,
cryptographically secure pseudorandom number generation,
digital signature scheme,
distributed function evaluation,
envelopes,
instance-hiding schemes,
locally random reducibility,
noninteractive zero-knowledge proof system,
oblivious transfer,
obliviously cryptographic multiparty unconditionally secure protocols,
one-way authentication,
one-way function,
one-way hash function,
one-way permutation,
one-sided statistical zero knowledge proof,

probabilistic encryption,
public-key cryptosystem,
random-self-reducibility,
secret sharing,
secret-key exchange,
secure circuit evaluation,
trapdoor function, and
zero-knowledge proof systems.

Unfortunately, the proliferation of cryptographic abstractions and focus on polynomial reductions between them has resulted in considerable confusion, particularly for practitioners. Which of these primitives have secure implementations in today's technology? What is their cost, and how can they be combined to solve specific problems?

Consider, for example, the secure channel model investigated in [**BGW88**] and [**CCD88**]. This model assumes the existence of authenticated, secret channels between principals, and is used to examine "unconditionally" secure protocols. (In particular, no complexity-theoretic or cryptographic assumptions are made.) But how are authenticated, secret channels implemented, if not via cryptographic means? If one admits cryptographic assumptions in the implementation of these channels, then what advantage is gained in not using those assumptions in the protocols that send and receive over the channels? Could more efficient protocols be devised that exploit those cryptographic assumptions?

Consider alternatively the proof of identity protocol devised by Feige, Fiat, and Shamir [**FFS88**]. On several occasions it has been suggested to me that this protocol could be used in specific systems to solve authentication problems. Unfortunately, although terminals and hand-held devices such as "smart cards" currently exist that implement the data encryption standard [**NBS77**], none that I know of generate true random numbers. If I am reduced to using DES to generate pseudo-random sequences, what advantage is there in replacing DES elsewhere in the protocol?

Given the infinite definitional possibilities, the existence of a practical implementation would seem to be a reasonable measure of the value of any particular member of the crypto-menagerie. What is needed is a concrete complexity theory of these and other primitives, with a focus on implementation.

6. Standards of proof

While I question the relevance of asymptotic theorems to practical cryptography, I applaud the *attempt* to define security formally and apply standards of proof to cryptographic systems. Determining the computational complexity of inverting any particular cryptographic function may be beyond current techniques, but the distributed protocols utilizing conjectured cryptographic properties raise other issues that can be more important to overall system security.

In this, the theory community has set an important example for practitioners. Amongst theoreticians, occasional errors have led to more rigorous standards and discussion of foundational issues. To cite one example, an early paper [**SRA81**] described how to play "mental poker" using cryptographic primitives. In [**Lip81**], Lipton demonstrated that the suggested protocols allowed cheating; the cryptosystem allowed red cards to be distinguished from black cards, even when face down! Responses to this and other errors has led to a theory that stresses the importance of adversarial models and of rigorous proof techniques.

The more practically-minded literature could benefit from serious consideration of similar issues. Most often, cryptographic protocols are presented without any formal discussion of potential attacks. Classical correctness arguments for cryptographic protocols seem to proceed as follows: "If it was possible to break DES, this protocol would be insecure. It is not possible to break DES. Therefore this protocol is secure." Occasionally, more sophisticated arguments are used: "The previous protocol fell to attack X. The present protocol does not fall to attack X. Therefore this protocol is secure."

It is not surprising that these proof techniques have led to numerous flawed protocols. For example, a key distribution protocol in [**NS78**] falls to a non-cryptographic attack in [**DS81**]. Alternative protocols immune to this particular attack were proposed in [**DS81**, **NS87**, **OR87**].

Essentially the same flaw exists in SUN's secure Network File System protocol [**Tay88**], which also has purely cryptanalytic weaknesses [**LO90**].

Examples of other insecure protocols include

- the CCITT X.509 protocol for signed secure communication [**CCI87**] is attacked in [**BAN88**];
- a key-management protocol proposed for an internet environment [**LS89**] is criticized in [**GNY90**] for failing to distribute authenticated keys;
- exponential key-exchange [**DH76**] is known to fall to an active, "man-in-the-middle" attack. A suggested fix, attributed to Rivest and Shamir in [**DP84**], falls to a slightly more involved attack [**BM90a**];
- a proposed revision to protocols in the Kerberos authentication system [**SNS88**] falls to a chosen-plaintext attack [**BM90b**].

Some work has been done in formal techniques for reasoning about cryptographic protocols. In the last century, Kerckhoffs stated the principle that cryptographic systems should be analyzed under the assumption that only the specific keying information was unavailable to the adversary—the encryption algorithms and system architecture must be assumed to be known to the adversary [**Kah67**]. Cryptanalysts have described more complex attacks, such as known- or chosen-plaintext attacks and the like. But work on "ping-pong" protocols was the first to extend Kerckhoffs' principle with the supposition that the entire communication network, and indeed some of the protocol participants, are under the control of the adversary [**DEK82**, **DY83**, **EG83**]. Noting that protocols may fall to such adversaries without any cryptanalysis, this work explored families of protocols that preserve simple secrecy properties in the face of such attacks. However, the focus was on characterizing the complexity of such proofs, rather than validating specific protocols of interest.

Later work of my own and others showed that more complex security properties can be modelled and proven by extending this technique [**DLM82**, **DM83**, **Mer83**, **Moo88**]. Formal verification techniques were applied with some success to this problem in [**Kem89**], and recently a new logical approach has been used to show that the key distribution solutions in [**DS81**, **NS87**, **OR87**] survive more than the single attack that defeats the original Needham-Schroeder protocol [**BAN88**, **GNY90**]. (The implications of the proof techniques of [**BAN88**] are explored in [**BAN90**], in this volume. Extensions of the techniques of [**Mer83**] are explored in [**TW90**], also in this volume.)

These approaches abstract away from specific cryptographic systems and validate protocols against a broad class of noncryptographic attacks. This seems to me a rich area for research of both theoretical and practical interest.

7. Distributed computing and cryptography

Cryptography is fundamentally concerned with the interactions of autonomous entities: the parties who wish to communicate and their adversaries. Within computer science, research in distributed computing focusses on the interactions of autonomous entities in the presence of an adversary, and hence cryptographic systems may properly be seen as an area of specialization within distributed computing.

This point of view emphasizes *systems* over *cryptography*, stressing the fact that any cryptographic primitive will be implemented in the context of a complex system. Following the metaphor of "steel doors in paper walls," the critical issue in practice is whether the system supports its users and defeats its adversaries.

The adversaries studied in distributed computing range from the fairly benign nondeterministic scheduler of concurrent programs, to more pernicious unreliable networks with unknown link delays and lost messages, and on to the Byzantine world in which worst-case analysis postulates protocol participants conspiring against the protocol itself. Traditional computer scientists have criticized the plethora of models that characterize the field, but should note that this is a necessary consequence of the phenomena under investigation. Small changes in model may fundamentally alter the computations possible within that model; no Church's thesis resolves the debate.

The consequent lesson extends to cryptographic systems as well. No one computational model, no single problem or even notion of what constitutes a problem will have universal application. Instead of *universal* tools, let us strive to develop practical, *general purpose* cryptographic primitives that engineers can turn to a variety of real purposes. In addition, we should develop methods for reasoning about distributed systems that contain embedded cryptographic primitives.

The resulting theory may not have the elegance or depth of the best abstract mathematics. But by enlightening and guiding the builders of secure systems, it can aspire to be a true applied mathematical discipline. At the same time, distributed computing as applied epistemology can lay claim to a rich intellectual history.

References

[BAN88] M. Burrows, M. Abadi, and R. Needham, *Authentication: A practical study in belief and action*, in Proceedings of Second Conference on Theoretical Aspects of Reasoning About Knowledge, 1988.

[BAN90] M. Burrows, M. Abadi, and R. Needham, *The scope of a logic of authentication*, these proceedings.

[BM90a] S. M. Bellovin and M. Merritt, *An attack on password-authenticated exponential key exchange*, AT&T Bell Laboratories Technical Memorandum, May 1990.

[BM90b] S. M. Bellovin and M. Merritt, *Limitations of the Kerberos protocol*, AT&T Bell Laboratories Technical Memorandum, May 1990.

[BGW88] M. Ben-Or, S. Goldwasser, and A. Wigderson, *Completeness theorems for non-cryptographic fault-tolerant distributed computation*, in Proceedings of the 20th ACM Symposium on the Theory of Computing, 1–10, Chicago, IL, May 1988.

[CCD88] D. Chaum, C. Crépeau, and I. Damgård, *Multiparty unconditionally secure protocols*, in Proceedings of the 20th ACM Symposium on the Theory of Computing, 11–19, Chicago, IL, May 1988.

[CCI87] CCITT, *The directory-authentication framework*, version 7, Technical Report, Draft Recommendation X.509, November 1987.

[DEK82] D. Dolev, S. Even, and R. M. Karp, *On the security of ping-pong protocols*, Information and Control **55** (1982), 57–68.

[DH76] W. Diffie and M. E. Hellman, *New directions in cryptography*, IEEE Trans. Inform. Theory **22** (1976), 644–654.

[DLM82] R. DeMillo, N. Lynch, and M. Merritt, *Cryptographic protocols*, in Proceedings of the 14th ACM Symposium on the Theory of Computing, 383–400, May 1982.

[DM83] R. DeMillo and M. Merritt, *Protocols for data security*, Computer **16** (1983), 39–50.

[DP84] D. W. Davies and W. L. Price, *Security for computer networks*, John Wiley & Sons, 1984.

[DS81] D. Denning and G. Sacco, *Timestamps in key distribution protocols*, Communications of the ACM **24** (1981), 533–536.

[DY83] D. Dolev and A. Yao, *On the security of public key protocols*, IEEE Trans. Inform. Theory **29** (1983), 198–208.

[EG83] S. Even and O. Goldreich, *On the security of multi-party ping-pong protocols*, in Proceedings of the 24th Annual Symposium on the Foundations of Computer Science, 34–39, November 1983.

[FFS88] U. Feige, A. Fiat, and A. Shamir, *Zero knowledge proofs of identity*, J. Cryptology (1988), 77–94.

[GNY90] L. Gong, R. Needham, and R. Yahalom, *A methodology for analyzing cryptographic protocols*, Technical Report, University of Cambridge Computer Laboratory, Cambridge CB2 3QG, England, March 1990.

[Kah67] D. Kahn, *The Codebreakers*, Macmillan & Co., New York, 1967.

[Kem89] R. A. Kemmerer, *Analyzing encryption protocols using formal verification techniques*, IEEE Journal on Selected Areas in Communications **4** (1988).

[Len89] A. Lenstra, *Experimental work on factoring*, a talk presented at the DIMACS Workshop on Cryptography and Distributed Computing, October 1989.

[LM89] A. Lenstra and M. Manasse, *Factoring by electronic mail*, Proceedings of Eurocrypt89 (Houthalen, Belgium; April, 1989), Springer-Verlag LNCS.

[Lip81] R. Lipton, *On the safety of cryptosystems*, American Mathematical Society Lecture Notes, January 1981.

[LO90] B. A. LaMacchia and A. M. Odlyzko, *Computation of discrete logarithms in prime fields*, 1990, manuscript in preparation.

[LS89] W. P. Lu and M. K. Sundareshan, *Secure communication in internet environments*, IEEE Transactions on Communications **37** (1989), 1014–1023.

[Mer78] R. Merkle, *Secure communication over insecure channels*, Communications of ACM **21** (1978), 294–299.

[Mer83] M. Merritt, *Cryptographic protocols*, Ph.D. thesis, Georgia Institute of Technology, February 1983, Technical Report GIT/ICS/83/06.

[Moo88] J. H. Moore, *Protocol failures in cryptosystems*, Proc. IEEE **5** (1988), 594–602.

[MRS88] S. Micali, C. Rackoff, and B. Sloan, *The notion of security for probabilistic cryptosystems*, SIAM J. Comput. **17** (1988), 412–426.

[NBS77] National Bureau of Standards, *Data encryption standard*, Technical Report, Federal Information Processing Standards Publication 46 Government Printing Office, Washington, D.C., 1977.

[NS78] R. Needham and M. Schroeder, *Using encryption for authentication in large networks of computers*, Communications of the ACM **12** (1978), 993–999.

[NS87] R. Needham and M. Schroeder, *Authentication revisited*, Operating Systems Review **21** (1987), 7.

[OR87] D. Otway and O. Rees, *Efficient and timely mutual authentication*, Operating Systems Review **21** (1987), 8–10.

[RSA88] R. L. Rivest, A. Shamir, and L. Adleman, *A method of obtaining digital signatures and public-key cryptosystems*, Communications of the ACM **21** (1988), 120–126.

[Sha79] A. Shamir, *How to share a secret*, Communications of the ACM **22** (1979), 612–613.

[Sha49] C. Shannon, *Communication theory of secrecy systems*, Bell System Technical Journal **28** (1949), 656–715.

[SNS88] J. Steiner, C. Neuman, and J. I. Schiller, *Kerberos: An authentication service for open network systems*, in Proceedings of the Winter USENIX Conference, Dallas, 1988.

[SRA81] A. Shamir, R. Rivest, and L. Adleman, *Mental poker*, in Ed. D. E. Klarner, editor, Mathematical Gardner, New York, NY, 1981. Wadsworth, Also MIT Laboratory for Computer Science Technical Report MIT/LCS/TM-125, 1979.

[Tay88] Brad Taylor, *A framework for network security*, Sun Technology, 47–49, Spring 1988.

[TW90] M. Toussaint and P. Wolper, *Reasoning about cryptographic protocols* (*extended abstract*), these proceedings.

AT&T Bell Laboratories
E-mail address: mischu@research.att.com

DIMACS Series in Discrete Mathematics
and Theoretical Computer Science
Volume 2, 1991

Feedback in Discrete Communication

Extended Abstract

ALON ORLITSKY

ABSTRACT. (X, Y) is a pair of random variables. Person $P_{\mathscr{X}}$ knows X, Person $P_{\mathscr{Y}}$ knows Y, and both know the joint probability distribution of (X, Y). Using a predetermined protocol, they communicate over a binary, error-free channel in order for $P_{\mathscr{Y}}$ to learn X. $P_{\mathscr{X}}$ may or may not learn Y. How many information bits must be transmitted (by both persons) in the worst case if only m messages are allowed?

$\hat{C}_1(X|Y)$ is the number of bits required when at most one message is allowed, necessarily from $P_{\mathscr{X}}$ to $P_{\mathscr{Y}}$. $\hat{C}_2(X|Y)$ is the number of bits required when at most two messages are permitted: $P_{\mathscr{Y}}$ transmits a message to $P_{\mathscr{X}}$, then $P_{\mathscr{X}}$ responds with a message to $P_{\mathscr{Y}}$. $\hat{C}_\infty(X|Y)$ is the number of bits required when communication is unrestricted: $P_{\mathscr{X}}$ and $P_{\mathscr{Y}}$ can communicate back and forth.

We prove $\hat{C}_1(X|Y) = \lceil \log \chi(G(X|Y)) \rceil$ where $G(X|Y)$, the characteristic hypergraph of (X, Y), can be simply constructed. We show that maximum reduction in communication achievable via feedback is almost logarithmic. For all (X, Y) pairs, $\hat{C}_\infty(X|Y) \geq \lceil \log \hat{C}_1(X|Y) \rceil + 1$, whereas, for a class of (X, Y) pairs, $\hat{C}_\infty(X|Y) = \lceil \log \hat{C}_1(X|Y) \rceil + 1$. We also mention, without proof, several other related results.

1. Introduction and definitions

Often, when a person conveys information to another, the recipient has some idea about the information sent. Although it is not the recipient's intention to convey any information, he might find that by telling some of his information, the *total* amount of communication can be reduced. This is illustrated by the following example.

EXAMPLE 1. A league has t teams named $1, \ldots, t$. Every week two random teams play each other. The outcome of the match is announced over the radio. All announcements have the same format: "The match between

A full version of this paper will appear in the IEEE Transactions on Information Theory.

team I and team J was won by team K" where $1 \leq I < J \leq t$ and K is either I or J.

$P_{\mathcal{X}}$ and $P_{\mathcal{Y}}$ are avid sports fans. One day, while $P_{\mathcal{Y}}$ listens to a match announcement, $P_{\mathcal{X}}$ grabs the radio from him. Consequently, $P_{\mathcal{Y}}$ hears the first part of the announcement: "The match between team I and team J" and $P_{\mathcal{X}}$ hears the second part: "was won by team K." $P_{\mathcal{X}}$ and $P_{\mathcal{Y}}$ agree that $P_{\mathcal{Y}}$ should know the winner (for it is his radio). They are looking for the most efficient way to do it.

If no interaction is allowed, $P_{\mathcal{X}}$ has to send a single message enabling $P_{\mathcal{Y}}$ to uniquely determine the winner. This message is based solely on the winner (for that is all $P_{\mathcal{X}}$ knows). Let $\sigma(i)$ be the message sent by $P_{\mathcal{X}}$ when he hears "was won by team i." If the messages $\sigma(i)$ and $\sigma(j)$ are the same for some $i \neq j$, then in the event of a match between teams i and j, $P_{\mathcal{Y}}$ cannot tell who the winner is. Also, if $\sigma(i)$ is a prefix of $\sigma(j)$ for $i \neq j$, then in the event of a match between teams i and j, $P_{\mathcal{Y}}$ does not know when the message ends. Therefore, the messages $\sigma(1), \ldots, \sigma(t)$ must all be different, and none can be a proper prefix of another. Hence the average one-way communication is at least $\log t$ bits, and the worst-case one-way communication is at least $\lceil \log t \rceil$ bits. The worst-case lower bound is clearly achievable since the one-way protocol instructing $P_{\mathcal{X}}$ to transmit the binary representation of K (well, the $\lceil \log t \rceil$-bit binary representation of $K-1$, to be precise) requires $\lceil \log t \rceil$ bits in the worst case.

Communication is very different once interaction is allowed. We describe a two-message protocol that requires only $\lceil \log \log t \rceil + 1$ bits in the worst case. $P_{\mathcal{Y}}$ considers the binary representations $I_1, \ldots, I_{\lceil \log t \rceil}$ and $J_1, \ldots, J_{\lceil \log t \rceil}$ of I and J. Since $I \neq J$, there must be a first bit location L where the binary representations differ: $I_L \neq J_L$. Using $\lceil \log \log t \rceil$ bits, $P_{\mathcal{Y}}$ transmits L. $P_{\mathcal{X}}$ responds by transmitting K_L—the Lth bit in the binary representation of the winning team K. The total number of bits exchanged is $\lceil \log \log t \rceil + 1$ bits.

Is there another protocol (using two or more messages) requiring fewer than $\lceil \log \log t \rceil + 1$ bits in the worst case? No. Using the general lower bound proved in Theorem 2, we will see in Example 2 that $\lceil \log \log t \rceil + 1$ bits are necessary with two or any number of messages.

In this paper we investigate some aspects of communication reduction achievable via interaction. Our model assumes two *communicators*: an *informant* $P_{\mathcal{X}}$ having a random variable X and a *recipient* $P_{\mathcal{Y}}$ having a random variable Y. The *random pair* (X, Y) is distributed according to a joint probability distribution $p(x, y)$ that is known to both communicators. $P_{\mathcal{X}}$ and $P_{\mathcal{Y}}$ want the recipient, $P_{\mathcal{Y}}$, to learn X with no probability of error. The informant, $P_{\mathcal{X}}$, may or may not learn Y.

To that end the communicators alternate in transmitting *messages*: finite sequences of bits. Messages are transmitted over an error-free channel and are determined by an agreed-upon, deterministic protocol. A *protocol for* (X, Y) (i.e., a protocol for transmitting X to a person who knows Y) enables communication in a distributed environment where, initially, $P_{\mathcal{X}}$ knows X, $P_{\mathcal{Y}}$ knows Y, and their knowledge about each other's random variables derives from the exchanged messages. It therefore guarantees that the number of messages and bits transmitted is always finite and that the following properties hold:

Separate transmissions: Each message is based on the random variable known to its transmitter and on previous messages.

Implicit termination: When one communicator transmits a message, the other knows when it ends, and both communicators know when communication is over.

Correct decision: When communication ends, the recipient, $P_{\mathcal{Y}}$, knows X.

For conciseness of the introduction, we postpone the formal definition of protocols to the next section. Presently, we define the minimum number of bits that must be transmitted in the worst case. The *support set* of a random pair (X, Y) with underlying probability distribution $p(x, y)$ is the set

$$S_{X,Y} \stackrel{\text{def}}{=} \{(x, y) : p(x, y) > 0\}$$

of ordered pairs occurring with positive probability. An *input* is an element of $S_{X,Y}$ viewed as value assignments to X and Y. For every input (x, y) the protocol used, ϕ, determines a finite sequence $\sigma_1(x, y), \ldots, \sigma_{m_\phi(x,y)}(x, y)$ of transmitted messages.[1] Since $P_{\mathcal{X}}$ and $P_{\mathcal{Y}}$ alternate in transmitting these messages, all even-numbered messages in this sequence are transmitted by one communicator and all odd-numbered messages are transmitted by the other. $m_\phi(x, y)$ is the number of messages exchanged for (x, y). The protocol ϕ is *m-message* if $m_\phi(x, y) \le m$ for all $(x, y) \in S_{X,Y}$. The *length*, $|\sigma|$, of a message σ is the number of bits it contains. The *transmission length* of the input (x, y) is

$$l_\phi(x, y) \stackrel{\text{def}}{=} \sum_{i=1}^{m_\phi(x,y)} |\sigma_i(x, y)| ,$$

the number of bits transmitted by both communicators when $X = x$, $Y = y$, and the protocol used is ϕ.

The *worst-case complexity of* ϕ is the supremum, over all inputs, of the number of bits transmitted during the execution of ϕ:

$$\hat{L}_\phi \stackrel{\text{def}}{=} \sup\{l_\phi(x, y) : (x, y) \in S_{X,Y}\} .$$

[1] For notational elegance we omit the su(b/per)script ϕ from $\sigma_i(x, y)$ Also, we do not assume that the same number of messages is transmitted for all inputs or that the same communicator transmits the first message for all inputs.

By the definition of protocols, $l_\phi(x, y)$ is always finite. Hence, when $S_{X,Y}$ is finite, so is $\hat{L}_\phi$. If $S_{X,Y}$ is infinite, $\hat{L}_\phi$ may or may not be finite. Many "interesting" random pairs have infinite support sets, yet lend themselves to finite-complexity protocols. One such pair is described in Section 4, Example 3. The results we prove hold for pairs with finite as well as infinite support sets.

The *m-message complexity of* (X, Y) is the minimum worst-case complexity of any m-message protocol for (X, Y):

$$\hat{C}_m(X|Y) \stackrel{\text{def}}{=} \inf\{\hat{L}_\phi : \phi \text{ is an } m\text{-message protocol for } (X, Y)\}.$$

It is the number of bits that the two communicators must transmit in the worst case if restricted to protocols that never require more than m messages.

$\hat{C}_1(X|Y)$, the *one-way complexity* of transmitting X to a person who knows Y, is the number of bits required in the worst case when $P_\mathcal{Y}$ cannot transmit to $P_\mathcal{X}$, that is, when no *interaction* is allowed. $\hat{C}_2(X|Y)$ is the number of bits required in the worst case when at most two messages are permitted: $P_\mathcal{Y}$ transmits a message reflecting Y, then $P_\mathcal{X}$ responds with a message from which $P_\mathcal{Y}$ must infer X. Since empty messages are allowed, $\hat{C}_m(X|Y)$ is a decreasing function of m bounded below by 0. We can therefore define $\hat{C}_\infty(X|Y)$, the *unbounded-message complexity of* (X, Y), to be the limit of $\hat{C}_m(X|Y)$ as $m \to \infty$. It is the *minimum* number of bits that must be transmitted for $P_\mathcal{Y}$ to know X, even if no restrictions are placed on the number of messages exchanged. A protocol for (X, Y) whose worst-case complexity is $\hat{C}_\infty(X|Y)$ is an *optimal* protocol for (X, Y). In summary, for all random pairs (X, Y):

$$\hat{C}_1(X|Y) \geq \hat{C}_2(X|Y) \geq \hat{C}_3(X|Y) \geq \cdots \geq \hat{C}_\infty(X|Y).$$

The results obtained in this paper concern the possible discrepancy between these quantities. We now review them, using the league problem of Example 1 for illustration. Casting the example in terms of the general model, $P_\mathcal{X}$ knows a winner $X_t \in \{1, \ldots, t\}$ while $P_\mathcal{Y}$ knows a match $Y_t \in \{(i, j) : 1 \leq i < j \leq t\}$ and wants to learn X_t. Here, and in the sequel, $X \in \mathcal{X}$ means that the random variable X takes values in the set $\mathcal{X}$. We saw that $\hat{C}_1(X_t|Y_t) = \lceil \log t \rceil$ and that $\hat{C}_2(X_t|Y_t) \leq \lceil \log\log t \rceil + 1$.

Most likely, there is a probability distribution p that determines the match and the winner. However the next section, which formally defines protocols and proves some of their basic properties, also shows that, as we consider only worst-case complexity and do not allow any errors, the precise values of p are irrelevant to $\hat{C}_m(X|Y)$:

COROLLARY 1. *For all* (X, Y) *pairs and all* $m \in \{1, \ldots, \infty\}$, *the* m-*message complexity* $\hat{C}_m(X|Y)$ *is determined by* $S_{X,Y}$, *the support set of* (X, Y).

Therefore, the m-message complexity of the league problem can be determined although we (implicitly) described only the support set of (X_t, Y_t); since all games are possible and the winner is one of the playing teams,

$$S_{X_t, Y_t} = \{(k, (i, j)) : 1 \leq i < j \leq t \text{ and } k \in \{i, j\}\}.$$

In Section 3 we consider the one-way complexity, $\hat{C}_1(X|Y)$ — the simplest complexity measure to analyze. We define $G(X|Y)$ — the *characteristic hypergraph of* (X, Y). $G(X|Y)$ is simply related to the support set $S_{X,Y}$ and will be instrumental in several subsequent proofs. As a first application we show that it determines the one-way complexity of (X, Y).

LEMMA 2. *For all* (X, Y) *pairs,*

$$\hat{C}_1(X|Y) = \lceil \log \chi(G(X|Y)) \rceil$$

where $\chi(G)$ *is the chromatic number of a hypergraph* G.

The proof slightly strengthens a result in Witsenhausen **[1976]** that showed that the minimum number of different messages sent in one-way communication is the chromatic number of a graph equivalent to $G(X|Y)$.

The characteristic hypergraph of the league problem with t teams is K_t, the complete graph on t vertices. This proves, again, that $\hat{C}_1(X_t|Y_t) = \lceil \log t \rceil$ as was shown in Example 1.

We saw that the two-message complexity of the league problem with t teams satisfies $\hat{C}_2(X_t|Y_t) \leq \lceil \log \log t \rceil + 1$. Therefore,

$$\hat{C}_\infty(X_t|Y_t) \leq \hat{C}_2(X_t|Y_t) \leq \lceil \log \hat{C}_1(X_t|Y_t) \rceil + 1.$$

In Section 4 we prove that this discrepancy is the largest possible. Interaction can never reduce the amount of communication to the logarithm of the one-way complexity.

THEOREM 2. *For all nontrivial*[2] *pairs* (X, Y),

$$\hat{C}_\infty(X|Y) \geq \lceil \log \hat{C}_1(X|Y) \rceil + 1.$$

Therefore, the two-message protocol described in Example 1 is optimal for the league problem, and

$$\hat{C}_2(X_t|Y_t) = \cdots = \hat{C}_\infty(X_t|Y_t) = \lceil \log \log t \rceil + 1.$$

The "almost-logarithmic" reduction achieved for the league problem is typical of a large class of random pairs. Let (X, Y) be a random pair. The

[2]A pair (X, Y) is *trivial* if $\hat{C}_1(X|Y) = 0$. That is, X is a deterministic function of Y.

support set of X is the set

$$S_X \stackrel{\text{def}}{=} \{x : \text{ for some } y, (x, y) \in S_{X,Y}\}$$

of possible X values. S_Y, the *support set* of Y, is similarly defined. $P_{\mathcal{Y}}$'s *ambiguity set* when his random variable Y attains the value $y \in S_Y$ is

(1) $$S_{X|Y}(y) \stackrel{\text{def}}{=} |\{x : (x, y) \in S_{X,Y}\}| ,$$

the set of possible X values when $Y = y$. His *ambiguity* in that case is

$$\mu_{X|Y}(y) \stackrel{\text{def}}{=} |S_{X|Y}(y)| ,$$

the number of possible X values when $Y = y$. The *maximum ambiguity* of (X, Y) is

(2) $$\hat{\mu}_{X|Y} \stackrel{\text{def}}{=} \sup\{\mu_{X|Y}(y) : y \in S_Y\},$$

the maximum number of X values possible with any given Y value. In the league problem, the maximum ambiguity is two: for every value known to $P_{\mathcal{Y}}$ (a game), $P_{\mathcal{X}}$ has two possible values (winning teams). Whenever $\hat{\mu}_{X|Y} = 2$, the characteristic hypergraph is a graph, and then, the bound of Theorem 2 is tight.

THEOREM 3. *For all* (X, Y) *pairs with* $\hat{\mu}_{X|Y} = 2$,

$$\hat{C}_\infty(X|Y) = \lceil \log \hat{C}_1(X|Y) \rceil + 1 .$$

This is as far as we prove in this paper. We now note, without proofs, several other results that can be proven. Stated differently, the last theorem says that for all random pairs with maximum ambiguity two,

$$\hat{C}_1(X|Y) \geq 2^{\hat{C}_\infty(X|Y)-2}$$

and a similar inequality holds for many other (X, Y) pairs. Therefore, the number of bits required when no interaction is allowed may be exponentially higher than the minimum necessary. Remarkably, just two messages (one feedback message) suffice to reduce communication to at most four times the minimum. For all (X, Y) pairs,

$$\hat{C}_2(X|Y) \leq 4\hat{C}_\infty(X|Y) + 2 .$$

Later on we contrast this with the corresponding results in communication complexity. If the maximum ambiguity is two, this result can be strengthened still. For all (X, Y) pairs with $\hat{\mu}_{X|Y} = 2$,

$$\hat{C}_2(X|Y) = \cdots = \hat{C}_\infty(X|Y) = \lceil \log \hat{C}_1(X|Y) \rceil + 1 .$$

As a special case we have the league problem. Its maximum ambiguity is two, and therefore it has the optimal two-message protocol described in Example 1.

The two-message protocol of the league problem exhibits a peculiar property. $P_{\mathscr{Y}}$, the recipient who wants to say nothing, transmits almost all the bits whereas the informant, $P_{\mathscr{X}}$, transmits almost none. This does not mean that $P_{\mathscr{Y}}$ must transmit more bits than $P_{\mathscr{X}}$. There could be other optimal protocols in which $P_{\mathscr{X}}$ transmits most of the bits. It can be shown, however, that for almost all random pairs (X, Y) with any given maximum ambiguity this is not the case. $P_{\mathscr{Y}}$ must transmit almost all the bits in order to achieve $\hat{C}_{\infty}(X|Y)$ or even to get close to it. The number of bits transmitted by $P_{\mathscr{Y}}$ can be appreciably reduced only if $P_{\mathscr{X}}$ transmits exponentially more than $\hat{C}_{\infty}(X|Y)$ bits.

The results obtained in this paper are related to two existing approaches in the study of communication. One branch of information theory assumes that a communicator wants to convey some random information X to another communicator who knows related information Y. Traditionally, the random pair (X, Y) is a collection of independent, identically distributed (i.i.d.) random pairs (X_i, Y_i), and the recipient is willing to tolerate some probability of not knowing X.

Communication complexity literature, on the other hand, assumes that two persons, one knowing X and the other knowing Y, communicate in order to determine the value of a binary function $f(X, Y)$. Only one instance ("episode") of the random variable pair is given, and the communicators want to know $f(X, Y)$ with no probability of error.

Following El Gamal and Orlitsky **[1984]**, we combine the two approaches. As in information theory, we assume that $P_{\mathscr{X}}$ wants to transmit X to $P_{\mathscr{Y}}$. As in communication complexity we assume that only one instance of the random pair is given and that no errors are allowed in determining the value of X.

A few comparisons are in order. The communication complexity problem is more symmetric as f depends on both X and Y. It is therefore natural to expect interaction to reduce communication. Indeed, Papadimitriou and Sipser **[1982]** showed a function for which one-message protocols require $\sqrt{t}/(2\log t)$ transmitted bits whereas there are two-message protocols for that function requiring only $2\log t + 1$ bits. Duris, Galil, and Schnitger **[1984]** showed that for every m, there is a function whose m-message complexity is $\Omega(\sqrt{t}/(m^4 \log t))$ but its $(m+1)$-message complexity is only $O(m \log t)$. Hence there can be an almost-exponential gap between m and $(m+1)$-message complexities. This contrasts with our case. Here $\hat{C}_2(X|Y), \ldots, \hat{C}_{\infty}(X|Y)$ are all within a factor of four from each other whereas only $\hat{C}_1(X|Y)$ can be exponentially higher.

To compare with information theory results, consider the related setup of El Gamal and Orlitsky **[1984]**. There, $P_{\mathscr{X}}$ and $P_{\mathscr{Y}}$ want to exchange their information: $P_{\mathscr{Y}}$ wants to learn X and $P_{\mathscr{X}}$ wants to learn Y. It was shown that, *on the average*, at least $H(X|Y) + H(Y|X)$ bits must be transmitted and that $H(X|Y)+H(Y|X)+3\min\{\log\log|S_X|, \log\log|S_Y|\}$ bits suffice for all distributions uniform over their support.[3] This resembles the result of Slepian and Wolf **[1973]** but does not allow any errors in determining X and Y and does not assume that X and Y are collections of i.i.d. random variables. In this paper we are concerned with worst-case complexity, rather than average, and we study the effect of interaction, rather than determine the minimum number of bits that must be transmitted.

2. Protocols

Protocols were informally described in the introduction. For conciseness, however, we left out the details. In Sections 3 and 4 we prove lower bounds on the complexities of probability distributions. These bounds rely on the precise definitions of protocols given in this section. The definitions follow those of Papadimitriou and Sipser **[1982]** (for communication complexity), El Gamal and Orlitsky **[1984]**, and Orlitsky **[1987]**, with adaptations to the present model.

For arbitrary elements $a_k, \dots, a_l$ we let $\langle a_k, \dots, a_l\rangle$ or $\langle a_j\rangle_{j=k}^{l}$ denote the $(l+1-k)$-element sequence whose ith element is a_{k+i-1}; for $k>l$ the sequence $\langle a_j\rangle_{j=k}^{l}$ is empty. A *message*, or *string*, is a (finite, possibly empty) sequence of bits. Let $\alpha_1, \dots, \alpha_k$ and $\beta_1, \dots, \beta_l$ be bits. The string $\langle \alpha_j\rangle_{j=1}^{k}$ is a *prefix* of the string $\langle \beta_j\rangle_{j=1}^{l}$ if $\alpha_j=\beta_j$ for $j=1, \dots, k$. It is a *proper prefix* if, in addition, $k<l$.

Let (X, Y) be a pair of random variables. The *support set* of (X, Y) is $S_{X,Y}=\{(x, y): p(x, y)>0\}$, and an *input* is an element of $S_{X,Y}$. A *protocol for* (X, Y) is a mapping ϕ that associates with each input (x, y) a finite sequence $\langle\sigma_1(x, y), \sigma_2(x, y), \dots, \sigma_{m_\phi(x,y)}(x, y)\rangle$ of messages satisfying the three properties described below. Since $P_{\mathscr{X}}$ and $P_{\mathscr{Y}}$ alternate in transmitting these messages, all even-numbered messages are transmitted by one communicator and all odd-numbered messages by the other. We extend the messages indefinitely by letting $\sigma_i(x, y) \stackrel{\text{def}}{=} \Lambda$ (the empty string) for $i>m_\phi(x, y)$. This simplifies notation and proofs since we can assume that $\sigma_i(x, y)$ exists for all i. The following properties must hold for all $(x, y), (x, y'), (x', y) \in S_{X,Y}$ and all $i \geq 1$:

2.1. Separate-transmissions property. If message i is transmitted by $P_{\mathscr{X}}$ then $\langle\sigma_j(x, y)\rangle_{j=1}^{i-1}=\langle\sigma_j(x, y')\rangle_{j=1}^{i-1}$ implies that $\sigma_i(x, y)=\sigma_i(x, y')$, and, if message i is transmitted by $P_{\mathscr{Y}}$ then $\langle\sigma_j(x, y)\rangle_{j=1}^{i-1}=\langle\sigma_j(x', y)\rangle_{j=1}^{i-1}$ implies that $\sigma_i(x, y)=\sigma_i(x', y)$.

[3] $H(X) \stackrel{\text{def}}{=} -\sum p(X=x)\log p(X=x)$ denotes the binary entropy of X. $H(X|Y) \stackrel{\text{def}}{=} \sum_y p(y)H(X|Y=y)$ is the conditional entropy of X given Y.

2.2. Implicit-termination property. If message i is transmitted by $P_{\mathscr{X}}$ then $\langle\sigma_j(x, y)\rangle_{j=1}^{i-1} = \langle\sigma_j(x', y)\rangle_{j=1}^{i-1}$ implies that neither $\sigma_i(x, y)$ nor $\sigma_i(x', y)$ is a *proper* prefix of the other, and, if message i is transmitted by $P_{\mathscr{Y}}$ then $\langle\sigma_j(x, y)\rangle_{j=1}^{i-1} = \langle\sigma_j(x, y')\rangle_{j=1}^{i-1}$ implies that neither $\sigma_i(x, y)$ nor $\sigma_i(x, y')$ is a *proper* prefix of the other.

2.3. Correct-decision property. $\langle\sigma_j(x, y)\rangle_{j=1}^{\infty} = \langle\sigma_j(x', y)\rangle_{j=1}^{\infty}$ implies that $x = x'$.

Several properties of protocols and complexity measures follow directly from these definitions and those given in the introduction. Some are described here. They are the present-model equivalent of results in El Gamal and Orlitsky **[1984]** and Orlitsky **[1986]**. First we give an obvious lemma that has many ramifications.

LEMMA 1. *If (X_1, Y_1) and (X_2, Y_2) are two random pairs such that $S_{X_1, Y_1} \subseteq S_{X_2, Y_2}$, then $\hat{C}_m(X_1|Y_1) \le \hat{C}_m(X_2|Y_2)$ for all $m \in \{1, \ldots, \infty\}$.*

PROOF. Every protocol for (X_2, Y_2) is also a protocol for (X_1, Y_1). As an immediate consequence we have

COROLLARY 1. *If $S_{X_1, Y_1} = S_{X_2, Y_2}$ for two random pairs (X_1, Y_1) and (X_2, Y_2) then for all $m \in \{1, \ldots, \infty\}$,*

$$\hat{C}_m(X_1|Y_1) = \hat{C}_m(X_2|Y_2) .$$

Two implications of this result are used throughout the paper:

(i) $\hat{C}_m(X|Y)$ is a function only of $S_{X,Y}$, the support set of (X, Y); hence in determining $\hat{C}_m(X|Y)$ the precise values of p can be ignored.

(ii) There are only finitely many "essentially different" random pairs with values in a finite product-set; hence when we mentioned towards the end of the introduction that the recipient must transmit many more bits than the informant, we could refer to "most random pairs."

These consequences were to be expected because of two assumptions made in formulating the problem. First, $P_{\mathscr{Y}}$ cannot make any errors in determining X: however small $p(x, y)$ is, if $X = x$ and $Y = y$, then $P_{\mathscr{Y}}$ must eventually know that $X = x$. Second, the complexity measure $\hat{C}_m(X|Y)$ is the number of bits exchanged in the worst case (rather than on the average).

Other results can be obtained with little work. If $\sigma_k, \ldots, \sigma_l$ are strings, we let $[\sigma_k \ldots \sigma_l]$ or, equivalently, $[\sigma_j]_{j=k}^{l}$ denote the string obtained by their concatenation. Let ϕ be a protocol for (X, Y). The *codeword* that ϕ

associates with the input (x, y) is the concatenation

$$\sigma_\phi(x, y) \stackrel{\text{def}}{=} [\sigma_j(x, y)]_{j=1}^\infty$$

of all messages transmitted under ϕ for that input. (Recall that ϕ is implicit in $\sigma_j(x, y)$.)

Theorem 1. *Let ϕ be a protocol for a random pair (X, Y). If one of $\sigma_\phi(x', y)$ and $\sigma_\phi(x, y')$ is a prefix of the other and $(x, y) \in S_{X,Y}$, then*

$$\langle\sigma_j(x', y)\rangle_{j=1}^\infty = \langle\sigma_j(x, y)\rangle_{j=1}^\infty = \langle\sigma_j(x, y')\rangle_{j=1}^\infty .$$

Proof. We show by induction on i that $\langle\sigma_j(x', y)\rangle_{j=1}^i = \langle\sigma_j(x, y)\rangle_{j=1}^i = \langle\sigma_j(x, y')\rangle_{j=1}^i$. The induction hypothesis holds vacuously for $i = 0$. Assume it holds for $i-1$, in particular $[\sigma_j(x', y)]_{j=1}^{i-1} = [\sigma_j(x, y')]_{j=1}^{i-1}$. Then one of $[\sigma_j(x', y)]_{j=i}^\infty$ and $[\sigma_j(x, y')]_{j=i}^\infty$ is a prefix of the other, which implies that one of $\sigma_i(x', y)$ and $\sigma_i(x, y')$ is a prefix of the other. If the ith message is transmitted by $P_{\mathcal{X}}$ then, by the separate-transmissions property and the induction hypothesis, $\sigma_i(x, y) = \sigma_i(x, y')$, hence one of $\sigma_i(x, y)$ and $\sigma_i(x', y)$ is a prefix of the other. By the implicit-termination property, neither $\sigma_i(x, y)$ nor $\sigma_i(x', y)$ can be a proper prefix of the other, hence they must be the same and $\sigma_i(x', y) = \sigma_i(x, y) = \sigma_i(x, y')$. If the ith message is transmitted by $P_{\mathcal{Y}}$ then, symmetrically, $\sigma_i(x, y) = \sigma_i(x', y)$ by the induction hypothesis and the separate-transmissions property, and, then, $\sigma_i(x, y) = \sigma_i(x, y')$ by the implicit-termination property, proving the induction step.

If ϕ is a protocol for (X, Y), and (x, y), (x', y) are distinct inputs in $S_{X,Y}$, then, by the correct-decision property, $\langle\sigma_j(x, y)\rangle_{j=1}^\infty \neq \langle\sigma_j(x', y)\rangle_{j=1}^\infty$. The next corollary implies that not only the sequences of messages, but even the codewords themselves, must be different.

Corollary 2. *Let ϕ be a transmission protocol for (X, Y). If (x', y), (x, y), $(x, y') \in S_{X,Y}$, and $x \neq x'$ then neither $\sigma_\phi(x', y)$ nor $\sigma_\phi(x, y')$ is a prefix of the other.* (*In particular, they cannot be equal.*)

Proof. Assume that either $\sigma_\phi(x', y)$ or $\sigma_\phi(x, y')$ is a prefix of the other. From Theorem 1,

$$\langle\sigma_j(x', y)\rangle_{j=1}^\infty = \langle\sigma_j(x, y)\rangle_{j=1}^\infty = \langle\sigma_j(x, y')\rangle_{j=1}^\infty .$$

The first equality and the correct-decision property imply that $x = x'$.

This enables us to apply traditional prefix-freeness results to our model. In Section 4 we will use it to apply Kraft's inequality; here, we prove a trivial yet useful lower bound on $\hat{C}_\infty(X|Y)$.

Equation (1) defined $P_{\mathscr{Y}}$'s ambiguity set $S_{X|Y}(y)$ to be the set of possible X values when $Y = y$. The last corollary implies that for all $y \in S_Y$, the multiset[4] of codewords $\{\sigma_\phi(x, y) : x \in S_{X|Y}(y)\}$ is prefix free.

COROLLARY 3. *For all* (X, Y) *pairs,*

$$\hat{C}_\infty(X|Y) \geq \lceil \log \hat{\mu}_{X|Y} \rceil .$$

PROOF. *Let* ϕ *be a protocol for* (X, Y). *Corollary* 2 *implies that for all* $y \in S_Y$ *the multiset* $\{\sigma_\phi(x, y) : x \in S_{X|Y}(y)\}$ *is prefix free. Hence, for some* $x \in S_{X|Y}(y)$,

$$\hat{L}_\phi \geq l_\phi(x, y) \geq \lceil \log \mu_{X|Y}(y) \rceil .$$

This holds for all $y \in S_Y$, *proving the corollary.*

3. One-way complexity

$\hat{C}_1(X|Y)$, the one-way complexity of a random pair (X, Y), is the number of bits $P_{\mathscr{X}}$ must transmit in the worst case when $P_{\mathscr{Y}}$ is not permitted to transmit any feedback messages. Starting with $S_{X,Y}$, the support set of (X, Y), we define $G(X|Y)$, the *characteristic hypergraph* of (X, Y), and show that

$$\hat{C}_1(X|Y) = \lceil \log \chi(G(X|Y)) \rceil .$$

Let (X, Y) be a random pair. For each y in S_Y, the support set of Y, Equation (1) defined $S_{X|Y}(y)$ to be the set of possible x values when $Y = y$. The *characteristic hypergraph* $G(X|Y)$ of (X, Y) has S_X as its vertex set and the hyperedge $S_{X|Y}(y)$ for each $y \in S_Y$.

Witsenhausen **[1976]** defined a graph that is closely related to $G(X|Y)$ and linked its chromatic number to one-way communication. Let ϕ be a one-way protocol for a random pair (X, Y). The codeword $\sigma_\phi(x, y)$ of an input (x, y) consists of the message $\sigma_1(x, y)$. By the separate transmissions property, $\sigma_\phi(x, y)$ is independent of y and we denote it by $\sigma_\phi(x)$; it is the message transmitted by $P_{\mathscr{X}}$ when $X = x$. Define

$$\Sigma_\phi \stackrel{\text{def}}{=} \{\sigma_\phi(x) : x \in S_X\}$$

to be the set of all messages $P_{\mathscr{X}}$ may transmit under ϕ. If x_1 and x_2 are adjacent in $G(X|Y)$ then for some $y \in S_Y$, both x_1 and x_2 are in $S_{X|Y}(y)$. By the correct decision property, $\sigma_\phi(x_1) \neq \sigma_\phi(x_2)$ for $P_{\mathscr{Y}}$ to be able to deduce X. Hence, σ_ϕ is a coloring of $G(X|Y)$ and so

$$|\Sigma_\phi| \geq \chi(G(X|Y)) .$$

On the other hand, any coloring of $G(X|Y)$ suggests a one-way protocol where $P_{\mathscr{X}}$ transmits the color of X. Hence there exists a one-way protocol

[4] A multiset allows multiplicity of elements. Hence, $\{0, 01, 01\}$ is prefix free as a set, but not as a multiset.

ϕ for (X, Y) with

$$|\Sigma_\phi| \leq \chi(G(X|Y)) .$$

Witsenhausen concluded that $\chi(G(X|Y))$ is the minimum size of Σ_ϕ, i.e., the minimum number of possible messages transmitted by $P_{\mathscr{X}}$ in a one-way protocol. This proves that $\hat{C}_1(X|Y) \leq \lceil \log \chi(G(X|Y)) \rceil$. However, the set Σ_ϕ is not necessarily prefix free.[5] According to the implicit-termination property, messages have to be prefix free only for each given value of Y. Therefore, the above implies only that $\hat{C}_1(X|Y) \geq \lceil \log \chi(G(X|Y)) \rceil - 1$.

A string α *extends* another string β if β is a prefix of α. A string is *maximal* in a set if no other string in the set extends it. The next lemma proves that even the set of maximal codewords in Σ_ϕ has size of at least $\chi(G(X|Y))$. This set is prefix free, hence at least one maximal codeword has length $\geq \lceil \log \chi(G(X|Y)) \rceil$.

LEMMA 2. *For all (X, Y) pairs,*

$$\hat{C}_1(X|Y) = \lceil \log \chi(G(X|Y)) \rceil .$$

PROOF. In view of the above, we prove only $\hat{C}_1(X|Y) \geq \lceil \log \chi(G(X|Y)) \rceil$. Let ϕ be a protocol for (X, Y). For each $x \in S_X$ let $\sigma'_\phi(x)$ be a maximal codeword in Σ_ϕ that extends $\sigma_\phi(x)$. The set

$$\Sigma'_\phi \stackrel{\text{def}}{=} \{\sigma'_\phi(x) : x \in S_X\}$$

is prefix free and is contained in Σ_ϕ. If x_1 and x_2 are adjacent in $G(X|Y)$ then for some $y \in S_Y$, both x_1 and x_2 are in $S_{X|Y}(y)$. Therefore,

(i) by the correct decision property: $\sigma_\phi(x_1) \neq \sigma_\phi(x_2)$,
(ii) by the implicit termination property: neither $\sigma_\phi(x_1)$ nor $\sigma_\phi(x_2)$ is a proper prefix of the other.

Therefore, neither $\sigma_\phi(x_1)$ nor $\sigma_\phi(x_2)$ is a (proper or improper) prefix of the other and so $\sigma'_\phi(x_1) \neq \sigma'_\phi(x_2)$. Hence, σ'_ϕ too is a coloring of $G(X|Y)$ so Σ'_ϕ is a prefix-free set of cardinality $\geq \chi(G(X|Y))$. Therefore, there must be an element in $\Sigma'_\phi \subseteq \Sigma_\phi$ whose length is at least $\lceil \log \chi(G(X|Y)) \rceil$.

This argument was implicitly used in Example 1 to show that $\hat{C}_1(X_t|Y_t) \geq \lceil \log t \rceil$. There, it was easy to see that all t messages have to be different and that no message could be a proper prefix of another. Both facts follow since the characteristic hypergraph in that case, $G(X_t|Y_t)$, is K_t, the complete graph on t vertices, whose chromatic number is t.

Unfortunately, this characterization of $\hat{C}_1(X|Y)$ might not be of much practical help in determining $\hat{C}_1(X|Y)$. Given a random pair (X, Y), its

---

[5]Indeed, protocols with codewords that prefix each other can reduce the *average-case* complexity.

characteristic hypergraph $G(X|Y)$ can be easily constructed but the chromatic number of a hypergraph is believed to be hard to compute.

4. Lower bound on $\hat{C}_\infty(X|Y)$

Example 1 showed that for some (X, Y) pairs $\hat{C}_\infty(X|Y) \leq \log \hat{C}_1(X|Y) + 1$. Can $\hat{C}_\infty(X|Y)$ be any lower? Are There (X, Y) pairs for which $\hat{C}_\infty(X|Y) \leq \log \hat{C}_1(X|Y)$? This section answers this question in the negative. A pair (X, Y) is *trivial* if $\hat{C}_1(X|Y) = 0$; that is, X is a deterministic function of Y.

THEOREM 2. *For all nontrivial (X, Y) pairs*

$$\hat{C}_\infty(X|Y) \geq \lceil \log \hat{C}_1(X|Y) \rceil + 1 .$$

Therefore $\hat{C}_\infty(X|Y) = \lceil \log \hat{C}_1(X|Y) \rceil + 1$ is the largest reduction in communication achievable via feedback.

Theorem 2 has a recursive proof that relates the length of a message to the chromatic number of the characteristic hypergraph remaining after it is sent. The proof is rather long and therefore is not given here. Instead we prove in this abstract a "bit" weaker result, namely that for all nontrivial (X, Y) pairs,

$$\hat{C}_\infty(X|Y) \geq \lceil \log \hat{C}_1(X|Y) \rceil . \tag{3}$$

Although very close to Theorem 2, this bound does not prove optimality of the two-message protocol of the league problem and other protocols that are not described in this abstract. Its proof however is simpler and more elegant than that of the stronger bound and is therefore given.

We conclude the section by showing that the league problem is not unique in achieving the bound of Theorem 2. The bound is attained with equality by all (X, Y) pairs with maximum ambiguity two.

The proof of Inequality (3) uses simulation: given an arbitrary protocol for a pair (X, Y), we simulate it by a low-complexity one-way protocol. Simulation protocols have been used in communication complexity, e.g., Papadimitriou and Sipser [**1982**]. There, however, all inputs are possible and interaction gain is obtained when the computed function is "irregular." Here, there is no function, and interaction helps only when the set of possible inputs is "irregular."

Let α and β be strings. We write $\beta \preceq \alpha$ ($\beta \not\preceq \alpha$) if β is (is not) a prefix of α and write $\beta \prec \alpha$ ($\beta \not\prec \alpha$) if β is (is not) a proper prefix of α.

LEMMA 3. *For all nontrivial (X, Y) pairs,*

$$\hat{C}_\infty(X|Y) \geq \lceil \log \hat{C}_1(X|Y) \rceil .$$

PROOF. Given a protocol ϕ for (X, Y) with worst-case complexity $\hat{L}_\phi$, we construct a one-way protocol whose worst-case complexity is $2^{\hat{L}_\phi}$. In

Equation (1) we defined $S_{X|Y}(y)$ to be the set of possible X values when $Y = y$. We similarly define $P_{\mathscr{X}}$'s *ambiguity set* $S_{Y|X}(x)$ to be the set of possible Y values when $X = x$. Recall also that $\sigma_\phi(x, y)$ denotes the concatenation of all messages transmitted under ϕ for the input (x, y).

$P_{\mathscr{X}}$, given X, sequentially considers all $2^{\hat{L}_\phi}$ sequences of $\hat{L}_\phi$ bits. For each such sequence α, he transmits:

$$f_X(\alpha) \stackrel{\text{def}}{=} \begin{cases} 1 & \text{if } \sigma_\phi(X, y) \preceq \alpha \text{ for some } y \in S_{Y|X}(X), \\ 0 & \text{otherwise.} \end{cases}$$

$P_{\mathscr{Y}}$ finds an $\hat{L}_\phi$-bit sequence α for which $f_X(\alpha) = 1$. He then finds an $x \in S_{X|Y}(Y)$ for which $\sigma_\phi(x, Y) \preceq \alpha$ and decides that $X = x$. To prove correctness of this protocol, we show the following:

(1) There is an $\hat{L}_\phi$-bit sequence α for which $f_X(\alpha) = 1$ and $\sigma_\phi(X, Y) \preceq \alpha$.

(2) If $x' \in S_{X|Y}(Y) - \{X\}$ then there is no $\hat{L}_\phi$-bit sequence α for which $f_X(\alpha) = 1$ and $\sigma_\phi(x', Y) \preceq \alpha$.

(1) holds because $(X, Y) \in S_{X,Y}$, hence $|\sigma_\phi(X, Y)| \le \hat{L}_\phi$. We prove (2) by showing that the existence of an α satisfying the two properties leads to a contradiction. If $f_X(\alpha) = 1$, then there is a $y' \in S_Y$ such that $(X, y') \in S_{X,Y}$ and $\sigma_\phi(X, y') \preceq \alpha$. If, in addition, $\sigma_\phi(x', Y) \preceq \alpha$, then one of $\sigma_\phi(X, y')$ and $\sigma_\phi(x', Y)$ is a prefix of the other. By assumption, we also have $(X, Y) \in S_{X,Y}$ and $x' \ne X$, contradicting Corollary 2.

As we already mentioned, the bound proved in the lemma is not strong enough to prove optimality of the two-message protocol of the league problem. However, we can use Theorem 2 to precisely determine $\hat{C}_m(X_t|Y_t)$ for all m in the league problem of Example 1.

EXAMPLE 2. It is now easy to see that $\lceil \log\log t \rceil + 1$ bits are necessary in Example 1 with two or even more messages. We saw that $\hat{C}_1(X_t|Y_t) = \lceil \log t \rceil$, and that $\hat{C}_2(X_t|Y_t) \le \lceil \log\log t \rceil + 1$. Theorem 2 implies that $\hat{C}_\infty(X_t|Y_t) \ge \lceil \log \hat{C}_1(X_t|Y_t) \rceil + 1 \ge \lceil \log\log t \rceil + 1$. Hence $\hat{C}_2(X_t|Y_t) = \cdots = \hat{C}_\infty(X_t|Y_t) = \lceil \log\log t \rceil + 1$.

Equation (2) defined $\hat{\mu}_{X|Y}$, the maximum ambiguity of (X, Y), as the maximum number of X values possible with any given Y value. We conclude this section by showing that for all (X, Y) pairs with maximum ambiguity two, the bound of Theorem 2 is tight. It is therefore the tightest general bound on $\hat{C}_\infty(X|Y)$ that can be expressed in terms of m-message complexities.

Theorem 3. *For all* (X, Y) *pairs with* $\hat{\mu}_{X|Y} = 2$,

$$\hat{C}_\infty(X|Y) = \lceil \log \hat{C}_1(X|Y) \rceil + 1 .$$

We demonstrate a two-message protocol whose worst-case complexity is $\lceil \log \hat{C}_1(X|Y) \rceil + 1$. *This proves* $\hat{C}_\infty(X|Y) \le \lceil \log \hat{C}_1(X|Y) \rceil$. *Theorem* 2 *provides the converse inequality.*

The protocol is essentially that of the league problem, but it uses colors instead of actual X*-values.* $P_{\mathscr{X}}$ *and* $P_{\mathscr{Y}}$ *agree on a* $\chi(G(X|Y))$*-coloring of* $G(X|Y)$ *and on a* $\lceil \log \chi(G(X|Y)) \rceil$*-bit encoding of each color.* $P_{\mathscr{Y}}$ *knows* Y *and therefore knows the two possible values of* X *and their (necessarily different) colors. He finds a bit location in which the encodings of the two corresponding colors differ and transmits that location using* $\lceil \log \lceil \log \chi(G(X|Y)) \rceil \rceil$ *bits. Then,* $P_{\mathscr{X}}$ *responds with one bit describing the value of that bit in the encoding of the color of* X. *The total number of transmitted bits is* $\lceil \log \lceil \log \chi(G(X|Y)) \rceil \rceil + 1$, *and Lemma* 2 *said that* $\hat{C}_1(X|Y) = \lceil \log \chi(G(X|Y)) \rceil$.

Example 1 illustrated a special case. For each Y value (a match) there were two possible X values (winning teams); hence $\hat{\mu}_{X|Y}$ was 2. This was a simple case to analyze since all two-subsets of S_X could occur. In general, $S_{X,Y}$ is much less regular.

Example 3. Modifying Example 1, assume an infinite league of teams named $1, 2, \ldots$. Two random teams I and J play each other and team $K \in \{I, J\}$ wins. $P_{\mathscr{Y}}$ knows who played; $P_{\mathscr{X}}$ knows who won. This time, however, teams I and J are always picked so that $|I - J| \le l$. (Perhaps the names correspond to locations, or strengths, and two teams too far apart in distance or strength cannot play each other.)

The vertices $1, \ldots, l$ form a complete subgraph of the infinite graph $G(X|Y)$; hence $\chi(G(X|Y)) \ge l$. On the other hand, the mapping $C(i) = i \bmod l$ is an l-coloring of $G(X|Y)$. Hence $\chi(G(X|Y)) = l$ and Theorem 3 implies that $\hat{C}_1(X|Y) = \lceil \log l \rceil$ and $\hat{C}_\infty(X|Y) = \lceil \log \log l \rceil + 1$.

One optimal one-way protocol instructs $P_{\mathscr{X}}$ to transmit the $\lceil \log l \rceil$-bit binary representation of $K \bmod l$. In one optimal two-message protocol, $P_{\mathscr{Y}}$ uses $\lceil \log \log l \rceil$ bits to transmit a location where the $\lceil \log l \rceil$-bit binary representation of $I \bmod l$ differs from that of $J \bmod l$, and $P_{\mathscr{X}}$ transmits the value of this bit for the winning team.

References

1. P. Duris, Z. Galil, and G. Schnitger, *Lower bounds on communication complexity*, Proc. of the 16th Annual ACM Symposium on the Theory of Computing (1984), 81–91.
2. A. El Gamal and A. Orlitsky, *Interactive data compression*, Proc. of the 25th Annual Symposium on Foundations of Computer Science (1984), 100–108.
3. A. Orlitsky, *Communication issues in distributed communication*, Ph.D. thesis, Stanford University, 1986.
4. C. H. Papadimitriou and M. Sipser, *Communication complexity*, Proc. of the 14th Annual ACM Symposium on the Theory of Computing (1982), 196–200.

5. D. Slepian and J. Wolf, *Noiseless coding of correlated information sources*, IEEE Trans. Inform. Theory, July 1973.
6. H. Witsenhausen, *The zero-error side information problem and chromatic numbers*, IEEE Trans. Inform. Theory (1976), 592–593.
7. A. C. Yao, *Some complexity questions related to distributive computing*, Proc. of the 11th Annual ACM Symposium on the Theory of Computing (1979), 209–213.

AT&T Bell Laboratories, 600 Mountain Ave., Murray Hill, New Jersey 07974

DIMACS Series in Discrete Mathematics
and Theoretical Computer Science
Volume 2, 1991

On Necessary Conditions for Secure Distributed Computation

RAFAIL OSTROVSKY AND MOTI YUNG

ABSTRACT. What assumptions are required to achieve an *unconditionally secure* distributed circuit evaluation in a fully connected network? This question was addressed with respect to the allowed number of malicious players [**BGW**, **CCD**, **RB**], given that *every channel* is unconditionally secure. In this paper we investigate whether the security of all channels is also a necessary condition.

[**BGW**, **CCD**] showed how secure computation can be achieved, provided that a constant fraction of the total number of players is honest. An insecure channel can be modeled as faults on both ends of the channel. Thus, as long as the number of such "faulty" players is smaller then the fraction established in [**BGW**, **CCD**], the channels can be made insecure. However, an insecure channel seems to be a much weaker fault than a corruption of both players. Thus, can a bigger fraction of insecure channels be tolerated? In this paper we show that this is not the case. That is, we show that in some cases the perfect security of multi-party protocols in a fully connected network requires *all* the channels to be physically secure. In particular, we show a simple protocol (for three parties) for which if privacy of even one channel is compromised, the protocol can not be computed securely. Thus, we establish that the security of *all* channels is not only sufficient (by the work of [**BGW**, **CCD**]), but also *necessary*. The lower bound holds even if players follow the protocol. That is, we establish our impossibility result even if all the players are honest but curious — if they follow the protocol exactly, but try to extract additional information "on the side". Thus, our result gives a pure security perspective of the impossibility. An additional feature of our result is its extreme simplicity, which is usually hard to come by for the lower bound proofs.

1. Introduction

This paper deals with feasibility results concerning the implementation of unconditionally secure computation in insecure communication environ-

1980 *Mathematics Subject Classification* (1985 *Revision*). Primary 68M10, 68P25, 68Q05.

Part of this work was done while the author was at the IBM Research, T. J. Watson Research Center, Yorktown Heights, NY 10598.

ments. That is, we examine the feasibility of multi ($\geq$ 3)-party secure computation. We concentrate on global computations in which all parties compute a private (possibly random) output.

The question of secure distributed computation received a lot of attention over the past decade, which culminated in the work of **[GMW1]** where they showed a way to compute any poly-size function on a fully-connected network of processors securely, under some general cryptographic assumptions, provided that more than $\frac{2}{3}$ of the processors are honest.

The cryptographic assumptions were then eliminated in the work of [**BGW**, **CCD**] where it was established that if every two processors can communicate secretly, one can achieve secure computation without any cryptographic assumptions for three or more processors (provided that either more than $\frac{1}{2}$ are honest while the rest are honest but may be curious, or that more than $\frac{2}{3}$ of the processors are honest in the case the rest of the processors may be Byzantine (malicious)). However, both the work of [**BGW**, **CCD**] and further extensions by [**RB**, **BG**] require each pair of processors to have a secure communication channel. In this work we examine whether this condition can be weakened, and provide a strong negative answer to this question.

That is, we show a gap between a network with physically secure channels and a network without such security measures. To do so, we exhibit a protocol for which there is no perfectly secure implementation on the second model even when only one channel is unprotected. The first model, on the other hand, is known to be universal for perfectly secure computations (even when up to $\frac{1}{3}$ of the participants are malicious [**BGW**, **CCD**].) This shows formally that adding physical security to *all* channels is not just sufficient but also *necessary*.

Notice that any insecure channel can be made secure using suitable cryptographic assumptions [**GMW2**, **GHY**]. The resulting protocol, however, is only as secure as the cryptographic assumption which was utilized. Instead, we are interested in the question of absolute security, independent of any assumptions. Our proof establishes that:

THEOREM 1. *Providing physical security to all channels is* NECESSARY *to the achievement of perfect security in distributed multi-party secure computation.*

Thus, our result justifies the model of physically secure channels as a model which achieves universality in the set of perfectly secure computation even when the parties are computationally unlimited, provided that *every* channel is secure. It also justifies the use of cryptography (and achieving only computational security) when such channels are not available.

The rest of the paper is organized as follows: In section 2 we describe our model. Section 3 explains our proof, while in section 4, we review recent and related results.

2. The model

We consider two models of computation for multi-party protocols. Both have computationally unlimited users in a fully-connected network. The first one has secure channels between each pair of users, while in the second model all (or some) channels are unprotected.

Both models have been used in various contexts in the past. For example, Feldman and Micali **[FM]** implemented a fast Byzantine Agreement protocol in the secure channel model and left an open problem whether such a fast Byzantine Agreement protocol (even with relaxed performance) can be implemented on the insecure channel model. (They also show a simulation of the private channel model in the insecure channel model using cryptographic assumptions, but here we are interested in perfect security.)

A bit more formally, we consider the model of multi-party protocols which is the standard system of communicating machines **[GMR]**. Each player is a probabilistic Turing machine with a private computation environment. They share communication tapes and communicate by writing messages on these tapes in a synchronous fashion.

Each pair of machines share a communication tape (for each such tape only two machines are allowed to write on it). When each machine has "read access" to all communication tapes this is the *insecure channels* model (or the bboard model); on the other hand, when each of the communication tapes can be accessed only by the pair of parties which are allowed to write on it, this is the *secure channels* model. A natural intermediate models with some private and some insecure channels can be defined as well.

A point worth mentioning is that the notion of secure channels can be somewhat relaxed. That is, the channels do not have to be totally secure, as we can adapt the wire-tap model of Wyner **[W]**. (He basically assumes a certain rate of being caught by the eavesdropper. By using linear codes according to the rate one gets that the users get the message while the eavesdropper does not.) Thus, the notion of "secure" channel can be interpreted in the above, weaker sense.

3. A simple proof of our result

We start with a review of Shamir, Rivest, and Adleman's impossibility of Mental-Poker **[SRA]**. This is a basic impossibility result (which seems to have been somewhat forgotten!) It shows that two players cannot deal a secret, disjoint, and random card hand based on information theory and open communication.

Shamir, Rivest, and Adleman's proof considers the minimal nontrivial scenario of two unfaulty (but possibly "curious") players, A and B, who try to deal a hand of one card to each out of a deck of three cards $\{x, y, z\}$. (This scenario can be extended to larger decks and any size of hands). Let the protocol *execution* M be the finite sequence of transmitted messages.

M should coordinate the cards drawn by each player (the cards drawn are a function of M and the player's internal computations). The hands should be drawn uniformly at random and be disjoint. Let x (y) be the actual card received by A (B).

Let S_A (S_B) be the set of candidate cards A (B) could have gotten, given M. S_A cannot contain only x since then B can compute the hand of A by simulating all possible computations of A consistent with the execution. S_A cannot contain all three cards since B will not be able to get any card disjoint to S_A: regardless of what card B gets, there is a computation consistent with M in which A may get the same card. Thus, S_A consists of two cards. Similarly, S_B must contain two cards. The total size of both candidate sets is four while the total size of the deck is three, thus there is an intersection between S_A and S_B, and there must be a computation consistent with M in which both players get the same card (in this case it is z). This contradicts the disjointness requirement which implies the impossibility.

We can now give an overview of our proof: consider the case of three nodes in the network. Note that if three players want to play and one channel is suspected not to be secure, they could use cryptography to solve the problem **[GMW2, GHY]**. But this solution relies on unproven complexity assumptions, while we are interested in retaining *perfect* (i.e., information-theoretic) security. A protocol for dealing cards (Mental-Poker) for three or more players which achieved information theoretic security was implemented, provided that all channels are secure in 1983 **[BaFu]**. The basic idea of our proof is to show that a three-player Mental-Poker is impossible if the channels are not secure.

We consider dealing of cards where there are three players and four cards in the deck. We start by assuming totally open communication. Given an execution (the protocol message sequence), none of the players can have only one card in the set of cards which are candidates to be taken to his hand consistent with the execution — this will violate security. The case of more than three cards in the candidate set is impossible as well (since if one player has more than three possible cards, then another player must have a nondisjoint card in his candidate set violating disjointedness of hands). Thus all players have two cards in their candidate set. However, again the deck is too small to provide disjointedness of the candidate sets, that is, there must be a computation consistent with the execution in which hands are not disjoint. Thus, the dealing protocol is impossible when all channels are insecure.

Can we make the result sharper and consider a network with only one insecure channel (while the rest are secure)? We assume the same scenario and problem as before with an intermediate model of a single insecure channel (say between A and B, while both channels to C are private). We have the execution which is the three sequences of messages over the three channels M_{ab}, M_{ac}, M_{bc}.

Again, in this case as before, no player may have a candidate set bigger than three. C may have a candidate set of size one. However, both A and B must have candidate sets of size two, since otherwise C who knows all the messages can determine their cards. The sum of the sizes of the candidate card sets from C's point of view is at least 5 while only 4 cards are present in the deck. (The other players see even less information than C and thus their view of the computation should also leave a candidate set of size 2.) This is a contradiction to disjointedness.

Thus, in this case, even one public channel prevents a perfectly secure implementation:

THEOREM 2. *There exist protocols which can not be executed securely in the information-theoretic sense on a fully-connected network if any one of the channels is compromised.*

This proves the necessity of secure channels in the case of computationally unbounded parties.

4. Related work

Recently, **[OVY]** considered two-party asymmetric games when one of the players is infinitely-powerful while the other is polynomially-bounded. Using the proof method similar to the above, they were able to show that information-theoretic Oblivious Transfer protocol is impossible to achieve. Moreover, noninteractive Oblivious Transfer was also shown to be impossible. On the positive side, they were able to show that if one-way functions exist, then any two-party asymmetric game (for example, Oblivious Transfer protocol) is possible to implement.

Further study of requirements for multi-party secure computation, when the network is not fully connected was done by **[DDWY]**, where they presented tight results on the required connectivity of the network in order to preserve security.

Acknowledgments

The authors thank Silvio Micali and Joan Feigenbaum for very helpful discussions on the topic of the paper.

REFERENCES

[BaFu] I. Barany and Z. Furedy, *Mental Poker with Three or More Players*, Info. and Cont. **59** (1983), 84–93.

[BGW] M. Ben-Or, S. Goldwasser, and A. Wigderson, *Completeness Theorem for Non-cryptographic Fault-tolerant Distributed Computing*, STOC 1988, ACM, pp. 1–10.

[BG] D. Beaver and S. Goldwasser, *Multiparty Computation with Faulty Majority*, FOCS 1989, IEEE, pp. 468–473.

[CCD] D. Chaum, C. Crépeau, and I. Damgård, *Multiparty Unconditionally Secure Protocols*, Proc. of 20th STOC 1988, ACM, pp. 11–19.

[DDWY] D. Dolev, C. Dwork, O. Waarts, and M. Yung, *Secure Message Transmission*, FOCS 1990, IEEE.

[FM] P. Feldman and S. Micali, *Optimal Algorithms for Byzantine Agreement*, STOC 1988, ACM, pp. 148–161.

[GHY] Z. Galil, S. Haber, and M. Yung, *Cryptographic Computations and the Public-Key Model*, The 7-th Crypto 1987, Springer-Verlag, pp. 135–155.

[GMW1] S. Goldreich, S. Micali, and A. Wigderson, *Proofs that Yield Nothing But their Validity*, FOCS 1986, IEEE, pp. 174–187.

[GMW2] S. Goldreich, S. Micali, and A. Wigderson, *How to Play any Mental Poker* , STOC 1987, ACM, pp. 218–229.

[GMR] S. Goldwasser, S. Micali, and C. Rackoff, *The Knowledge Complexity of Interactive Proof-Systems*, STOC 1985, ACM, pp. 291–304.

[OVY] R. Ostrovsky, R. Venkatesan, and M. Yung, *On The Complexity of Asymmetric Games*, manuscript.

[RB] T. Rabin and M. Ben-Or, *Verifiable Secret Sharing and Multiparty Protocols with Honest Majority*, STOC 1989, ACM, pp. 73–85.

[SRA] A. Shamir, R. Rivest, and L. Adleman, *Mental Poker*, Technical Memo MIT (1979).

[W] A. D. Wyner, *The WireTap Channel*, Bell System J. **54** (1981), 1355–1387.

MIT Laboratory for Computer Science, Cambridge, MA 02139
E-mail address: raf@theory.lcs.mit.edu

IBM Research, T. J. Watson Research Center, Yorktown Heights, NY 10598
E-mail address: moti@ibm.com

DIMACS Series in Discrete Mathematics
and Theoretical Computer Science
Volume 2, 1991

Secure IX Network

JIM REEDS

ABSTRACT. This paper sketches a design for a network of computers running the McIlroy-Reeds **ix** system. The emphasis is on modularity and decentralization; security does not rely much on central key distribution. It assumes that there are multiple overlapping domains of authority, and relies only loosely on an ultimate common organizational loyalty. This work is speculative. It is heavily influenced by the networking arrangements in the Research 10th Edition UNIX[†] system.

1. Single machine ix [*]

When we began working on **ix** [**MR1**, **MR2**], M. D. McIlroy and I simply wanted to add to the usual UNIX system model a stricter file access policy, a variant of the military security classification system. We believed that a no-frills implementation of this part of the Orange Book [**DOD**] requirements for a secure computer would satisfy most real security needs of most users, even if it might *not* satisfy the Orange Book people themselves. We also believed that our new access restrictions could be kept largely orthogonal to the existing scheme of `rwx` bits, which we left essentially intact. The new access policy could be airtight and draconian in its preservation of security labels (and the intellectual property rights they represent), even if on the same machine, at the same time, the usual UNIX system concepts of `userid`, `setuid`, `root accounts`, and `rwx` file permission bits were subverted.

After three years of part-time but intense work we have not changed those beliefs, but we have expanded our notion of what needs to go into a "no-frills implementation." Our resulting system, like all other attempts at secure operating systems, ends up with a two-tier structure. There is the generality of user programs, including all programs written by ordinary users and most

1980 *Mathematics Subject Classification* (1985 *Revision*). Primary 68M10.

[†]UNIX is a trademark of Bell Laboratories.

[*] Some details of single-machine **ix** given below are, for exposition's sake, simplified. The true description is in the on-line manual pages and in our technical report [**MR1**]. **Ix** is *not* pronounced like the German word *ich*.

of the programs in the public program directories. Then there are the privileged programs used to administer the security system, covering functions like logging users in, changing users' security clearances, and so on.

The distinguishing property is that the privileged programs must break the usual security rules, or viewed another way, that the kernel must be assured by a privileged program that some particular violation of the usual rules is not in fact a breach of security. Files, for instance, are not usually allowed to drop in security classification level. Terminal ports are files in the UNIX system, so when a terminal port used in a classified login session becomes free at the end of the session, before it may be used for a new, unclassified, login session it must be declassified by a privileged program. Ordinary disk files might be declassified from time to time for the usual reasons; this again needs a privileged program. The kernel cannot itself know when such actions are acceptable: it relies on the privileged programs to tell when to deviate from its worst-case application of the usual rules.

Trusted computing base. The presence of these privileged programs complicates things enormously. Obviously questions like "how do I know that a baddie hasn't tampered with a privileged program," or "how do programs become privileged," or "how do new releases of privileged programs get installed on the system" are relevant. The easy answers (essentially the same in all secure operating systems) are: Giving or removing privileged status to files can only be done by a privileged program. A privileged program can not be removed or changed, other than to have its privileged status removed. The program that first runs at boot time, *init*, is privileged. The privileged programs thus form a self-nominating closed "committee" which, together with the kernel as an *ex-officio* member, runs the computer. The jargon for this committee is TCB: trusted computing base.

This in turn leads to the hard questions. How does the TCB know which information from the outside world it should act on, and which is spurious? How does the computer user know he is talking to the TCB and not an imposter? How does one privileged program communicate with another, in such a way that each recognizes the other's privilege? **Ix**'s answers to these questions are based on two mechanisms, one in the kernel, the other coded into the privileged programs, both of which seem easily extendable over a network. Hence the TCB's iron reign can be extended over a network, and hence so can **ix**'s security services.

PEX. The first of these wonder mechanisms is a form of mandatory exclusive file locking, which we call PEX for "process exclusive." Any file may be marked for exclusive use by a process in which it is open, so long as no other process has done so first. The exclusivity lasts until the process explicitly drops it or until the file is closed or the process exits. A special twist occurs in pipes, each end of which may be independently PEXed. A pipe will not carry data unless both ends are PEXed or neither end is PEXed: an attempt to read or write on a half-PEXed pipe results in an error. When a pipe end is PEXed the other end is given indicia of privilege of the PEXing process. All this is done synchronously and independently of the usual stream [**R**] discipline. Thus a privileged process communicating on a pipe can tell if it has a unique partner process at the other end, and whether the partner process is privileged. A privileged program, for example, can refuse to collect a password unless it can PEX the standard input. If talking to an IO device unPEXed to any other process, the PEX call succeeds and no interloping process that also has the device open can steal the password. If talking to a pipe (say, to a window on a windowing terminal) the PEX bid will be accepted or rejected by the process at the other end of the pipe. If accepted, the privileged program can now tell if the other end is also in the TCB (as a trusted terminal multiplexor running secure windows would have to be), in which case the password dialogue can go forward, and so on. Using these means, parts of the TCB can recognize each other, can know when they are talking to users, and—although the details are clumsy—can prove to users that they are indeed talking to the TCB.

This can be thought of as a generalization of the Orange Book's "trusted path" mechanism, and as an alternative to Biba-style "inverse labels." (Biba inverse labels are described in pages 69–71 of Gasser [**G**]; the labels track trustability or provenance of data rather than secrecy.)

The notion of a PEXed pipe is nothing other than that of a secure communications channel between identified parties, an end goal of both classical and modern cryptology and of secure network design. The novelty is in making this service available to user processes, protecting themselves from eavesdropping, forging or spoofing by other processes. In its current single-machine form, the writ of PEX ends at the machine boundary, and cryptography is not needed to implement this new operating system feature. (New to the UNIX operating system, at least.) For PEX to go over a network to another machine would require at least a special protocol for the kernels to use in discussing the PEXity of their ends of the cross-machine pipe, and also possibly cryptography to identify and authenticate the end machines and to protect the data in transit.

Privilege server. The second special mechanism for privileged process control in **ix** is a *privilege server* embodying a particular design for denoting, recording, and exercising users' rights. The main idea is that although the TCB is all-powerful, it doesn't have any security interests of its own, save self-protection and economic control of the local hardware resources. The TCB is a custodian of users' rights, which might originate off-machine, possibly created under an authority separate from the management or ownership of the local host computer. In **ix** these fiduciary responsibilities of the TCB are managed by the privilege server.

The privilege server centralizes *authorization* calculations, much the way an authentication server centralizes authentication services. Authorization calculations often take a stylized form: a resource's owner passes a credential to a user, who later presents the credential together with a particular resource usage request to the custodian of the resource. In **ix**, the privilege server is the custodian of most users' rights (other than routine file access rights implied by user id and process label). For each request, the privilege server must check that the credential indeed authorizes the request, that the privilege server itself is authorized to act on the request (which includes checking whether the resource in question has been entrusted to the privilege server), as well as authentication information, such as whether the issuer of the certificate is the owner of the resource, and so on.

Requests for privileged services are made to the privilege server as text strings, which are also statements in a trivial computer command language, *nosh*. (This is a restricted, feature-starved "secure" shell with fewer possibilities for latent subversive side effects than found in the usual interactive shells *sh*, *csh*, or *ksh*.) If the requester has a right warranting the command string in question then the privilege server executes the command. Corresponding to each right, then, is the set of *nosh* command strings it warrants.

More precisely, a "right" is a regular language. Rights are recorded in a privileges file as pairs (R, Q), where R is a regular expression* (specifying the set of *nosh* commands warranted by the right) and where Q is a predicate applied to: the user, the execution environment of the current invocation of the privilege server, the status of the user's connection to the server, and (optionally) a protocol execution status. When a request s is presented to the server, it is executed only if a pair (R, Q) can be found such that s is an element of R and such that the predicate Q evaluates true. Thus "anyone" who satisfies Q may exercise R.

For ease of subdivision and delegation, we organize our privilege file as a rooted tree. Node (R_1, Q_1) may be above (closer to the root than) node (R_2, Q_2) only if language R_2 is contained in R_1. Thus, sub-nodes correspond to sub-rights, and if you can exercise a right at a given node you automatically may do anything you could do by exercising rights at sub-nodes.

Our command language has statements to edit the privileges file, so it is possible to formulate rights to change rights. In particular, it is easy to formulate a right to edit only a sub-tree of the tree of rights. Allowed edit commands are: diminish the set of rights at a node, delete a node or sub-tree, create a sub-node with rights equal to the parent node, and change the Q part of a node. Thus, editing can only reparcel or dilute existing rights, but not create new ones. (Since privilege file edits are relatively infrequent there is no practical performance loss in forbidding concurrent edits, or forbidding privilege calculations during edits.)

* Abuse of notation to follow: I make no notational distinction between a regular expression R and its corresponding language, so sometimes R really means $L(R)$.

To delegate a right means simply to create a sub-node in the tree of rights.

The Q predicate might require given login ids, ask for a password, require successful completion of a challenge-response protocol, or insist that the privilege server is being invoked by a particular named program. Q specifies the *authentication* needed to enjoy the rights in question.

A weak point in this scheme lies in the formulation of rights as regular expressions: extreme care must be taken to ensure that the *nosh* command language statements accurately catch the real meaning of the rights in question. In particular, the manual describing the TCB and the *nosh* language must be accurate, and worse, the meaning of command-line arguments and options to privileged programs may never be lightly changed, lest established rights be overthrown or inadvertently widened.

An example. Here is how the privilege server helps administer a security classification compartment. Suppose some users of an **ix** machine start a new project and want to create a security compartment to guard their work on the computer. This new security compartment shows up outside the computer as a new classification keyword stamped on documents and inside the computer as a new bit field in the security labels carried by files and processes. Say project leader Alpha wants to create a compartment `BETA` for his project; what steps does it take to teach the TCB about this new compartment?

To begin with, the TCB's only interest in `BETA` is in issues of operating system resource exhaustion: is the keyword `BETA` already in use for some other security compartment and is there an unused label bit field on the local machine to represent `BETA`? The usual solutions to these problems apply: categories might have hierarchical names (keywords like `ADONIS.PICCOLO.BETA` are less likely to be preempted), and only certain users may consume label bit fields by creating new security classifications. So among the rights already stored in the privileges file is an entry $(R_{\mathtt{mkcat}}, Q_{\mathtt{mkcat}})$ giving project leaders the right to run the privileged *mkcategory* program:

$$R_{\mathtt{mkcat}} = \mathtt{mkcategory.}$$

$$Q_{\mathtt{mkcat}} = \mathit{login\_id} \in \{\mathtt{Alpha,\ Rocky,\ Boris,\ Natasha...}\}.$$

So Alpha presents the request

```
mkcategory BETA
```

to the privilege server, which runs the *mkcategory* program in such a way that *mkcategory* knows this invocation is an authorized invocation. Note that so far the privilege server has only been guarding the local machine's operators' interest in preventing resource exhaustion, and not any security interest *per se*.

Mkcategory has two functions. One is to allot a bit field in the machine's internal representation of security labels and bind the name `BETA` to it, registering this in an official list. The other function is to register Alpha as the "owner" of `BETA` by placing a new entry $\beta = (R_\beta, Q_\beta)$ in the privileges file.

(The *mkcategory* program itself has the right to edit part of the tree of rights, according to a $Q_{\texttt{mkcat2}} = \text{invokerprog} \equiv \texttt{mkcategory}$.) To begin with, *mkcategory* finds out from Alpha what formula to use for Q_β, that is, how future commands from Alpha about BETA will be recognized. Alpha may provide any formula for Q_β he wishes: he may simply specify a password, or may specify that possession of Alpha's *login_id* suffices, may present the public key by which future commands may be verified, *a la* RSA, and so on. The R part of the new right is always the same for a newly created category, and expresses the union of these rights:

> Exerciser may access data marked BETA by logging on with the appropriate bit set in his process label.
>
> Exerciser may declassify category BETA from files, by executing a privileged command of the form `downgrade BETA`,* which clears the BETA bit from the named file.
>
> Exerciser may specify network addresses that may receive BETA data.
>
> Exerciser may edit this node β in the tree of rights.

Now project leader Alpha has a private security classification label all of his own. He can make classified login sessions, he can create secret files readable by no one else, he can declassify them.

Soon, however, Alpha wishes his assistants Mr. Gamma and Ms. Delta could access his secret files, too. He invokes his right to edit node β (by presenting whatever credentials he earlier spelled out in Q_β) and creates a sub-node, call it $\beta/access$, whose R part consists solely of the exerciser's right to read and write data marked BETA. The Q part is again at Alpha's discretion, who (say) chooses the formula

$$Q_{\beta/\texttt{access}} = \mathit{login\_id} \in \{\texttt{Gamma, Delta}\} \& \mathit{shows\_password}(\texttt{cyto97plasm}).$$

(Alpha need not add himself to the list in $Q_{\beta/\text{access}}$ because he already may exercise the superior right β, but might want to do so because for simple file access $Q_{\beta/\text{access}}$ might be easier to use than Q_β.) Note that Alpha has extended only his access rights to Gamma and Delta: as desired, Gamma and Delta can read and write BETA secrets, but they cannot change the list of people so cleared.

The project prospers, and when new assistants Eps through Lamb show up boss-man Alpha tires of editing $\beta/access$. So he appoints Ms. Delta as his BETA-clearance officer, by creating a new node $\beta/clearance$. $Q_{\beta/\texttt{clearance}}$ only lets Delta in. $R_{\beta/\texttt{clearance}}$ only allows the exerciser to edit the predicate $Q_{\beta/\texttt{access}}$.

At appropriation time some good press coverage is needed, so Alpha appoints Gamma his publicity manager, whose job of course includes shrewdly sequenced leaks of BETA data, which means a new node $\beta/declass$ is formed, with a $Q_{\beta/\text{declass}}$ for Mr. Gamma alone, and with $R_{\beta/\text{declass}}$ allowing BETA-downgrade rights to the exerciser.

What would it take to extend these activities to another computer? Obviously at set-up time the remote file servers need to reconcile their differing internal representations of file security labels: it is almost guaranteed that the bit slot allotted to represent category BETA will differ on all machines. But before BETA files may be traded the two machines should really check to make sure that what each knows as category BETA is really Alpha's BETA, by trading and verifying credentials signed by Alpha, according to the recipe spelled out in Q_β.

2. Networked IX

The general shape of a network of **ix** machines is clear. If a pair of machines trust their network connection, and trust each other's TCBs to enforce the same basic security policies, then they may extend PEX service and remote file system service as sketched above. A minimal version might consist of the following ingredients:

- A LAN offers secure networking within the confines of a single department.
- The individual **ix** machines are run by the same systems staff, who run identical software on the machines, so any of the machines can trust any other's TCB as much as it trusts its own.
- Terminals are at known network locations at known physical locations.

Within such a network different machines can carry varying mixes of secret data: some label categories may exist on all machines, other categories may exist on single machines only, other categories yet may exist on other subsets of machines. The user communities may be heterogeneous: not all users may have accounts on all machines, nor need all users of a given machine have access to the same security categories. Such a setup might be appropriate in a small department, or in a rigidly run branch of the government.

A more ambitious network might include subnets of the above description but would also have insecure network links, a variety of terminals in unknown or uncontrolled locations, a variety of computers with differing software, some of which are in isolated secure physical locations. Such a network would need a measure of cryptographic boost to give untappable connections, or connections to known endpoints. While it is unreasonable to hope that the computers all run exactly the same system software there is still a chance that their security software is the same. If two machines each believe the other's TCB there is a possibility that they can trade security services. To prove that partner machines have correct TCBs some appeal to authority is needed. Depending on details, machine A might trust B if B is at a known network address, or if B has a document attesting B's honesty, signed by an authority A trusts, or (what is really a variation of this) if B can communicate at all with A when A uses cryptographic keys it was provided with by a trustworthy authority.

In an ambitious network user terminals and user authentication pose a real problem: there is no general way for a network or a computer to tell the difference between a terminal and a work station or heftier computer. Any command purporting to come from a user at a terminal might really come from a hostile computer, which can play the **ix** protocols for dishonest purposes. Terminals on the network are thus treated as computers: unless they are at certain special secure network addresses on a trusted network, they must prove their *bona fides* before they are given PEX service, and hence before they may be used to get favors from the privilege server.

Little special software is needed for networked **ix**, given single-machine **ix** and given regular UNIX system networking facilities. As hinted earlier, a protocol for the TCBs to manage cross-machine PEX would be needed, possibly as a stream [**R**] module. And to handle remote file systems, for example, a form of "power of attorney" protocol is needed, by which one machine can prove to another that it has authority from a third party known to both. To be usable there must be user software to make it convenient to create (say) RSA keys on demand, and so on.

3. Special terminals and user authentication hardware

In a network of **ix** machines, terminals at unknown or uncontrolled network locations must be treated as potentially hostile computers, which of course makes logging in, authenticating users, and reading secret data over a terminal difficult. Here is a possible solution to these problems, relying on special hardware, prompted by our experience with windowing terminals in single-machine **ix** [**MR3**].

The main idea is to use special purpose secure computers as terminals, together with smart-card-like user identification tokens which are also special purpose secure computers.

The terminal and screen software is part of the TCB. The TCB is unprogrammable (in ROM, say) and contains secret cryptographic keys in an uninspectable store; the whole packaged in a tamper-proof container. The TCB can enforce a primitive form of **ix**'s file access policy (each multiplexed terminal process and associated windows, say, has a label, with label inequalities obeyed on mouse-initiated cross-window copies or "snarfs"). Also, a form of PEX is available: if a screen layer is accessible by exactly one terminal process, and if the keyboard is accessible only by that terminal process, then a distinctive unforgeable visual mark may be placed on the screen layer (a flashing border, say).

The "user authentication tokens" are small special purpose computers with their own TCBs and tamper-proof memory. A token can be plugged into a special terminal, and has a light visible to the user when the token is plugged into the terminal.

This hardware is used to help several authentications. There are as many as four parties with differing security interests: user, user token, terminal, and host computer. The user token must be convinced that its legitimate user is present. The terminal and host must like each other's TCBs enough to set up cross-machine PEX. The host must communicate through the terminal to the user token, but the terminal will not play PEX unless it trusts the token, and so on.

Most of these security interests are satisfied by multiple applications of, say, the Feige-Fiat-Shamir [**FFS**] protocol, where the terminal, host, and token successively play differing roles. The FFS protocol has two roles: the "prover," who has a certificate issued by an authority, and a "verifier" who checks the certificate without—and this is the big trick—actually seeing it. The authority knows the factorization of a modulus N. The modulus N, but not its factorization, is known ahead of time by the verifier. What the verifier knows at the end of the protocol is that whoever prepared the certificate knew the factorization of N.

The terminals and tokens carry certificates from their manufacturers signed according to a modulus $N_{\mathtt{term}}$, characteristic of the brand name of the terminal. This modulus $N_{\mathtt{term}}$ is known by all the host computers. This prior distribution of public authenticating key is not a burden because the number of distinct brands of secure terminals will remain small.

User identification tokens also carry certificates attesting to the identity of their owners. These certificates are signed with a modulus N_{dom} characteristic of the security domain in which the user lives. There is nothing wrong with a user identification token carrying several such certificates valid in different domains. Computers also have one or more certificates signed by the same moduli N_{dom}. The assumption is that the same authorities that certify users are able to certify computers. Roughly, if you have an account on a machine, there is at least one N_{dom} you and the machine have in common.

Here is how to set up a login session with such equipment. First, the token and terminal authenticate each other with respect to modulus $N_{\mathtt{term}}$. They tell the user that they like each other by visual signals: the light on the token is lit, a special icon or message is displayed on the terminal. Then the token has a chance to demand a password from the user, typed via the keyboard of the now-trusted terminal. Then the token tells its N_{dom} values to the terminal. Terminal and host computer negotiate to find a common N_{dom}, then the computer proves its *bona fides* to the terminal using modulus N_{dom} and the terminal proves to the computer that it is a special terminal with modulus $N_{\mathtt{term}}$. The computer and terminal now set up the cross-machine PEX protocol on their link, and the user proves his identity to the computer either by typing a classical password or by letting his token prove the user's credentials using N_{dom}.

A simplification is possible in the case where there is only one security domain which knows about all trustable computers. Then the user token is not needed: the single modulus $N_{\mathtt{term}}$ can suffice for all applications of Feige-Fiat-Shamir.

Conclusion

The foregoing describes a general architecture for a network of secure computers, offering far more security than is commonly found in the UNIX system, offering users a measure of distributed security services with a minimal overhead of centralized bureaucracy.

How large an organization could such a net serve, before the methods of user authentication, delegation of rights and authorities, and system administration sketched above become too cumbersome? How much work would it take to build such a net, given the existing pieces?

I have had chats with Baldwin, Coutinho, Feigenbaum, Fernandez, Fraser, Grampp, Kurshan, McIlroy, Merritt, Pike, Presotto, Ritchie, Thompson, Wilson, Zempol, among others, to whom I am grateful for ideas and helpful criticism.

References

[DOD] Department of Defense Computer Security Center, *Department of Defense Trusted Computer System Evaluation Criteria*, US Department of Defense, Fort Meade, MD, 15 August 1983.

[FFS] U. Feige, A. Fiat, and A. Shamir, *Zero-knowledge proofs of identity*, J. Cryptology **1** (1988), 77–94.

[G] M. Gasser, *Building a secure computer system*, New York, Van Nostrand Reinhold, 1988.

[MR1] M. D. McIlroy and J. A. Reeds, *A Security Model for Files and Processes in the UNIX System*, Bell Labs Technical Report, 14 April 1987.

[MR2] M. D. McIlroy and J. A. Reeds, *Multilevel security with fewer fetters*, UNIX Around the World: Proc. of the Spring 1988 EUUG Conference.

[MR3] M. D. McIlroy and J. A. Reeds, *Multilevel windows on a single-level terminal*, Proc. UNIX Security Workshop, August 29–30, 1988.

[R] D. M. Ritchie, *A stream input-output system*, AT&T Bell Laboratories Tech. J. **63** (October 1984).

AT&T Bell Laboratories, Murray Hill, NJ 07974
E-mail address: reeds@research.att.com

DIMACS Series in Discrete Mathematics
and Theoretical Computer Science
Volume **2**, 1991

Reasoning about Cryptographic Protocols

Extended Abstract

MARIE-JEANNE TOUSSAINT* AND PIERRE WOLPER**

ABSTRACT. We present a modelization of the probabilistic knowledge of the participants in cryptographic protocols. This modelization can be used to establish the security of the protocols. It is based on the assumption that the underlying cryptographic system is perfect and is an extension of the "Hidden Automorphism Model" introduced by Merritt.

1. Introduction

So far, a lot of effort has been devoted to the study of cryptographic systems. The goal has been to develop cryptographic systems that are as secure as possible. Currently, a fair amount of research is still devoted to increasing the security of existing cryptosystems [**QD89**, **SB88**, **BO88**] and to the underlying mechanisms: pseudorandom generators [**GGM86**, **HS85**, **GKL88**], one-way functions [**NY89**, **IR89**], and the relations between these notions [**Lev85**, **ILL89**]. As a result of this work, one has a fairly good idea (which further discoveries might modify) of what cryptographic systems can be used in order to achieve a given level of security. Unfortunately, this is not sufficient for a very simple reason: if the cryptographic system is used in an incorrect protocol, security can be compromised even if the cryptographic system is perfect.

These considerations prompted Merritt [**Mer83**] to separate the security of the protocols from the security of the underlying cryptographic functions: he studied the problem of reasoning about cryptographic protocols, assuming the underlying cryptographic system to be perfect. For this, he introduced a model to formally represent the state of knowledge of the participants in

1980 *Mathematics Subject Classification* (1985 *Revision*). Primary 94A60, 68P25, 68Q60, 03B45, 03B70.

*Research Assistant for the National Fund for Scientific Research (Belgium).

**The work of this author is partially supported by Esprit project SPEC (3096).

a cryptographic protocol. In this model, the cryptographic system is represented by an algebra, and the hypothesis that the system is perfect is modeled by the fact that this algebra is isomorphic to a free algebra. At a given point in the execution of a cryptographic protocol, the knowledge of a participant about the cryptosystem being used depends on what objects he can identify in the free algebra. This is represented by a set of automorphisms on the algebra, hence the model is known as the " Hidden Automorphism Model."

This model was elaborated upon in **[MW85]**. There, mostly to make the model more intuitive, the knowledge of a participant in a protocol is modeled not by a set of automorphisms, but by a set of isomorphisms between two algebras: one representing the cryptosystem and one representing the participant's view of the cryptosystem. The more a participant knows, the smaller the set of isomorphisms he thinks possible. So, no knowledge corresponds to the set of all isomorphisms and complete knowledge to a set containing just one isomorphism.

The example used to illustrate these concepts in **[MW85]** is a coin-flip protocol. Not surprisingly, the property that was proved of this protocol is that the result of the flip is Heads (or Tails) with probability 1/2. However, the reasoning that was done about the probabilities was informal and intuitive and not incorporated into the model.

In this paper, we start by further refining the model of **[MW85]** and present an improved representation for the knowledge of a participant. Next, we attempt to give a precise and formal treatment of probabilistic properties. We found two distinct sources of probabilistic information. The first is linked to the structure of the protocol and to the random choices made by the participants. We represent it by considering the execution tree of the protocol where the different branches correspond to different random choices of the participants. The second is linked to the knowledge the participants have about the cryptosystem. The problem there is to show that, given the state of knowledge of a participant, some states of the execution tree are indistinguishable or, in probabilistic terms, equally likely.

This confronted us with some technical problems. Indeed, the main hypothesis we had to model is that in the absence of knowledge, the distribution of the possible values of an element is uniform. (This is exactly the type of property the coin-flip protocol relied upon for the distribution of the keys.) Unfortunately, in our modelization, the set of these possible values is denumerable and, as is well known, it is not possible to define a uniform measure on an infinite countable set. This problem was solved by introducing a specific family of measures. This family of measures is obtained as the limit of uniform measures on finite sets and captures the "intuitive" uniformity used when reasoning about the protocols.

This paper is organized as follows. In Section 2, we present our refinement of the model of knowledge in cryptographic systems defined in **[MW85]**.

Then (Section 3), we analyze a simple coin-flip protocol from the point of view of participants' knowledge. In Section 4, we introduce the concept of execution tree and relate it to the participants' states of knowledge. This enables us to establish the security of the coin-flip protocol described in Section 3. The measure on countable sets used in this proof is then formalized in Section 5.

2. Modeling states of knowledge

This section introduces our model of cryptosystems and of the knowledge participants in protocols can have about them. This model is essentially the one introduced in [**MW85**]. However, we refine it and present it with (we hope) an improved notation.

2.1. Modeling the cryptosystem. A cryptosystem is seen as an algebraic system called the *crypto-algebra* $\mathscr{C}$. Its constants correspond to the plaintexts and keys. We distinguish the set of enciphering keys $\mathscr{K}_e$ and the set of deciphering keys $\mathscr{K}_d$. There is a bijection (denoted b) between these sets. In secret-key cryptography, the enciphering key is the same as the deciphering key; thus $\mathscr{K}_e = \mathscr{K}_d$, and the bijection b between $\mathscr{K}_e$ and $\mathscr{K}_d$ is the identity relation. In public-key cryptography, the enciphering key is different from the deciphering key; the bijection b is often a mathematical relation in modular arithmetic. For example, in the RSA system, the bijection b is the operator computing the inverses in arithmetic "modulo the Euler totient function" [**RSA78**]. Here, for simplicity, we suppose that the plaintexts and ciphertexts belong to the same set $\mathscr{M}$. (Note that $\mathscr{M}$ could have been divided in two sets $\mathscr{M}_p$ and $\mathscr{M}_c$ as is done for the keys.)

The operators of the crypto-algebra $\mathscr{C}$ are usually the enciphering function $e : \mathscr{K}_e \times \mathscr{M} \to \mathscr{M}$ and the deciphering function $d : \mathscr{K}_d \times \mathscr{M} \to \mathscr{M}$. The functions e and d are linked by some relations. For example, if we consider encryption in a secret- or public-key cryptosystem, we have

$$(1) \qquad d(k_d, e(k_e, m)) = m, \qquad \forall m \in \mathscr{M}, \quad \forall k_e \in \mathscr{K}_e$$

and for

$$k_d \in \mathscr{K}_d \; : k_d = b(k_e).$$

A specific cryptosystem and hence crypto-algebra is characterized by the particular sets of messages and keys as well as the encryption and decryption functions being used.

Following [**MW85**], we also consider an idealization of the cryptosystem. It is the quotient by the relations (1) of the free algebra of the same type as the crypto-algebra. This algebra represents the structure of the cryptosystem. We will denote it by $\mathscr{F}$.

There is an epimorphism (surjective morphism) denoted ϕ between the free-algebra $\mathscr{F}$ and the crypto-algebra $\mathscr{C}$. Indeed, in the real cryptosystems, the messages have a limited size. For example, in the DES they are 64 bits long and in RSA they belong to $[0, n[$ where n is the chosen modulus and is thus finite. On the other hand, closing under the functions e and d produces an infinite number of distinct elements in the free-algebra. Thus, several elements of the free-algebra have sometimes to correspond to a single element of the crypto-algebra.

We do not want to deal with real cryptosystems but rather with a "perfect" cryptosystem. This "perfection" will be modeled as in [**MW85**] by assuming that the crypto-algebra is isomorphic to the free-algebra and hence that ϕ is an isomorphism rather than an epimorphism. Intuitively, this hypothesis means that there is complete independence between the keys: the knowledge of some keys and some correspondences "plaintext — ciphertext" doesn't give any information about the other keys or the other messages that are enciphered by unknown keys.

This ideal condition is not often satisfied in practice. Indeed, some cryptosystems actually being used have known collisions (i.e., two identical ciphertexts for two different plaintexts or two different keys) ([**QD89**, **QG89**, **Dam88**]). However, finding such collisions requires an enormous amount of computing power, which means that a participant in a cryptographic protocol can only know a few particular collisions that he does not choose. Thus our assumption that the cryptosystem is "perfect" is not unrealistic. Moreover, our goal is not to investigate the failures of specific cryptographic algorithms but to analyze the security of the cryptographic protocols independently of the cryptosystem. This type of analysis does not absolutely guarantee the security of the global protocol, but it will at least detect an incorrect use of the cryptosystems.

We consider an infinite set of messages and keys. A crypto-algebra isomorphic to this free-algebra could be one where keys and messages are represented by arbitrary length strings of bits and where the encryption and decryption functions are unknown functions (at least to these authors) having all the right properties.

It probably seems a little ridiculous to distinguish between the free-algebra and the crypto-algebra since they are isomorphic. It turns out that this will be useful for modeling participants' knowledge as we now describe. An element of the free-algebra is a string that contains a lot of useful and easily computable information that cannot be obtained in the crypto-algebra. For example, it doesn't require a Cray to figure out that the decryption of $e(k, m)$ is m, but it better be essentially impossible to figure out that the decryption of 10010000111100101010000011111 is 1000100100100100000111100111101. So, there is a lot of information in the isomorphism between the crypto- and free-algebras. It is essentially what participants know about this isomorphism that will determine their knowledge. We will view knowing an element of the crypto-algebra as knowing its representation in the free-algebra.

2.2. Modeling participants' knowledge. To model a participant's knowledge about the cryptosystem, we thus need to represent partial information about the isomorphism between the free-algebra $\mathscr{F}$ and the crypto-algebra $\mathscr{C}$. The isomorphism is a subset of $\mathscr{F} \times \mathscr{C}$. Thus, one natural form of partial knowledge about the isomorphism is a finite subset of $\mathscr{F} \times \mathscr{C}$ that can be extended to a full isomorphism. We use the following definition.

DEFINITION 2.1. A *simple state of knowledge* about a cryptosystem is a finite subset of $\mathscr{F} \times \mathscr{C}$ that can be extended to a full isomorphism.

For this definition to be useful, two points have to be elaborated upon. The first is how to represent a simple state of knowledge. The second is which assumptions are made about what a participant can compute from his state of knowledge.

To represent a simple state of knowledge, we could give the corresponding elements from the cross product of the free- and crypto-algebras. However, we don't care about the specific crypto-algebra being used; we want our model to be independent of the crypto-algebra. Moreover, our reasoning about the protocol will be done in terms of the free-algebra. We will thus only give the free-algebra component of the pairs of elements. In order to define what use a participant can make of the information in his state of knowledge, let us examine how a participant achieves a given state of knowledge.

We want to represent the knowledge of a malicious participant in (or an eavesdropper on) a cryptographic protocol. It is useful to think in the following terms. The malicious participant is trying to find the isomorphism that exists between the crypto- and free-algebras. In more vivid terms, he is trying to label each element of the crypto-algebra with an element of the free-algebra. How much labeling can he do?

For plaintexts and keys, the labeling is immediate. For ciphertexts, it depends on how much the participant can compute. With infinite computing power he could recompute the whole isomorphism from the bijection on the plaintexts and keys. This amounts to breaking the cryptosystem by exhaustive computation and should be ruled out. Nevertheless, we want to assume that the malicious participant will do some computation. For instance, if he knows that an element x of the crypto-algebra corresponds either to $e(k, a)$ or to $e(k, b)$ and knows $\phi(k)$, $\phi(a)$, and $\phi(b)$, he will pretty easily determine whether x is $\phi(e(k, a))$ or $\phi(e(k, b))$. To distinguish between these two situations, we will assume that our malicious participant *does* compute everything, but *only with* some elements, namely those that are in his state of knowledge. This is essentially the notion of *Revealed Reduct* of **[Mer83]** and **[MW85]**. Thus, to be an accurate representation, a participant's state of knowledge will have to contain only elements he is aware of or that play a special role in the protocol. These considerations are formalized in the following definition.

DEFINITION 2.2. In a simple state of knowledge $K \subset \mathcal{F} \times \mathcal{C}$, the *known fraction of the isomorphism* is the closure of K under the operations of the free- and crypto-algebras.

EXAMPLE 2.1. Consider the state of knowledge $\langle a, b, k \rangle$ for a private key cryptosystem with the usual functions e and d. This implies that $e(k, a)$ and $e(k, b)$ are in the known fraction of the isomorphism and that if the participant sees an element of the crypto-algebra that is either $\phi(e(k, a))$ or $\phi(e(k, b))$ he will recognize it.

Unfortunately, the model we have described so far is sometimes not sufficient. We might see an element of the crypto-algebra and not be able to label it with an element of the free-algebra. However, we might have some information about it. For instance, we might know that it is one of two elements. Even if we know absolutely nothing about this element, it might still be important to remember that we have seen it since it might reappear later in the protocol. We might also only be aware of the existence of an element of the crypto-algebra of a given type (e.g., a key) even though we have never seen it. We thus need a more general definition of states of knowledge. The most natural is the following.

DEFINITION 2.3. A *state of knowledge* about a cryptosystem is a subset of $\mathcal{F} \times \mathcal{C}$.

Compared to Definition 2.1 we have simply relaxed the restriction that the subset of $\mathcal{F} \times \mathcal{C}$ be finite and extensible to an isomorphism. As for simple states of knowledge, we have to solve the problems of representation and interpretation.

For cardinality reasons, not all states of knowledge can be finitely represented. However, in practice, only states of knowledge with a restricted structure appear. We will thus only represent states of knowledge defined by a subset of $\mathcal{F} \times \mathcal{C}$ that is the union of three parts of the following form.

(i) Pairs (a, b) that define a one-to-one mapping on a finite subset of $\mathcal{F}$ and $\mathcal{C}$. These will be represented by the free-algebra component of the pair.

(ii) Pairs (x, b) where x ranges over a subset of $\mathcal{F}$ and b over a finite subset of $\mathcal{C}$. These will correspond to a finite number of elements of the crypto-algebra that the participant has seen but is unable to label unambiguously by an element of the free-algebra. These elements will be represented by a variable (denoted by a letter of the end of the alphabet $x, y, \dots$) ranging over the free-algebra together with constraints on this variable. These constraints can be inclusion in a subset of the free-algebra or equality and inequality relations between variables. This last type of constraint is useful when a state of knowledge contains several variables and when we have information on whether these variables might or might not correspond to the same element of the free-algebra.

(iii) Pairs (a, x) where a ranges over a finite subset of $\mathscr{F}$ and x over a subset of $\mathscr{C}$. These will correspond to a finite number of elements of the free-algebra the participant is aware of, but for which he doesn't know the corresponding element of the crypto-algebra. These elements will be represented by a variable (denoted by a tilded symbol $\tilde{a}$) ranging over the crypto-algebra together with constraints on this variable.

States of knowledge that can be described as above will be called *representable.*

In order to define the information contained in a state of knowledge, we need to remember that a participant can only infer information from a one-to-one mapping between parts of the free- and crypto-algebras. We will thus view a state of knowledge as the set of its restrictions that are one-to-one mappings between subsets of $\mathscr{F}$ and $\mathscr{C}$. These one-to-one mappings are like simple states of knowledge except that they might not be extensible to full isomorphisms between the algebras. (Indeed, there is usually only one restriction of the state of knowledge that corresponds to the "real" isomorphism.) We will thus call these simple states of *belief* rather than simple states of knowledge.

DEFINITION 2.4. A *simple state of belief* compatible with a knowledge state $K \subset \mathscr{F} \times \mathscr{C}$ is a maximal restriction of K to a one-to-one mapping.

Note that for representable states of knowledge, the corresponding simple states of belief will be finite. A participant with a given knowledge state considers all the underlying simple belief states as possible. He will thus know some information if it is known in all these belief states. This leads to the problem of defining what a participant can infer from a simple belief state. It might seem reasonable to use a definition similar to Definition 2.2. However, this would have unacceptable consequences. Indeed, by computing the closure for all his belief states, a participant could determine which of these are consistent (can be extended to an isomorphism) and rule out those that are not. This will often give him considerable information. What makes this unreasonable is that the closure has to be computed for a potentially infinite number of belief states. It is reasonable to assume that the participant will compute the closure for a finite bounded number of his belief states, but not for all of them. In what follows, we will adopt the simple position that the participant does not compute the closure of any of his belief states. In a more complete version of this paper, we will relax this assumption and assume that a participant can compute the closure of a finitely bounded number of his belief states.

3. A simple example of cryptographic protocol

To illustrate the definitions of the preceding section, we apply them to a simple coin-flip protocol also used as an example in [**MW85**]. The cryptosystem being used is a secret key system and thus $\mathcal{K}_e = \mathcal{K}_d = \mathcal{K}$.

We assume that two users A(lice) and B(ob) want to flip a coin by telephone. Each user (A and B) doesn't trust the other.

(i) A chooses a key k and sends $e(k, T)$ and $e(k, H)$ to B ('T' for "tails" and 'H' for "heads").
(ii) B picks and sends $e(k, T)$ or $e(k, H)$ to A. (We assume here it is $e(k, H)$, for example.)
(iii) A sends k to B and knows the answer (H) of the coin-flip by applying the transformation $d : d(k, e(k, H)) = H$.
(iv) B also gets the answer H in the same way and verifies that A didn't cheat in Step 1.

Let us now analyze the successive knowledge states of the participants in the protocol. We will denote by $K_{X,n}$ the representation of the knowledge state of participant X at step n of the protocol. The successive states of knowledge of the participants are the following.

0. The protocol assumes the participants know which messages of the crypto-algebra are used for representing T and H. These elements are thus part of the initial state of knowledge of each participant,

$$K_{A,0} = K_{B,0} = \langle T, H\rangle.$$

1. At the end of the first step, we have

$$K_{A,1} = \langle T, H, k\rangle$$

and

$$K_{B,1} = \langle T, H, x, y, \tilde{k}\rangle$$

where

$$\tilde{k} \in \mathcal{K} : x, y \in \{e(\tilde{k}, T), e(\tilde{k}, H)\}, \qquad x \neq y.$$

A's state of knowledge is simple (in the sense given in Definition 2.1) and quite straightforward to understand.

The representation of B's state of knowledge might require some explanation. B knows that a key exists and is used by A to encipher T and H. He can fix the representation of that key in the free-algebra but he doesn't know the corresponding key of the crypto-algebra. (If he did know, the protocol would fail.) Thus, we represent this key by a variable $\tilde{k}$ ranging over the set of keys of the crypto-algebra.

The introduction of the variables x and y can be explained as follows. B receives two streams of bits, thus two elements of the crypto-algebra; he knows that one is the encryption of T under $\tilde{k}$ and the other the encryption of H but he doesn't know which corresponds to which. Thus, here the representation in the crypto-algebra is fixed but not the corresponding element in the free-algebra.

B's state of knowledge corresponds to an infinite number of simple states of belief, one for each possible value of $\tilde{k}$, x, and y. Only one of these states of belief (the one corresponding to the actual values of $\tilde{k}$, x, and y) is consistent.

2. At the end of the second step, the knowledge states of the different participants have not changed: B only transmits an element already sent by A.
3. Finally, at the end of the protocol,

$$K_{A,3} = K_{A,2} = K_{A,1}$$

and

$$K_{B,3} = \langle T, H, k \rangle.$$

4. Using knowledge states to analyze protocols

In the preceding sections, we have introduced a formalization of what participants know about the cryptosystem when executing a cryptographic protocol. We will use this representation to reason about the correctness of the protocol, but we first need a complete representation of what can happen when the protocol is executed. This representation will take the form of the tree of possible executions of the protocol.

4.1. The protocol execution tree. The protocol execution tree is the tree of possible global states of the protocol. In a protocol that uses choices, the various branches of the protocol execution tree will be assigned probabilities. We illustrate this notion on our coin-flip example.

First note that in the coin-flip protocol, the step "A sends $e(k, T)$ and $e(k, H)$ to B" is somewhat ambiguous. In any implementation, the messages will not be sent simultaneously. They are sent one after the other. What matters is that the order is random and gives no information to B about which message is which. A more precise description of the protocol is thus the following.

(i) A chooses randomly a key k in $\mathscr{K}$ and different messages m_1, m_2 in $\{T, H\}$. A sends $em_1 = e(k, m_1)$ and $em_2 = e(k, m_2)$ to B.
(ii) B picks u in $\{em_1, em_2\}$ and sends u to A.
(iii) A sends k to B and they both know the answer a of the coin flip by applying the transformation d to u.

At the first step of the coin-flip protocol, A has the choice of either sending $e(k, T)$ or $e(k, H)$ in first position. There are thus two possible states after the first step. At that point, B can choose either of the messages he has received and send it back. This leads to four possible states at the end of the protocol as illustrated in the following figure.

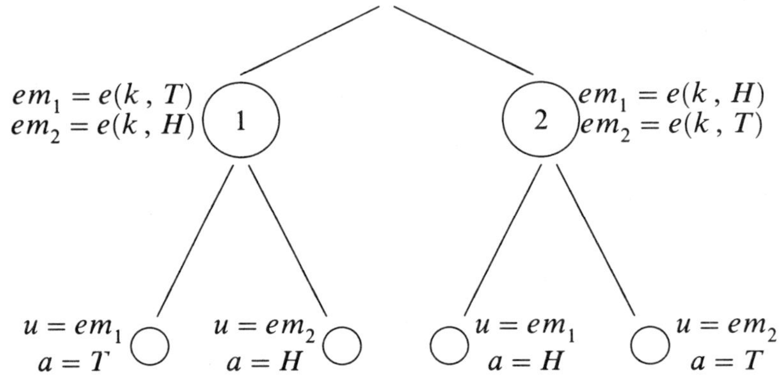

The choices made by A and B during the execution of the protocol are assumed random. We can thus assign probabilities to them. If the participants are honest, the situation is as represented in the figure below.

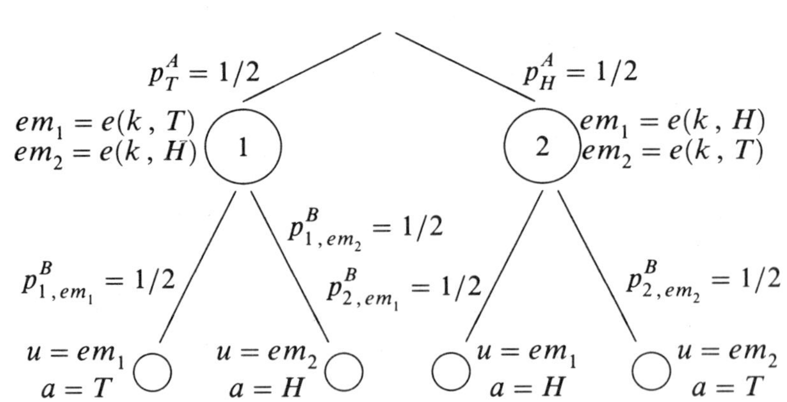

Malicious participants would try to bias the result of the coin flip by using a nonuniform choice policy in some states of the protocol. Let us thus analyze the execution tree under this hypothesis. The most general situation is illustrated in the following execution tree.

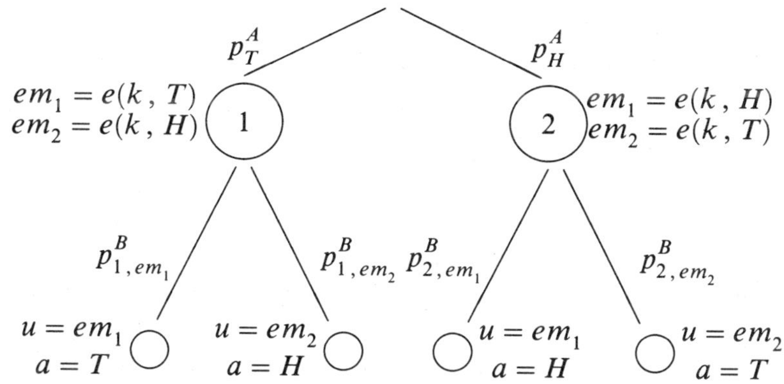

4.2. An analysis. From the probabilities assigned to the choices of the participants, one can by standard techniques derive probabilities on the states of the execution tree. From these probabilities, one can derive the probability that the outcome a of the coin-flip is H or T. One obtains

$$a = T : p_{1,em_1}^B p_T^A + p_{2,em_2}^B p_H^A;$$
$$a = H : p_{1,em_2}^B p_T^A + p_{2,em_1}^B p_H^A.$$

These two probabilities can certainly be different if Participant B can choose different probabilities in States 1 and 2. Intuitively, this is not possible since he is choosing between encrypted messages. We will make this precise very shortly, but let us assume it is the case and go ahead with our analysis. If we have that

$$p_{1,em_1}^B = p_{2,em_1}^B = p_{em_1}^B \quad \text{and} \quad p_{1,em_2}^B = p_{2,em_2}^B = p_{em_2}^B,$$

the probabilities of obtaining T and H are the same if and only if

$$(p_{em_1}^B - p_{em_2}^B)\,(p_T^A - p_H^A) = 0.$$

Thus no participant can cheat the other since it is sufficient for one participant to choose his probabilities evenly to guarantee a fair outcome to the coin flip.

4.3. States of the protocol and states of knowledge. A state of the protocol is an assignment of values to protocol variables. We will distinguish between cryptographic variables that range over elements of the crypto-algebra and the other variables of the protocol. We will call the values of the cryptographic variables the *cryptographic state* of the protocol. The problem we are facing is to determine when two protocol states that only differ on their cryptographic state are distinguishable to a participant in a given state of knowledge. In our framework, elements of the crypto-algebra, as such, have little meaning. The useful information is in the free-algebra elements corresponding to the crypto-algebra. Thus in order to distinguish between protocol states, a participant will attempt to replace the crypto-algebra elements by free-algebra elements using his knowledge of the isomorphism ϕ between the free- and crypto-algebras. This leads to the following definitions.

DEFINITION 4.1. A *cryptographic protocol state* for a protocol with a set M of cryptographic variables is a function $CS : M \to \mathscr{C}$.

DEFINITION 4.2. Given a partial one-to-one mapping $\psi : \mathscr{F} \to \mathscr{C}$, the *free-algebra image under* ψ *of a cryptographic protocol state* $CS : M \to \mathscr{C}$ is a function $FCS : M \to \mathscr{F}$ such that $\forall m \in M$, $FCS(m) = \psi^{-1}(CS(m))$. If for some m, $\psi^{-1}(CS(m))$ is not defined, $FCS(m)$ has the conventional value $\bot$.

Note that in our analysis of the protocol, we have actually described free-algebra images of the protocol states rather than the protocol states themselves. When doing this, we are taking the role of an external observer with perfect knowledge of the isomorphism ϕ. Thus whether we describe the states or their free image is irrelevant.

We can now turn to the definition of indistinguishable states. In a simple state of knowledge, it is sufficient to require that both states have the same free image under the mapping defined by the state of knowledge.

DEFINITION 4.3. Two cryptographic protocol states are *indistinguishable* in a given simple state of knowledge for which the known fraction of the isomorphism is ψ if they have identical free-algebra images under ψ.

Note that one frequent way for free-algebra images to have identical values is for them to have the undefined value $\bot$.

For general states of knowledge, the situation is a little more complex. What is needed for protocol states to be indistinguishable is the existence of underlying belief states compatible with each of the protocol states.

DEFINITION 4.4. Two cryptographic protocol states are *indistinguishable* in a given state of knowledge if, for each of the protocol states, there is at least one belief state such that:

- the belief state defines a mapping ψ;
- where it is defined, the free-algebra image of the state under ψ coincides with the free-algebra image of the state under the actual isomorphism ϕ.

It appears immediately that States 1 and 2 of the coin-flip protocol are indistinguishable according to this definition. This can be viewed as completing our analysis of this protocol.

Nevertheless, there are reasons to be dissatisfied with Definition 4.4. If many more simple states of belief of the participant point to one protocol state than to the other, it seems natural for the participant to believe he is in that state. This leads us to a stronger definition of indistinguishable states. This definition requires a measure on the set of simple belief states of a knowledge state. We would like this measure to be uniform in order to reflect the fact that we view all instantiations as equally possible. If the set of these instantiations is finite, defining a uniform measure is immediate. If it is countably infinite (as is often the case), such a uniform measure does not exist. In the following section we will see how a measure that approximates uniformity can be defined on infinite sets. For the time being, let us assume that such a measure exists.

Given a measure on the set of belief states underlying a participant's knowledge state, we define *probabilistically indistinguishable protocol states* as follows.

DEFINITION 4.5. Two cryptographic protocol states are *probabilistically indistinguishable* in a given state of knowledge if, for each of the protocol states, the sets of simple belief states such that:

- the belief state defines a mapping ψ;
- where it is defined, the free-algebra image of the state under ψ coincides with the free-algebra image of the state under the actual isomorphism ϕ

have the same measure.

As we will see, this condition is satisfied for States 1 and 2 of the coin-flip protocol if one uses the measure introduced in the next section.

5. Defining a measure on countable sets

Our goal here is to define a measure on countable sets that is a natural extension of the uniform measure on finite sets. We will apply this measure to the sets of simple belief states corresponding to the knowledge states of the participants in a cryptographic protocol.

Consider B's state of knowledge after Step 1 of the coin-flip protocol. There is an infinite set of simple belief states corresponding to this knowledge state: one for each possible combination of values for $\tilde{k}$, x, and y. If $\tilde{k}$ could only take a finite number n of possible values (i.e., if there were only finitely many possible keys), there would be only $2n$ possible belief states and a uniform measure would assign $1/(2n)$ to each of these. One would like to take the limit of these measures when n goes to infinity. Unfortunately, that would assign a measure 0 to all elements and the measure of the whole set could not be 1.

Nevertheless, in some cases, taking the limit seems quite reasonable. For instance, it seems natural to state that the probability of picking an element that has a specific value from a countable set is 0, even though it cannot be 0 for all specific values. (This is sometimes called the "lottery paradox.") The way we resolve this paradox is to take limits of the probabilities defined in the finite case, but only to do this for the probabilities of a limited set of properties.

Because of their structure, it is possible for the purpose of defining our measure to view simple belief states as k-tuples of values from the crypto- or free-algebra. As we pointed out in Section 2, if the state of knowledge is representable, k is finite. Thus we need to define a measure on a set of k-tuples where each component ranges over a finite or countably infinite set. Precisely, let $D = D_1 \times \cdots \times D_k$ be the domain on which we want to define a measure. We assume that $D_1, \ldots, D_j$ are finite and of respective cardinality $d_1, \ldots, d_j$ and that $D_{j+1}, \ldots, D_k$ are countably infinite. We do not lose generality by assuming that D is

$$[1, d_1] \times \cdots \times [1, d_j] \times \omega \times \cdots \times \omega$$

where ω denotes the set of the strictly positive natural numbers.

We want to define a measure on D (called the "uniform" measure) as the limit of the uniform measures defined on a series of finite sets that converge to D. Intuitively, the most natural way (for our purpose) to define such a series is to consider that at each step we add an element to each infinite component of D. We consider thus the series $\{D_m\}$ defined by

$$D_m = [1, d_1] \times \cdots \times [1, d_j] \times [1, m] \times \cdots \times [1, m].$$

Let us consider properties p_i such that

$$\lim_{m \to +\infty} \Pr\{x \in D_m : p_i(x)\}$$

exists for the usual uniform distribution on sets of finite size. We first give a definition of independence for such properties.

Definition 5.1. We say that two properties p_1 and p_2 are *independent in D* and we write

$$\text{“ Independence}_D(p_1, p_2)\text{ ”}$$

if

$$\lim_{m \to +\infty} \Pr\{x \in D_m : p_1(x)\} \neq 0,$$
$$\lim_{m \to +\infty} \Pr\{x \in D_m : p_2(x)\} \neq 0,$$

and

$$\lim_{m \to +\infty} \Pr\{x \in D_m : p_2(x) \mid p_1(x)\} = \lim_{m \to +\infty} \Pr\{x \in D_m : p_2(x)\}.$$

The " $\text{Independence}_D(.,.)$" relation is a symmetrical property:

$$\text{Independence}_D(p_i, p_j) \equiv \text{Independence}_D(p_j, p_i).$$

Consider a finite or countable number of properties p_i $(i = 1, \ldots, q, \ldots)$ such that either

- they are pairwise independent, or
- $\lim_{m \to +\infty} \Pr\{x \in D_m : p_i(x)\} = 0$.

(Note that only a finite number of properties can satisfy the second condition; the others have to be pairwise independent.)

From these properties we define an *induced measure* on the countable set D by

$$\mu(\emptyset) = 0,$$
$$\mu(\{x \in D : p_i(x)\}) = \lim_{m \to +\infty} \Pr\{x \in D_m : p_i(x)\}$$

for any $i = 1, \ldots, q, \ldots$.

Of course this measure will depend on the set of properties chosen initially. Let us establish that we indeed have a measure and determine which sets are measurable. We have the following two propositions.

PROPOSITION 1. *The set of measurable sets contains the initial sets*

$$\{x \in D : p_i(x)\},$$

and is closed under the classical finite operations on sets (finite intersection, finite union, complementation, difference of two sets).

PROPOSITION 2. μ *is a measure.*

To prove this, we use the theory described in [**Mun74**] and establish that μ is finitely and denumerably additive.

REMARK. Defining the measure from independent properties as we did makes things rather simple. It can be possible to relax this condition and start with nonindependent properties. This is possible if we have convergence of the limits, not only for the initial properties, but also for their Boolean combinations. For example, if $D = \omega$, it is possible to generate a measure with the following properties:

$$\mu(\{x \in \mathrm{N} : x \text{ is a multiple of } n\}) = \frac{1}{n} \quad \forall n \in \omega.$$

5.1. Application of the measure to the coin-flip protocol. We want to use the measure we have just defined to establish that the Protocol States 1 and 2 are probabilistically indistinguishable by B. The set of simple belief states of B is isomorphic to

$$[1, 2] \times \omega.$$

We consider one property:

- p_1 is true of all belief states that define a free image of the protocol state that coincides with Protocol State 1.

It might seem natural to also consider the following property:

- p_2 is true of all belief states that define a free image of the protocol state that coincides with Protocol State 2.

However, this property is definable by Boolean operations in terms of p_1 and is thus not necessary for defining the measure.

We have that

$$\mu(\{x \mid p_1(x)\}) = \lim_{m \to +\infty} \left(\frac{m}{2m}\right) = \frac{1}{2}$$

as expected.

6. Conclusions and comparison with other work

Besides what can be found in [**Mer83**] and [**MW85**], little work has been done on general tools for reasoning about cryptographic systems. This is however an important problem because many more people will be confronted with the problem of using correctly an assumed-to-be-ideal cryptosystem than of designing such cryptosystems.

There has been some work on proving the security of cryptographic protocols. An early reference is [**DY83**] where a theoretical analysis of the security of public-key protocols is given. Successful attacks on specific protocols have been published [**EGS86**, **Moo88**]. However, these attacks are closely linked to the cryptosystem and do not illustrate a failure of the protocol that is independent of the underlying cryptosystem.

Recent work uses logical frameworks for verifying cryptographic protocols [**BAN89**, **Kem89**, **MCF87**, **Var89**]. The difference with our work is that, in these contributions, the properties of the cryptosystem that ensure security are modeled by axioms [**BAN89**, **Kem89**] or explicit relations [**MCF87**, **BAN89**]. We rely on a model of the cryptosystem that enables us to derive the properties that ensure security.

One of our contributions has been to show how the modelization of [**Mer83**] and [**MW85**] can be extended to handle probabilistic information. We believe this will make this modelization more appealing and more widely usable. Indeed, a large number of properties that one wants to prove about cryptographic protocols are probabilistic in nature.

Because our method separates the protocol security from the security of the underlying cryptosystem, we believe and hope that it can be applied to more complicated examples. Moreover, our approach is quite compatible with the current trend in cryptographic research of defining some cryptographic primitives and building protocols with these primitives [**CK88**].

A problem is that separating the protocol from the cryptosystem is not always easy when the protocol is built on a very specific cryptosystem.

A step in making our approach more usable would be to provide a method for systematically constructing the execution trees and participants' states of knowledge from the protocol. Such a method is currently being developed and will be described in a later paper.

Acknowledgments. We would like to thank M. Merritt for several helpful and positive discussions about this work.

REFERENCES

[BAN89] M. Burrows, M. Abadi, and R. Needham, *A logic of authentication*, Technical Report 39, Digital — Systems Research Center (SRC), 1989.

[BO88] E. F. Brickell and A. M. Odlyzko, *Cryptanalysis: a survey of recent results*, Proc. of the IEEE **76** (1988), 578–593.

[Bra88] G. Brassard, *Modern cryptology—a tutorial*, Lecture Notes in Computer Science #325, Springer-Verlag, 1988.

[CK88] C. Crépeau and J. Kilian, *Achieving oblivious transfer using weakened security assumptions (extended abstract)*, in 29th Annual Symposium on Foundations of Computer Science, IEEE (1988), 42–52.

[Dam88] I. B. Damgård, *Collision free hash functions and public key signature schemes*, in Lecture Notes in Comput. Sci. Advances in Cryptology — EUROCRYPT'87, **304** D. Chaum and W. L. Price, eds., Springer-Verlag, (1988), 203–316.

[Den82] D. E. Denning, *Cryptography and data security*, Addison-Wesley Publishing Company, 1982.

[DY83] D. Dolev and A. C. Yao, *On the security of public key protocols*, IEEE Trans. Inform. Theory **29** (1983), 198–208.

[EGS86] S. Even, O. Goldreich, and A. Shamir, *On the security of ping-pong protocols using the RSA*, Lecture Notes in Comput. Sci. Advances in Cryptology — CRYPTO'85, **218**, H. C. Williams, ed., Springer-Verlag (1986), 58–72.

[GGM86] O. Goldreich, S. Goldwasser, and S. Micali, *How to construct random functions*, J. ACM **33** (1986), 792–807.

[GKL88] O. Goldreich, H. Krawczyk, and M. Luby, *On the existence of pseudorandom generators*, 29th Annual Symposium on Foundations of Computer Science, IEEE (1988), 12–24.

[HS85] J. Hastad and A. Shamir, *The cryptographic security of truncated linearly related variables*, Proc. of the 17th Annual ACM Symposium on Theory of Computing (1985), 356–362.

[ILL89] R. Impagliazzo, L. A. Levin, and M. Luby, *Pseudo-random generation from one-way functions (extended abstract)*, Proc. of the 21st Annual ACM Symposium on Theory of Computing (1989), 12–24.

[IR89] R. Impagliazzo and S. Rudich, *Limits on the provable consequences of one-way permutations*. Proc. of the 21st Annual ACM Symposium on Theory of Computing (1989), 44–61.

[Kem89] R. A. Kemmerer, *Analyzing encryption protocols using formal verification techniques*, IEEE Journal on Selected Areas in Communications **7** (1989), 448–457.

[Lev85] L. A. Levin, *One-way functions and pseudorandom generators*, Proc. of the 17th Annual ACM Symposium on Theory of Computing (1985), 363–365.

[MCF87] J. K. Millen, S. C. Clark, and S. B. Freedman, *The Interrogator: protocol security analysis*, IEEE Trans. on Software Eng. **13** (1987), 274–288.

[Mer83] M. J. Merritt, *Cryptographic protocols*, Ph.D. thesis, Georgia Institute of Technology, 1983.

[Moo88] J. H. Moore, *Protocol failures in cryptosystems*, Proc. of the IEEE **76** (1988), 594–602.

[Mun74] M. Munster, *Théorie générale de la mesure et de l'intégration*, Bull. Soc. Roy. Sc. Liège (1974), 526–567.

[MW85] M. Merritt and P. Wolper, *States of knowledge in cryptographic protocols (extended abstract)*, unpublished manuscript, 1985.

[NY89] M. Naor and M. Yung, *Universal one-way hash functions and their cryptographic applications*, Proc. of the 21st Annual ACM Symposium on Theory of Computing (1989), 33–43.

[QD89] J.-J. Quisquater and J.-P. Delescaille, *How easy is collision search?*, application to DES, EUROCRYPT'89, 1989.

[QG89] J.-J. Quisquater and M. Girault, *2n-bit hash-functions using n-bit symmetric block cipher algorithms (abstract)*, EUROCRYPT'89, 1989.

[RSA78] R. L. Rivest, A. Shamir, and L. Adleman, *A method for obtaining digital signatures and public-key cryptosystems*, Comm. of the ACM **21** (1978), 120–126.

[SB88] M. E. Smid and D. K. Branstad, *The Data Encryption Standard: past and future*, Proc. of the IEEE **76** (1988), 550–559.

[Tou89] M.-J. Toussaint, *Reasoning about probabilistic properties of cryptographic protocols (extended abstract)*, abstract of the talk at the F.N.R.S. day on Computer Security, May 1989.

[Var89] V. Varadharajan, *Verification of network security protocols*, Computers & Security **8** (1989), 693–708.

UNIVERSITÉ DE LIÈGE, INSTITUT MONTEFIORE, B 28, B-4000 LIÈGE SART-TILMAN, BELGIUM

E-mail address: u515902@BLIULG11.BITNET